D0898990

THE SAVAGE WAR

Take up the White Man's burden—
The savage wars of peace—
Fill full the mouth of Famine,
And bid the sickness cease;
And when your goal is nearest
(The end for others sought)
Watch sloth and heathen folly
Bring all your hope to nought.

—Rudyard Kipling, "The White Man's Burden"

THE SAVAGE WAR

The Untold Battles of Afghanistan

Murray Brewster

John Wiley & Sons Canada, Ltd.

Library and Archives Canada Cataloguing in Publication

Brewster, Murray
    The savage war : the untold battles of Afghanistan / Murray Brewster.

Includes bibliographical references and index.
Issued also in electronic formats.
ISBN 978-1-11811-593-0

    1. Afghan War, 2001—Participation, Canadian.
2. Canada—Armed Forces—Afghanistan.   I. Title.

DS371.412.B73 2011   958.104'7   C2011-902933-2

ISBN 978-1-118-11593-0 (cloth); 978-1-118-12206-8 (ePub); 978-1-118-12207-5 (ePDF); 978-1-118-12208-2 (Mobi)

Production Credits
Cover Design: Michael Chan
Cover Photo Credit: Murray Brewster
Composition: Thomson Digital
Printer: Friesens Printing Ltd.

Editorial Credits
Executive Editor: Don Loney
Production Editor: Pauline Ricablanca

John Wiley & Sons Canada, Ltd.
6045 Freemont Blvd.
Mississauga, Ontario
L5R 4J3

Printed in Canada

1 2 3 4 5 FP 15 14 13 12 11

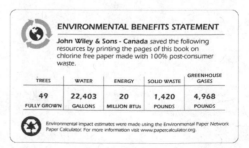

ENVIRONMENTAL BENEFITS STATEMENT

John Wiley & Sons - Canada saved the following resources by printing the pages of this book on chlorine free paper made with 100% post-consumer waste.

TREES	WATER	ENERGY	SOLID WASTE	GREENHOUSE GASES
49	22,403	20	1,420	4,968
FULLY GROWN	GALLONS	MILLION BTUs	POUNDS	POUNDS

Environmental impact estimates were made using the Environmental Paper Network Paper Calculator. For more information visit www.papercalculator.org.

To My Family . . .

Table of Contents

A light summer rain pecked at the assembly of veterans, dignitaries and villagers in Pourville, France, on a warm summer day in August 2007. A crowd had gathered at the war memorial beside the seaside community's idyllic, stone church, just behind the empty, silent beach. Everyone was there to listen to Canada's Veterans Affairs minister reflect on the long-past, but not forgotten, battle of Dieppe. Soldiers who'd survived the slaughter huddled under umbrellas and were draped with see-through, plastic, disposable bags to keep the rain off. Everyone rightfully fussed over them. They listened solemnly and politely as Greg Thompson spoke. On that horrific day in August 1942, 903 Canadians died. With the hindsight of history, it is celebrated as a victory.

Some of the vets seated in wheelchairs looked as though they'd nodded off until the minister intoned the well-worn narrative: For every life sacrificed at Dieppe, ten lives were saved two years later at D-Day by what the Allies learned. You could sense some of the old soldiers shifting uncomfortably in their seats before the sound of a metal cane banging defiantly on the pavement rang through the crowd.

"Bullshit," said one vet, his jowl-creased face red with anger.

He growled loud enough that some of Thompson's staff standing nearby cringed and then smiled painfully, but the minister never missed a beat. He kept right on speaking. I was never sure whether he'd heard the protest.

The reality of that vet's experience did not match the politically acceptable narrative, the same narrative that has been handed down to us through the years. Canadian soldiers who lived through the nightmare of the Balkans in the 1990s would say the same thing. They were dropped into the middle of a shooting war while everyone back home celebrated and called it peacekeeping. The disconnect between the stories we tell ourselves and the gritty, often uncomfortable reality was my prime motivation for what you are about to read.

The war in Afghanistan is like few other wars, in terms of its length, complexity, ignorance and sheer brutality. It has featured aspects and events that even today defy understanding. Despite boatloads of newspaper ink and thousands of hours of airtime, our collective appreciation of what the country has been through remains painfully shallow and fleeting.

Many of my recollections of my time covering Afghanistan have been refreshed through the time and generosity of the hundreds of people whom I've interviewed. Some of them have been quoted anonymously—or "on background," as it's called in the world of journalism. Without their patience, contributions and courage, some of the elements of this narrative would not have been possible. In almost all cases, these sources are senior government officials, diplomats or officers who are still serving or whose positions depend upon absolute discretion. They have contributed, without malice, to my understanding of this war, and hopefully to yours as well.

The country's combat mission in Afghanistan dragged on for more than five years and throughout that time I had the privilege and sometimes the burden of seeing it up close, both on the mean streets of Kandahar and in the equally hard-nosed back rooms of Ottawa. Sometimes, it feels as though I've covered nothing but Afghanistan. What you are about to get is my unvarnished take on what I've witnessed. Make no mistake: this is not a history book. I'll leave history to the historians to sort out. My objective in writing this account was to give you a sense of what it looked and felt like to be in the midst of the tempest. If what you are about to read makes you angry, makes you cry, makes you laugh or even prompts you to fling this volume across the room, then I will have accomplished my goal. Bronze it or burn it when you're done, but read it. Because war and the blood spilled these last few years is too important to forget—or be left to a cyclone of spin. Despite what some would have us believe, war is never neat, never tidy, never fully understood. If this book makes you pause for a moment in the day-to-day hubbub to reflect on the events of the last few years—even for a short moment—then it will truly have been worth the effort.

Kandahar, Afghanistan
July 2011

In order to get to Osama bin Laden's former compound on the outskirts of Kandahar, you have to drive through a garbage dump—actually two garbage dumps. One of them is a true dump, the smelly, discarded refuse from nearby Kandahar Airfield (KAF); the other is a graveyard of rusted, dilapidated Soviet and Taliban-era military equipment, all trashed unceremoniously around the remains of a former radar station. It seemed fitting and somewhat ironic to me that the place where an adolescent al-Qaeda matured into a terrorist behemoth would be nestled at the end of a road of refuse.

On the way to Tarnak Farms, which sits isolated at the very edge of the majestic Registan Desert, we stopped at a local Afghan National Army (ANA) post. The commander offered chai tea, bread and one of his soldiers to accompany us on the brief, kidney-rattling journey to the camp that had in its heyday been one of six terrorist training grounds in Kandahar province. It was, he explained, a bit of a shrine for militants, although U.S. air strikes had long pulverized to dust many of the eighty buildings within the fortified walls. Afghan troops from the nearby camp routinely patrolled its ruins to shoo away leftover fanatics and keep the curious from blowing themselves up among the unexploded munitions that still littered the site.

Even before we had finished the pleasantries, the Afghan soldier flopped into the front passenger seat of our translator's car and propped his AK-47 rifle between his legs. He smiled at the three of us as we crammed into the back seat. No doubt he was happy to be relieved from the mind-numbing chore of standing watch over the southern desert for hours on end. Guard duty is tedious for even the most simple-minded, but looking out at the vast wasteland where shifting red sands intersected with the hard-baked brown soil of Kandahar must be uncommonly punishing.

Screeching country music, a favourite of our driver, blared from the tape player as the car rattled and shook along a road that was hardly more than reiterated tire indentations in the desert. The music was loud enough to wake the dead, or at least loud enough to let them know we were coming. I leaned forward and stared through the filthy, cracked windshield as the high walls of the compound loomed in silhouette against the late February sky. A few skeletal buildings peeked above the three-and-a-half-metre mud ramparts. The entire place looked like a sinister medieval fortress and the deep shadows of the late afternoon only added to its menacing quality.

The car slipped through a stream swollen by the winter rains, although to our eyes it was hardly bloated. The water barely licked the hubcaps. We rolled through the heart of the dump, past piles of plastic bottles that winked in the sunshine, past scattered junk and past garbage bags full of rotten food. It was an afterthought to close the car windows and we haplessly held our breath against the waves of pungent air trapped inside the cab. The windows weren't cracked open again until we dipped into a dry riverbed. The tires spewed gravel as the car churned up on to a more defined roadway, one that ran the perimeter of the compound.

The Afghan soldier motioned to the fist-sized holes punched in the two-metre-thick walls by armour-piercing shells. Those holes gave us our first unobstructed view of the pitiless field of rubble inside. We passed one section of the earthwork that had collapsed entirely—no doubt under the weight of American bombs. Prior to the September 11, 2001, attacks on New York and Washington, the Americans were reluctant to hit Tarnak Farms. The fear was they'd kill innocent bystanders. There was no such hesitation post–9/11. Cruise missiles, laser-guided bombs and eventually artillery rained down on the place in a fire-and-brimstone spectacle that only Dante could have imagined. It was said that scores of al-Qaeda Arabs were killed. Their bodies are buried in a cemetery in the city's poorest district, where sympathetic Afghans still visit to pay their respects to these "martyrs." But the target of the rage, the one most wanted, had fled months before to the safety of eastern Afghanistan before he disappeared entirely.

The road narrowed when the car rounded the corner and the pathway was squeezed between the remains of the wall and a deep, dry irrigation ditch that ran the length of the south side of the compound. Beyond the canal lay a largely flat, anemic green field dotted with scrub brush. A squat, mud-walled building about three metres high and three metres square—that looked as though it had been fashioned by a child's sand pail—sat beside a rickety bridge on the opposite bank of the ditch. Two thin wooden staffs, lashed together with black electrical tape, formed a flagpole that strained to hold up the Afghan standard against a solid, warm wind that blew in from the desert. Three men sat cross-legged atop the structure and turned around with the sound of the engine. Only one was dressed in the pale blue, woolen uniform and coat of the Afghan National Police (ANP). As we got out of the car, the cop picked up his AK-47 and assessed us carefully. A second man, a civilian, remained seated in seeming indifference. The third man, plump and balding, ambled down a crude, four-rung ladder to the ground.

"Wait here," said Jojo, our driver and translator. His full name was Javed Yazamy, but he preferred to be called by his nickname.

Jojo and the soldier walked toward the Afghan, who approached in an unhurried manner. Greetings were exchanged and the man spoke happily with the soldier, but kept a wary eye on the three "foreigners" standing beside the car. The man also spoke pleasantly with Jojo, whose small, wiry frame made him seem like a dwarf next to the soldier and the stranger. Once our reason for being there was made clear, the man came over and was introduced as Abdul Ghafoor, the local police commander who also happened to own farmland near the compound. He smiled in a way that made me wonder exactly what Jojo had told him—or offered to pay.

Ghafoor insisted on acting as our guide. We were free to look around, he told Jojo in Pashtu, but he warned us to be mindful of the unexploded cluster bombs that were apparently sprinkled all over the former al-Qaeda obstacle course at the centre of the community. We slipped back into the car and drove the remaining 500 metres into the compound with the police commander and the soldier trailing on foot.

A rusted, burned-out hulk that had at some point or another been a passenger vehicle sat in the open, its shaped metal peeled back and twisted like tinfoil, its tires and major components incinerated. Two nearby buildings, mere skeletons, were the largest structures in the area. Both had had their roofs blown away.

As I got out of the car, I was immediately struck by the eerie silence of the place. It was like entering a tomb. The wind, blowing hard enough to bow the flagpole at the police outpost, seemed to purposely avoid this area. I looked for a rational explanation—a wall, a berm, something to justify the dead air that surrounded us—but I found nothing. The wall on the south face of the compound, which would have given shelter from the harsh desert elements, had been largely obliterated. By rights the wind should have howled through, but we had stepped into a vacuum, a place so hated and so evil that it felt as though nature had abandoned it entirely.

The scene to my right stopped me cold. The shapes, lines and colours of the training course were instantly familiar, as they would have been to anyone who watched television news footage in the aftermath of 9/11. This place had been burned into my memory in those days, and seeing it up close felt like a wide-awake nightmare. Some of the surrounding structures had changed, either flattened or reduced to their frameworks, but the single concrete training wall, over which fledgling terrorists had crawled, remained defiantly erect. The blistering Afghan sun and repeated pummelling by U.S. bombs and missiles had blanched its green and brown camouflage paint. A little farther away, the barbwire obstacles under which trainees were expected to crawl had also survived the high-explosive onslaught. Despite the elements, despite the fury, despite the weight of U.S. military might, these potent symbols of misery and the spilling of innocent blood endured. It was little wonder the jihadists drew such inspiration from this place.

The Afghan government owned the land immediately surrounding the complex and leased it to businessmen like Ghafoor, who'd tried for years to lure tenant farmers to the fields. But they wouldn't come—at least not many. The few who did worked only one season before quickly retreating as though chased away by the ghosts of Tarnak. But it wasn't fear of the supernatural that spooked them as much as what the place represented. In an illiterate culture symbols are more powerful than words and those bombed-out buildings spoke more loudly to most Afghans than anything we could say. As long as the buildings stood, the site suggested the Taliban and al-Qaeda would return.

"You don't want to be walking over there," Jojo reminded me, with the police commander at his side.

Bin Laden had moved his followers here in 1998 from Nazim Jihad, an al-Qaeda training camp near Jalalabad, after the Northern Alliance threatened to attack the city, Ghafoor explained through Jojo.

The building in front of us had been al-Qaeda's administrative office. We skirted a waist-high pile of smashed bricks and concrete for a closer look, but going inside was out of the question—the second-floor ceiling hung by only a few threadbare steel rods and braces. The building had been picked clean by U.S. Special Forces soldiers who occupied the site after the Taliban were routed in Kandahar. It was said that the last wills and testaments of Mohammed Atta and Ziad Jarrah, two of the 9/11 hijackers, were found amid these ruins.

Staring at what remained of that rectangular building, it was hard to maintain a journalist's dispassion or avoid a flood of bitter memories. I felt the police captain's eyes on me. Jojo had long disappeared to help my television colleagues, who were poking around the remains of a nearby larger building. Part of me wanted to explain to Ghafoor why I looked so angry, but the language barrier was insurmountable and besides, there was a deeply skeptical air about him. For all of the suffering I had witnessed in New York that September, the furrowed lines on his leathery face and the dead light in his eyes suggested he could attest to worse. I flipped open my notepad and jotted down a few thoughts in the hope that it would help me escape his gaze. It worked. Bored with my silent scribbling, Ghafoor wandered across an open concrete pad that had once been used as a vehicle park for bin Laden's caravan of armoured SUVs.

"Are you a reporter?" The voice spoke from someplace in the back of mind.

"Yes," I remembered replying.

The woman who stood before me in my mind's eye was petite and pretty with wavy, coarse, light brown hair. Her brown eyes and freckled cheeks were red and swollen. I remember her clutching a poster, rolled up like a scroll. There was a breathless, hoarse quality to her plea.

"Can you put his picture on TV?" she begged. "Everyone told me this was where the media was. Maybe he's in the hospital. Please, you've got to help me."

"Who?"

"My brother; he was in the North Tower. Please you've got to help me."

Everything about those days in New York crashed into my mind. Even as I stood in the shadow of bin Laden's compound, I could still taste the thick dust that coated the city and hung in the air for days after the attack; the smell of burned plastic, burned dust; the screaming people who stampeded in terror down 5th Avenue outside of Madison Square Garden, fleeing the towers and the hundreds of false alarms in the days afterward. I remembered walking away calmly from those scenes with the thought that none of it seemed real, that I must be drunk. I'd never come away from an experience so exhausted, so angry and so utterly changed as I did from Manhattan on those gloriously sunny September days.

The woman had approached me outside of the Manhattan Armory, where posters of the missing had been plastered all over the wrought iron fence and brownstone sides like some implacable wallpaper.

"Please, you've got help me. I don't know what else to do. He's not come home since the day of the attack. We can't reach him."

Thousands of people died in New York that fall, but this women's brother was the one I carried with me.

She unrolled the homemade poster and shoved it into my face, oblivious to the fact that I wasn't carrying a camera. His name was Paul; that's all I remember. The ink lettering and the photograph were faded, no doubt from having run hundreds of copies.

The broadcast microphone in my hand made her think I was a television reporter, but there was no cameramen anywhere near us, which would have been a giveaway at any other time. But at this time, in this moment, she had tunnel vision. There was an uncomfortable silence while I tried to figure out how to tell her that I was only a wire-service reporter, not someone who could put her brother's face on television. I remember distinctly how she wouldn't let me look away. Her eyes bore directly into my conscience.

"You have to help me," she insisted, as though her life depended upon my answer.

"I don't work for television. I'm sorry."

She began to cry. My words sounded more like a condolence than a simple reply. I'd never felt so helpless, nor at such a loss for words. It was only a passing encounter in what had been almost two weeks of mayhem in that wounded city. The woman was a total stranger, yet her grief-stricken face and excruciating loss would haunt my memory as though we'd known each other all our lives.

Little did I know that six years later I'd be standing at the source of her misery. My two colleagues from CTV were fascinated by the remains of the largest building, which at three storeys high was the compound's defining landmark. With every crunch of broken masonry beneath their boots they could hear history. For cameraman Al Stephens, the former al-Qaeda hideout was a visual feast of huge craters, pitted walls and broken columns. A lanky, bear of a man affectionately known as "Big Daddy"—courtesy of his two daughters—Al zipped back and forth shooting every detail.

A cruise missile had crashed through the roof and exploded after the attacks on New York and Washington, Ghafoor explained. The evidence was before us: a two-metre-deep hollow where the floor had once been. Two of the four walls were blown out completely. It was here that al-Qaeda's senior leadership had met to discuss important matters, he claimed. I stepped through the hinged doorway and gaped up at the non-existent roof.

"The world's major terrorists would meet in the only building in southern Afghanistan that can be seen clearly from orbit?"

Jojo translated my skepticism in what seemed like an awfully long, apologetic way. Ghafoor just laughed.

"When they were here, they had nothing to fear."

He was right. These men knew the Americans didn't have the stomach to bomb this place. The Americans knew bin Laden was here. They had grainy surveillance footage from an unmanned drone showing the al-Qaeda leader and his entourage walking to the mosque at the compound. The CIA had meticulously planned a commando-style raid—led by a friendly, well-financed Afghan tribe—to capture bin Laden and spirit him to the U.S. to face justice for the embassy bombings in Africa in the late 1990s. Afghan spies had plotted out the houses where bin Laden slept with each of his wives and tried to guess where he would be on the night they attacked. But after two dress rehearsal exercises in the States, the plan was called off. Popular lore had it that scrapping the plan to snatch the world's most wanted terrorist was a political decision made by a scandal-plagued president worried about the optics of the inevitable civilian casualties. But there's little evidence that the ill-fated proposal ever reached President Bill Clinton's desk. Administration officials said there were misgivings about whether the ragtag band of Afghans would succeed in carrying out the assault. According to George Tenent, the former director of the CIA, the judgement to shut down the operation was made at a much lower level.

"If only these walls could talk," observed CTV's Tom Clark as he squinted up into the light streaming through the open beams.

Not only had the blasts peeled away the whitewash on everything, they had randomly stripped the mud plaster from the remaining walls down to the brick. It looked as if it had been scratched away by giant, raging fingers.

Tom, one of the most thoughtful guys I've worked alongside, looked grim as he stepped around the crater in the centre of the room. It felt as though we had disturbed the dead, a sense that was only heightened when we wandered out the opposite side of the building toward some of the huts the Arabs had called home.

Embedded in the mud, weeds and pulverized bricks a few paces away I found a woman's discarded sandal. Tattered bits of *keffiyehs* and other scarves stuck out from beneath heaps of rubble, something that made me wonder whether their former owners were buried under tonnes of mortar. Cooking pots—blackened and dented—as well as other household items lay where they had been dropped at the moment the apocalypse descended. A diesel-powered well pump sat silent and abandoned. Something clinked underneath my boots. I froze and looked down. Part of me wanted to close my eyes in anticipation of a blast, but the apprehension was replaced with a feeling of stupidity when I realized I was standing atop half-buried spent shell casings. I knelt down and scooped up a handful of the cartridges.

Ghafoor appeared out of nowhere behind me. He said something and from farther away Jojo translated. The building to my left had apparently been the place where al-Qaeda stored its weapons for training. It still had most of its roof, but no walls. At least a third of the ceiling had collapsed and now hung precariously by its twisted steel rods, frozen in time like some cascading waterfall of debris. The entire building was supported by half a dozen quivery pillars. At the far end, the Afghans had erected one of their makeshift flagpoles. I noticed then how many of the buildings had the red, black and green standard on them. It was as if the Afghans were trying to tell the world that they had reclaimed this loathsome little piece of the soil.

Before al-Qaeda moved in, Ghafoor explained, the compound belonged to the Ministry of Agriculture, which had used it as an experimental farm. The largest building, which dominated the compound, had been a bakery in the days before and during the Soviet occupation. By the time Taliban supreme leader Mullah Omar allowed bin Laden and his followers to take possession, the complex had already been abandoned for some time, cast aside during the civil war that tore the country and the government to shreds. Al-Qaeda turned the building into a meeting hall where, local legend had it, the 9/11 attacks were planned.

"He seems to know an awful lot," I said, with half a smile. "Are you sure he wasn't one of them?"

Jojo simply laughed and didn't translate. Ghafoor aped him, although he didn't seem quite sure what was so funny.

Over the next half an hour, my television companions turned the pudgy police commander into an honest-to-goodness tour guide, having him point out areas of interest and give a little history lesson. His unabashed tutorial would be cut together with Tom's voiced-over impressions in a piece that was supposed to air that night.

I wandered. Taking photographs, notes and a little Web video, I was happy to be alone and stay out of the camera shots. I found a medium-sized rubble pile and, when it was clear there was nothing to impale me, I climbed to the top and sat down. The sun played against the ruins, sending a checkerboard of long shadows across the compound. My eyes traced the pattern in much the same way one looks for shapes in the clouds. But the distraction was short-lived. All I could think about was New York—that beautiful, loud, overbearing city. The very lifeblood of American identity coursed through that place and al-Qaeda had gone for the jugular. But the war they started had bled all over each of us, regardless of where we came from. If you talked to Americans, those in the intelligence agencies and military, they said the war had started much earlier than 9/11, with the African embassy bombings of 1998 and the attack on the USS *Cole* two years later. Canadians officially pegged the start of the war as October 10, 2001, the date troops first set foot in Afghanistan. Some academics say it really didn't start for "us" until the spring of 2006, when Canadians began fighting and dying in the arid grape fields of Panjwaii. But those of us who rushed to New York in the hours and days after the twin towers collapsed knew right there and then that nothing in our world was ever going to be the same. A new, violent and dark chapter of history opened before our eyes. It was a total break with the past, startling, brutal and furious. The heady days of the 1990s instantly seemed distant and trivial. Even the dangerous Cold War years took on a quaint, comfortable quality in the shadow of those crisp, autumn days and all that followed.

I gazed at Tarnak Farms with its jagged ruins against the crimson sky and marvelled—this, apparently, was where it had all begun. Maybe. I suspect no will ever know precisely where and when the plot was hatched. Al-Qaeda isn't likely to publish a comprehensive history any time soon and the sketchy inside accounts that are available suggest the plan came together piecemeal, rather than in an epiphany moment. But history and people in general need a focus, a sense of order—a beginning, middle and end. At least here one could start to sort through all that had happened and make sense of it, if ever one can make sense of war and terrorism.

The low rumble of a pair of Dutch F-16 jet fighters taking off from Kandahar Airfield interrupted my reflection. Without 9/11, none of us would be here—not the journalists, and not the soldiers flying those planes and manning KAF. A painful reminder of that fact lay just beyond these walls.

From my dusty perch it wasn't possible to see the field where four Canadian soldiers had been killed in a 2002 training accident, but the flat stretch of scrub-brushed land where an American pilot mistakenly dropped a 250-kilogram bomb had been visible from the road. We comforted ourselves following their deaths and the many that came after with the notion that these men had died fighting the terror and fear unleashed on the streets of New York and Washington. We comforted ourselves with the notion that the Afghans had been freed from a brutal Taliban regime, one that enslaved women and deliberately kept its people ignorant. We were bringing light where once there was darkness. At least that's what we told ourselves.

Jojo waved at me from the parking lot where Tom and Big Daddy had set up the camera for one last interview with Ghafoor. They wondered if I wanted in. I gingerly climbed down from the hill and joined them, although I wasn't sure I'd write anything; Tarnak Farms had been written about many times before and I assumed there was nothing left to learn.

It took a moment for me to fish my recorder out of my pocket. Ghafoor stroked his long, thin beard and seemed genuinely pleased to be the centre of attention. Being interviewed on camera in the street may be commonplace in North America, but in Afghanistan it was a rare occurrence indeed.

Before the tape rolled, there were the perfunctory pre-interview questions, the most amusing of which were those related to his age. Ghafoor wasn't sure how old he might be. Many Afghans, especially in rural areas, could only guess. Watches and calendars had little meaning in a land that time had forgotten. Some of the younger Afghans calculated their age by the number of years that had passed since the Soviets left, as though that was when life began.

The interview lasted only a few minutes and Ghafoor, with Jojo acting as his voice, filled in some of the narrative blanks for Tom's piece. I was curious about the al-Qaeda days. Had he ever met bin Laden or Ayman al-Zawahri, the terror group's deputy commander?

"No."

Local Afghans, even Taliban fighters, were not allowed into the compound and rarely mingled with their Arab "guests," as he described them. Every outsider was a guest in Pashtun culture. He said the segregation was strict, especially after an Afghan cook apparently betrayed bin Laden's travel plans in the late 1990s. The spy incorrectly predicted where the terror chief's convoy was headed. His information brought down a rain of cruise missiles on the wrong training camp in the eastern part of the country. At the last moment, bin Laden changed his destination, choosing to go to Kabul in the aftermath of the U.S. embassy bombings in Africa. The cook was apparently not punished, an act of mercy that stunned the Afghans and heightened their appreciation of the man. Whether the tale was true or not didn't seem to matter; it was often repeated.

Finished with his portion of the interview, Tom wandered off to get more cutaway shots of the compound, leaving Jojo and me standing with Ghafoor.

I wondered whether the locals had any inkling of what al-Qaeda had been up to during the long years it was headquartered here. All of the gunfire and practice bombings of the training must have made some people curious, I contended.

No, very few people lived in the area and they essentially minded their own business, Ghafoor suggested. A millennium of conquest and occupation by world powers had genetically removed nosiness from the Afghan character. Much of what he'd learned about what went on at the compound came from Afghan militia who were among those to occupy the site after the Taliban were defeated.

"They have done some very terrible things and many thousands of people have died," I said. "Were you afraid of them? Did they give you any reason to fear them?"

Ghafoor smiled and shook his head.

"No, not at all," he replied through Jojo. "They were very nice guests. They brought medicine when we were sick. They were kind. They helped us, like you people."

I flicked off my tape recorder and stared at him.

"We are nothing like them," I insisted quietly.

Ghafoor just gave a vacant smile.

We're Not in Kansas Anymore

The gasp is almost universal. When you tell somebody you're going to Afghanistan—be it family, friends or complete strangers—the reaction is instantaneous: a mixture of shock, horror, excitement and, in some cases, envy. But usually it starts with the gasp, as if they'd just witnessed a traffic accident.

"God bless you," said a U.S. customs agent after I explained the purpose of my trip to Virginia in the winter of 2006. I was headed to a war-zone boot camp on a remote farm in the Shenandoah Valley.

"Godspeed," she added as she stamped my customs form.

While I had been given many expressions of good luck on assignments, no one had ever issued such an urgent, breathless blessing, even when a colleague and I had gone charging into New York City in the hours after 9/11. And "Be careful" was the most anyone said for Hurricane Katrina, in a tone that made you feel as though you were crossing the street. The stories with exotic place-lines somehow seemed more dangerous.

In the weeks leading up to the training course, friends and family spoke to me with the ginger words usually reserved for terminally ill patients—or those who'd lost their minds. As it turned out, those who argued most strenuously against going ended up being the ones who listened in full rapture to the tales of "what it's like over there" and fed on the shadowy romance of it all. But in the beginning, if I wasn't being berated directly, I could count on semi-weepy e-mails, including one from my oldest friend, who struggled to understand why I would volunteer for such an assignment.

It's occurred to me more than once that you have to be either slightly touched or insensibly determined to want to put the words "war correspondent" on your CV. A senior Canadian officer whom I admire once described it by saying that cops, soldiers and journalists, unlike others, run toward gunfire, not away from it. That tribute sounds nice and on the surface it is sometimes true, but scratch just a little at the veneer and you find out how hollow the glamour can be and how crazy the life can become. Going in, you never know how much it can change you. Events, comments and scenes that would have horrified you in a previous life become routine, sometimes even funny. Then there are moments when the work, the thrill of the story, provides an adrenaline rush like no other. There are correspondents I know who've been sucked so far inside the beast that eventually the line on the resume is all they have left of themselves. Others have had the courage to walk away. But you never fully escape. Maybe it's more accurate to say that a little piece of you gets left behind with each story. Still, there was no question that I was going. My time in New York, in the aftermath of 9/11, had left me determined to reach out and touch this war, to breathe it until I understood it.

The first gulps of air on this journey were taken in the Virginia countryside, where I was expected to complete training on how to navigate in a war zone. The Hostile Environment and First Aid Course was mandatory preparation for an embedded assignment with Canadian troops in Kandahar. For a week, we were bombed, shot at and kidnapped. The course, run by a group of salty ex–Royal Marines, was a brutal introduction to the pitfalls and intricacies of covering a story amidst an assortment of threats. I learned to overcome my uneasiness at the sight of blood, and that I was quite calm when an automatic rifle was being shoved in my face at a checkpoint. I also learned rather quickly that I did not like being kidnapped with a black canvas bag over my head. And as I knelt in a muddy field with a gun to the base of my skull I vowed that I would never be in this position for real.

Weeks later, as my plane touched down in Dubai—the major transit route for world-weary correspondents covering Afghanistan—I found myself thinking about statistics. It's funny how you don't "think" about "it" when you are signing all of the papers and liability waivers that the government and your employer shove in front of you. The likelihood of something happening to me in Afghanistan seemed pretty remote, at least that's what I told anyone who would listen, including myself. In any given week, there were only so many times you could be outside the protection of fortified bases and outposts. And of those times there were only so many bombs and bad guys to go around. Still, it was tough to convince some folks of these facts. My rationalizations were—in the opinion of friends and family—the postmodern way of whistling past the graveyard.

Despite whatever bravado I tried to display, I found the coffee cup shaking in my hand the morning I was to depart Dubai for my first trip to Kabul. I was the only westerner on the Ariana Airlines flight. There was no assigned seating and I was promptly shown to the back of the ancient Boeing 737. Safety standards on Ariana were somewhat lax, I noticed, when the fasten seatbelt sign lit up. Or didn't. The plastic covers over the lights above most seats in the aircraft were gone, leaving only tiny, naked bulbs.

The only pre-flight announcement involved an angry-sounding man— possibly the pilot—shouting almost indiscernibly over the loudspeaker: "Close the door!"

Bearded flight attendants in white, short-sleeved shirts shooed children, who had been running in the aisle, to their seats. One of them, a ten-year-old girl, sat next to me. A young, beardless man with a kind but nervous face sat on the opposite side, looking out the window. It was evident by the way he spoke and gestured to the child that he was her father.

With the engines fired up, we rumbled on to the taxiway. It was then that I noticed that our row—second from the back—had no seatbelts. The buckle portions appeared as if they had been ripped off with a jagged knife. I looked at the man sitting next to me. He shrugged.

When the aircraft roared down the runway, the vibration of our seats seemed extraordinary. As the nose pitched upward, I found out why. The entire row hadn't been bolted to the deck and the seats tipped backward. Instinctively, I grabbed the headrest in front of me, as did my Afghan companion. We held on—fingernails dug into the cushions—until the jet levelled off at its cruising altitude. The front legs of our row hit the deck with a metallic thump. The little girl next to me squealed with delight, as though we had been on a roller coaster. The man next to me gave a relieved smile.

"Are you American?" he asked in halting English.

"No, Canadian."

He seemed even more relieved, shook my hand and said, "That's good. I don't like Americans."

The flight whisked over the still waters of the Persian Gulf and out above the sun-baked coastline of Iran. Many of the passengers got up and mingled, as though the flight were one big family reunion. I was introduced several times over to approving nods as the "Can-ay-dee-ann." A middle-aged man, whom I was told was a cleric in Wardak province west of Kabul, seemed to take a particular interest in me. He talked at length in Pashtu with my seatmate and gazed at me for what seemed like a very long time before he smiled and returned to his seat.

"He doesn't believe you and thinks you are American," said my new-found friend, who finally introduced himself as Rahim. "He also doesn't like Americans."

"He's welcome to see my passport."

"No need. We trust you."

"Do you go to Kandahar by bus or plane?" Rahim asked.

"On a UN flight."

"Good. The road is becoming not safe."

Kabul is located at the bottom of a bowl between snow-capped mountains. Our rickety jet skimmed along the rim of the peaks until the pilot put the aircraft into a sudden corkscrew dive that arched around as though we were being sucked down a drain. This time, Rahim was the first to snatch the headrest. The dive was a combat manoeuvre meant to confuse incoming missiles, although it occurred to me that something important could have fallen off, flinging us into a death spiral. My cheeks fluttered with the force of gravity until, at what seemed the last minute, the pilot levelled out, dropped the landing gear and gently put us on the tarmac.

The jet taxied past several American F-16 fighter-bombers parked near the terminal and I noticed Rahim looking at them for what seemed like a long time. "Five years; they have done nothing to help us," he muttered, realizing that I had been watching.

The arrival terminal was still a work-in-progress. It was chaos, made all the more aggravating by the fact that Afghans seemed not to understand the concept of a queue. They cut in front of one another with little attention or regard. There was a lot of shouting and waving fists. I thought it best to just stand back and let them fight it out in the half-completed hall, where the new walls and slate-grey tiles already seemed worn and dingy.

Two harried, exhausted customs agents sat almost on top of each other behind bulletproof glass in a cubicle no bigger than a closet. It wasn't until I got closer that I realized one of them was white. He sat hunched next to an Afghan and seemed to be showing him what to do. They were both dressed in the pale blue winter coats of the country's customs service. The man motioned me forward, even though there were still several screaming Afghans in front of me. He gave my passport and visa only a cursory glance before throwing them back at me under the glass. There was no stamp, nor sticker. He ran a hand through his mop of greasy hair and waved me on.

The dimly lit baggage collection area was even more of a mess. Frenzied relatives and passengers clung to one another as though it was a miracle we were all alive. Perhaps it was. Young Afghan boys in dirty Western soccer shirts weaved their way in and out of the crowd and tried to match, by guess-work, the bags on the conveyor belts with their owners. As someone reached for his or her suitcase, one or several of the boys would pounce in the hope of getting there before the owner. Elsewhere in the world, such activity might be considered attempted robbery, but in Afghanistan it was evidence of the entrepreneurial spirit. Once they had your bag, the boys acted as though they would carry it to ends of the earth for a nice tip in U.S. greenbacks, usually a dollar. The boy who snatched my bag was skinny and much paler than the other children. My duffle bag probably weighed more than him. He spoke tough-sounding, halted English and assured me that he could get a cab. It wasn't necessary, I told him. We passed several filthy Toyota Corollas, older models that had been converted to taxis. Drivers sized up the passengers with a brutal glare. My young porter may have been prepared to go on, but for him the earth ended when the pavement did, at the dirt parking lot. There, behind a steel gate, was Manilay, the local I'd arranged to meet me.

"Salam aleikum, brother." Manilay knew me right away. Since I was the only bewildered westerner in sight, it probably wasn't a great leap. "Welcome to Afghanistan."

He shooed my young baggage handler away once I had slipped the boy a couple of bucks and then threw my duffle bag into the back of a beaten-up, grey sedan. The car bumped out on to the wide boulevard connecting the airport to the rest of the city. My eyes were drawn to an old, faded and dented Soviet MiG fighter perched atop a pedestal. The thoroughfare, with brown, untended grass and crumbling curbs, had seen better days.

It wasn't until we got to the traffic circle that the full extent of Kabul's never-ending misery became apparent. Manilay slowed the vehicle and twisted in his seat for a better of view of the oncoming traffic and I looked through the front windshield at what seemed like hectares of ruins, half-smashed buildings and jagged piles of rubble. Smoke from the cooking fires burning amid the vestiges of homes and apartments wafted into the slate-coloured sky and created a shifting, ugly grey pall over the city. I watched as a boy in a tattered baseball jacket and no shoes carried a crumpled tin pot up and over a hill littered with broken bricks. A woman in a filthy, threadbare burka appeared out of nowhere at the passenger window. With boney, outstretched fingers she asked for money through the mesh faceplate of the enveloping cloak. With her other hand, she held on to her toddler. "Tell her to go away," Manilay insisted. The hesitation in my face forced him to repeat the order.

She clawed frantically at the window. Her plea became a demand and as she began to shout her voice turned into a shrill, impatient wail. The sound reminded me of a wounded animal.

Manilay put the car in gear and sped away. Once through the traffic circle, he gave me an impatient look.

"I don't think you will like it here," he said.

"Why do you say that?"

"People here are very poor, very desperate, and you just cannot keep handing them things because they will always want more," he declared without a trace of sympathy.

"But that woman—"

"That woman should be with her family. Her husband is probably dead. Maybe he was Taliban or something."

"And what if the rest of her family is dead? What if she can't go home?"

The nuances of the woman's tragic life was something Manilay either wasn't prepared to consider or was eager to ignore. We rode the rest of the way to the guest house in relative silence.

Once I was settled in my room, a shabby ten-foot by ten-foot space, with unevenly cut doors and threadbare curtains, Manilay suggested we sit and have coffee. A few minutes later we were out of the musty room and into an airy dining area, a bright open space with windows that looked out over the garden. A man in a beige shalwar kameez, a knee-length shirt and winter jacket tended the flowerbeds. Beyond the bare trees and brownish grass was the compound wall. It was topped with razor wire. Grey clouds were breaking up and intermittent waves of sunshine flitted across the garden. Soaring snow-capped mountains completed the panoramic backdrop.

Strong coffee to which I added healthy dollops of sugar and cream was served from a silver urn. The waiter, who doubled as the check-in clerk, brought a tray of sweets, which Manilay eyed.

It was the first opportunity I'd had to assess him without the swirl of the Kabul spectacle. He was big for an Afghan, both in height and proportion—not fat, but definitely nourished compared with some of the rawboned figures we had passed in the street. He walked with the heavy-footed gait of a big person, but with slightly rounded shoulders. His eyes were small and inquisitive. He smiled after taking a sip of his coffee.

"So why do you come to Afghanistan, brother?"

"To tell stories," I replied, noting how he kept watch over the sweets.

"What kind of stories?" He was too polite to ask to share the plate, especially since I had paid no attention to it.

"All sorts. I am here to cover the army, but am very interested in writing about the Afghan people."

"What do you know about the Afghan people?"

My answer came out like a well-practised dissertation. I waxed about recent history, politics and some of the ex-pat Afghans whom I'd met. It might have sounded impressive to Western ears, but the distant, skeptical look on Manilay's face told me I didn't fool him. My soliloquy lapsed into dry-throated silence. I took a sip of coffee and slid the cookie tray at him.

"Do you pray?" he asked after devouring a couple of shortbread sweets.

"Occasionally."

It was his turn to launch into a dissertation. He spoke passionately and convincingly about the deep spirituality of Islam and insisted with emphatic hand gestures that it was far superior to the Christian faith. I listened without comment, but then challenged some of his perceptions when they descended to deliberate caricatures of Western religion. He seemed genuinely startled by my willingness to debate. He snatched more cookies and we argued until the setting afternoon sun turned the room a shadowy crimson.

When it became clear he wasn't about to convert me to Islam on the first day, Manilay steered the conversation away from religion and toward more practical matters. Manilay was to be my guide, my translator, my driver and cultural advisor over the three days I was to spend in Kabul. He turned out to be a very good "fixer" and I came to appreciate his steadiness and insights all the more when I got to Kandahar, where the people and the place were more precarious. We planned the stories we were going to do in the coming days and our conversation slowly petered out. Something clearly weighed on Manilay's mind. He stared out the window in silence.

"You will not like it here," he said after a couple of moments.

"You've said that already."

He looked straight at me. "May I give you advice?"

After a slight nod of my head, Manilay spoke with a forceful conviction that seemed to rise up from the very tips of his toes.

"If you are going to tell stories of the Afghan people you must understand how important Islam is to their lives and you must understand what that means," he said with an unflinching gaze. "And you must understand that this is not Canada. Afghanistan is a broken place after thirty years of war, but there are many parts where people have not changed for centuries. They do not believe in the same things as you and do not see things as you do."

"So you think I will not like it because people are not like me?" I folded my arms across my chest. "That is an awfully shallow assessment. It usually takes people a couple of days to come to that conclusion about me."

The self-mocking tone made him smile. He grabbed the last shortbread cookie on the way out the door.

* * *

Kabul in the spring of 2006 felt like a slaughterhouse that had been taken over by new owners. Everywhere you turned you found reminders of carnage from days past: buildings smashed to rubble by warlord Gulbuddin Hekmatyar's guns when the city refused to bend to his iron will; the city's main stadium, where the Taliban gleefully stoned to death women whom they accused of immoral behaviour. It sat silent and empty. If you peeked around the side you could see the goalposts used as makeshift scaffolds for public hangings. It was said the bodies dangled in the breeze like so many pieces of meat and served as reminders of the Taliban's awful authority. The stockyard feel of the place had yet to dissipate even though almost five years had elapsed since the hardline regime had been chased from power.

It was into this menagerie that hundreds of thousands of returning refugees poured, an influx that, over the years, had given the city streets an artificial verve. The place felt alive when in many districts it was still a putrid carcass. There was choking traffic and the markets, including the famous bird market, bustled on a daily basis. But there was little or no sanitation in the burgeoning neighbourhoods that seemed to explode on either side of the dirt pathways. There was running water for only three hours a day and electricity was just as intermittent. Into these suburbs were tossed a jumble of returning people with no social cohesion. Doctors lived alongside street sweepers, who were beside thieves and drug runners. Even the once leafy Share Nau district, north of the river where the city's elite had once lived, was a tangled mess. The sixteenth-century Babur Gardens along the slopes of the Asmayee mountain, once the jewel of Kabul, lay in disrepair. The cold, dry air that swooped down from the mountains never seemed able to purge the city of the clouds of smoke from brick kiln fires, the smell of diesel fuel, sewer, garbage and mustiness.

Reconstruction had a tendency to mushroom in some districts, where the ruins of old, historic buildings were swept aside and replaced with a few shiny, modern offices. These Manhattan-like corridors were cut and stitched haphazardly on to the landscape, as a hack surgeon might bind an old wound. Some called it progress. Most just called it ugly. For the thousands of Western diplomats, aid managers and military officers who zipped back and forth between fortified compounds in their armoured SUVs, the sight of steel and glass was comforting and familiar. It offered them a continuity with the outside world. It also gave them purpose. That was what they were here to see. They were going to build and build and build. Yet the problem   even back then—was that with so much money sloshing around behind compound walls, everyone seemed to forget what they were building for. Beyond the dilapidated borders of the city, just a few dozen kilometres in any direction, was the real heart of Afghanistan—mountain and desert villages that had remained largely untouched for two thousand years. Visiting them was like visiting the far side of the moon. It was a world so foreign, so incomprehensible that it was almost not to be believed. So, almost everyone just kept building in Kabul.

It was generally agreed that President Hamid Karzai's mandate ended at Kabul's city limits, and in 2004 and 2005 a lot of planning went in to extending his writ. It would be done through force of arms under the auspices of the North Atlantic Treaty Organisation (NATO), the European-based military alliance that had won the Cold War without firing a shot in anger. But Afghanistan was new territory, and NATO had never run an operation outside of its continental borders. The plan was to expand step by step throughout the country, first bringing security and then allowing for reconstruction and the delivery of aid. Everyone assumed, of course, that the Afghans were eagerly awaiting this helping hand.

On my second day in Kabul the sky dawned a thin, faultless blue, the kind you only witness high in the mountains. Manilay and I had agreed to do some colour stories on the city. I was, at first, content to amble the compound's winter-scorched garden, but eventually I got restless waiting for Manilay and wandered out through the gate. The guards and I exchanged stupid grins, and mumbled incoherently to one another. An Afghan cop with an AK-47 stretched across his lap and a filthy flask of tea leaned back in rickety wooden chair and stared blankly at me. He was the last sentinel before a street teeming with people. Some of the passersby stopped to gawk at the westerner dressed in blue jeans and a windbreaker. Soon a crowd stood silently at the end of the alcove, some with mouths agape. It was as if I were an alien delivered into their midst. We stared at each other across the shaded concrete archway. In that moment, I discovered how monkeys in a zoo must feel. One man, in a blue nylon Adidas jogging jacket, with a light beard and a Beatles-style mop-top, smiled at me. His friend, who wore a black knit winter cap and a powder-blue baseball coat over his shalwar kameez, scratched his heavy beard. Two men in turbans talked among themselves. My cellphone rang; it was Manilay, wondering where I was.

"Waiting outside the gate for you." It was an innocent enough comment, but the sputtering at the other end forced me to hold the phone away from my ear.

"What? Get back inside the compound, right now!"

"Everything is fine," I replied.

"No, it is not."

"There's a cop right next to me."

"I don't care. You're crazy. Get inside the compound and I will be there in five minutes."

A moment later, Manilay came crashing through the crowd and hauled me by the sleeve out to his grey Toyota. Even though he had been in a hurry to retrieve me, he had locked the doors behind him and now found himself fumbling with the keys. He almost shoved me into the passenger seat.

"Don't ever do that again," Manilay snarled as we drove away. He gripped the steering wheel and stared straight ahead, unable to look at me. "What kind of reporter have they sent me?"

"No one there posed a threat."

"You never know who is watching or what they will do."

"You're just being paranoid," I said.

"Yes, and so should you be." He steered the car into a traffic circle, and, taking a deep breath, he recounted how four Macedonian aid workers had been snatched off the streets of Kandahar just a few days earlier. The Taliban murdered them, dumped their bodies in the desert and told the police where to find them. In an added twist, the insurgents booby-trapped the bodies. Seven police officers were killed trying to recover the remains.

Since 2004, the Taliban had conducted sporadic, minor attacks in Kandahar. They were considered not much more than a nuisance to the U.S forces in the region. Far more sinister was the campaign, started the year before, to murder pro-government mullahs and other tribal elders. The assassinations would tear to shreds the very fabric of village society in southern Afghanistan, with the body count reaching into the hundreds over the next few years. Most non-governmental aid groups packed their bags around the time the *shabnamehs*—threatening night letters—were nailed to their doors. It was a positively medieval form of intimidation, something you'd expect in a fifteenth- or sixteenth-century European village. And it worked, mostly. When it didn't, when the aid workers refused to be frightened, that's when the bloodshed started.

We drove for a couple of hours and ended up at a vending stand across the street from the old soccer stadium. The rickety cart, an improvised affair hammered together with different bits of wood and paint, was tucked up against a stone wall. There were two cardboard boxes of potato crisps, plastic plates, cups and several steaming tin pots of tea. The owner was a slight man with kind eyes and a trim, shocking white beard. Gathered around him were several younger men who sat on the waist-high wall. A man in a knit cap stared distantly at the ground. It was not an unfamiliar air; I'd seen the same look on the faces of the homeless in Canada. I didn't speak until we got back in the car.

"What were all of those guys hanging around for?"

"They come and wait there for work, but there is none today," Manilay said as I looked back over my shoulder. "It is very bad here; half of the people don't have work."

The sun beat through the windows and the air in the vehicle was heavy as we drove the city. Cracking the windows, even a little bit, invited someone to drop a grenade or stick a gun through the opening. I made small talk with Manilay, but I could not shake the horrible sense of isolation that gripped my chest. As I stared through the smudged window at hardscrabble neighbourhoods, the biblical-looking men with the fierce expressions and the wandering livestock, I wondered just what on earth any of us in the West had in common with these people who'd been ground under the boots of history. All my talk the previous day about chronicling the plight of the Afghans seemed simple-minded.

The farther we went into the city, the heavier traffic became. Not far from the guest house, we were held up by a large, white flat-bed truck. Manilay sought to distract me by pointing out the line of cabs parked along the street in front of a bombed-out brick building wedged between a line of tumble-down shops. Two of the yellow and white taxis were new, one adorned with flaming red decals like a stockcar. The driver, a short man in a grey woolen top, dipped his hand into a greasy, yellow bucket and slopped soapy water on to the Toyota. He lathered it lovingly. It was an ordinary scene, something that could have played out on the driveway of any proud car owner back home. Anywhere else, it would hardly be worthy of note; here, it represented a desperately sought-after normalcy.

A young boy, no more than ten, scampered from a ruined building, hopped a concrete drainage ditch, and ran between the taxis right up to our car. He peered at us with wondrously large, brown eyes. His expression was hard at first, but the shifting sunlight remoulded it into a pitiful pout. He held out his hand.

I looked over at Manilay, who sat stone-faced behind the wheel. He stared at the child for what seemed a long time. It was hard to tell what was going on behind those narrow eyes. He reached down into the cup holder, pinched two small Afghanis bills between his fingers and held them up to me.

"Give him this," he said quietly.

With the window rolled down a crack, I slipped the money to the child, who smiled and disappeared back into the labyrinth of smashed bricks. I looked at Manilay, who didn't hesitate to meet my gaze. Neither of us said a word.

The Gathering Storm 2

There is something breathtaking yet terrifying about the approach of a sandstorm. The blue desert sky is replaced by a milky overcast, and the clouds—as if summoned by some ancient, long-forgotten gods—gather in great mounds of steel blue and grey. The wind rises slowly until you can hear the snap of flags straining against their poles. Great shifting curtains of dust rise in the laneways and along the roads, forcing trucks and armoured vehicles to turn on their lights. Sometimes there is an advanced wave of hail; others times there is lightning as the sky grows darker in a swirling, billowing menace that boils like witch's brew. There is no real barrier against the fine, powdery sand that pricks your eyes like a thousand tiny knives and blasts the complexion of your cheeks to a ruddy, red glow. The grit and grains build up on your tongue. You want to spit, but opening your mouth only invites more of the same. The rising crescendo of wind and sand rustles and shivers canvas tent covers. All around you is a sound like someone cracking a freshly starched sheet over a bed. Sometimes it goes on for hours. Everything around Kandahar Airfield seemed to be at a standstill during those storms.

You just hunkered down, tried to stay inside and cursed anyone who opened the tent door.

* * *

In the spring of 2006, the Taliban conducted—for want of a better description—research and development for suicide bombs on the streets of Kandahar, with the local population as the guinea pigs. It started soon after I hit the ground in the southern city and only weeks after Canadian troops raised their tents. Homemade bomb-making is a crude, imprecise science; it's never certain whether enough explosive has been added. The appearance of Canadians with their light armoured vehicles (LAVs) confounded the bomb makers. They'd long ago figured out how to destroy the thinly plated G-Wagon jeeps, but with the LAVs, their best efforts resulted only in blown tires.

Shortly after the arrival of the LAVs, the army picked up intelligence chatter that the Taliban had been scouring the black market for something to take on the troop carriers. In conjunction with the shopping trip, they launched a relentless wave of suicide attacks. The goal? To find the right mixture of old Soviet munitions—or bombs—that could blow a hole in the vehicle.

As the Taliban experimented, Afghan civilians paid the price. The bomb makers watched, either from a safe distance or on video tape, to measure the destruction and figure out how much more punch to add. It seemed like Jojo and the other fixer who acted as our eyes and ears in Kandahar called every day to report from the scene of a bombing. Sometimes they'd be on the verge of weeping: shopkeepers, teachers, children, it just went on and on. The chaos, screaming and tears were so common that spring it almost made you insensible. Jojo, who could get to the latest site faster than any of us and blend in more discreetly, would eventually show me the scenes, sometimes days afterward, and even then we found messed-up people. It was horrifying and it took months for many of us covering the war to be battered into a sense of cynicism and despondency. But like the bomb makers themselves, we got there eventually.

Taxis were the suicide-bomb vehicles of choice in those days. The pervasive white, yellow and black Toyota Corollas made the perfect cover. At first there were two guys: one to drive and the other to pull the switch. But since the volunteer pool for suicide missions was inevitably shallow, the Taliban rigged up remote detonators. Eventually bomb makers would move on to donkeys, which made a horrible mess, bicycles and even wheelbarrows.

The Taliban, for all their pious pretense, were not above hiding weapons caches in cemeteries. The thought was that no Western soldier would dare disturb a Muslim burial ground. One day, a vest went off accidentally when it was being retrieved. The *Globe and Mail*'s Christie Blatchford and her photographer Louie Palu happened to be a few blocks away and were able to get to the scene. Both looked harrowed and sullen when they eventually came through the door at KAF. Christie didn't have much to say and soon disappeared, but Louie was wound tight like a spring and he talked to release the tension.

They had come across what was left of the bomber, or the guy who was supposed to bring the bomber his vest. Most of the man was still there, spread-eagle on the ground. Although his face had been blown off, the skin had ripped away from the skull almost perfectly, to the point where Louie thought it looked like a rubber mask. The Afghan cops held it up and examined it for identification. Bits of flesh, chunks that looked like red Jell-O, were scattered all about. Some pieces hung from the crooked wooden sticks the Afghan used as grave markers. Years later, Louie told me that he couldn't stand the sight of meat, especially cooked meat. He'd become a vegetarian.

"It's fucked, man," he said that day in the tent. "Why would anybody want to do that to themselves?"

None of us had any answers.

After that day, the story didn't come out too often, but when it did, Louie seemed to like to tell it over breakfast to new colleagues. He was like that: hilarious, irreverent, but also someone deeply moved by the insanity around him whose only defence was to pour either acid wit or expletives on the misery. He saw more up-close combat than any Canadian journalist of the war. Louie's words came back to me months later, in early 2007, when I had my own chance encounter with the remains of a suicide bomber. Coming back from the Canadian provincial reconstruction team (PRT) base, I got to the scene of a bombing at the same time as the Afghan cops, but before troops arrived to put up a cordon. The bomber had been ripped clean in half. I had no idea where his legs and hips had gone, but the rest of him was still intact, lying face up in the dirt. His clothes had been ripped off by the blast and his chest, spongy beard and frizzy black hair were sprinkled with dust that reminded me of icing sugar. His eyes were still open, staring at the sky. I vaguely recall a kid wandering around, half stupid from the explosion, with a man's sandals in his hand.

I remember repeating Louie's lament.

"That's just fucked, man. Why would anybody do that?"

"Because they are all crazy. That's all they know is crazy," Jojo later said to me.

I'm sure Louie would have liked the answer.

* * *

Forward Operating Base (FOB) Robinson sat atop a sandy, dusty plateau in Helmand province, west of Kandahar. To one side was a cliff that dropped off to an open plain. The land sloped gradually upward toward a series of small compounds and the nearby village of Sangin. The most discernible landmarks in that tiny bit of wasteland were two semi-ruined mounds known as Castle Ruins and the Fortress. The U.S. Special Forces defended the base along with a scratch group of Afghan troops and police—whom I later discovered were often stoned. Sangin was the westernmost tip of the Taliban's infiltration route into southern Afghanistan and the outpost was meant to act as a plug to prevent insurgents from spilling into the Helmand River valley.

By the time a section of Canadian troops was airlifted in to FOB Robinson late on March 28, 2006, the base was under siege. It had been attacked twenty-one times since mid-February and commanders knew the place was eventually going to go up in flames. They had conducted a reconnaissance two weeks prior and realized the area was going to be trouble. As internal Defence Department documents later revealed, the local populace was largely behind the Taliban, "due to intimidation."

A resupply convoy headed to FOB Robinson had been ambushed and mauled by the Taliban early on the 28th and eight Afghan army soldiers were killed. A quick-reaction force of thirty-eight guys from 7 Platoon, Charlie Company, 1st Battalion, Princess Patricia's Canadian Light Infantry (1 PPCLI) was sent to shore up the defences. Once on the ground, the Canadians mingled with the U.S. Special Forces and trainers who were there to work with the Afghan troops. The arrival of the Canadians was like a tonic for American commanders, who judged that the Taliban would have seen the incoming helicopters. They predicted: "There's no way they'll hit us tonight."

That night was clear and cool, but very dark. The low-light conditions were made even worse by the talcum-like sand that, once disturbed, seemed to hang in the air like a gritty curtain.

When there was an explosion outside of the compound—an occurrence the Canadians were assured was normal at Sangin—a nighttime patrol to feel out insurgent positions was planned. Five minutes later there was another blast followed by a hail of tracer fire that lit up the night sky. The patrol was cancelled and the Canadians rushed across the assembly yard to reinforce the south and north gates.

A section of Canadian soldiers moved outside the north gate and ran past a Humvee, the ubiquitous U.S. four-wheel drive-gun truck, parked at the northeast corner. One of the Canadians hollered to get the attention of the two Special Forces operators crewing the vehicle.

The dozen or so Canadians flopped down into the cover of a two-metre-high berm that faced the Taliban lines. Within seconds they had drawn fire from two positions. The Americans behind them, including those in the mentoring compound, returned fire over the heads of the Canadians.

There was a pause before the Canadian troops, firmly dug into the dirt, opened up on Castle Ruins.

Through his gunsight, an American soldier watched the battle unfold. He saw the incoming fire, witnessed the Canadians take up position and stared in horror as the Humvee in the northeast corner belched five to six bursts out of its powerful M240B machine guns—directly at the berm.

The guys who survived recalled hearing the zing of bullets smashing into the dirt around them, sixty rounds in total. One Canadian was hit in the leg. He could tell by the way his body twisted that the fire was coming from behind. Shocked, he jumped to the other side of the berm, where Taliban bullets had landed only moments before. Another soldier was hit in the left leg and left side. He too turned toward the American compound.

Someone yelled, "Get down!"

The bloodied Canadians shouted for the Americans to stop. Someone grabbed the radio and screamed into it, but no one could raise the gun truck. The withering fire ended as inexplicably as it started. Suddenly the Humvee's twin barrels swung around and unleashed a blast toward the roof of the compound where the American mentors were located.

The entire radio net was alive with an urgent, desperate and angry plea: "Check fire! Check fire!"

Thirty seconds later all gunfire ceased.

Private Robert Costall, the section's C9 gunner, had been hit. He was found in the prone position, slumped over his machine gun. He'd died instantly from a bullet to the back of the head and one to the chest. Sergeant 1st Class John Stone, a fifty-two-year-old American medic and reservist, also died instantly.

The soldier lying exposed within sight of the Taliban whipped a bandage from his kit and slipped back over the berm to his comrades. The other wounded man shoved a pressure bandage against his side and secured a tourniquet to his leg. As the casualties were carried from the field, a U.S. A-10 jet rumbled out of the darkness and delivered a bomb square on to the Taliban position. When the ear-splitting concussion faded, everything went quiet. The wounded were brought inside the compound and loaded on to another Humvee for transport to the helipad. A medevac chopper—a nine-liner in military parlance—was on its way.

* * *

Lying on my cot, I was vaguely aware of the creeping grey dawn outside the canvas walls. The blistering Afghan day had yet to begin. It was cool and comfortable. I'd cast off my sleeping bag at some point during the night and was curled on the thin mattress that cushioned our collapsible cots. The steady, rhythmic breathing of my sleeping colleagues could be heard over the distant rumblings of the camp. A TV cameraman let loose a throaty snore. I could hear the sound of boots on the gravel. The flap moved and a blinding halo of light forced me to sit up.

"Sorry to disturb everyone," said a disembodied voice. It was one of the public affairs officers. "You're going to have to get up. There's been an incident."

Everyone dressed quickly and in silence. It was unusual to be rattled out of bed that way. A motley, bleary-eyed collection of journalists presented itself at the white, two-storey Canadian headquarters building. We were briefed by the general in charge of the Canadian contingent. Brigadier-General David Fraser—a quiet and unassuming man with an understated manner in front of the press—broke the news about the previous night's battle in a brief statement. He was short on detail and his answers to questions even shorter. Where? Sangin. We'd never heard of it, but it sounded exotic and dangerous. We were given Costall's name, although we weren't initially told about the

American soldier. No one said anything about the possibility of friendly fire; that wouldn't come out for days.

No journalist had been allowed to accompany the relief force, a sore point among those of us eager to get outside the wire. It was the first time I actually felt like a hostage of the army. They could tell us as much or as little as they wanted, and they often chose the latter. In this case, they chose to say nothing, or next to nothing, which was probably worse. News, especially big news, abhors a vacuum.

The firefight in Sangin was tiny compared to the great battles of the past, but it was still significant. It was the first time in a generation that Canadian soldiers had taken casualties in a pitched battle with a sworn enemy. Troops had taken part in engagements in Cyprus in the 1970s and Croatia in the 1990s, but those were peacekeeping missions. So far, Afghanistan had only seen friendly fire deaths, suicide bombers, roadside bombs and accidents. Faced with the results of an honest-to-goodness battle, we wanted to know everything, and we wanted to know it now. The best the army could offer in terms of narrative was that Costall had died defending his comrades.

"We will not forget his sacrifice," Fraser intoned. "Our thoughts are with his family today and with the families of the injured."

The scrum was over as quickly as it began. We wandered back to the work tents, the only sound that of our hiking boots as they crunched over the smooth rocks and gravel. We filed what little we knew. Eventually we tried to talk to the soldiers, but anyone who knew anything was still in Sangin and those that knew something in Kandahar weren't talking in specifics. When 7 Platoon arrived back at KAF a few days later, they were barred from talking to us.

Sangin was my first experience with how hopelessly and wilfully inarticulate the Canadian military could be. Individual soldiers, I found, were wonderfully colourful and quotable, but the Canadian military as an institution seemed quite pleased to have a stranglehold on information and the movement of journalists. And then it would complain—sometimes in bitterly personal terms—about how it was portrayed. The cloak under which the institution often hid was "operational security"—or OPSEC. It was a convenient blanket for a variety of sins, and it was initially thrown on the events in Sangin. In the end, it was left to Fraser's chief of staff, a British colonel, to explain to the Canadian media the circumstances surrounding the death of a Canadian soldier.

The Chai Tea House was an airless concrete building with rattling steel doors situated close to the camp's main gate. It was the perfect location to hold meetings with Afghan elders and Kandahar reporters. It was inside the wire but not too far inside—in enough to make the Afghans feel included in their war, but still remote enough from the headquarters, where the real decisions were made, to demonstrate that they weren't sitting at the same table as the big people.

Colonel Chris Vernon called the news conference principally to brief the Afghan media. We were invited almost as an afterthought. Vernon's refined velvet accent and cool good looks made him a hit with many of my female colleagues. He didn't seem to mind the attention. With his mussed mane of salt-and-pepper hair, khaki uniform and shoulder boards, there was a dash of matinee idol about him. Although he was low-key and appeared a bit distracted, he was clearly very sharp. As the British Army's spokesman during the 2003 invasion of Iraq, Vernon had famously declared, ahead of his own government, "Militarily we have won the war—no significant resistance remains either in Basra or Baghdad." The good colonel was well schooled in military and political warfare, but what made him particularly endearing and useful to us was that he could string a sentence together. In fact, he could string a sentence together beautifully. For a time there, it was like listening to Churchill.

When asked about Sangin, he painted a compelling portrait of a desperate, pitched battle with the Taliban in the middle of night on an isolated desert hilltop.

"Did we expect a Taliban attack on the base? Yes," said Vernon, using both hands for emphasis. "The size and the tenacity with which it was carried out may have slightly exceeded our estimates."

He filled in all of the details. He took questions, challenged our assumptions and even delivered an enlightening soliloquy on counter-insurgency warfare. He was smart, quotable and comfortable in front of the camera. More than anything, he wasn't afraid to articulate and defend his comments. We couldn't take notes fast enough.

It was clear Vernon considered the Taliban an inferior fighting force, but he couldn't hide how impressed he was—or maybe it was surprise.

"The only thing I will say, there is no doubt they are brave," he said.

His brutally honest answers were all the more refreshing because he didn't try to shovel mindless optimism at us, the kind that dismissed facts.

Vernon clearly laid down the markers for this war, carefully distinguishing between counter-insurgency and counterterrorism, drawing a line between the way Washington saw Afghanistan and the way NATO defined it—although he was smooth enough not to make a direct comparison.

It was well known that U.S. generals wanted Canadians to "whack" the bad guys during their time running Kandahar on behalf of the coalition, but Vernon spoke about tackling the region's crushing unemployment rate as the way to win. He pragmatically pointed out that the Taliban was largely a mercenary force with commanders who wintered in Pakistan. They returned every spring with offers of U.S. $500 and a motorcycle to anyone who carried a gun for them. They could be beaten, he intoned, if the international community could deliver aid and reconstruction quickly.

"We are in a race with the Taliban to provide young, fighting age males between eighteen and twenty-five more suitable employment."

The Afghan journalists, with more immediate concerns, pressed him on civilian casualties. Vernon denied there were any. Yet his answer was so precise and so ironic that it stayed with me. I couldn't help but think of it when the investigations into Sangin reached their conclusion.

"Our rules of engagement for the United States Armed Forces, the British Armed Forces and the Canadian Armed Forces are pretty strict. Our soldiers and our airmen are held to account through military courts of justice. Soldiers are not on a free licence to use lethal force," Vernon declared.

The Canadian investigation, released in August 2007, found U.S. Special Forces operators had opened fire on the Canadians because they thought the berm had been overrun. They believed Costall's machine gun was firing at the mentoring compound. Canadians never found out exactly which of the two gun truck crewmembers pulled the trigger; the Special Forces guys refused to talk. The board of inquiry relied on their written statements to Pentagon investigators. The final report found that the soldiers from 7 Platoon occupied areas that overlapped with the Humvee's arcs of fire, but that "no safeguards [were] in place to preclude the gun trucks from firing on friendly forces." And since the Americans refused to testify it was "not possible to confirm whether the soldiers who manned the gun trucks were informed of the lay out of friendly forces." With an acerbic touch, Canadian investigators noted that other Americans had told them the berm was routinely used as a defensive line by the Afghans. "It was not unusual to have a friendly force manning the north," said the final Canadian investigation report into the incident. In other words, the Special Forces operators should have known better.

No one was charged and no one faced discipline for the events in Sangin that night. The American base commander was rebuked for not having a better defensive plan, but the Canadian investigation concluded that "no one person or persons met the requirements of blame." Everything was fine. The message was clear: Move along. Don't look here.

Each of us got the sense, within days of the battle, that the U.S. Special Forces was calling the shots. Christie Blatchford, Louie Palu and Rosie DiManno accompanied the battle group commander to FOB Robinson during the hurried reinforcement of the base days after the battle. They were booted out. I had been slated to accompany the artillery but was yanked off the convoy before it even left KAF. Weeks later, when I finally did get to Sangin, I was told to avoid the Special Forces compound unless I didn't "want to be seen again." Months later, a CBC colleague landed at another base, west of Kandahar, with a healthy contingent of Canadian and American Special Forces and was immediately told to "get the fuck off." In that case, it was the Canadians doing the evicting. They didn't care whether the reporter walked or hitched a ride with the Taliban. There was no fighting taking place; he just wanted her gone. We all got good at picking these guys out, the ones who didn't want to talk, who thought we were trying to sensationalize things. You could see them coming a mile away at KAF and other bases, with their sunglasses, bushy beards and holstered Beretta 9mms—or Glocks—sticking out from underneath untucked shirts. Some were like huge teddy bears, despite the fierce hillbilly-on-steroids look. But then there were the other bloody-minded ones—guys who didn't talk to you, but at you. They strutted around Afghanistan as though this was their personal fight, so war-wasted that the only thing that kept them going was the chance to "smoke some *hajjis*." It would be years before that culture of impunity was reined in by U.S. General Stanley McChrystal.

* * *

It was close to dusk the night after the battle when we were told there would be a repatriation ceremony for Private Costall. We would be allowed to cover it as long as we obeyed strict guidelines and made ourselves invisible.

Sufficiently cowed, we waited in the tent for the appointed hour. The bagpiper tuned up on the patio of the wooden café behind us. The longer we waited the more still it became outside the grey-green canvas walls.

Finally, I opened the steel door of the tent and stepped into the musky evening. It was dark and the air seemed heavy, as though the heat of the day had refused to disperse. A cloud of sand flies and moths buzzed in the face of the floodlights. The public affairs officers, dressed in fresh fatigues, collected us. The TV guys slung their cameras on to their shoulders and their reporters picked up the tripods. The rest of us grabbed our notepads and tape recorders. We walked through the gate and out on to the road. A long, uninterrupted column of soldiers passed in front of us. They marched toward the flight line, their boots scuffing the dirt roadway and kicking up a veil of dust that grew wider and higher as each rank passed. We stood for a moment as hundreds of them walked by in one unbroken column of khaki camouflage. Faces were difficult to make out in the dusty umbra and that gave the ranks an inhuman, almost mechanical aura. They seemed like a force of nature, a sandstorm blowing along a dry riverbed between a canvas mountain of tents.

We joined the procession and walked to where the avenue intersected in a "T" with the main airfield road. When we reached the tarmac, I stood still for a moment, wide-eyed and completely taken in by the scene.

All three thoroughfares spilled troops into a pool at the flight line, where they briefly congregated in a heaving grey mass before streaming out toward a solitary transport plane on the floodlit taxiway. They moved smoothly and efficiently. There were no gaps in the ranks; arms and legs locked in unison. There were Canadians, Americans, Romanians, Dutch and British. There were thousands of them. As soldiers divided themselves into nations, the beige river that had surged before us tightened into steel ribbons underneath the flush of the white lights.

"Your left, your left, your left, right, left," an American-accented voice called in the distance.

Some of the soldiers coming on to the field gave us the once-over as they passed. A few of the Americans sneered. Others looked disgusted, but the expression soon disappeared behind a mask of indifference.

"What the fuck are they doing here?" said one voice, heard in passing.

They halted at the open back of the C-130 Hercules and formed two giant columns on either side of the ramp. The cargo bay of the aircraft was lit with soft orange lights and a giant Canadian flag hung at the back. One of the aircrew stood with his arms folded, looking out at the assembly. We were ushered to the base of the ramp. The last to arrive were the padre in his combat fatigues and communion sash, a colour party with regimental flag and the bagpiper.

The airfield was now completely silent, save for the distant tweeting of birds. Air traffic control shut down the base. We stood with our eyes cast to the pavement and listened to the wind. Thin wisps of sand blew across the flight line. We waited. After what seemed like a long time, the low, steady growl of a diesel engine could be heard somewhere in the darkness. A single point of light appeared to our right and it grew with the engine sound. A low, dark silhouette inched along the tarmac behind a column of soldiers with the cadence of a hymn. As the shadow reached the glare of the floodlights, it morphed into an armoured vehicle that turned and presented its open back to the assembly. Clearly visible through the hatch, and bathed in the interior red combat lights of the cabin, was Costall's steel casket, tightly wrapped in a Canadian flag. The vehicle passed back into shadow and stopped just outside of the soft white light. Six pallbearers stood waiting. The parade came to attention as the casket was lowered tenderly onto a stand. That's the thing about soldiers: they can be crude; they can be rough; their job is to be violent and some of them revel it in. Yet they are capable of such poignant displays of compassion that your heart almost bursts to witness them.

The padre's homily echoed over the loudspeaker through the hushed desert night. Captain Harry Crawford talked about what you'd expect: the love of Christ, redemption, sacrifice. He sermonized on family and loss, but also about the choices all of us make in this life. His words crashed into my conscience like a freight train.

Robert Costall had chosen to be there. All of us had chosen to be there. Costall may not have wanted to be on that hill, and he most certainly didn't want to die at that moment in his young life, but he chose the life of a soldier. It is a cold, cold moment when it strikes you that the choices you've made could get you killed. There were hundreds of interesting and unique ways to die in such a stinking, miserable place. You could be shot, or have your flesh ripped apart by a bomb or booby trap. There were bone-crushing accidents in armoured vehicles or helicopters. For journalists who ventured off the base without the army, there were more intimate ways to die—like being stuck with a grungy knife and having your throat slit like a chicken, the way the

Taliban did to inattentive cops. There was kidnapping and possible beheading on the Internet. And disease.

"He has paid the ultimate price for trying to build a better future for the nation we are now in," said Crawford as he solemnly ended the memorial. "May those who knew him learn to smile at his memory."

Saying you want to go quickly, without any pain, is almost a cliché. But in a place like this, the cliché becomes a prayer. In the end, that was all any of us could do: pray. Pray for a swift, quick end, one without malice or irony. Deep inside, you also wanted a passing that meant something, but in this godforsaken land that was almost too much to hope for. As the piper struck up his lament, we were all left cold and wondering. What was in store for us?

"Task Force Afghanistan!" the camp sergeant major screamed. "To your fallen comrade . . . salute!"

The pallbearers lifted the casket to their shoulders and slow-marched between the stiff columns of impassive faces. The piper and a soldier bearing the beret of the fallen man stepped gracefully behind them. The soft white flush of the airfield lights occasionally left a phosphorescent hue on the flag as the troops carried their heavy burden up the metal ramp and into the open bay.

* * *

Coffee was always a necessary ritual. Standing in line at the Green Bean one day I noticed an attractive young woman in U.S. Air Force fatigues. She had a rifle slung over her shoulder. With her blond hair pulled back in a ponytail, she looked like she belonged on a beach somewhere in California, not here. But her face was drawn and grim, as though she hadn't slept.

As the line snaked its way through the tiny seating area, I caught her glancing back at me, or rather at my white and blue identification badge.

"You're a journalist?" She had a deep, rich Texas accent.

"Uh-huh." I was never good at conversation before my first coffee. "Let me guess. You're with force protection for the air element."

"You're good."

"That's why they pay me the big bucks."

"Really?"

"Not really."

She ordered her drink—a chai latte—and then fumbled through her pockets. No cash. She gave me a weak smile. I paid.

"It's okay. You look like you could use a shot of caffeine."

"That bad?"

It was one of those trick questions guys should never answer. I just shook my head and chose to say nothing.

"I was on duty in one of the OPs on the other side of the strip," she said. "They were testing the wire all night."

The Americans maintained a series of sandbag, plywood and corrugated tin outposts on the far side of the airfield. Strung behind layers of razor wire, the defences were meant to deter anyone from sneaking up through the desert and launching an attack.

I was stunned. Kandahar Airfield was one of the most heavily guarded places in all of Afghanistan, yet the Taliban were poking around the wire looking for soft spots. I don't know why but it came as a shock. Maybe somewhere in my subconscious I'd actually bought the line that the Taliban were a spent force, a disorganized band of turban-wearing, death-worshipping zealots. They weren't to be taken seriously, at least in a military context. One of my colleagues got himself in trouble for quoting the battle group commander as saying that a "spring offensive" by the Taliban was imminent. It was the word "offensive" that made soldiers livid. It bestowed on the Taliban a certain undeserved equality. These guys wore sandals, had no radios or body armour; they opened up with AKs and blew their load in one clip. They would "shoot and scoot," never really holding any territory. They died by the dozens. That's not an army, our people insisted.

It was an infuriating academic argument that made you want to scream. The often-repeated mythology—how wild-eyed Pashtun tribes had defeated everybody from Alexander the Great to the Russians—was treated as irrelevant or downright defeatist by almost everyone of any importance. Yet throughout that spring none of us escaped the feeling something ancient and awful had been awakened. The storm was gathering.

"What Does Sorry Mean to Me?" 3

During the first month of the Canadian battle group's deployment, Kandahar city often had the feel of a ghost town. A ramshackle archway, which has since been torn down, marked the southern approach. A wide boulevard ran underneath it, but there was hardly any traffic on the days I went in, especially as the evening neared. Bits of trash and empty plastic water bottles blew across the paved highway and collected in the concrete drainage ditches that ran the length of the thoroughfare. Junk also piled up in the squalid, unpaved dirt alleys that snaked in between empty and boarded-up shops, no more than corrugated tin hovels. It was as if someone had conducted nuclear testing in a seventh-century bazaar. The city's medieval verve was only enhanced by the smell that hit you upon reaching the "golden arches," the name given to the entrance. The place reeked of roasted meat, rotting vegetables, open sewers and wood fires. You never forget the stench and it seemed to seep into the very fabric of your clothes.

The wide avenue that rolled past the governor's palace featured a generous median that had once contained grass and flowers. It was now parched, the turf starved into lifelessness. The trees were wilted and the streets were full of the fine powder that passed for desert sand in this part of the world. The soldiers called it moon dust. It was as though nature sensed the city was near death and intended to reclaim it grain by grain.

Canadians would later put the local unemployed to work sweeping the streets with thatched brooms. They would also pay for public garbage cans emblazoned with a maple leaf that looked strangely like a marijuana leaf. The Taliban quickly learned these were great places to hide bombs and the cans were discarded. The grand mosque Mullah Omar had intended to build stood silent and incomplete. Steel supporting rods stuck out of the poured concrete base and swayed in the breeze. A few blocks away, the counterpoint to this fundamentalist vision also stood abandoned and lonely: a Western-style park complete with Ferris wheel and built by the first post-Taliban governor. The Taliban forbid anyone from going there. The park stood in the shadow of the city's soccer stadium where, during the reign of the hardliners, stoning and public executions took place. If there was ever a place that seemed on the verge of a nervous breakdown, it was Kandahar in the spring of 2006.

When people did venture out of their walled-off compounds and tightly packed, hardscrabble homes, it was with trepidation. They got what they needed at the few shops that were open and scurried back as quickly as their sandaled feet would take them. But Afghans have a fascination with the morbid and the macabre. They would sometimes stop and talk with each other about the latest suicide bombing or killing. They wanted to know every grisly detail and talked about the event with the same intensity as we discuss sports rivalries. Most days, there was a lot to talk about. The spot where a Canadian diplomat's jeep was blown up by a suicide car bomber was treated almost like a tourist attraction, a place where people would come and gawk. The fixers and translators who drove disguised Western journalists around would capriciously point out the place. The city was not safe for anyone with white skin and when we travelled without the army we dressed in a shalwar kameez, if you were man, or burka if you were a woman. Flak vests were stuffed between you and passenger doors to guard against random attacks and stray bullets. These precautions—superficial to the trained eye—did little to enhance your survivability; they just made you feel better.

Wherever you looked there were bombed-out buildings and collapsed compounds. Those that weren't smashed had scattered pockmarks from gunfire. If you were travelling with the army, Afghan kids would sometimes wave. On other occasions they'd throw rocks at your vehicle. Air sentries—the soldiers who stood in the LAV's open hatches—would curse and throw water bottles at the kids or anyone else who got too close for comfort. The adults stared with a grudging patience that we often mistook for disinterest. Others wore an expression of open contempt, a black gaze that cut right through you. It made many of us fidgety.

Kandahar was mysterious, dangerous and thoroughly incomprehensible. Soldiers would hold up their hands at traffic stops, palms facing oncoming cars and pedestrians, but what we took to be the universal sign for "stop" was actually the Afghan gesture "come here." Only when your palm is facing downward does it mean halt. In those early days, it felt like we were all blindfolded and stumbling through a room full of machetes and hot pokers. We saw the Taliban everywhere, whether they were there or not.

I had been in Kandahar only a few hours when the first shooting happened. A patrol of Canadian soldiers killed a man during a routine stop at a traffic circle. The suspect vehicle had been "barrelling" toward the parked armoured vehicles and refused to stop, reporters were told. Soldiers thought it was a suicide bomber, at least until they heard the shrieks of the family of the mortally wounded man.

Days later, I sat cross-legged on the filthy concrete floor of a guest house. There were no rugs or thin cotton mattresses, and within a few minutes my backside started to ache and my legs cramped. It amazed me how the Afghans could sit on their haunches for hours. Hard, white sunshine streamed into the room from two open windows. The air was close and hot, even though it was technically still winter. Outside there was the sound of traffic.

Nisar told his story.

Rising out of bed each morning, the notion that this could be our last day on earth is usually the furthest thing from our minds. Even when you live in one of the most dangerous cities in the world, the thought of death is strangely remote. The idea that one could get killed doing something routine—buying a cup of coffee, picking up a newspaper or driving home after dinner with a friend—is just as foreign in Kandahar as it is anywhere. Dying is something that happens to somebody else. At least that's what we tell ourselves.

Nisar's father, Nasrat Ali Hassan, a mechanic and itinerant labourer, had just finished a charming evening in the company of friends. It was late, but the forty-two-year-old insisted he and his family go home. Foreign troops were in the city and they would "protect us from bandits or the Taliban," his second-eldest son remembered him saying.

Ali, his wife and several children packed into a *tuk-tuk*, a covered, three-wheeled motorized rickshaw, one of the fleet taxis that buzz the dusty streets and alleyways.

It was dark. There are few street lights in Kandahar city, especially in the jumbled collection of neighbourhoods that unfold in the northern and eastern districts.

Unbeknownst to the Hassans, a Canadian army patrol from the nearby PRT base had stopped in a traffic circle to check on a pair of lonely, terrified ANP officers hunkered down at the makeshift traffic stop.

The cops were happy to see the Canadian soldiers. Outside of the confines of the reconstruction base or Kandahar Airfield, soldiers on patrol or in convoys rarely liked to stop. It is better to keep moving in order to avoid an ambush or some individual clown taking potshots at you. A halt is never good, especially at night when it seems like all of the walls have eyes. But stopping there was important. The cops were badly outnumbered and the Taliban had just begun a killing spree targeting police, a spasm of violence that left forty-one policemen dead, shot or blown up at their checkpoints, mostly at night. Without uniforms, body armour or radios, often wearing sandals and sometimes wrapped in blankets to keep warm, these mostly illiterate ex-militiamen maintained a lonely vigil at posts throughout the city.

The taxi carrying Ali and his family zipped out of the shadows and entered the traffic circle from a street on the opposite side of the police barricade. Within seconds the *tuk-tuk* was between the police guard post and the convoy. It made for an opening between two of the armoured vehicles in much the same way a suicide bomber would. An alert sentry on the last LAV in the convoy tightened his grip on his weapon. He had only a few seconds to determine whether this was an innocent incursion or a deadly Taliban trick. The soldier waved and shouted in Pashtu.

"Stay back!"

Nisar said they never saw any warning signs.

The soldier opened up, aiming three shots at the engine block of the flimsy scooter. A ricocheted bullet struck Ali in the abdomen and the taxi came to a halt just a few metres from the back of LAV.

Amid the frightened screams, the Canadians and their Afghan interpreter—or terp—tried to figure out what had just happened. Judging by the blood and the sight of the wounds, Ali's wife, Semen Gul, later said she believed her husband had been shot at least four times. It is possible that small, twisted pieces of hot steel sprayed from the front of the taxi as it was hit, striking Ali.

With his father mortally wounded, Nisar scrambled out of the vehicle to confront the Canadians. The terp told him to stay back, otherwise the troops would shoot him as well.

"It was not our fault. It was not our fault," the teenager repeated through the translator. "We didn't see anything."

He pleaded with the soldiers to take his father to the city's dilapidated hospital, which was only a short ride away. By this time an army medic was examining the wounded man, who was still conscious. Although bleeding profusely, Ali's injuries were pronounced serious but non-life-threatening. The patrol commander, fearful of driving to an unknown part of the city at night with the Taliban possibly lurking in ambush, refused the teenager's pleas.

The family hailed another taxi. Ali slipped into unconsciousness on the ride to Mirwais Hospital and died three hours after being admitted.

The day after the shooting, Ali was buried in a small, dust-choked cemetery at the edge of the city. During the funeral, one of his children fainted and had to be carried away from the open white coffin. After laying him to rest on the sun-baked ground beneath a pile of rocks, his family erected flags, strips of green and white cotton tied to wooden sticks. The white pennant represented martyrdom—a statement that Ali had died before his time.

"I don't have a husband," Semen Gul sobbed afterward in an interview with the *Toronto Star*'s Rosie DiManno. By custom, male reporters were not allowed to talk to Afghan women.

"I have nobody to protect me. What am I to do? You say sorry. What does sorry mean to me? Will sorry feed my children?"

Nisar repeated his mother's statement.

The words cut through me like a knife. I looked up from my notebook.

"I told them we were not terrorists," Nisar said in a quiet, defeated way, as if still pleading with the soldiers.

Although time had passed, the event was still raw and had festered into a poison on his conscience. As we sat there, so many emotions were at play in his brown, raw-boned face. There was the frightened boy, the angry young man, the helpless child, the protective son. All of it burst forth in a startling portrait of misery. Our interview was over. He couldn't look at me, nor I at him. My presence reminded him of the soldiers who'd killed his father. And I wondered about the unwritten tribal code of Pashtunwali, which governs the lives of many in this part of the world. By birth I was considered a brother to the one who pulled the trigger, even though I had never met the man. Blood feuds in this country had begun over much less than an accidental shooting and in this case Pashtunwali demanded revenge. I wondered how the boy would seek his reckoning or whether he'd simply roll over and take it, one more outrage to swallow in a place already drowning in toxic bile.

I closed my notebook and turned off the tape recorder.

Nisar's account differed sharply from the "official version" released in the aftermath of the shooting, but that wasn't entirely surprising. The army that had worked so hard for over a decade to rid itself of the stain of the Somalia scandal—the torture and murder of Shidane Arone—had a potential public relations disaster on its hands.

The military investigated and found that the soldier acted appropriately. He thought the taxi was a suicide bomber and responded with measured brutality. If only the bullet hadn't ricocheted. There were attempts to make amends to the family with cultural gifts and a cash payment, which journalists were told of but sworn to secrecy over. Letting us into the cone of silence was a calculated move. The army's intent was to get us to stop pestering them and make the story go away. Officially, keeping the payment under the radar was meant to prevent the family from being targeted by thieves and thugs. As with many trumped-up claims of security, though, there was a touch of the absurd at play. Kandahar is a gossipy, small town and many who knew the victim's family would have noticed they were not immediately cast into poverty following Ali's death. Word travels fast in Afghan circles and such a realization would have had far more impact than any scribbling by Western journalists.

A week or so after the shooting, huge, brightly coloured signs appeared on the backs of Canadian G-Wagon jeeps. Written in Pashto, they warned drivers to keep a safe distance from military vehicles. There was a silhouette drawing of a soldier holding up his hand—palm facing outward—to reinforce the message. The army was eager to trumpet this lesson-learned and proudly noted it to all of us at a briefing.

I turned to Rosie DiManno.

"That ought to be very helpful in a city with a sixty-five per cent illiteracy rate," I said.

At times, it was as if the army was oblivious to the world outside its own sand-filled bastion walls. To events like Ali's shooting, officers and soldiers responded with sympathy, not empathy. And then there was the natural Western reflex to whip out the chequebook, as if somehow money would make it all better. The Afghans eagerly took the cash, fooling all of us into thinking they were just as cynical as we were about these things.

The pattern would repeat itself over and over and over again. A wild-eyed old man wandering in the middle of the road with twine sticking out from his vest, threads that soldiers mistook for the wires of a bomb; the Afghan policeman who inadvertently stuck his head above a wall as a convoy was passing; the elderly man on the motorcycle who got too close to the compound where President Hamid Karzai was holding a meeting. The man turned out to be one of Karzai's early teachers, who had just wanted to say hello.

Chest-thumpers quite rightly point out that the Taliban killed—accidentally or intentionally—double the number of civilians as Western forces. What they didn't say was that the insurgents did so without the moral caveat that they were there to "help." We rode into Afghanistan promising freedom, democracy, prosperity and justice. It was the latter that resonated most. Afghans have never truly experienced the other three, but they could understand justice. If someone had wronged them, they expected that person to pay without exception, qualification or excuse. The grudging admission of our mistakes and sanguine requests for forgiveness did not go unnoticed.

* * *

When I conducted interviews without the army's assistance, most took place at the Intercontinental Guest House. The name makes it sound fancier than it was. The hotel was a spartan series of low-lying, whitewashed buildings surrounded by neat walkways and bushes, a head-snapping contrast to the unkempt, filthy streets outside the compound walls.

At the time I interviewed Nisar, I had been in town on only one other occasion and Rosie had graciously loaned me the use of her fixer Jojo. He drove a white Toyota sedan with tinted windows. Even still, I dressed as an Afghan in a shalwar kameez and those rather airy balloon pants. My choice of a *pakol*—a spongy woolen cap worn by northerners—did raise Jojo's eyebrows, but he was polite enough not to say anything. Turbans, I soon discovered, were more popular in southern Afghanistan. The air in the back of the car was stifling with the windows snapped shut.

The traffic barrier leading out of the hotel to a busy thoroughfare consisted of a single steel post that was raised and lowered by a drawstring. As I had come to expect, guards with AK-47s manned the gateway. It was strange how it already seemed normal. One of the dishevelled guards, with a thick ammunition belt around his waist and an even thicker beard, stopped our car and asked a question. The response almost sounded like a wisecrack. The guard laughed and raised the barrier.

"What did he say to you?"

Jojo was one of the smoothest and most westernized Afghans I'd ever met. His nickname was bestowed on him during his days sweeping the floors and translating for U.S. Special Forces.

"What did he say to me?" Jojo ran through the translation in his head. "He asked if you were armed."

"And what did you tell him?"

"I told him you were a stupid journalist and refused to carry a weapon because you believe the pen is more powerful." He laughed at his own joke.

Jojo's black hair was neatly combed back and gelled. His thin brown face, large eyes and knowing smirk made him an attractive, instantly likable guy. He spoke flawless English with only the slightest Afghan lilt and could swear up a storm. Although he had scruff on his face, it looked as though he had trouble growing a full beard.

Jojo was a hustler and looked the part. He talked fast, drove even faster and from what I could tell lived very close to the edge. He boasted about his contacts and how the Taliban would talk to him but no other local journalists. That was an obvious exaggeration, but one I allowed since my life was largely in his hands. One of the Taliban commanders had even given him a coat, a sign of respect. But at the same time, he insisted he was still in good stead with the Americans, who realized how valuable his contacts were.

He worked primarily for the CTV television network, shooting video in the aftermath of the frequent suicide attacks and bombings. But Jojo would work for anyone who paid him, driving, translating and arranging interviews. He made a lot of money off the *Toronto Star*, as near as I could tell. The *Globe and Mail* also used him. He eagerly said I could use him too, but with so much call on his time it was evident I would be at the bottom of his priority list. Still, I ended up working with him many times.

To solve my immediate problem, it was recommended I hire Abdul Raziq Khan, a cousin to the local AP reporter, Noor Khan. Everyone was related to everyone in Kandahar, I would discover. The fixers were always doing favours for one another, recommending each other, sharing rides together, exchanging quotes, and generally covering for one another. It was a tight little circle that Western journalists came to be suspicious of, but we tolerated it because there was no alternative. None of us spoke Pashtu and even those seasoned in the demolition derby of Montreal driving blanched at the thought of taking on Kandahar streets. One journalist, a veteran of Afghanistan who used to shave his head completely bald and spoke in the acronym-laced babble of someone that had been here way too long, was so notorious in his mistrust of the fixers that he once proposed walking to the gate and simply hopping in a taxi. "Fuck the fixers," he would say. We talked him out of it.

"Khan is a good guy," Jojo assured me.

I had met Khan face to face a few days earlier in the parking lot across the street from the governor's palace. He had a wide, pleasant face with only the hint of a beard, deep-set eyes and a heavy brow that often presented a brooding expression. That could change in an instant if he was struck by something funny or ironic. Then his face would light up with a droopy grin. The contrast was amazing. We had met behind an ornate, white fence that partially shielded us from passing traffic. I had gone into town with two other reporters and their fixer. Khan and I shook hands, but he looked around nervously throughout the conversation. The longer the meeting went on, the paler Khan became. His manner made me uneasy. I hesitated to hire him and ended up using Jojo for the interview with Nisar. On reflection, however, it became evident that my choice of meeting spots had unsettled Khan. I had chosen a location out in the open, on the off chance that Khan wasn't as trustworthy as reported. But what seemed safe to me—a busy street, in plain view of everyone, including my colleagues and probable Taliban watchers—was a risk for him. Yet he stood there, slightly embarrassed and occasionally scratching his tussled mop of hair. I left that meeting with Khan noncommittal, but by the time Jojo dropped me back at Kandahar Airfield, I'd decided he was the one I was going to trust with my life on a regular basis.

* * *

A few months later, Khan led me along a dim, empty corridor at the Noor Jahan Hotel. He fished around in a pouch for the keys to his room—or his office as he liked to call it. One of the things I learned about Afghans was that they glommed on to any status symbol, no matter how trivial, and flaunted it like a badge of honour. We passed several rooms with shoes and sandals piled up outside. Shafts of light came from underneath the unevenly cut doors and sliced across the unswept concrete floor. The air was heavy and smelled of cooked lamb and burned coffee grounds from the hotel restaurant two floors down. I could hear voices. Some were loud and it sounded like they were angry, but Pashtuns always sounded angry, even when they were pleased. In this case it was pretty clear they were debating. We finally stopped outside a battered and gouged wooden door. It was a faded blue. As Khan opened it, I slipped off my hiking boots. He looked at me and shook his head. The boots would have to go inside. Anyone walking past and seeing them would automatically know a westerner was around. Khan cast a critical eye on my shalwar kameez, which had bits of sparkling cotton around the collar. He covered his eyes in obvious exasperation and dragged his hand the length of his face.

"Sir, I will get you a more appropriate outfit," he sighed.

"Am I an embarrassment?"

"Yes sir."

We went into his room and closed the door. There was only one window, which Khan covered with a frayed, light blue, woolen blanket. There was no bathroom. A worn Persian rug covered the concrete floor, almost from corner to corner. The walls looked as though they had been painted a glossy, industrial white perhaps thirty years ago. It was hard to tell with all of the nicks, scrapes and smudges. We sat on thin, colourful floor mattresses; it wasn't long before my rear end started to ache. Khan had a neat pile of clothes in one corner of the room, a few pillows, a single wooden stand with a few personal items and his laptop. At night the room was lit by a naked electric bulb that dangled from the ceiling.

"I don't know what brother Les was thinking when he bought that," Khan said and pointed at my outfit. Everyone was called brother and he referred now to my colleague and good buddy Les Perreaux. "We must get you something more professional. And we must get you sandals. What size do you take?"

He lit a cigarette and before I could answer there was a knock at the door. Both of us rose when it opened. Four men were lined up in the hallway. One was on crutches, although it took me a second to realize it. The flash of aluminum caused my heart to skip a beat. You always looked for weapons. I saw no rifles or handguns as they entered; a good sign. Khan mumbled his traditional greetings and hugged each of them, carefully holding his cigarette away from the flowing robes.

"These are the gentlemen I told you about," he said to me and then urged them in Pashtu to sit down.

"Salam aleikum," I said to each of them as they walked past and assumed places on the floor.

The tender-looking man on crutches had a lame left leg. He was the last to be seated. Pain was evident on his face as he arranged himself on the far mattress. Khan introduced him as Fida Mohammed.

The one seated next to him, the shortest of the lot with dark skin and close-set hazel eyes, was identified as Norul Haq. He managed a half smile when Khan pointed to him and he adjusted his bejewelled, brightly coloured *kufis*—or prayer cap.

The other two bearded men wore dark brown turbans and stern expressions. They sat hunched with their knees pulled to their chests. One had a green woolen blanket draped over his shoulders like a cape. The other kept the tail of his turban swept up around his neck. Khan introduced them only as villager elders from Tulakan, about sixty kilometres southwest of the city.

Khan spoke a few animated words to the visitors and then stepped out to arrange lunch with the kitchen. Haq chortled something in response. The two elders said nothing. They simply stared at me—or through me—with a chilling, dead expression I had seen many times on the street. I smiled awkwardly, an attempt to lighten the mood. Seeing no response or friendly sparkle in their eyes, I picked the eldest of the two village leaders and met his gaze. I forced my expression to harden into the same impenetrable, dark contemplation. A couple of drops of sweat trickled down my back. It's impossible to say how long this contest of wills went on. Time just seemed to stop. It ended when a noise in the hallway caused the elder to look toward the door. After that he lost interest in me and picked at a plate of nuts and dates Khan had set on the floor.

My shalwar kameez was neatly pressed, crisp and relatively new, regardless of how garish Khan considered it to be. I wore it partly out of comfort and partly from a misguided notion that if something went wrong it would give extra seconds of cover, or at least cause confusion for anyone who intended harm. In my estimation it was also a sign of cultural respect. A young Afghan police recruit said to me once that since I wore the shalwar and dressed like an Afghan I should also convert to Islam. I asked him if he wore Western clothes, would he convert to Christianity. He seemed stunned. Khan chuckled at that incident. But now, faced with the villagers' fiery glares, it was hard not to feel like some kind of imposter. I did not smell of sweat or desperation the way these men did. My shalwar had not been lived in. I felt sad as I watched them try to ignore me.

Khan's return immediately lightened the room. Lunch was served and the formalities of Afghan hospitality were respected before we got down to business. With his cheerful demeanour, Khan looked oddly out of place among those angry villagers. He offered the men cigarettes and they chatted with him in Pashtu. Haq said something that startled him and he laughed long and loud, drawing each breath from deep in his gut.

"They think you are CIA," Khan announced.

I wanted to laugh, but stayed serious.

"I'm Canadian."

"They do not know the difference. You are white. You are all foreigners, in their eyes."

The men were from just outside of Tulakan, deep in what the army considered Taliban territory, if there was such a thing in this war without fronts. It sat in Panjwaii district, a stretch of parched farmland that had until the Soviet occupation been quite fertile and rich. But the Russians, as part of their campaign to pacify the area, blew up many of the centuries-old irrigation canals. The result was drought—a condition that persisted for years. If scorched earth wasn't enough, the Soviets in the late 1980s de-populated whole villages, forcing tens of thousands of farmers to flee their land and communities. Many compounds still sat abandoned because only a few thousand souls returned home after the withdrawal. These men were among them. But the area was also a notorious nest for the Taliban, who found ample places to hide among the deserted homes.

When lunch was over Khan broke out more cigarettes. Both elders leaned back against the wall, one wiping his greasy fingers on his shirt and rubbing his distended belly in satisfaction. Haq spooned leftover yogurt into his mouth. Mohammed had barely touched his meal. I sipped a clear glass of chai tea and looked questioningly at Khan. He nodded.

The elder started. He began by talking about the weather. Every Afghan story was twice as long as it had to be. It's just the way it is. The temperature in May climbs until most of southern Afghanistan takes on a blast-furnace quality during the day. The nights are only marginally better. It was on one of those airless evenings that Fida Mohammed, the village teacher, returned home with his family after celebrating the wedding of a relative.

I started to write.

A man of delicate features and a gentle disposition, Mohammed had for most of his thirty-five years been able to avoid the waves of violence that rolled through his village. He was happy being a teacher, even though the Taliban often made threats. With his wife and three children, he lived a relatively quiet life. His pride and joy was his youngest son, four-year-old Mehmood, who was notorious throughout the village for his mischief-making. The child was a source of pleasant exasperation for his parents, who described him as a "naughty boy."

They lived in a mud-walled compound along with three other families at the edge of the village.

On the night in question, it was almost midnight, yet everyone was still awake and glowing with excitement about the wedding. Mohammed sat for a while in the relative darkness, looking up at the stars and gossiping with his family and neighbours.

It was so hot that particular evening that the men decided to sleep on mats and blankets outdoors. Somewhere beyond the compound there was an intermittent burst of gunfire; farther away was the low rumble of jets.

The elder became quiet and looked at Mohammed, who picked up the story. He said he told his wife that the shooting and the jets were nothing unusual. He urged her to go to sleep. What happened next occurred in a dreadful, dream-like slow motion.

"We were not warned by any person; it just happened," Mohammed said, with Khan translating.

Although he didn't see it, he heard the whoosh of the first missile. It exploded just outside of his compound with a thunderous clap. Mohammed sprang to his feet and ran to a bench that allowed him to poke his head just above the mud wall. The dust and smoke kicked up by the blast raised a grey curtain in front of him. The roar of jet engines prompted him to turn around and scream for his family to run to the far corner of the compound—the farthest point away from the incoming aircraft.

Mohammed spoke so softly in recounting the story that at times it was hard for Khan to make out what he was saying.

Haq then took over the narrative. He was a wheat farmer who lived in an adjacent compound. The first chest-crushing explosion took his breath away and was followed by two additional blasts that systematically demolished a trio of earthen-walled buildings all in a row. His brother and his family were in a fourth building, next in line. His brother lit a lamp, hoping the aircraft that plunged out of the darkness would realize they had attacked the wrong target.

"At least they could see we were human beings; we were civilians, women, children and that we were not Talibans," Haq said.

The move proved fatal for his brother.

"Even when we were seen by them, we were bombed again," Haq said. "When they saw them in light, again they attacked."

Mohammed was thrown to the ground by one of the explosions. A piece of hot, sharp steel sliced the tendons in his left foot. Bleeding, he dragged himself through the smoke and dust to find his family. His wife had taken two chunks of shrapnel to the neck, but was still alive. Thorny pieces of the same munitions had lacerated the feet of his two older children. Mehmood was sprawled a few metres away, his little body punctured in several spots by fragments. Mohammed was dumbfounded. Just before he passed out, he remembered screaming his son's name.

When he awoke in a bed at Kandahar's Mirwais Hospital, Asadullah Khalid was standing over him. Mohammed had never met the governor of Kandahar before and wondered who he was. The awkward moment seemed to go on for a long time, Mohammed said. He was barely conscious when Khalid shoved a wad of money—roughly U.S. $425—into his hand. The scene was witnessed and dutifully recorded by the Afghan journalists who accompanied the frantic governor to the hospital in the aftermath of what had been, at that time, the worst loss of civilian life since the end of the civil war.

No one wanted to talk about Mehmood, Mohammed said.

Over the next couple of days he asked about him repeatedly, but everyone, including his wife, "made up some pretense" and wouldn't tell him. Although he didn't need to be told his son was dead. Mohammed had seen the little body. Eventually a relative did confirm the worst, but only as Mohammed was spirited away to a Pakistani hospital, where he received specialized treatment on his battered left foot and leg. The instant compensation given to him by the governor paid for that surgery. To care for the injuries of his wife and two surviving children, Mohammed sold his land. If he was to walk again without crutches, the doctors told him, he would need another surgery in Pakistan. Unable to afford the further care, he said he would continue to hobble around on crutches. Largely destitute, he and his family moved into a squalid rental flat in a makeshift district of Kandahar city, which was already overrun with refugees from the fighting to the west. Some, like Haq, chose to return home, but not Mohammed. The roof of his house in Tulakan had fallen in and his petition to the Afghan government for compensation had been ignored.

Sixteen people died that night and fifteen others were wounded—the result of a wayward air strike called in by U.S. Special Forces chasing Taliban commanders in some of the nearby compounds of Azzizi. Both Mohammed and Haq said there had been no extremists hiding with them.

"If they had proof we were Talibans, then they could shoot us, but they had no proof." Mohammed's voice was loud and bitter for the first time.

The U.S. took responsibility, which it would do repeatedly throughout the war in dozens of other incidents that enraged Afghans. It was one of the things that nearly drove their president crazy—to the point where he privately declared he'd join the insurgents. It would be years before the use of air strikes, conveniently brutal weapons and one of the few Western advantages over the Taliban, was seen as a mission killer. To watch one happen was awe-inspiring. It was quick, efficient, devastating, a machine that wouldn't stop. Air strikes were the crack cocaine of the battlefield and something outgunned NATO soldiers had to be weaned from. But by the time they were reined in, the rot in terms of goodwill had become gangrenous. Never mind that the Taliban were monsters who cut off the heads of collaborators and used children as suicide bombers; the Afghans expected us to behave differently. They truly held us to a higher standard, at least in the beginning. That was the thing with this place; it has a way of pushing you hard against a wall and squeezing the optimist out of you.

Whenever I told the story of the Fida Mohammeds back at Kandahar Airfield, invariably the first question I got was whether these people were part of a Taliban IO—information operation. The first few times it happened, my head rattled in amazement, but after a while I got used to it. The army and the government just didn't want to hear it. In 2007, a staffer in the Prime Minister's Office (PMO) e-mailed a reporter in-field complaining about a story in which Afghans protested a civilian death. The journalist was accused of making it up, of being anti-military—that was until the video feed of the protest hit the television networks. The lovely antiseptic term "collateral damage" was nowhere in the messaging strategy. It would be naive to suggest that the Taliban don't engage in deception, but more often than not, NATO gave them ample propaganda fodder.

The U.S. gave $6,000 to the families of the Azzizi-Tulakan air strikes and expected the Afghan government to cover the additional rebuilding costs, including the $4,000 allotted per home. The cash was part of a pool of money spent at the discretion of the provincial governor. Claims would often take months to be considered, if they were considered at all. Khan badgered provincial officials and kept hounding them even when it seemed the families had written off any chance of compensation. He checked in regularly with Mohammed and promised to keep on top of the governor's office.

"We have to do something, sir," he told me more than once.

"You shouldn't have promised them anything," I said one day as we left his "office" following another interview.

"I did not promise success, sir, only that we try," he said. "We are journalists. We must try to help the people."

I stopped, leaned against the open door of the sedan and looked Khan straight in the face.

"The money for compensation is clearly in the governor's hands and he doesn't want to part with it. Forget about his officials and at the next news conference, ask him why."

Khan's face lit up and he ran an open palm through his rumpled hair. He had evidently already thought this tactic through but wanted my permission to pursue it.

"Thank you, sir. I was thinking exactly the same thing. Now, please get in the car before somebody shoots you."

The opportunity to ask that question came and went several times over the ensuing weeks and each time Asadullah Khalid either ignored or would not recognize Khan. I realized later how guileless we were in actually believing Khalid would care about a handful of families in an area still considered rebellious and sympathetic to the Taliban. Eventually even the officials would hang up on Khan when he called.

Months later, I was working late in the media tent. It was one of those rare nights when it rained in Kandahar. The overhead fluorescent lights were turned out and I pecked away at the laptop under a single desk lamp hooked to a tent pole with a spider clamp. The rain pounded against the canvas and the occasional violent gust of wind shook the place. The storm had started before sunset and began, as they always did in this desert, with a dust storm.

My cellphone chirped its happy tune, a ring oddly out of place in such a grim corner of the world. But I couldn't figure out how to change it. The backlit call display showed that it was Khan.

Nothing in particular had happened. He just wanted to talk. Evidently, he'd been thinking about the families. It was hard to know sometimes what spirit moved him or why certain things came to his mind when they did. I let him talk without interruption.

"You sound disappointed, brother," I said after he finished. "You really expected it to happen? You thought Khalid would pay."

"Yes sir, I did."

"I'm sorry you are disappointed."

"So am I."

I finished the story that was on my screen, turned off the light and walked back to the sleeping tent in the pouring rain.

Perceptions *4*

We trudged along a dirt road between fenced-off compounds with the enthusiasm of prisoners on the way to the gallows. We had been summoned. When you're an embedded journalist in Afghanistan and the general in charge calls for you, there is no RSVP. You just show up on time.

The Canadian media corps at Kandahar Airfield in the spring of 2006 was an intimate group of anywhere between five and fifteen journalists, photographers and cameramen. Over the years many of us would become regulars. But on this day in early April, there were just five reporters who'd been told that the general commanding all of southern Afghanistan wanted to see us. It took all of five minutes to walk the five hundred or so metres between the two media work tents and the headquarters for Regional Command South—known affectionately in this acronym-laced hell as RC-South. We were accompanied by the senior Canadian army public affairs officer. We entered through the gate in a newly erected chain-link fence and passed through a wood-framed guard hut, where we were required to surrender our cellphones. We crossed a cement courtyard that looked so clean I was certain you could eat off of the ground. I was almost afraid to walk across it for fear of leaving a trail that some poor private would have to sweep up. Clad in hiking boots, mud-splashed cargo pants and sweaty T-shirts, the five of us no doubt brought to mind images of the Peanuts cartoon character Pig-Pen.

Once inside the command post, we were met by a British officer who stared at us as though the barbarians had succeeded in storming the gates. After handshakes and introductions, he cast a bemused, critical eye over our group.

"It's very good to have all of you Canadians here," he said with an iron-toothed grin. "A G8 country; nice to see you finally pulling your weight in the world."

The public affairs officer clasped his chest with an instant cardiac arrest, I'm certain.

"Can we quote you on that?" I asked.

"Of course you can," replied the officer, refusing to be outdone. My startled colleagues and I reached for our notepads and pens.

"But," he said, finger raised in a well-practised manner that told me he'd played this game before, "I would prefer you quote me on background as a *senior British officer.*"

It was the most elegant climbdown I'd ever witnessed. But this *senior British officer's* ever-so-refined verbal slap felt pretty raw. It still smarts today and part of me doesn't know why. Maybe it's the naive streak in the Canadian psyche that believes everybody likes and respects us because we're inoffensive. We always say "please" and "thank you" to the world, never "fuck you." Or maybe it was our sometimes-pathological urge to be respected by the big boys; sort of like being the Oscar-accepting Sally Field of the international community.

Throughout my time covering the war, I got used to the thin streams of condescension that often trickled out of people's mouths. Sometimes, it was heaped on. Other times it was sprinkled out through repetition, like with the American brigade commander who told me later in the war that Canadians had better stop with this withdrawal talk and get on the bandwagon or be run over by it. Once in awhile it just drizzled on: a British general shocked a friend of mine by describing his visit to Saskatchewan as a trip to the "Third World." It was enough to infuriate those of us not career-bound by diplomacy or tied to the National Defence Act. The instinct was to give them the finger, but one day my photographer buddy Louie Palu pointed out a historical precedent that he said made him wonder why we even bothered.

"Look at D-Day with Hollywood. We didn't exist," he said. "It was the Brits and the Yanks; meanwhile we're getting our asses handed to us in Orotona and Dieppe. We're good for cannon fodder. Why do we keep showing up at these things just to get bitch-slapped?"

Canada had among the highest casualty percentages in NATO throughout the war, yet most Americans and Brits were gobsmacked to discover we were in Kandahar.

Louie had laid bare one of the aching sores of the Canadian psyche: The perception that we've often fought the wars of other nations with little or no recognition. The Second World War example was perfect. History looks at it as a good war, with a clear, unambiguous morality. The Dutch and French, whom we liberated, love us and remember. But I recall being at the fiftieth anniversary of D-Day in Portsmouth, England, where the town was bedecked in the Union Jack, the Stars and Stripes and the tricolour of France. There wasn't a Canadian flag in sight at the place where Canadian troops embarked.

The frequent snubs are not something we talk about openly. We just stew in our own resentment and smile sweetly. But some have suggested that this resentment manifested itself during this war, when poll after poll showed that a majority of Canadians wanted their soldiers to return to the days of blue-beret peacekeeping. At least then we felt appreciated, even if it was in our own minds, and even if that kind of peacekeeping pretty much no longer existed.

* * *

Whenever Khan was confounded by technology he always got the same strained look. He'd clench his tongue between his teeth and scowl at the device as if to scare it into working. Satellite phones, notoriously temperamental, always frustrated him.

"Something the matter?" I asked.

"Everything is perfectly alright, sir," he said as he redialled the number. He was met with a beeping sound, hit the "end" button and sighed.

I couldn't leave it alone.

"What? The Taliban do not have call waiting or voice mail? What kind of second-rate insurgency is this?"

Khan just glared at me.

Interviewing the Taliban was always a dodgy prospect. To do it in person was a kidnapping wish at best, a death wish at worst. Even westerners with deep experience in the region—those with intimate knowledge of the complex tribal system, those that could take advantage of the rivalries and desires for glory—ended up clapped in irons. Sending an Afghan journalist as a surrogate, aside from the obvious journalistic concerns, was perilous. The fire-breathers labelled them as collaborators and swiftly cut off their heads. The ditches around Kandahar and Helmand were littered with the headless corpses of locals whom the Taliban considered traitors. Some were freelance reporters and translators, but there were also human rights workers who had been concerned, ironically enough, about the plight of militants.

The Taliban were capricious in dispensing their brand of justice. Whether you lived or died depended on the whim of the local commander. Higher authorities sometimes intervened simply because a captured Western journalist had great propaganda and monetary value. In the spring of 2007, Mullah Dadullah, the Taliban's notorious, bloodthirsty military commander, turned the kidnapping and ransoming of westerners into a cottage industry. I was in Kandahar when an Al Jazeera English TV crew, on its way back from Helmand province, was taken. The gunslingers seized the cellphone of the reporter, an ex-BBC staffer, and it looked pretty grim until the Brit was able to convince them he worked for the Qatar-based news network. On that basis alone, he and his crew went from being "prisoners" to being "guests" of the Taliban. The crew was let go after a couple of days; the reporter showed up at KAF looking as though the blood had been permanently drained from his face.

There was a lot of debate within military and government circles about reporting what the Taliban had to say. Some on-line postings likened it to treason and called for Western journalists to be thrown in the dungeon for distributing such blasphemy. They questioned the methodology. I always found that rich, coming from a government that's message control throughout the war was so strict that interviews—even telephone interviews with officials—were cast aside in favour of e-mailed, bullet-point responses. The system of avoidance became so sophisticated that government communications "specialists" would, when faced with an interview request, create a series of anticipated questions, answer them with non sequiturs and send the response before the journalist even had an opportunity to open his mouth.

Interviewing the Taliban was seen as playing straight into their IO campaign. Apparently the Western public that would consume the Taliban's words were either more gullible or more stupid than their grandparents and great-grandparents, whose censored news reports had routinely quoted the claims of German and Japanese radio.

The deployment of Canadian troops to Kandahar in 2006 was initially scheduled to last only a year. That was what Paul Martin's Liberal government agreed to before it was dispatched by the electorate on January 23, 2006. The new Conservative government, led by Stephen Harper, wanted to extend the deployment until February 2009 and was eventually badgered into laying the matter before the House of Commons for a "take notes" debate.

It was in the context of letting the folks back home hear what the *enemy* had to say about Canada that I'd asked Khan to contact the Taliban's spokesman for the southern region. At the time, they had two "official" spokesmen—one for the south, the other for the eastern half of the country. They could be contacted by satellite phone and all of the fixers in Kandahar had their numbers. Some of us at KAF came to refer to it as 1-800-TALIBAN. They were always interviewed from an "undisclosed location," which, given the nature of the insurgency, was assumed to be a cave somewhere. But on the few occasions that I sat with Khan, listening and recording the conversations, I could hear street noise. Horns honked, motorcycles sputtered, people hollered in the background. I later learned that one of the spokesmen owned a prosperous bakery in Peshawar and only moonlighted as a mouthpiece. These men were the furthest things from cave dwellers you could imagine.

Qari Yousef Ahmedi had a harsh, guttural voice that made the hair on the back of your neck stand up. He spoke in long, uninterrupted sentences that were part statement, part sermon, part artful streams of consciousness. I'm sure Khan dreaded the interviews more than I did. His arm would get tired of holding the receiver and once in a while he'd let the phone sit on the armrest until the feeling returned to his hand. Ahmedi just kept talking, oblivious to anything but the sound of his own voice. The first time we spoke, Khan did a pre-interview and we recorded the second one, a plan that forced him to endure the ordeal twice. He vowed we'd never do that again.

Canada was a rich but weak nation, Ahmedi insisted, one without the will to fight the kind of war the Taliban envisioned. He lay out in clear, direct terms what their strategy would be for the coming expansion of NATO into southern Afghanistan.

"We think that when we kill enough Canadians, they will quit [the] war and return home," he said.

In the minds of the Taliban, Canada was NATO's weak link, and if they pushed us hard enough, they thought, the whole effort would collapse. He suggested the Taliban respected and feared the Americans, but considered Canadians to be "women." What startled me was how aware he was of the nuances of Canadian politics. He rhymed off the names of the prime minister and Opposition politicians without pause. The thought that Canada would reconsider and debate its troop commitment once soldiers were in the field was cause to sneer. Canadians might consider debate a strength of democracy, but it was viewed as a sign of "indecision and confusion" by the Taliban. They sensed a lack of resolve and were determined to make us bleed. They intended to stick the knife in as often as they could and give it the occasional twist. Throughout the years I heard from soldier after soldier who swore that whenever the political debate heated up at home the Taliban would step up ambushes and bombings. We talked; they bled.

During that first interview, Ahmedi trotted out a well-worn phrase: "You have the watches, but we have the time."

It was such a cliché that even Khan made a face when we later pored over the translation in the back of his car. Yet there was something so unsettling, so genuine about it that I found it hard to ignore. Ahmedi wanted me to believe that it was over for us before it had even started, and that our experience would be the same as the Russians and the British before them. That sort of historical shading made it easy for Ottawa, Washington, London and points between to dismiss the idea. Canadian and British officers who responded directly to the comments painted the Taliban as cornered, marginalized into rural pockets, an insurgency that was struggling to find money and recruits.

"The reason we think the Taliban are falling apart is because the pattern of attacks we're seeing is not coordinated," said Major Quentin Innis, a Canadian whose job that spring was to convince the local Afghan media to buy the coalition line.

In other words, there was no method to their madness, and without a method, there was no threat. As I transcribed the quotes, it felt as if I was writing history—not the backward kind but the forward variety, the type where everything unfolds in slow motion, the nightmare where you scream and no one hears. That was, as I discovered over the years, the quintessential Afghanistan experience.

* * *

Stephen Harper went to Kandahar Airfield in early March of that year to deliver a message of his own. The Conservatives had ridden to power a few months earlier on a promise to rebuild the military and refashion Canada's foreign policy into a more activist agenda.

"You can't lead from the bleachers. I want Canada to be a leader," the prime minister said.

It was music to the ears of the thousand soldiers who stood on the loose rocks under a clear blue sky to listen to the speech. Many whom I talked with afterward felt he was declaring their time as peacekeepers over. They had finally been let loose to fight the war that began on September 11, 2001. In Harper and the Conservatives, most in the military felt they had found their political soulmates. The prime minister, in turn, genuinely admired soldiers, their discipline and their determination, and the black-and-white way they looked at the world. Harper hit all of the right notes that day. He touched on their patriotism and desire to make a contribution.

"Your work is about more than just defending Canada's national interests. Your work is also about demonstrating an international leadership role for our country."

Making Afghanistan Harper's first international trip was certainly symbolic. It spoke volumes to those who stood under the blazing Afghan sun, to the Conservative political base back home and to the rest of Canadians. Even though the Liberals had put the troops in Kandahar, the mission presented Conservative insiders with a golden opportunity and they threw their arms around it in an unrestrained embrace, appropriating for better or worse what Paul Martin had begun.

Harper insisted that Canada was in Afghanistan for the "long haul" and that Ottawa was committed to helping turn a failed state into a "democratic, prosperous and modern country." What he didn't know—or failed to recognize—was that such ventures, under the very best of conditions, are excruciating, decades-long exercises. Even still, he laid down the infamous political marker that would repeatedly come back to bite him.

"There will be some who want to cut and run, but cutting and running is not my way and it's not the Canadian way," he said and the troops applauded. "We don't make a commitment and then run away at the first sign of trouble. We don't and we will not, as long as I'm leading this country."

At first blush, it seemed that skeptical allies and the Taliban were the natural audience for that kind of how-the-West-was-won talk, but Conservative insiders who helped craft what became known as the "cut and run speech" had a slightly different agenda. They were laying the groundwork. Throughout their time in office, a number of important policy questions would be viewed through the political prism of the Tory desire to supplant the Liberals as the country's natural governing party. To do that, insiders said, the party needed to identify itself with "strong" national institutions.

"The Liberals had medicare and the CPP and we needed to have our brand on something," a former senior official said. "We chose the military and the RCMP and poured what we had into backing them."

Doing the right thing and living up to international obligations in Afghanistan were always part of the equation, the insiders insisted, but the domestic political calculation was just as important. From the outside, it was hard to tell some days which took precedent. The Tories held on—sometimes precariously—to their minority government, but also determined to wage their long-term war of attrition with the Liberals as they battled the Taliban. The reflex to eviscerate political opponents and critics was strong and often unchecked. It poisoned the discourse and prompted equally outrageous retorts from the Opposition. It's one of the reasons debate throughout the war, with painfully few exceptions, never rose above narrow political self-interest.

* * *

The Martin government decided to go to Kandahar in the spring of 2005, and it was announced publicly, if not somewhat prematurely, by Defence Minister Bill Graham. It was only after the head of the army conducted a survey of the place in the summer that the decision came back to cabinet for final approval. According to Liberal insiders, the formal decision to place troops in Kandahar was made in a unanimous show of hands, on August 26, 2005, in the ballroom of a Winnipeg hotel. It was the final, unflinching approval and it came in one of those travelling circus cabinet shows the prime minister seemed to love. It was a strange place from which to launch the country's most dramatic military operation in half a century, wedged on the agenda between softwood lumber and cucumber sandwiches. Much has been written about how Martin's government never expected Kandahar to turn into a cauldron, and it's hard to get two people in Ottawa to agree about their perceptions and recollections of how the country ended up there. The longer I spent on the ground, the more intrigued I became.

I spent my spare time pouring through old stories, interviews, transcripts and Hansard records.

Just about everyone, it seemed, had a score to settle. Jean Chrétien, in his prime ministerial memoir, blamed Martin's dithering and insisted he would have kept Canada out of the "killing fields of Kandahar." Others pointed the finger at silver-tongued chief of defence staff General Rick Hillier, whose arguments supposedly convinced Martin that southern Afghanistan was the place to be. Still others cast it as an act of appeasement, a gesture to placate Washington, which was supposedly annoyed with Canada for sitting out the Iraq war. The arguments, claims, denials and counter-denials, especially when things were going badly in 2006 and 2007, were churned out almost faster than we could report them. The Conservatives may have wanted to own the war, but the Liberals were silently relieved to let them have it. The longer it went on, the higher the casualty count, the more collective amnesia took over. History is heavy with attrition. At least that was the political calculation for the Liberals as they plotted their eventual return to power.

When there was a spark of remembrance, the political maxim of deny and deflect would take over. The messaging was: We knew Kandahar was going to be tough, but not that tough. Yet in the months before they were defeated in 2005, Martin's government approved $278.3 million to outfit the army for the conflict. They bought armoured patrol vehicles, new artillery and slapped extra protective plating on existing troop carriers. Bill Graham did a round of speeches and interviews in the fall of 2005 to warn that there would be casualties.

"I think there's no question that the mission in Kandahar is a much more dangerous mission than the one here in Kabul," Graham told reporters in a conference call from the Afghan capital on October 12, 2005. Prior to making the remarks, he had met with President Hamid Karzai and his Afghan defence counterpart.

"And, as you know, when we move our troops to the Kandahar region they will be actively engaged in providing stability in the region and actually it will be more in the nature of a combat mission where they will be out looking for people who are doing exactly this type of thing to try and destabilize the country and they'll be on the lookout for them."

Graham placed a heavy emphasis on development through the newly established Canadian provincial reconstruction base in Kanadahar, but said the job of soldiers would be to meet the Taliban in the field and destroy them.

"So there's no question but that is the nature of that mission and it will bring those consequences with it. We know from reports that have already been made some of our forces have already been engaged in that type of operation and we expect will be engaged in more."

It was a perfect description of a counter-insurgency war.

When Rick Hillier retired in 2008, I interviewed Paul Martin. He said when he hired Hillier for the top military post, he wanted the Forces to become a useful instrument in the country's foreign policy, beyond traditional peacekeeping. The problem was that Martin, his cabinet and his political advisors had no ideas on how to turn this notion into a vision for the future. The solution partly presented itself in a strategy paper written by Hillier, who was then head of the Canadian army and freshly returned from Afghanistan, where he had served as commander of the International Security Assistance Force (ISAF) in Kabul.

"I had a view of the role of the military in supporting us in peacekeeping and peacemaking in fragile states," Martin said of his first meeting with Hillier at 24 Sussex Drive.

He recalled how the two faced each other on yellow couches in the living room of the official residence.

"General Hillier essentially took over and articulated far better than I could how he saw it. And it was at that moment I said, 'Look it, we've got complete agreement.'"

The deployment to Kandahar fit with the vision the two laid out together, but that didn't mean Martin was without concerns and conditions. He was adamant the mission last only for one year and that the army be freed up to go elsewhere—perhaps a humanitarian intervention in Darfur or a peacekeeping mission in Haiti. He recalled that the defence chief made a forceful and passionate argument for taking a lead role in Kandahar, which was by that time the only high-profile NATO assignment left. During a roundtable interview at the CP bureau in Ottawa in 2006, Hillier laid out some of the arguments he made within government. Prior to stepping into Kandahar, he said, his goal was to raise the profile of the Canadian Armed Forces. A prominent place in the Afghan mission not only helped a down-trodden people wrestle their country from the grip of fanatics, it restored a dejected and marginalized Canadian military as a national institution within the conscience of the nation. It also demonstrated to our allies that Canada was a reliable international partner. There were times, Hillier recalled, when it was tough to find staff officers to fill posts at NATO headquarters in Brussels.

"We were almost invisible at NATO," he said.

Behind the toothy grin and self-deprecating style lurked a sharp political mind, and Hillier knew the Canadian public would be more willing to support the military and fork out for the equipment it needed if it could be seen in action.

"The profile needed to be raised so Canadians could at least recognize the Canadian Forces and once they got a look at them, understand the incredible value that those Canadian Forces and the men and women therein brought to the country. Our little, tiny strategy, if you will, was: Recruit the nation."

The decision to send Canadian troops into battle is made by the executive branch, not Parliament. Over the last several years, the public has been lulled into thinking the House of Commons actually has the power to decide. But that power rests with the prime minister and, to a lesser extent, the federal cabinet. Despite becoming public champions of democratic debate on the Afghan mission, the Conservatives never changed the legislation and happily perpetuated the misunderstanding. The very first extension, passed in a vote on May 17, 2006, came about because of hectoring by the Opposition. And for a while there, when the Conservatives looked like they were going to lose the vote, they threatened to ignore it. The second debate—in March 2008—was the result of the prime minister's blue-ribbon panel, known as the Manley Commission, which looked into the future course of the mission. It resulted in the current extension to 2011.

In the United States the president must ask Congress for a declaration of war. It is the country's elected representatives—for better or worse—who decide to put their young men and women in harm's way. When Canada went to war in Kandahar, the decision was made by a prime minister whose minority Liberal government was perpetually on the brink of collapse. The closest the country ever got to a democratic discussion about what is inarguably the most solemn undertaking of a nation—to shed the blood of its young people and the blood of others—happened in a "take notes" debate just days before the Martin government fell. Such a debate is an occasion for MPs to discuss an important issue, but not vote on it. It is one of those impenetrable Parliamentary traditions that seem so out of step in our hyper-aware, twenty-four-hour news-cycle sense of democracy.

* * *

One evening, about halfway through the war, I sat on my bunk at a forward operating base in Panjwaii, laptop on my knees and satellite dish plugged in outside. On the screen was a transcript of that "take notes" debate.

November 15, 2005, was a chilly night in Ottawa and MPs who scurried to the late debate on Afghanistan had to dodge a mixture of snow and freezing rain for the long hike up Parliament Hill. Many of those with offices nearby chose to stay warm and dry by using the underground tunnel that connects the West Block with the Centre Block, where the Commons resides. The debate started promptly at 7 p.m. and lasted exactly five hours and five minutes. It took place in the shadow of a non-confidence motion, which ended thirteen days later with the defeat of the Liberals.

In retrospect, it is uncanny how prescient the MPs were that night. Conservative Leon Benoit led off for his party and expressed frustration that Canadian soldiers had been plucked out of the relatively safe confines of Kabul and sent to the most dangerous part of Afghanistan without so much as an explanation. If Canadians were being asked to fight, he suggested, the decision deserved a fulsome, convincing explanation beyond the canned speeches and media response lines about "providing stability and good government" for Afghans.

"Here we are having this debate in the House today and yet the minister has not given the most basic explanation to Parliament and to the Canadian public as to why the government has made this change," Benoit said. "I would really appreciate if the minister would take this opportunity to explain finally why the government has taken this decision."

Former brigadier-general and soon-to-be Conservative defence minister Gordon O'Connor chimed in and said the Liberals had meandered into the Kandahar commitment without realizing all that was involved in NATO's "high-risk" expansion to the south. Like any good military man he wanted to see "a clear political and military strategy" and definitions for success. Only a few months later it was O'Connor who struggled to describe what success should look like.

Although Paul Martin was clear that the mission would last only one year, O'Connor pointed out that commentators, academics and government officials were suggesting the international community's commitment to Afghanistan could run for ten to twenty years.

"It is obvious that the government does not have an idea how long the commitment will go on," O'Connor told the Commons. "What really irritates me about the government's management of the military commitment to Afghanistan is that it has created a crisis situation and it is running out of time. The government knows it has made a hasty decision without thinking through the consequences."

Bill Blaikie, the veteran Manitoba New Democrat and the party's respected defence critic, said the mission didn't look like peacekeeping.

"It might be called peace building, but it is more like war fighting," he said.

The burly Manitoban also worried that the military commitment at the provincial reconstruction base overshadowed the civilian elements.

Defence Minister Bill Graham joined the debate late. He said he recognized that an imbalance between soldiers and aid workers existed, but justified it by saying "people living in the area want stability and they want it now."

They touched on what would become the lightning-rod issue of prisoner treatment and Graham startled the Commons when he announced he was going to set up an arrangement whereby those captured on the battlefield would be handed over to Afghan authorities. It was the first anyone had heard of it. There was hand-wringing about whether the army was suitably equipped for combat, but in the end there was little anyone could do. The redeployment of troops was already well underway.

When the Peace Tower bells tolled midnight, the MPs gathered their papers, put down their earpiece translators, slipped on their overcoats and stepped out into the late evening dampness. A thick fog had blanketed the Hill while they'd been inside. Hardly anyone was on the street and even fewer in the rest of the country had noticed what took place.

When I finished reading the transcript, I switched off my laptop and emerged from the reinforced bunker into the heavy, velvet blackness of Panjwaii. As I lit a cigar behind a Hesco bastion—a wire-encased barrier that reminded you of sandbags on steroids—I watched the orange fizz of an illumination round dwindle and curl across the sky. I felt as though I was looking up from the bottom of a deep well. Somewhere in the darkness there was the deep throbbing of outgoing artillery. It was going to be a long night.

Moral Murk 5

The Chinook helicopter is a great lumbering monster with two powerful rotor blades and turbo engines that deliver a screeching whine so potent it feels, after only a few minutes, as if someone has taken an electric drill to the side of your head. Earplugs were always necessary, but ultimately useless. On some long hauls, the noise could be so irritating you were tempted to claw at your ears just to end the misery. I could never tell how much of that desire was really the noise, or just the result of nerves as we headed toward a landing zone. On the way back to base, the engine sound was the same, but nowhere near as convulsive. On particularly bad days you even welcomed it, as much as anyone welcomes drilling in the side of their head.

The wait to get on a Chinook, no matter when and where you were going, was always interminable. They seemed to take forever to warm up. Everyone would stand in two neat columns under the blazing sun and wait for the order to scurry past the tail gun—a .50-calibre machine gun—and up the ramp into the cavernous bay. Marching toward the open back, the wind from the blades was violent enough to knock you down and tear away loose objects, like ball caps and notepads. That usually happened to civilians and prompted air gunners and ground crew to shake their heads. When you crossed the tarmac, tiny bits of sand would burrow into your cheeks. Stepping on to the ramp would ease the harsh wind, but the scalding engine exhaust washed over you like some pre-battle baptism.

It was Easter Sunday 2006 when I sat hunched in the red mesh seat of a Royal Air Force (RAF) Chinook as it thundered low over the desert, pointed toward Sangin. The rotors were powerful and violent and I felt the concussion as the air slammed on to the hard-baked soil and bounced back up at us. There was an eclectic mix of Canadian, American and British troops onboard, as well as cargo pallets. The chopper was FOB-hopping. It had several base deliveries to make that day before returning to the confines of KAF. Forward Operating Base Robinson, the scene of the first major battle of the Canadian deployment, was the first stop. The pilot bobbed, weaved and looped his way to the besieged outpost in a trip that felt as though it took forever. I looked out one of the bulbous side windows on final approach and was struck by the utter isolation of the base. I wondered why anyone in his right mind would want to possess such an unloved little plateau, let alone die for it.

There was a pop and hiss just before we landed and through the open back hatch I could see twin curling smoke trails and the star-like sparkle of shells. The pilot fired off counter-measures to confuse any potential incoming missile. The Taliban were rumoured to have dug up some long-buried Stinger missiles given to the mujahideen during the Soviet war. The reports were credible enough for the CIA to offer a U.S. $250,000 reward to the Afghan warlords who turned them in. I had worked with Jojo on that story and prayed like hell that greed had won out over jihadist zeal.

There was a gentle bump as the chopper arrived, but didn't quite land. The nose stayed elevated and pointed tentatively skyward, ready to leap back into the air at the first sign of trouble, although the door gunners near the front did relax, allowing the barrels of their .50-calibre machine guns to droop. The tail gunner, who'd sat on his haunches throughout the flight, stood up and coiled his rubber headset cable around one hand, motioning frantically for us to get off. We spilled out the back of the helicopter like pieces of paper shaken from a tilted trash can. The blade wash lifted a thick curtain of milky, grey dust that seemed to envelope the entire area. A dozen soldiers and civilians scrambled a few metres from the ramp, dropped to one knee and crouched to shield themselves from the violent gusts as the helicopter heaved into the air like an untamed horse. It was gone within seconds, but the dust cloud lingered as soldiers slipped on their packs and checked their weapons.

I stood up and watched the dust settle on the oversized stones of the helipad. Sangin revealed itself stubbornly, grain by grain. The hot, heavy, early morning breeze failed to entirely whisk away the murk. It was only when we started walking toward the gate that the place came into focus. A LAV sat at the edge of the wide-open helipad, its 25-mm chain gun pointed toward the edge of the cliff.

Almost the entire Canadian battle group had been rushed to the remote base in the aftermath of the fight that killed Robert Costall and John Stone. As I walked among the slit trenches, berms and strategically placed armoured vehicles, soldiers looked up, half-surprised to see civilians, let alone a journalist. Some gave tired, vacant smiles and one or two waved. Their attention, however, was on the green slope that led toward Castle Ruins, the Fortress and the village of Sangin. The field, which ran right up to the base and kissed the razor wire, was full of poppies that were close to harvest. The green bulbs swayed hypnotically whenever there was puff of wind.

The opium poppy was the lifeblood of Afghanistan's corrupt narco-economy. When the Soviets withdrew in the 1980s, their scorched-earth policy combined with season after season of drought to turn the once-lush river valley and farms to dust. Poppies need very little water to thrive and during the Taliban years they were so plentiful and their effects so potent that the hardline Islamists at first outlawed their cultivation. But once deposed, they realized the cash value of the opium and heroin trade and their brutal, single-minded objections vanished. Drug money filled their war chest with an embarrassment of riches. Even the non-ideologues saw the profit-making potential and in the years since the overthrow of the Taliban, Afghan drug cartels and private armies had sprung up throughout the south. Kandahar was the Taliban's spiritual home, but Helmand province was its pocketbook, the place that would fund the endless jihad.

From the moment the U.S. and its allies set foot in the region they faced the poppy conundrum. The American solution, as with everything, was to blow it up. Slashing and burning poppy fields was their preferred method for starving the Taliban of their main source of income. Later in the war, I discovered Canadian diplomatic cables that showed how Washington pressured Hamid Karzai's government to accept an aerial spraying eradication plan, similar to what the Soviets had done in the 1980s. Canada and other allies quietly counselled him to reject the idea. Depriving dirt-poor farmers—who may have been only sympathetic to the Taliban at that point—of their livelihood would have been a huge mistake. The all-too-likely popular uprising could have made the current war seem like a picnic.

Geographically, Sangin was at a crucial nexus. It was not only at the tail end of the Taliban's Ho Chi Minh Trail, it was also a major transit route for the drug trade. Standing on one of the Hesco barricades that day, I could see the Helmand River—which flowed south and west and spilled into a basin in neighbouring Iran—in the distance. It was the superhighway of illegal drug exports. The Taliban and the Iranians hated each other. The objection wasn't so much personal or diplomatic as it was theological, a mutual loathing between Shiite and Sunni, the different sects of Islam. But when it came to Iranian drug cartels, it was the old maxim "the enemy of my enemy is my friend." The two sects were united in their desire to screw the Americans and make money doing it. The Iranian regime was careful to disavow the unholy alliance, but American military commanders repeatedly pointed out how Tehran never discouraged it either.

The Canadians in Sangin were under strict orders not to disturb the poppy crop, said Major Bill Fletcher, commander of Charlie Company, 1 PPCLI. We stood together and watched a farmer wander among the waist-high bulbs. If at all possible, the soldiers' armoured vehicles were not to chew up the fields.

"We don't want to incite them," Fletcher said.

Fear was good. It was healthy. At that point in the war, few wanted to openly admit that this place was an enigma—one gigantic, sun-baked, stinking riddle. The message from the top was always optimistic, usually without qualification and delivered with the subtlety of a steamroller: We are here and we are in charge and we are going to fix this place. Whether the farmer in front of us, who was squeezing the poppy bulbs to see if they were ripe, felt the place needed fixing was often irrelevant. Yet it was coming face to face with his reality that was most sobering for the troops and anyone who followed in their wake.

An unsettled calm had descended over Sangin with the arrival of the Canadian relief force. Fletcher attributed the stability to the intimidating presence of the LAVs and the pair of brand new 155-mm artillery guns that conducted regular firing exercises into empty fields as a demonstration of force. Some of the militants thought responsible for the March 28 attack on the supply convoy—the fight that led to Costall's and Stone's deaths—were captured not long after Charlie Company arrived. They were paraded into the compound, hooded and restrained by plastic zap straps, and made to kneel in a sandy area sectioned off by razor wire.

"The ANA hated them," Lieutenant Jon Snyder recalled as the two of us sat in the shade of a Hesco bastion and tried to escape the hard heat of the day. He motioned to the Afghan soldiers, who had their own segregated portion of the compound.

Snyder, twenty-four, was in charge of 8 Platoon. He was from British Columbia and happily advertised the fact he'd always wanted to be a soldier. There was a certain undeniable panache about him. Maybe it was his enthusiasm that struck me. He spoke confidently, convincingly and articulately. The head of the army, Lieutenant-General Andrew Leslie, would later confide that Snyder's guts, intelligence and ability to improvise stood out to the upper echelons of the military during that first tour. He was convinced the soon-to-be Captain Snyder would one day occupy his seat.

"The Afghans went nuts," Snyder said, describing a recent joint patrol. "We captured this Taliban and we knew we had the real deal because we opened up his jacket and found letters and documents inside."

He described how the letters, written in Pashto, were taken from the fighter and examined by the Afghan soldiers.

"They were signed by Taliban commanders, recommending him to village elders wherever he was going. They said he was brave and he should be treated well because he had proven himself by killing, I think it was eight Afghan army soldiers."

The Afghan soldiers, some of whom liked to chew on the poppy leaves to get a high, were furious.

Snyder looked at me. His unshaven, sun-reddened baby face hardened with irony.

"They wanted to shoot this guy on the spot and we had to stop them," he said. "I told them, you're not going to do that, he's going back to KAF, and we had to guard the guy until we got him on a chopper."

Months later, in following a court case involving Amnesty International and the B.C. Civil Liberties Association, I discovered copies of those letters. The two human rights groups tried to halt the handover of prisoners to Afghan authorities. Whenever the debate was in a full-throated rage in either the courtroom or the House of Commons, I would think about Snyder and the way he looked at the Afghan soldiers that day. The Conservatives would deem questions and criticism about the handling of prisoners as an attack on the integrity of the troops. The public, they intoned, really didn't care whether these monsters that'd killed "our boys" were tortured. It was just Afghans torturing Afghans. Who cares?

It was an appeal to our lowest instincts. Yet never was the divide between the reality of the field and the rhetoric back home greater than on this issue. It wasn't that the soldiers didn't hate the Taliban. They did. There wasn't a turn-the-cheek sentiment when they slaughtered troops and innocent civilians. Most everyone wanted revenge in one form or another. Afghanistan had a way of doing that to you. It wore you down. With enough time, enough blood and enough misery, you snapped across a line where the once unthinkable was justifiable. Sometimes it was tough to notice when someone had gone over that line. Sometimes they went and never came back. It manifested itself in phrases like, "Some motherfucker is going die for what happened." I heard it often enough. It was acceptable coming from soldiers vacant and wasted by combat. It was cringe-worthy when it came from someone who spent the war in line for an iced cappuccino. But it was obscene when mouthed by the starched, manicured and finely coiffed back home. The Conservatives had us believing that courage was standing up to Taliban machine gun bullets and rockets, and medals were deservedly pinned on many a chest for those actions. But it took real guts for Jon Snyder and his men to stand between those outraged Afghan soldiers and their captives.

Sitting against the Hesco that Easter Sunday, with the wire mesh digging into my back, I asked Snyder what he thought about the orders that required him to hand over all prisoners. He shrugged his shoulders with a resigned heave. Government policy and politics wasn't within his lane and the army always encouraged soldiers who talked to the media to stay within their lane.

* * *

The previous December, General Rick Hillier had signed a memorandum of understanding with the Karzai government. It bound Canada to hand over all prisoners to local Afghan authorities, be it the army, the police or the country's notorious intelligence service, the National Directorate of Security (NDS). The British and the Dutch signed similar deals. With events at Guantanamo Bay and Abu Ghraib still fresh in many minds, the thought of handing prisoners to the Americans sent shivers down political and human rights spines. The Canadian agreement was nearly identical to those signed by the allies, with one notable exception. It did not give Canadian authorities—military or otherwise—the automatic right to check on the fate of those handed over. The Canadian military argued repeatedly over the years that once a prisoner was out of its hands, it was no longer responsible, especially when individuals were transferred to the custody of their own countrymen. To ensure that international law was respected, Canada's civilian agencies had to follow up through much more opaque diplomatic channels.

But at the time Jon Snyder faced his dilemma, there were virtually no Canadian civilians on the ground in Kandahar. Most had been withdrawn following the assassination of diplomat Glyn Berry the previous January. They didn't start returning to the PRT base in Kandahar until late April and even then it was only one mid-level staffer by the name of Richard Colvin. By that time a wide body of human rights reports on prison conditions within Afghanistan were warning repeatedly of torture and summary executions. The U.S. State Department authored a particularly stark report in 2005. Canada's own Foreign Affairs Department had a similar assessment in its annual classified human rights report. Whether the authors of the Canadian agreement had to access to or considered those reports is unclear. When the agreement was drawn up, Amnesty International Canada raised an alarm with the Liberal government before it was thrown out of office. The human rights watchdog said the Canadian government's legal responsibility did not end when a prisoner was transferred. International law considers it a war crime for a state to hand over a prisoner to either suspected or certain torture.

Much was made of the fact that Hillier and not the country's ambassador in Kabul signed the deal on December 18, 2005. It was used as an illustration, as the prisoner fiasco unfolded, by bitter and frustrated Foreign Affairs staffers of how the military and the defence chief in particular had big-footed the mission. Oddly enough, classified documents I viewed later in the war showed that no one at Foreign Affairs, with one notable exception, raised a finger to revise the agreement and some fiercely resisted changing it even when it developed into a raging political inferno. There were, however, second thoughts about the wisdom of the agreement among soldiers, specifically those whose job it was to track and implement the policy.

"I had visions of, we turn over this really bad guy that's been trying to kill us or had killed military soldiers and he goes out the back door as soon as they leave the base, out the back door, the back of the car, or he's shot dead somewhere down the side of the road," Major Kevin Rowcliffe later told Military Police Complaints Commission (MPCC) investigators. "Who knows? If you don't do any follow-up, who knows?"

Rowcliffe was the military police policy advisor in 2006 at Canadian Expeditionary Force Command (CEFCOM), the country's Ottawa-based overseas headquarters. He'd spent considerable time in Afghanistan on previous missions and testified the agreement "raised a whole bunch of concerns" in his mind, which he said he raised "up the chain of command"—meaning to his boss at the time, Lieutenant-General Michel Gauthier.

"I was making him aware of these concerns as well, that we're handing them over but we don't know what happens afterward and the message I was getting back [was] that we need to hand them over," he told investigators.

Gauthier later testified to a public inquiry. He said he didn't recall Rowcliffe bringing up those specific concerns and pointed out they had no first-hand accounts.

"From my perspective we didn't know factually that Afghans were tortured," Gauthier testified.

The International Committee of the Red Cross (ICRC) during the spring of 2006 expressed concerns to Canadians in Afghanistan that it wasn't getting timely information about the increasing number of prisoners being detained and handed over to Afghan authorities. The humanitarian agency was bound to check on the welfare of prisoners and report—in the strictest of confidence—to individual governments about the conditions and abuses it uncovered. The ICRC waited, in some cases, weeks before it was notified by Canada, and sources said when the information arrived it was often "shoddy and incomplete." It made it almost impossible to track prisoners turned over to Afghan custody.

Even while Canada's special forces were handing prisoners to the Americans, prior to December 2005, the agency complained in the strongest terms about the quality of the information. It issued several diplomatic notes, copies of which I later viewed, and warned that reporting practices needed to improve. The arrival of Richard Colvin in Kandahar gave the agency a direct point of contact and an outlet for its frustration.

Colvin arranged for two meetings. The first was between the agency Kandahar representative and the deputy commander of the PRT base, Major Eric Liebert. The follow-up happened on June 2, 2006, and involved senior task force officials, including the military lawyer and a political advisor attached to KAF headquarters. What they heard shocked them. Since the Red Cross is bound by convention not to tattle, the officials gathered around the table reportedly spoke in coded diplomatic language. But it was enough for Colvin to write two of the memos that later created a political firestorm. Neither memo, both of which I saw in uncensored form, used the word "torture," but the implication was there. What Colvin's memos did not contain were specific, individual allegations, a point his critics made ad nauseam.

Watching these events unfold was the fledgling Afghanistan Independent Human Rights Commission (AIHRC). The agency was one of the Canadian government's favourite feel-good funding projects and often pointed to as an example of the kind of nation-building work that Ottawa did best. Head of the commission's office in Kandahar was the soft-spoken, dignified Abdul Qadar Noorzai. He estimated publicly at the time that approximately one-third of the prisoners handed over ended up being tortured, especially if they were in the hands of the ill-equipped, illiterate, underpaid and brutal local police.

Afghan authorities have "two kinds of attitudes," he later told my CP colleague Bob Weber in an interview. "When they come into my office, they behave very officially; when they go back to their offices they behave in another way."

Nobody listened.

Yet the events of spring 2006 were enough for Rowcliffe to declare, in hindsight, that his worst fears were confirmed.

"That's when I kind of felt there's definitely a flaw in the Canadian position, the government position," he said.

The Canadians would later pack up and leave FOB Robinson to the British Army, but they never seemed to escape the moral murk unleashed by events there. A University of Ottawa law professor and human rights advocate would later use the Access to Information Act to accuse Canadian soldiers of directly abusing prisoners at the base. But the claim—investigated and dismissed by the military—was a mere sideshow compared to the legal, ethical and political juggernaut of transfer to torture. The notion conjured up the worst imaginable shame in a country that had convinced itself over the decades of its moral superiority and enlightened ways. It just wasn't possible that we were no better than the Americans, British and a host of other allies who'd fought most of the dirty little wars of the last century, the ones Canada scrupulously avoided.

* * *

The army kept me on a tight leash in Sangin because of the previous trouble with the U.S. Special Forces and the duelling friendly-fire investigations. It sent along a young, affable public affairs officer by the name of Captain Mark Peebles, who had a gift for mangled quotes but was just so likeable and helpful it was easy to forgive the sin. The army had certain things it showcased whenever it allowed you to go someplace and on that particular Easter Sunday it was the guns. They were quite proud of the new 155-mm howitzers purchased in a hurry by the former Liberal government from the U.S. Marine Corps. They were lightweight and deadly accurate. Peebles took me over and introduced me to the forward operations officer.

Captain Nichola Goddard sat on the open back of her LAV with a member of her crew. For a moment I thought she was a hallucination, but somewhere in the back of my mind, I remembered my CTV colleague Lisa LaFlamme telling me about her. Even still, I was startled. My first reaction was silent admiration; I knew artillery spotters were always at the cutting edge of the fight. They were at the front of the front and the job was among the most dangerous in the military. Sitting and chatting with Goddard made me think of some stories I'd written a decade before, about the horrific experiences of the first woman infantry officer, Captain Sandra Perron, who was tied to a tree and beaten by her fellow soldiers in 1992. The fact that Goddard now sat before me in the middle of a war zone seemed both remarkable and gently inspiring. She had serious eyes with a hint of mirth, yet carried herself with a natural authority. A lot of women in the military, especially combat arms, had an edge, an implied desire to demonstrate they had more stones than you or any of their male comrades. There was no trace of that in Goddard. She seemed perfectly comfortable in her own skin. And her troops looked as though they respected her. It was evident by the conversation that she fussed over them; several times she referred to them as "my crew." It wasn't a statement of possession as much as an expression of belonging. She looked as though she belonged.

We chatted for a while and I took a few pictures and some quotes for a story that moved later that day. There was a tinge of sadness about being away from family at Easter, but her face lit up with a huge, genuine smile when she spoke about her parents in Calgary and her husband. The conversation meandered from the mundane to the remarkable: new showers at the FOB, routine patrols, the thrill of calling down fire with new guns. There was delight in her voice when she described the moments when indifferent Afghan villagers realized that they were dealing with Canadian soldiers, rather than Americans or some other nationality. The unspoken subtext was that change was coming and we could make a difference. It was a point of pride often repeated by soldiers early in the mission and it occasionally made you wince because it sounded so parochial. Yet coming from Goddard, the words were fresh and unaffected. She believed it was possible. When I stumped through the heavy sand on my way out the gate at Sangin, considering all I'd heard that day, I wanted to believe too. I wanted so much to believe.

Fighting Season 6

We bounced around in the rear of the Bison armoured vehicle for hours. It was late April 2006 and the airless heat of spring was already upon us. The convoy commander had wanted to push through the hardscrabble maze of Kandahar city and its surrounding suburbs before stopping for a break. When the back ramp finally came down, we stumbled out of the dusty, diesel-choked metal cocoon to stretch our legs. It was one of those stunning Afghan mornings. The sky was a bright blue and we were surrounded by desert that was itself framed by serrated mountains. There wasn't a lick of vegetation, even at the edge of the paved, double-lane highway. It was a wasteland—a beautiful, frightening wilderness that had been ground into lifelessness. You always felt small in the face of such vistas, but you also felt secure. There was no building, not even a rock that someone could use to set up an ambush.

It was while lounging against the rear tire in the shade of the Bison that I first heard another convoy wasn't having such a carefree moment. The vehicle commander stuck his head over the side. A convoy travelling from Shah Wali Kot, where we were heading, had been hit and there were casualties. Everyone tightened up. Most of the soldiers, who moments before had been wisecracking and harassing each other, slipped on their game faces, those impenetrable masks of silent tolerance. The air sentries, who stood guard out the rear open hatches of the armoured vehicles, took extra care to double-check their weapons.

We were back inside the Bison on its uncomfortable benches and rolling again when one of the air sentries stuck his head down and pointed skyward. There was a spare hatch in the centre and I poked my head out just as a U.S. Apache helicopter gunship rumbled low and disappeared over the line of vehicles ahead of us. It was followed seconds later by an American Black Hawk with the Red Cross symbol on the door. It too vanished into the distance where the road curved to the left and slinked toward a green-edged river valley. Choppers travelled in pairs and unarmed ones were always guarded.

We weren't plugged into the vehicle's communications system so we had no idea how bad it was until we arrived at our destination, a firebase under construction in the hinterlands. The place was occupied by Alpha Company, 1 PPCLI, and they were in a bloody-minded mood. The ramp went down again and we climbed out into the dusty, rock-strewn mountain bowl that was to be FOB Martello. The soldiers were spooling up a patrol into the nearby village of Gumbad. They were pissed and they wanted answers. Four of their comrades lay dead in a dry riverbed—a wadi—just outside the community. A powerful bomb, likely made of an old Soviet shell, buried in the hard-packed soil had split open a lightly skinned G-Wagon. The explosion was big enough to upend the jeep. The day before, Brigadier-General David Fraser had paid a visit to the place, bringing along promises of aid and development. The gesture was repaid in blood and the Red Devils—as Alpha Company was known—wanted payback. In their minds, at least at the time, there was still a separation between the villagers, who often looked at us with unmistakable contempt, and the Taliban, who acted out their hatred with fury. It hadn't dawned on them yet that the helpless shrugs and tearful protests of innocence from some village elders were just as malicious, just as much a tactic as the bombs.

Looking back, one of the officers I knew said that this was the biggest thing about those first few months. Nobody seemed to fully understand the nuances of what was going on. They had some good hunches, some good perspectives and "some trusted Afghans who provided insight, but not a complete understanding." It was something that always stuck in his mind.

The convoy that had been hit was going south while we had been heading north. Richard Fitoussi, a documentary filmmaker, was travelling with the guys returning from Gumbad. Thin, soft-spoken and with thick-rimmed glasses, he's since given up a career of shooting portraits of Bay Street and Wall Street titans to take pictures of Cambodian refugees. He couldn't get over how the guys with everything in the world looked so miserable, while the people with nothing seemed to light up with the most radiant smiles. He had the famous *National Geographic* picture of the green-eyed Afghan girl tattooed on his upper arm, just below the shoulder. Richard hated riding in Bisons and LAVs because you couldn't see where you were going. Stepping inside one of those things always felt like giving up control over your fate. Richard's lumbering, heavily shielded vehicle was directly behind the lighter-weight G-Wagon when it struck the bomb.

"There was this huge explosion that seemed to suck all of the air out of the LAV and it was hard to breathe with the pressure against my chest," he recalled.

The two air sentries started yelling. There were a couple of bursts of weapons fire and Rich wondered for a minute whether they'd been caught in a full-fledged ambush, but the firing ended almost as quickly as it started.

"The LAV stopped. They dropped the ramp. I kept asking, 'Is it bad? Is it bad?' They wouldn't answer me."

For twenty breathless minutes, no one answered him. The soldiers confined him to the chalky, diesel-smelling semi-darkness of the Bison cabin while the sickening aftermath of the attack swirled around him. Troops scrambled to render first aid, recover the dead and secure the area.

"At first, I was freaked out," Rich said, remembering how he passed the troops extra first aid kits and ammunition, "but then I calmed down and there was this sense of serenity. It was really strange."

Soldiers take comfort in the regime of their training; Rich grabbed his camera and hit "record."

"My immediate reaction was to hide behind my camera and get to work, start shooting, get to work and hide behind the 'do your job,'" he recalled.

As each agonizing minute ticked by, Rich wondered about the fate of the four men in the G-Wagon, with whom he'd spent the better part of two weeks. These were guys whose pictures he'd taken. He'd shared meals and swapped stories. When the news did come, it was from one of the soldiers guarding him from the attack site.

"One guy just whispered in my ear that three guys were dead and one is in bad shape," he said. "I started to cry because some of these guys had kids. I don't. I feel a little bit guilty because why them and not me?"

Corporal Matthew Dinning, Bombardier Myles Mansell, and Lieutenant William Turner were the three men who lost their lives in the vehicle just fifteen metres ahead of him. Corporal Randy Payne, whom Rich was told by other soldiers had fought valiantly to survive, died after being air evacuated to the coalition hospital at KAF. It was the worst one-day combat loss for the Canadian army since the Korean War more than half a century earlier.

Eventually, Rich was allowed out of the vehicle and witnessed the carnage for himself. He stood alongside that lonely stretch of desert trail and threw up in the shadow of the Bison.

* * *

The attack happened on a Saturday. As time went on, most of us would come to loathe that day of the week. Saturdays seemed to be when all of the nasty, freaky stuff happened. I don't know of any study or report that parsed the numbers, but you just kind of got that vibe. The soldiers talked about it too, like police and hospital workers talk about the full-moon effect on calls and emergency room admissions. Some of the guys speculated that it had to do with Friday being the Muslim holy day. The story went something like this: The Taliban and their surrogates file into the mosques, lap up all of the jihad zeal and then turn it loose the next day. The end of the week always sucked. And so, in preordained fashion, a week after the massacre, the battle group was locked in a seventy-two-hour-long firefight west of the city in Panjwaii, a district that would, over the next five years, become soaked in blood.

The guys in Bravo Company, 2 PPCLI led the way. They swept into a pair of villages about twenty-five kilometres outside of Kandahar city, an area the provincial governor had been told was full of Taliban. The troops considered this mission to be progress. Two weeks earlier, the hot-tempered governor Asadullah Khalid, a favourite of the Americans because he truly relished killing Taliban, had led a ragtag group of ANP and locally hired guns out to the village of Senjaray. It was a slaughter, and the battle group was forced to rescue them. This new mission saw the soldiers and the Afghan cops working together. But it hardly mattered.

From the moment they set foot in the sun-baked villages, the Taliban were shooting at them. Some of the cops promptly fled, leaving the soldiers to fight on. For three adrenaline-pumped days they went at it. Canadians rained down artillery and called in U.S. Apaches with their fearsome 30-mm cannons. Still the Taliban stood their ground. Dead fighters were dragged from the battlefield before soldiers could see what damage they'd inflicted. Some of the guys seemed spooked by this; others were frustrated. Often the only evidence they'd find was pools of blood that turned the sand a moody black. Sometimes there was broken glass from a vehicle, maybe a few spent cartridges or a discarded water bottle, but that was it. When it was all over, Major Tod Strickland, second-in-command of the battle group, stood beside his bullet-grazed and dented LAV with an almost punch-drunk expression.

"A soldier's luck is a funny thing—sometimes you got it, sometimes you don't," Strickland said.

They were lucky. Despite the tumult of that weekend's pitched battle, nobody was killed. And yet, as April rolled into May the mad kaleidoscope of firefights, patrols, frightened villagers, grinding poverty, sweat and fear only spun faster. The worse it became, the more the soldiers clung to their training. They loved their training. They'd heard all about the three-block war—the latest and greatest military theory of battling insurgents while delivering humanitarian relief. But now they were living it. It wasn't pretty. Every morning they'd roll out of their scrapes—the modern version of trenches—shake off the dust, eat bagged rations and mount up. Yet what they did every day was the furthest thing from what they'd planned.

"I don't think anyone can ever really appreciate the worst five minutes of absolute chaos," said Captain Jay Adair, who was second-in-command of Bravo Company in spring 2006.

"You're firing at the enemy in one direction, you're handing out blankets and food to locals, you're caring for wounded, when the original mission was to come [to a village] and have a shura [a meeting]."

What was sensed, but not yet fully understood, was that the battle group was about to be sucked into the sands of Panjwaii and Zhari, two bellicose rural enclaves west of Kandahar city. It was there that the Taliban not only found a home, not only drew their spiritual strength, but found legitimacy. They were often welcomed with open arms by villagers, predominantly Noorzai tribesmen angry that they had been marginalized by the Karzai clan, including the political godfather of Kandahar, Ahmed Wali Karzai (AWK).

The arrival of hardened Taliban fighters from Pakistan that spring was solace for some of the villagers. For others it was the beginning of a reign of terror. Say what you want about the Taliban, but they brought order—brutal, sometimes murderous order. They set up a tax collection system, known as a zakat, and conducted their business in an orderly manner. It was a refreshing change from the shakedowns locals endured at the hands of ill-equipped and underpaid Afghan police, many of whom were outsiders from far-flung parts of the country. They promised to protect one of the few livelihoods left—poppy farming—and they exploited the governor's vow to burn the crops. The hardliners also brought the imposition of Sharia law, something welcome in this devout realm that was nothing more than a jumbled, sprawling maze of arid grape fields, mud compounds and dusty footpaths. The Taliban had been born among those squalid lanes and hovels and rode a wave of fury and orthodoxy to control almost all of the country. Mullah Omar had been born in Sangasar, a low-lying town in Zhari. Local villagers offered up their young men as tribute to everything the Taliban brought with them. Some were recruits, some were conscripts, but for all of the talk over the years from NATO commanders about foreign fighters and outside influence, the one unmistakable fact was that the bulk of the Taliban fighting force was made up of locals from in and around Kandahar.

One particularly notorious commander, Mullah Baqi, staked his ground in Panjwaii. He attacked troop and supply convoys along Highway 1, known as the Ring Road because the paved all-weather highway circled the entire country. Baqi was a nasty piece of work, someone who killed villagers indiscriminately if he suspected them of collaborating. He maintained an iron grip on the district and knew when someone unfamiliar wandered into his territory.

In the aftermath of the gun battle at Senjaray, Khan and I stumbled around looking for leads and made plans to interview Afghan soldiers, cops and villagers in both Zhari and Panjwaii. The day we were supposed to travel, I dressed in my shalwar kameez only to be told the road was too dangerous and Khan would go with his cousin. He arrived back close to dusk, called and said he wanted to pray before discussing the interviews. He rang back within half an hour, squealing into the phone. The Taliban had tracked down his number and threatened to kill him. He had committed the unpardonable sin of travelling "their territory" without permission and they said no villagers in Senjaray could be quoted in whatever story he did. Not only had he interviewed soldiers and cops in several villages, he'd spoken with local residents and, desperate to appear legitimate, told them he worked for The Canadian Press.

"What do we do, sir?" he asked.

"We do nothing," I told him without blinking.

We met the next day. He gave me the tape and the notes and I tucked them away. They never saw the light of day.

There were bastards all over the place, but what was most startling to me was that the Taliban actually staked territory. They laid a claim, drew a line and stood their ground. Some of the guys around the battle group estimated that there were no more than a hundred Taliban in both Zhari and Panjwaii at the time. The underlining message was that they were no threat. Later, I learned the assessment was based upon hand-me-down American intelligence. As April rolled into May and the firefights piled up, a bitter, cynical crust started to develop on the backs of some of the guys. What they were being told didn't match what they saw. Jay Adair was diplomatic about it all, but he remembered clearly how everything changing almost overnight. Where once Bravo Company patrols had ranged unmolested as far as Maiwand district, the most westerly jurisdiction in the province, they found themselves, after the poppy harvest ended, under almost constant attack.

"We couldn't go down most roads without getting in a firefight," Adair said.

The 1 PPCLI battle group was spread out all over the province that spring. The Red Devils were in the rugged mountain creases of Shah Wali Kot, where the Americans, based upon their past experience, expected the Taliban to be concentrated. U.S. commanders pressured Lieutenant-Colonel Ian Hope, the battle group commander, and the Canadians to focus on the area, and in March had ordered up a major sweep of the largely empty valleys and mountain passes. The Canadians ended up chasing shadows. Bravo Company was "penny-packeted," as one officer described it. It patrolled Kandahar city and rural districts to the west, right out to the province's border with Helmand. It also provided protection for the provincial reconstruction base and soldiers to staff a joint coordination centre with Afghan security. Charlie Company was Hope's firefighting unit and was often shoved anywhere it was needed, such as FOB Robinson in Helmand. In early May Hope met with a trusted

ANP commander, Captain Massoud, who warned him that Taliban had built up in Panjwaii and Zhari and speculated that they were preparing to attack Kandahar city itself.

Originally just one municipal unit known as Panjwaii, the Afghan government ordered the region west of the city divided in early 2006 at the Arghandab River, which sliced across the parched landscape almost east to west. Zhari district was created north of the river, and the area south of the divide remained as Panjwaii. The Arghandab had been reduced to a gravel-bedded trickle after four years of drought, but the land that straddled each bank was a green checkerboard of irrigation ditches, dirt tracks and tangled fields. It was laboriously stitched with a web of interconnected, mud-walled compounds and spidery, dried-out streams.

By the time NATO arrived, the Taliban, always on the lookout for empty real estate, had turned some of the compounds abandoned during the Soviet era into bomb-making factories. The isolated little hovels were perfect hideouts. From the air they were just mounds of ruin in a ruined country. But the compounds had been built for extended families, with mud-walled buildings and deep, dried, out wells—convenient places to hide weapons caches. The farmers that were around kept their mouths shut and went about their business as normally as they could, tending their grapes, wheat, melons, poppies or marijuana, which grew to enormous heights. If troops did snoop, the land was once again a natural blessing. Many of the fields were walled in and made excellent defensive lines. Most featured grape-drying huts, large two-storey structures with iron bar doors and mud walls that had hardened to the consistency of cement. They were natural pillboxes. The grape fields were rock-ribbed with a series of two-metre-high berms on which farmers hung their vines.

It was into the morass of Panjwaii and Zhari that the Canadians launched their battle group in May 2006, and there it would remain, more or less, for five bloody, ponderous years. The operation envisioned by Hope was a hammer-and-anvil approach. One company of soldiers formed blocking positions while a second unit swept through a location and squeezed the Taliban up against the first. To start, Hope selected a cluster of villages in Zhari known as Nalgham. Located on the north bank of the Arghandab, it was a place where sources said the insurgents had congregated. The operation was code-named Bravo Guardian and the two companies—roughly 300 soldiers—marshalled at the Kandahar PRT base in the pre-dawn hours of May 17, 2006. The LAVs and G-Wagons rumbled through the silent streets and out into the countryside with little fanfare. They moved in two convoys.

Jay Adair commanded Bravo Company for the operation while his boss, Major Nick Grimshaw, was on leave. His G-Wagons and soldiers were spread out in a three-kilometre blocking line north of the villages while Jon Snyder's section and the rest of Charlie Company swung south and then punched north. As the soldiers got in to position, just as the sun was coming up, they faced an unnerving site: a stream of ragged-looking civilians—old men, women and children—plodded along the roads and through their lines. Later, the soldiers figured out that the villagers had been warned to get out of their homes—a sure sign that there was going to be fighting. An intelligence tip prompted the battle group to move farther east toward Bayanzi, also on the north bank of the river. When Charlie Company's LAVs rolled in from the south, one was ambushed by a swarm of well-concealed Taliban. A short, hard firefight ensued, in which the armoured vehicle was pummelled by rocket-propelled grenades (RPGs), machine gun and AK-47 fire. Bravo also came under fire and ended up in a series of rolling gun battles that lasted most of the day. All of it played out as the merciless Afghan sun rose to its full 50°C fury. The battlefield was a furnace.

Bravo's heavy weapons team—the mortars and the machine guns—were under the command of Sergeant Jason Boyes. A veteran of Afghanistan, he'd fought high in the mountains with the Americans in 2002 as they chased the remnants of the Taliban and al-Qaeda. He'd seen firefights before, but nothing like Bayanzi. There was so much fire—a fog of lead everywhere you turned. But what struck him most was how undisciplined the Taliban seemed. They'd empty their clips in one burst and scurry for cover. When we spoke later, he said he'd often wondered what the Taliban would have been like if they'd actually stood and fought. As that particular day unfolded, however, he thought to himself it wasn't so bad.

"It's a rabble, a disorganized rabble," he said.

But the rabble was cagey and still quite deadly. The Taliban liked to spring traps and surprises either at sunset or at night. The tide of battle ebbed and flowed all day and had eased by the late afternoon. Nichola Goddard and her crew, in their specially outfitted LAV, had called down artillery fire on Taliban positions for hours. At sunset, they were tucked in with a line of vehicles belonging to Bravo, facing Bayanzi, when the Taliban sprang. In an instant, the entire line was engulfed in a haze of tracers and RPGs. Goddard, who was standing in the turret, was killed instantly.

"My Sunray is down!" came the call over the radio. Sunray was the code name for a vehicle commander.

Jay Adair heard it, but was too consumed by the fight to react. Like Boyes, he marvelled at scene in front of him, a steady eruption of fire, smoke, cinders and waves of boiling air. Without warning a van burst out of the pandemonium on the Taliban side of the line and drove straight for the soldiers.

"And of course, everyone's initial reaction is, suicide bomber," said Adair. "Why else would a van come out toward us when we're firing?"

One of the soldiers snapped off a few rounds into the engine block and the vehicle lurched to halt just shy of the Canadian line. The doors flew open and a terrified family—father, mother and children—leapt out into the middle of the firefight. No one could believe his eyes. The shooting subsided on both sides and as the last gunfire reports echoed into the twilight, the Canadians snapped into action, manoeuvering their vehicles to protect the bewildered family. The family stumbled off the razor's edge.

"I'll never forget the look on their faces and the fact we stopped [firing] and [got the] vehicles postured to get them back safely," Adair said. "The restraint that was shown, and I saw it with my own eyes, the restraint that was shown was absolutely incredible."

The family didn't look back; they just kept going. And once they had plodded through the Canadian line, the firing resumed as though it had never been interrupted.

Adair delivered the story with the urgency of someone recalling an incredible dream. I didn't want to interrupt him and when he finally paused it was a long pause, the kind that makes interviewers uncomfortable.

"You know what's strange about this whole thing?" he finally said. "When the Afghans are scared, they don't go to the Taliban. When there's an incident, they don't go to the Taliban. They don't seek refuge behind the Taliban, they seek refuge behind us."

Every once in a while guys would blurt out something like that. It was so genuine, so heartfelt that you couldn't help but be converted, even if it was only for the afternoon. They held on to stuff like that. They had to, because the alternative was worse.

Later that night, the soldiers looked out toward Highway 1 and watched the headlights of civilian vehicles as they played across the desert. The Taliban presumably carted away their dead and wounded as the Canadians wrapped Nichola Goddard in a body bag and prepared to chopper her remains back to Kandahar Airfield.

Later, Khan told me he remembered the Canadians rolling back in to the city the day after the battle. He was amazed. Afghans came out into the streets and cheered and clapped as the armoured vehicles rumbled past.

* * *

The battle in Bayanzi was followed by what seemed like an endless series of patrols and short, sharp firefights. The Taliban would lie in wait and open up with a shower of AK-47, mortar and RPG fire. But it was a tease. They'd go on just long enough to tempt the artillery or helicopter gunships and then withdraw before retaliation could be brought to bear. It was a game of cat and mouse. Who was the cat and who was the mouse depended on the day. Around that time, soldiers uncovered huge weapons caches and even primitive first-aid stations in a place called Pashmul. The mere mention of the name would later elicit expressions of wasted horror from almost every soldier who trod its foul ground, but in early June 2006, it was still undiscovered.

The battle group probed in western Panjwaii and fought in Nalgham. Each reported contact was dutifully passed up the chain to what some of the guys described as the "Big Giant Heads" at Bagram Airfield, outside of Kabul—Combined Forces Command. The name rang with authority and the acronym CFC-Alpha sounded even better. But the collection of American colonels and generals who ran the war didn't believe what they were reading. Those Canadians—what do they know about fighting a war? There couldn't be that many Taliban in Kandahar province. Intelligence said so. The Canadians had to be exaggerating. The conventional wisdom of most U.S. officers was that NATO troops wouldn't hunt down the Taliban as aggressively as they did. The Americans were utterly insensible to the gravity of events in western Kandahar and to prove it, they ordered the Canadian battle group out of the area and into the mountains of Shah Wali Kot to sweep the same empty valleys and stony passes that had been empty in March.

The last time I saw Ian Hope before going home that spring, we sat outside the Green Bean coffee hut right next to the flight line and talked over the roar of turbo props. He said nothing of the mounting frustration with the Americans. Even years later, when I asked about it again, he refused to dump on them.

That day we debated the merits of reporters travelling with the troops as opposed to on their own in Kandahar with fixers. Since I was going to Parliament Hill in Ottawa, I asked if there was anything I could get for him there.

"Yeah," he said, without missing a beat, "helicopters."

I thought he was joking. As it turned out, he wasn't.

Some days were surreal. You'd wake up in the morning, your boots covered with talcum sand and the ringing of jets and helicopters in your ears. By lunch you'd be strolling the polished marble and gilded hallways of Dubai's Mall of the Emirates, where each window burst with jewellery, high-end clothes and other trappings of obscene wealth. The journey back to the real world was mind-bending, no matter how many times it happened. I always found it hard to believe that the place where I had begun my day and the place where it ended were on the same planet, let alone within two hours of each other.

Passing through a succession of airports, it was possible to keep tabs on the progress of the war. Details would pour into my BlackBerry with the same precision and ease as sports scores. I learned about Nichola Goddard's death on my BlackBerry and remember staring incomprehensibly at the screen for a very long time.

When I looked up, one of the airport's flat-panel TV screens was showing images of the war. I was waiting for my duffle bag in the brightly lit arrival section when the picture cut away to the House of Commons and the prime minister. Stephen Harper looked combative. I couldn't hear everything in the CBC reporter's voice-over, but I knew that Parliament was about to vote on an extension. Harper vowed to extend the mission end-date by two years, with or without the support of the Commons. The Conservatives had only grudgingly agreed to the non-binding debate in early April, but had since been bludgeoned into allowing a full-fledged vote. It was something they resisted even though they'd tried to force Paul Martin's government into holding a similar vote not quite two years earlier.

If the government lost and unilaterally extended the deployment, Harper promised to call an election within a year and put the decision for war or peace into the voters' hands.

"We cannot walk away quickly," the prime minister said. "If we need further efforts or a further mandate to go ahead into the future, we will go alone and go to the Canadian people to get that mandate."

He waved the terrorism flag.

"The events of September 11, 2001, [were a] wake-up call, not just to Americans but to people in all free and democratic nations. Canada is not safe from such attacks, and we will never be safe from such attacks as long as we're a society that defends freedom and democracy."

The proposal was to extend the exit date in Kandahar from February 2007 to February 2009.

Afghanistan was one of the Conservative's "key institutional pieces," something that would set them apart from their rivals. Yet staff in the PMO realized within weeks of taking power that public support for a full-fledged war in Kandahar was not there.

"We were trying to avoid all the debates in Parliament because frankly we couldn't really win them in the public sphere," a former staffer told me. "The PM, throughout this, he just wanted to fight the good fight. It was ideological for him. He didn't really care" what the Opposition said.

It didn't help that the hand-picked defence minister, the good soldier Gordon O'Connor, was said in published reports to privately have his doubts. There was talk that he was worried about the impact heavy combat would have on the army, but senior staffers around Harper said O'Connor showed no sign of it with them.

"He brought the full range of his political and military experience to the question," said Ian Brodie, Harper's former chief of staff. "I was impressed with his analysis. And he fully supported the decision."

Doubts were quelled when strategists inside the PMO realized a Commons vote afforded them an opportunity to expose divisions within ranks of the Liberals, who'd authorized the mission in the first place.

Thirty Liberals, including interim leader and former defence minister Bill Graham, fell in line behind the Conservatives. Not unexpectedly, the Bloc Québécois and the NDP were opposed. The final tally was 149 to 145. There should have been a mood of celebration among Conservatives, but the news of Goddard's death was out and I'm told everyone in the foyer of the Commons spoke in hushed tones, a contrast to the usual messy cacophony.

Graham said he wanted specifics. His party supported the troops and the deployment, but the MPs had voted "with a gun" to their heads. More Liberals would have come onside, Graham insisted, had they been able to talk a bit more. Even at that nascent stage, the Liberals clearly felt the heavy grinding of history against the weight of their decision to go in to Kandahar. Jack Layton was equally milquetoast.

"A two-year commitment without the questions answered, no exit strategy, no sense of the chain of command, NATO is not in charge yet . . . I think a lot of Canadians are going to be disappointed."

It was one of those rare occasions when Harper stopped to talk to reporters from the stairs in the dim marble foyer.

"I think . . . the support for the mission is a lot stronger than the vote" results, the prime minister said.

There aren't many things more discouraging in politics than when someone reads the tea leaves and gets it wrong. In fact, within weeks of Harper's return from the "cut and run" speech in Kandahar, staff in the PMO knew that public support for the mission was teetering on the edge of a cliff. The Conservatives conducted extensive opinion research, the results of which guided just about every public step they took throughout those critical early months and beyond.

"We had this weird dual personality on the Afghan file," said a former staffer who did a lot of long-term political planning.

On the one side, there was Harper and a select number of cabinet ministers who possessed a "damn the torpedoes" mentality, an approach the opposition happily played up. Then there was the cadre of campaign-hardened political staff and advisors who, as the researched rolled in the door, realized with horror that the public wasn't with them, and that Afghanistan was a huge political liability. The party and the government that lived and breathed political messaging, advertising and signage abruptly found itself having to pull its punches. An in-the-works marketing campaign to sell the country on the merits of the Kandahar mission was scrubbed.

"When I say campaign, I mean PR blitz and the whole thing on the Afghan mission because we saw it as a political wedge," said the staffer, who spoke on background. "When we got back [from the Kandahar trip], the market research was so atrocious that we had to change gears."

The opinion research released that spring by various pollsters suggested Canadian were divided on the fight in Kandahar; many still saw their soldiers as peacekeepers. Most alarming to PMO strategists was that Afghanistan seemed to be a "no return issue." People who supported the deployment were solid and mostly among the Conservative base. Those who were against it were just as dogged in their view. The so-called soft supporters worried the politicos the most; the numbers told them that when these people decided to turn against the war, there was no coming back.

"One of the things that market research told us was that we were going to bleed people over time," said the staffer. "We couldn't possibly hold the support for the mission. So we had to change gears and that's when we tried to shift the communications toward humanitarian and all that sort of stuff."

The research was startling and disheartening to true believers—those who wanted to change the international face of Canada into something a little more rock-jawed and chiselled. The Kandahar file was, as it turned out, an archetypal experience for the Conservatives in government. Afghanistan represented "a whole host of issues where the public has not been conditioned to where the party wanted to take the country," the strategist recalled.

The entire political spin machine—the one that would over the years take a flame-thrower to the image of successive Liberal leaders, hammer Economic Action Plan ads into the consciousness of television viewers and pound economic stimulus signs into the ground for all to see—was told to stand down on the war. Staffers assumed a "defensive posture" almost overnight.

"We went from hammering this to managing this. That's probably the better way of putting it," insiders said. "It became less of an offensive from a political perspective and more of a 'manage the risks associated with it' [situation]."

In Conservative-speak, "managing" meant optics. It meant directing the image. The first target was the flag atop the Peace Tower on Parliament Hill, which had been lowered to half-staff for every casualty since 2004.

The order came down in mid-April not to lower the flag whenever a soldier was killed, even though Conservatives had insisted on the policy in the first place. Government insiders bristled at the mention of the contradiction and at the resulting blowback.

"We were trying to manage this issue so it wasn't going to kill us," said the senior official.

Lincoln Dinning, the father of Corporal Matthew Dinning, felt the heavy hand of that management. Before he died, Matthew had talked to his father about what it meant to soldiers to see Parliament's flag brought to half-staff to honour them. Angered by the change in policy, Lincoln wrote to Harper's office and expressed his dismay. He said he never received a response. The day before he and his wife Laurie were to drive to Canadian Forces Base (CFB) Trenton for Matthew's repatriation ceremony, they received a call from their Liberal MP, Paul Steckle.

"You realize there won't be any media there because Mr. Harper has banned the media," he told Lincoln.

The grieving father was startled and disturbed by the call. He told Steckle: "That could be, but I certainly never requested it."

As he stood with the families of the soldiers killed alongside his son, Lincoln quietly canvassed them about whether they had requested keeping the media beyond the gates.

"Nobody had any idea and nobody had specifically not asked the media to come," Lincoln recalled afterward.

They waited in one of the cavernous hangars under the peroxide glare of the giant ceiling lights. General Rick Hillier and his wife paid their respects, as did Afghanistan's ambassador, the smooth and eloquent Omar Samad.

"I thought that took balls for him to come, but he said, 'Thank you for your son's service to our country,'" Lincoln recalled.

Hillier said the military would do whatever it could to help the families through the crisis, a comment that stuck with Lincoln and inspired him to challenge the federal government a year later to fully cover the costs of military funerals.

It didn't fully dawn on him until he shook hands with Defence Minister Gordon O'Connor that the flag and the media ban might have been connected as part of a deliberate political strategy meant to soften the impact of the war on public opinion. Upset that his son's death was being consumed by a communications plan, he had the arrival of the caskets videotaped.

Days later, Lincoln took a stand during Matthew's funeral at the local hockey rink in Wingham, Ontario.

"Now I'd like to show you some of the video that Mr. Harper wouldn't let you see close up of Matthew's arrival home," he said before playing the tape for the thousands of mourners assembled on the cement floor and in the bleachers.

Lincoln would later roll his eyes at the resulting headlines.

"Oh, 'course the next morning in the paper, 'grieving father slams the prime minister,'" he recalled.

There were essentially three kinds of military families: those who withstood the indignity of losing someone precious and silently bore the political and bureaucratic injustices; those who fumed privately; and those who fought back regardless of the consequences or judgements. In the aftermath of Dinning's funeral, political staff in Ottawa were aghast. They later described the episode as a "stunt" and went so far as to privately dismiss Lincoln Dinning as a "well-known Liberal."

The military establishment was privately beside itself over the ban and watched with unease as television satellite trucks lined up beyond the fence at Trenton and shot video with telephoto lenses. The government got hammered by the coverage, especially the references to the ban being similar to the Bush administration's policy.

I had been in Kandahar when the edict was first announced, but watched it in its full fury on the home front during Nichola Goddard's repatriation. Afghanistan is often like living in a bubble. Not much of the day-to-day racket, the incessant noise that seems to preoccupy our lives and conversations, makes much of an impression over there. But the decision to close Trenton to the public intruded on the war. Maybe it spoke to the very keen sense of mortality you feel in place like that. Among the troops, the policy of keeping the media at bay was not unpopular. Journalists were considered vultures on the subject of casualties. You could feel it in the looks that came from beneath helmets or over shoulders amid the tight circles where the soldiers would sit when they didn't want to acknowledge your presence. It was unsparingly direct and forthright. There were some guys who resented being paraded in front of us to talk about dead buddies and they hated it even more when we'd print their words. Closing off Trenton, they reasoned, was the proper way to protect the families. Yet some felt the decision should be up to relatives, an acknowledgement that it was cathartic to grieve in public.

Among the older troops, there was an almost unanimous sense that the ramp ceremonies in Kandahar needed to stay public. Those guys remembered the bad old days of Bosnia, when casualties—wounded and dead—were shipped home anonymously.

"We want you guys to see; we want everybody to see what happens to us," one exhausted soldier said. His face was blank, but his eyes were angry.

The sentiment was shared right at the top. General Rick Hillier later wrote about how the PMO tried to shut down media coverage of Goddard's repatriation. He wouldn't allow it. The policy was eventually changed to allow the families to decide whether they wanted the media around, but the poison was in the well and there was no putting it back in the bottle. In his memoirs, Hillier wrote extensively about his battles on behalf of the military with Ottawa "mandarins" and "bureaucrats" whom he never named. Yet anyone within earshot of the Langevin Block, the imposing sandstone, Gothic government nerve-centre, knew the bile was being directed at several high-ranking officials within the Privy Council, the bureaucratic arm of the Prime Minister's Office, and at Foreign Affairs. The general was careful not to criticize Harper, whom he portrayed in a very business-like manner, or the Conservative party, which showered the military with new equipment and adoration. As much as Hillier was portrayed as being in the hip-pocket of Harper's government, his memoirs displayed more warmth and personal affection for Paul Martin, the man who'd appointed him to the military's top job. He also wrote glowingly about Bill Graham, the defence minister with whom he worked the closest.

"The accounts in the Hillier book about his battles with PMO communications, those sound fairly accurate from where I was sitting," said a Tory insider.

"We were frustrated because on one hand we were seeing images of caskets, but on the other hand, the military wasn't releasing things like the number of terrorists killed—or anything like that."

The images of the flag-draped caskets vexed the spinners and political strategists because they were so powerful. The media and the public were mesmerized and the Conservatives didn't know how to counter it. The bleeding of political support predicted in the research did indeed take shape in the late spring of 2006. One potential solution was to release body counts to the public.

"One of our theories on this was, they had to see the scorecard," said a former senior official. The average Canadian had "nothing to compare," no estimation of damage on the other side.

"Unfortunately there was no way for the public to . . . I hate to say it . . . keep score on how well we were doing over there."

Some in the military were astounded and horrified at the request. When I heard about it later in the war, I was amazed. There was something almost pathological about counting the bodies of your enemy to prove that you were winning. It suggested there was nothing that good spin and talking points couldn't fix, as long as the data points danced with them. The military pushed back, arguing that body counts had been thoroughly discredited during the Vietnam War. Never mind that gathering that kind of information in Kandahar was next to impossible. It wasn't like other wars, where the dead were left to rot in the fields. The Taliban cleaned up after themselves and if there were visible corpses, it was never clear who was a bona fide Taliban and who wasn't. It was a statistician's nightmare, even without the cynicism that seemed to have swallowed itself whole.

There is a hilarious and sad footnote to this discussion. Late in the war, a groundbreaking study conducted by the political science department at the University of Laval found that the so-called Trenton Effect had little real impact on the public's perception of the war. Yet in politics, the perception of a perception can sometimes be dangerous and Harper's inner circle was worried. As one senior official later told me, they trusted the military to fight the war on all fronts.

"All the issues about the parade of coffins, body counts and so on should be seen in the context of that—the PM was content to let Rick [Hillier] run the entire effort," said the official, who would only speak as a Conservative insider.

What wasn't clear to the PMO as the conflict spiralled downward was "what the CF [Canadian Forces] had in mind for managing the home front."

One incident that hammered that home for Harper's inner circle was when Hillier remarked that the war in Afghanistan would go on for decades. The prime minister felt compelled to publicly remind the defence chief that those decisions were made by the civilian leadership. Hillier tiptoed backward and qualified the statement by saying that NATO and not necessarily Canada would be engaged that long.

"Even that caused a hell of a lot of heartburn," said the official. "I've never met anyone in the party who wanted an open-ended war."

* * *

I asked Jack Layton one evening how he found out the army was going to Kandahar.

"Paul Martin called me to tell me," he said, pointing out that when the call came, the decision was already a done deal.

Layton was miffed. Those kinds of decisions belonged in Parliament, not beneath the recessed crystal chandeliers and tapestry rugs of a hotel ballroom in Winnipeg, he said.

Martin presented it as continuation of the role the army had played in Kabul.

"He generally characterized it within the ambit of the mandate that had been ours to date, except that it would involve more troops and in a different location," Layton recalled.

What he knew of Kandahar, Layton said, he didn't like, but he was prepared to go along. Under previous leader Alexa McDonough, the party had supported going after al-Qaeda in the dark days following the 9/11 terrorist attacks. Layton's doubts, however, started with that vacuous phone call.

"I was concerned because I felt that it wouldn't be possible to go to Kandahar and have the same kind of role that we had previously," he said. "I told him I was concerned."

Almost immediately Layton noticed the gap between the assurances he received from Martin and the "murderers and scumbags" rhetoric he heard from General Rick Hillier. The comments, made early that summer, didn't fit with how the mission had been described to him. When Defence Minister Bill Graham chimed in with his own warnings about casualties in the fall of 2005, Layton and his handful of MPs went from concerned to uneasy to fidgeting in their seats. In the months leading up to the deployment, Afghanistan was a regular item on the agenda of NDP closed-door caucuses. The fact that they couldn't square what was being said made them suspicious.

"That was all a part of how our party moved toward the position that we should be bringing our troops home. It took a while for that position to evolve."

Layton said the fact they did not come out swinging right away on the Kandahar deployment was a sign of his party's "pragmatic idealism." But there were times when they were itching to scream their opposition. Halfway through the winter election campaign in 2005, at a stop in St. John's, Newfoundland, the NDP leader laid it on thick. He called for the Kandahar deployment to be halted until Martin could explain the goals. I asked some of Layton's senior staff shortly after his statement whether that meant they'd wanted the deployment cancelled altogether. They said yes, but quickly backtracked.

With the election of Harper in January 2006, Layton expected to be invited along with Bill Graham, who replaced Martin as Liberal leader, to talk with Stephen Harper about Afghanistan. It never happened. In hindsight, Layton said he wasn't surprised; it wasn't the prime minister's style. As the years unfolded the two never had an in-depth conversation about the war, not even in private. Whenever the topic was brought up, Harper would just smile and say, "We're going to have to just agree to disagree on that, Jack."

At one point in the conversation, the old political science professor in Layton came out. He knew from previous wars that they should have been talking, but he figured it was up to the prime minister to make the overtures.

"Most governments when you're in a war context, the structure of the relationship changes and there's this kind of understanding that we're at war," he said. "We were already sworn in as Privy Councillors. They could have shared certain kinds of information. There was none of that."

Opposition leaders were routinely briefed about important policy matters, PMO insiders said. What Layton was suggesting was that there should have been some kind of war cabinet—or a loose arrangement where the other parties were brought into the decision-making process.

Would it have made a difference to the emerging political divisions on Parliament Hill? Layton wasn't prepared to speculate.

"We could have taken the leadership of the parties into confidence and had honest and frank discussions about where we stand and what lay ahead. It doesn't always produce consensus, but sometimes [it] could help to shape the discussion into a more productive direction."

By the time Nichola Goddard was killed, pressure had built to the point where Layton felt it was time to take action. McDonough, now the party's foreign affairs critic, led the most vocal faction in caucus to demand the troops be brought home. Her long-standing work with parliamentarians for nuclear non-proliferation and disarmament gave her great cache within the party. She pushed hard for Layton and the rest of the caucus to take a stand.

"That's how the position evolved because it became increasingly clear as time passed that this war was becoming a quagmire and we couldn't just stay there because it wasn't going to be won in the foreseeable future."

During select interviews in early June 2006, Layton started floating the position that the NDP wanted the troops out. As his political campaign gathered steam over the summer, the military looked on in frustration and alarm. The summer fighting season kicked in to high gear in Kandahar and the army conducted a series operations in Zhari. By the end of August, eleven more soldiers were dead. Throughout it all the Conservative government seemed to go to ground. Aside from prepared statements on casualties, Gordon O'Connor gave no interviews on Afghanistan that summer, except to news agencies in Australia and New Zealand. Public statements by the government were limited to big-ticket defence purchases. It was left to Hillier to defend and explain to the public what was happening in Kandahar. Did he feel he was being hung out to dry that summer? His memoirs are silent on the topic and he skirted the question whenever I asked him. Hillier may not have felt the government was making him wear the unfolding potential catastrophe, but his staff did.

"He has no problem defending the mission or speaking on behalf of the men and women in uniform, but until recently the government had not stepped up to the plate," said one senior advisor to the general at the time.

In the newly Conservative, tightly spun Ottawa, that was the equivalent of a bitch-slap, and when I ran with the story that summer it was treated as such.

Some around the general openly fretted that the public perception was hardening and that Kandahar was becoming "Hillier's War." Sources in both the military and the PMO said the frustration boiled over in a September 6, 2006, meeting called to discuss reinforcements.

According to insiders, Hillier complained that critics of the war—meaning Layton—had enjoyed "an open field" during that summer to "degrade support for the mission."

On the record, the general wouldn't confirm the account, but he gave Harper's government a lesson in PR: "You're clearly going to have to work constantly to keep Canadians satisfied so that they know and understand what we're doing and support it."

But from inside PMO, the view was that Hillier was in charge of running the war. Staffers whose job it was to manage the message recognized they'd crawled into a bunker.

"It was always a crisis," said one official. "I think the reason there was so much silence was because we were trying to figure out how to transition the communications politically from a hard terrorism message to, you know, about women voting and all that stuff."

The result? There was no consoler-in-chief during that awful summer. The country that had not been at war in half a century was left to figure out for itself why its sons and daughters were coming home in caskets.

* * *

"I don't think there was a true recognition on just how difficult it was going to be to turn back the wave of insurgency," Peter MacKay told me later in the war.

We sat in his wood-panelled Parliament Hill office, having one of several conversations about the turbulent early years of the war.

MacKay said he knew Afghanistan was going to be trouble from the moment he opened his transition briefing books in the winter of 2006. In fairness, he used the bureaucratic-speak "dominant issue" and "extremely challenging." The first phone call he received after being sworn in as foreign affairs minister was from Condoleezza Rice, the U.S. Secretary of State. The first item on the agenda was Afghanistan.

"The deployment down to Kandahar, my understanding from the briefings, came after much consternation within the department and within the previous government about not having gone to Iraq," he said.

There was "almost a sense of 'we have to do something more significant than we have thus far.'"

MacKay said he doesn't believe there was a true appreciation of how fierce, persistent and determined the Taliban were going to be—not around the cabinet table, not in the halls of Parliament, and not at National Defence Headquarters.

In early May 2006, with his Liberal and NDP critics in tow, MacKay took his first trip to Kandahar and Kabul. He sat down with President Hamid Karzai, whom he'd never met before. They chatted in stiff, high-backed, Queen Anne–style chairs before an unlit, grey marble fireplace in the heavily guarded presidential palace. Karzai wore a sport coat over his white shalwar kameez. He was without his trademark green-and-purple cloak and his *karakul*, the grey wedge cap he usually wore. In photographs after the meeting, the president looked tired. MacKay said later he left with the distinct impression that the enormity of events that spring in Kandahar had just begun to dawn on Karzai. Although the Pashtun leader had been in power four years, his writ had never fully extended to the south and NATO was to impose it for him by force of arms. It was one thing to talk about it, as they had done for years; it was another to actually stand back and watch it unfold in a bloody, slow-motion nightmare.

"We were all seized with the size of the challenge," said MacKay.

When they talked about Canadian casualties, Karzai teared up when he expressed his appreciation.

"He was very emotional."

Much has been made about Karzai's state of mind over the years, whether he suffered from depression or even bipolar disorder. Was he on prescription medication? Why did he cry so much in public? MacKay took a pass on characterizing what he saw.

"I can only imagine the pressure he was under," he said.

Together with Bryon Wilfert of the Liberals and Alexa McDonough of the NDP, MacKay visited a girl's school in Kabul. It seemed worlds apart from Kandahar, where they had visited the provincial reconstruction base as well as the main airfield. During the stop, MacKay met Richard Colvin, one of only two foreign affairs staffers in the city at the time. He had arrived on the ground only a few days before the minister arrived.

Dragging along the Opposition critics and stuffing them into green, ill-fitting flak jackets and helmets was meant to lay the groundwork for a bipartisan understanding, MacKay said. He knew he might not go the full distance to all-party co-operation, but the political calculation was that some of the sting might be washed out of their critiques.

"I wanted to give them an opportunity to see first-hand what we were up against," he said.

It went over like a lead balloon.

McDonough, a fellow Nova Scotia MP whom MacKay had earlier told to stick to her knitting, was unconvinced. She noted almost all aid organizations had pulled out of the embattled city ahead of the military buildup and in anticipation of violence.

"One can see that the resources are heavily weighted on the military [and] security side instead of the aid side," she said.

By the time they returned to Canada, MacKay said he realized that all bets were off.

He said he was "sorely disappointed" at the critics' response.

Operation Medusa 8

By late August 2006, the headlines had started to scream at you. What seemed like a never-ending series of increasingly brutal firefights and bombings spilled across front pages and on to television screens—a cascade of violence so intense, so unexpected that it stilled much of the usual political burble. History uninterrupted, unvarnished, the kind you can't turn off or away from, intruded into those hazy, late summer days with the sharpness of a branding iron.

Among those who followed the mission, there was a debate on when exactly the country realized it was at war. Some argued for the very first firefight in Sangin, the one that killed Private Robert Costall. Skeptics scoffed, saying it was later, around the time of Captain Nichola Goddard's death. Measuring the pulse of a sleeping nation is never precise. Some academics and politicos insisted the acknowledgement in the public's heart, if not its mind, went all the way back to cabinet's approval of the Kandahar mission. But this was not the kind of war you could put a time stamp on. There was no start clock, mostly because everyone wanted it to be something other than what it was. By late summer that year, there was no debating or hiding from the realization that Kandahar had turned into a bloody morass. Yet, in the politically correct world of Ottawa, politicians and mandarins refused to use the word "war." Afghanistan was a "mission," an "operation," an "exercise," an "intervention." The last one used to crack me up; it made it sound as though we were packing the Afghans off to rehab, even if it was Ottawa that was lodged in deep, intractable denial.

Arguments about timelines occasionally got right down into the weeds and extended to specific battles. There are some who say that the largest battle to that time in the war—Operation Medusa—began not on September 2, 2006, as the official record states, but a few weeks before. The revisionists call what happened in Bazaar-e-Panjwaii on August 19, 2006, "Pre-Medusa" and painted it as a warm-up for the big show. It happened on the very cusp of the handover between Lieutenant-Colonel Ian Hope's 1 PPCLI battle group, which had been bloodied almost from the moment it hit the ground, and Lieutenant-Colonel Omer Lavoie's incoming team of the 1st Battalion, Royal Canadian Regiment. The firefight in and around the dust-bowl farming town was an orphan. It belonged to nobody, or so it seemed.

The district centre is a series of low slung, sun-bleached cement buildings surround by a concrete wall and razor wire. It sits on the outskirts of the community, where farmers bring their stock to market. It was supposed to be the place where the district leader met with staff and villagers, but with the local Noorzai tribes still clinging to the Taliban, the place sat almost empty, a striking emblem of the hollow promises of good governance.

A few days before the battle, Hope led his replacement on a tour of the area. His tight, swift-moving column of light armoured command vehicles pulled up to the base of Ma'sum Ghar, the soaring, dark volcanic peak that looms over Bazaar-e-Panjwaii. The place always seemed spooky to me. The coarse, dark brown rock appeared black, even in the blinding Afghan sun. It was chilling, somehow.

Lavoie got his first taste of what the tour was going to be like at sunset that day when, during a stop at the newly established Patrol Base Wilson, an 82-mm mortar round whistled in and exploded right next to his vehicle. Shrapnel punctured the LAV's machine gun and wounded its gunner.

"It was a close call," Lavoie recalled.

Hope saw his friend Captain Massoud for the last time during that farewell tour. The Afghan cop, whose wily spirit and spiderweb of cellphone contacts had proved invaluable, had been living in a hilltop fighting position with his detachment of police for a week. Massoud came down to greet Hope and brought with him a disturbing report, one final intelligence gift.

The militants had planned to attack Kandahar city directly, but battle group operations in early August had disrupted them, according to Massoud. The Taliban were everywhere in Panjwaii and Zhari and multiplying fast. Hundreds had been mowed down in the battles of the spring and summer, yet they kept coming on like a force of nature. Some of the guys described them as a freak legion of zombies. The Americans, to Hope's relief, realized over the summer that the two districts had spiralled out of control and had started to dedicate more resources to supporting the Canadians and the thinly sprinkled Afghan security forces. Massoud had not been home to see his family in Kabul for almost six months, but he told Hope he was willing to stay to defend Panjwaii. He said if he expected his men to stay, they had to see he was committed to doing the same. Hope admired that.

Two days after their meeting Hope handed over command of the battle group to Lavoie, who ordered Major Mike Wright to position himself and his men on the heights of Ma'sum Ghar. The job was to find the mortar team that had taken the pot shot at them and was keeping up daily harassment. The Taliban, right around that time, unleashed a tempest on the town that stood in the shadow of the big rocks.

"It was very difficult to figure out where the enemy was coming from because of the fact they were coming from the south [which] was not what we were expecting at all," Wright said.

The Taliban quickly overran the ANP outposts.

"As I was giving orders on the radio, my LAV gunner was firing at a rock formation where we could see a guy skirting back and forth where the police had been. [My gunner] was the one who was basically able to see the Taliban in waves trying to go up to the top of Ma'sum Ghar."

Hope, back at KAF and ready to leave for home, went to the tactical operations centre and listened to the radio traffic as the fierce battle was underway. While he was still in command the day before, he'd ordered Alpha Company of 2 PPCLI placed in Bazaar-e-Panjwaii to support Massoud's beleaguered police detachment. The fighting became thick and Hope was told at one point that Massoud and the small number of ANP and ANA were cut off. Determined not to let down the man who'd helped him so much, he marched 500 metres from the plywood operations centre through the dusty laneways of KAF to the RC-South headquarters, where he asked NATO commanders to order the platoon to move to support the Afghans. He also wanted Canadian artillery to fire in support. He got neither. In one last gamble, Hope went to the American control centre for unmanned aerial vehicles (UAVs) and convinced the duty operator to zero in on Bazaar-e-Panjwaii. The Predator in the sky that day had Hellfire missiles on its wing tips.

"Together we tracked several enemy groups before using two missiles to destroy two of them," Hope recalled. "I had the operator search Massoud's fighting post. I confirmed that there were still ANP in place despite their having taken casualties. I prayed for him that night and stayed with the UAV unit ready to help them track any other visible targets until the enemy firing stopped and reports informed us that the Taliban had given up the attack."

It wasn't until the next day Hope heard through the governor's palace that Massoud had survived the attack. He never heard from the police commander again.

* * *

The fight in Bazaar-e-Panjwaii served to reinforce the local Afghan leadership's growing doubts about NATO. This was especially true for Governor Asadullah Khalid, who was always itching for a fight with the Taliban. It irritated Khalid that the Canadians were not willing to embrace his hell-bent-for-leather style. His wild-man ways had military disaster etched all over them, according to many officers I spoke with. Yet he "complained of inadequate coordination between ISAF and Afghan national security forces," according to secret Foreign Affairs documents I viewed later in the war.

At a meeting of southern governors in Kabul during mid-August 2006, and in the presence of NATO's Afghanistan commander, Lieutenant-General David Richards, Khalid complained bitterly about what he saw as a lack of resolve by the Canadians. He pointed to the roadside bombing in Shah Wali Kot the previous April to make his case.

"Canadian forces 'stopped in their tracks,' he said, after four [Canadian] soldiers were killed," the diplomatic report quoted him as saying. "ISAF is too focused on development rather than security."

In his harangue, Khalid ignored the fact that at least three operations had been mounted in Zhari and Panjwaii since the Shah Wali Kot bombing, with almost a dozen casualties. Instead, he focused his frustration on the recently completed U.S.-led Operation Mountain Thrust—the same operation that

Ian Hope's men had dubbed Operation Waste of Time. The operation to sweep empty mountain passes of the Taliban had been useless, Khalid declared. On that point, at least, Canadian soldiers were in agreement.

The governor wasn't the only one complaining. Ahmed Wali Karzai, the president's half-brother and leader of the provincial council, also made noise. Both men had deep ties with the U.S.—both with the military and the CIA. They trusted and respected American firepower and their determination to lay waste to anything and everything Taliban. They wanted a military force backing them that gave no quarter and wasn't concerned about niceties. The pair, whose covetous, brutal clawing for power and money in Kandahar had stoked the fires of rebellion, was skeptical about NATO. The U.S.-led war on terror, Operation Enduring Freedom (OEF), with its focus on thumping bad guys, suited their purposes quite nicely. The military alliance, with its focus on good governance and nation-building, was greeted with derision.

"At meetings in Kandahar and Kabul, senior Kandahari leaders—including Governor Asadullah Khalid and presidential brother / provincial kingpin Ahmed Wali Karzai—have suggested that NATO's ISAF is 'unwilling to take the fight to the Taliban,'" said the cable written on August 28, 2006.

"In front of ISAF officers, [Canadian] officials and key tribal elders in Kandahar, AWK reportedly said that 'the coalition kicked out 20,000 Taliban [from Afghanistan] and now ISAF can't even get rid of Taliban from two districts.'"

Senior NATO commanders and diplomats were aghast and irritated.

"ISAF vigorously rejects suggestions that NATO is unwilling to take the fight to the Taliban," said the summary, which also noted that U.S. rules regarding artillery and air support remained unchanged despite the transition.

Richards, a Brit who would later go on to be the chief of the general staff, acknowledged the threat posed by the Taliban buildup in Zhari and Panjwaii and confirmed that driving the insurgents from the area was his "number one military requirement."

An operation had been planned and Richards told the meeting he expected an improvement in the security situation within two to three weeks.

American Brigadier-General Stephen Layfield, Richards's operations chief of staff, was even more put out by the criticism. The former commander of the U.S. Rangers rhymed off statistics about the number of firefights that had taken place and "dismisses as 'nonsense' and 'ridiculous' the suggestion that ISAF is less willing to fight than OEF."

The Dutch ambassador, whose troops had just arrived in Uruzgan, the mountainous province north of Kandahar, responded to Wali Karzai's allegations with cold fury.

"In that context, Dutch [head of mission] strongly criticized Afghan officials who 'play games' by accusing NATO of weakness," said the diplomatic cable.

Richards said he saw it as a problem of optics and suggested better information operations, including the publication of Taliban body counts, to dispel the perception that NATO was having the stuffing kicked out of it in the south.

"The perception has built up that NATO is suffering more casualties than the Taliban," Richards was quoted as saying. He pointed to Canadian casualties in Kandahar as a specific example.

"Unfortunately, *there may be a need for body counts* to counter public misperceptions."

As September 2006 unfolded, Richards got his body count and then some. The fight of August 19 in Bazaar-e-Panjwaii made clear that both sides had committed themselves to a showdown. The Taliban were in Pashmul and were not going away; neither was NATO. An offensive was inevitable, and nobody on the ground doubted it would come. Brigadier-General David Fraser worked on the plan almost all of August, pulling together approximately 1,400 troops from the various nations scattered across southern Afghanistan. The core of the fighting force belonged to Omer Lavoie's RCR, but there were also elements of the U.S. 10th Mountain Division in the form of Task Force Grizzly and special forces troops. The Dutch contributed troops and artillery, which supported the Canadian batteries. The Danes also kicked in a few dozen troops.

The plan was called Operation Medusa, after the wild-haired Gorgon of Greek mythology. According to legend, anyone who gazed upon her face would be turned to stone. In ancient times, shields were emblazoned with her image to ward off evil. It was a fitting allegory for the story NATO wanted to tell about Kandahar. Turning the Taliban stone cold was to be Job One, and unlike moments before and since, the pretense of nation-building was abandoned. Troops were locked, loaded and ready to kill. Armies were always best when you pointed them in one direction and told them to blast something, the guys would joke, and this was to be a conventional battle, not the ghostly dance of counterterrorism soldiers had fought to that point. It was also the kind of fight that lent itself to headlines and TV clips. People back home could quickly and easily make sense of it. Good guys versus bad guys. There was no clutter, ambiguity or qualification. When the headlines hit, you could almost taste the excitement in every drop of ink.

The plan was relatively straightforward. The Taliban would be encircled north of the Arghandab River and pounded to oblivion. Estimates on how many militants had twisted themselves into the contoured grape fields, irrigation ditches and narrow laneways varied wildly. The first number was 200, but when the fighting got in to full swing, excited public affairs officers claimed it was more like 700. Two Canadian companies led the huge hammer-and-anvil assault. One dug in to the north of Pashmul while the other punched up from the south. U.S. and other NATO units were set up in blocking positions to catch fleeing insurgents as they tried to escape. Three days of shelling and bombing were to precede the ground attack.

General Rick Hillier took the plan to the prime minister the day before the troops jumped off from their starting points, according to PMO insiders. They described the closed-door meeting as "very casual." The general walked in alone with a single map and presented "a totally optimistic assessment" of what was to come. Hillier told Stephen Harper that he had instructed the ground commander to "make haste slowly" and that the operation would unfold "step by step" and the army would "not to rush into anything," a senior Conservative insider later told me.

What irked Harper's inner circle in hindsight was how late they were brought into the loop.

"This was the first we heard of Medusa from a Canadian, although by this point the operation was already being announced on the BBC and CNN," said the official.

* * *

The guns opened up on September 2, 2006. They were followed quickly by the planes—American A-10 Thunderbolts, known affectionately as Warthogs for their slow, lumbering ways. Anyone who's ever seen a Thunderbolt in action never forgets. A splash of Roman candles belches from its nose. The sound is memorable too. The deep, throbbing bass of an A-10 Gatling gun, a seven-barrel 30-mm cannon meant to tear open the guts of tanks, can send cold shivers down your back. Their mission was to bomb and strafe targets in the kill zone.

Charles Company, led by Major Matthew Sprague, seized ground south of the Arghandab River shortly after sunrise. They took fighting positions on Ma'sum Ghar and other hills surrounding Bazaar-e-Panjwaii. Their orders were not to cross the river. From the rocky slopes, the troops were perfectly situated to have "eyes on" the village of Pashmul itself. The place was still and seemed deserted, save for a small band of Taliban who took potshots across the river as the Canadians dug in around their armoured vehicles.

The battle plan called for an air strike on the village if it was determined civilians had fled the area. The bombs were to be aimed at known Taliban positions. One of the objectives of the eventual ground assault was the White Schoolhouse. It, along with the Yellow Schoolhouse farther to the north, had been turned into fortified positions by the Taliban over the summer. The White Schoolhouse was labelled Objective Rugby and on day four of the operation, Charles Company was expected to splash across the Arghandab River and seize it. The previous battle group had lost four soldiers in their attempt to overrun the site in early August. With that in mind, the troops were happy to let the artillery and the Warthogs do their work.

Brigadier-General Fraser arrived at Ma'sum Ghar by late afternoon on the first day for a conference with his battle group commander. The volume of fire coming from across the river had eased and there seemed to be very little movement in Taliban territory. At that moment, Fraser made a snap decision, one of the most controversial of the war. He scrapped the further artillery and air bombardments and ordered Charles Company to cross the river and seize the White Schoolhouse. A platoon was sent out to map a suitable crossing point. Fraser reportedly pressed for an immediate assault, but Lavoie resisted. The attack was scheduled for the next day. Aside from losing what he saw as a critical softening-up period, during which the Taliban would have been chipped away, Lavoie worried about the lack of intelligence on enemy positions.

Later, Fraser said he came to his decision based upon his own observations and after hearing the views of not only Lavoie, but the other battle group commanders and Afghan authorities—the same Afghans who had been trash-talking NATO, and Canadian troops in particular, for not being aggressive enough. The secret Foreign Affairs communiqués I viewed show that ISAF headquarters in Kabul was also impatient for the operation to get underway. General Richards emphasized the need to "push hard." Fraser acknowledged the pressure, but dismissed it as factor in his decision to throw out the first part of the plan.

Charles Company pushed across the shallow, gravel-bedded river almost right in front of Ma'sum Ghar shortly after sunrise on September 3, 2006. Combat engineers opened up breaches for the infantry, and the assault force, which included Afghan troops and their embedded U.S. trainers, spilled into the surrounding fields. Their orders were to advance on the White Schoolhouse, observe and then attack. NATO had dropped leaflets the day before, warning local residents to flee. The Taliban knew they were coming and Charles Company plowed right into a three-sided ambush. It was a bloodbath.

A rocket-propelled grenade punched through the window of one of the G-Wagons, killing Warrant Officer Rick Nolan. An 82-mm recoilless rifle split open an armoured vehicle and killed Sergeant Shane Stachnik, who had been standing in one of the open air sentry hatches. Private William Cushley and Warrant Officer Frank Mellish, who had come forward to help Nolan, were both killed when an anti-tank round slammed into a front-end loader where casualties were assembled. There were dozens of wounded. One of the LAVs, pressed into service as an ambulance and carrying Nolan's body, drove into a ditch and never got out. It was abandoned and soldiers had to go back later to retrieve Nolan.

The radio was full of pleas for help. The Taliban, holed up at the White Schoolhouse, slipped in and out of the towering marijuana fields that surrounded the position. The Canadians fought back. On their flanks, they lashed out at an enemy that was dug in deep among trenches and thick mud-walled grape huts. The 25-mm chain gun on the LAV, which normally chewed through a target, made only dirt splashes on the sides of some of the ancient hovels. Sprague calmly ordered artillery fire and air strikes, but the Taliban were well fortified. At one point, a U.S. jet dropped a 1,000-pound bomb that skipped over its target and landed among the Canadian lines. It didn't go off. The two platoons of Charles Company withdrew from the kill zone and retreated back across the river. Out of the fifty soldiers that made the crossing that morning, there were more than twenty casualties, including dead and wounded.

That morning, soldiers who had been excited to fight as their fathers, grandfathers and great-grandfathers had fought—in an old-fashioned frontal assault—got a real taste of what it was like. The attack across the Arghandab River was the first company-sized combat operation for Canadians since the Korean War. It had the further distinction of being the first large-scale NATO combat assault in the alliance's history. It was also a tragedy. The attack didn't succeed, but guys I've spoken with throughout the years—guys who were there—insist it wasn't a defeat either. Many talk about the long odds they faced and the hundreds of Taliban they killed. One soldier stands out in my recollection. He talked about how before Medusa, he didn't really like firing his C8 rifle. Unlike in training, the hard reality of operations was that you were going to kill somebody. If he'd gotten through his tour without having to fire, he said, that would have been fine. After Medusa, however, he didn't want to stop shooting. There was no compunction, no hesitation. You couldn't take the rifle out of his hands. I am still struck by how much his story says about fear, and about the kind of guts it takes to cross a shallow, emaciated river into the unknown.

* * *

Throughout the night and early morning of September 3 and 4, 2006, American jets and attack helicopters bombed and strafed Taliban positions north of Charles Company's position. They chewed up the arid grape fields and laid waste to the White Schoolhouse. Some of the guys who watched said it was like all of Panjwaii and Zhari were on fire that night. The place burned and it burned nicely—not with cold vengeance, but with a clear-eyed rage. It's thought that hundreds of Taliban died in the bombardment, some inside the school, others in the marijuana fields and irrigation ditches. Abandoning all reservation about body counts, military commanders pulled out a bloody scorecard and claimed as many as 200 insurgents had been incinerated over those two days.

The sense of urgency to extract some type of vengeance extended to the American A-10 pilots who kept up the vigil in the skies that night. Two of the tank-busting jets, based out of Bagram Airfield, had been on station for hours when the eastern sky started to show the first milky traces of dawn. The pilot of the lead plane, a veteran of sixty combat missions, had on his night-vision goggles the entire time, picking out targets in the luminescent green soup. The arrival of dawn prompted him to switch off the visor. The ground was obscured by haze and smoke from previous bombings, but he decided to make one more pass. The only thing he could see through the windscreen and dull glow of his cockpit display was a pillar of smoke, what he assumed was the smouldering leftover of the target from his previous run. He pressed the trigger.

"Splash," the pilot said, referring to the fountains of earth kicked up by the armour-piercing rounds.

In fact, what he'd hit was a garbage fire lit by soldiers. The men were still huddled around it for warmth.

Within seconds the Canadian air-ground controller with the troops screamed into the radio, telling the pilot and his wingman, who was lining up a follow-on attack, to abort.

The cockpit transcripts were part of a 5,000-page freedom of information request I made to the Pentagon. Even years later, they make chilling reading.

"I, ah, got confused by, I saw smoke coming from another position. I rolled in on the wrong spot," the pilot said after being told friendly troops had been hit.

The soldier on the radio, after confirming the pilot had switched his guns to "safe," demanded to know what happened: "Can you tell me why those rounds came in on a friendly position?"

What do you say when you realize you may have killed perhaps dozens of people? The first instinct is probably denial, but that wasn't this man's style.

"That was pilot error. I had the smoke coming up from that position and I mistook [garbled]," was the answer.

The mistake cost the life of Private Mark Anthony Graham, a former Olympic sprinter. There were thirty others wounded, including company commander Matthew Sprague. One soldier, who survived the attack, told U.S. Air Force investigators that it looked like fireworks were raining down on them.

"I heard the A-10 and looked over my left shoulder," the soldier said in a sworn statement just days after the tragedy. "I saw a shower of 'white roman candles.' The impact began one hundred metres behind me, southwest of the [garbage] fire and continued toward and into the fire."

He said he felt what he thought were punches. The next thing he knew, he was lying on the ground surrounded by other bodies and pools of blood. The pilot had strafed an entire platoon and its tactical headquarters with 30-mm cannon fire, effectively wiping out Charles Company as a combat force.

The debrief transcript showed the veteran airman was utterly devastated by the accident. He accepted his responsibility, unlike the defiant Major Harry Schmidt, the pilot who mistakenly killed four Canadian soldiers at Tarnak Farms in 2002. The pilot at Ma'sum Ghar was so distraught that he proposed to fly down to Kandahar and personally apologize to the soldiers of Charles Company. The idea was nixed by his senior officers, and the U.S. Air Force went to great lengths to protect him and his identity.

A joint American and Canadian investigation was launched. Each nation's final report couldn't have been more different in style, if not in actual substance. The incident could have been prevented "had the pilot checked" his electronic combat display in the cockpit, the final Canadian board of inquiry investigation said. But the U.S. team twisted itself in knots to avoid accepting the blame. Even a generous reading of the transcripts left me with the impression the team was looking for some way to pin the accident on what they saw as hapless and inexperienced Canadian soldiers. The Pentagon report showed American investigators focused much of their attention on perceived deficiencies with the Canadian military and the Canadian soldier on the ground who directed air strikes.

The pilot was asked, "Did you have any apprehension or hesitation or any we'll say nagging issues coming down working with the folks down around Kandahar?"

The pilot told them he had no qualms about working with the Canadians, and since they had suffered terrible casualties a day before the friendly fire incident he "felt some pressure to support them."

U.S. military officers paid close attention to deficiencies in equipment. They complained the Canadians did not have proper identification markers, and that the air controller had been in continuous action for seventy-two hours with only four hours of sleep. They weren't impressed the Canadians had only one soldier to coordinate both aircraft and artillery fire. In the American military there are always two.

Questions were raised about the training. At one point, the Canadians were described as "probably not the best" joint tactical air controllers.

"Were you comfortable with the inputs he was giving, the level of control and the manner with which he exercised his authority? Do you think he could have done better?" the pilot was asked.

The pilot answered: "I think we all obviously could have done better because the outcome shows that. I think there's things on both sides we could have done."

At last report, the pilot involved in the Mas'um Ghar tragedy had received no censure.

"You Have to Spend to Save" *9*

The guys of Bravo Company, 1 RCR, followed the painful disintegration of Charles Company on the radio during the first few days of Operation Medusa. Later, they told me that the steady drip of casualties and setbacks was like the Chinese water torture. From positions north of Pashmul, they heard the explosions and gunfire, saw helicopters and jets zip past and listened to the cries for help. There was nothing they could do. Their orders were to sit tight as Regional Command South figured out how to regain control of an operation that had gone horribly wrong. One element of Bravo had been sent to guard the crash site of a British Nimrod spy plane, an accident that had resulted in the loss of fourteen crew members. The ghastly duty only reinforced the feeling of abandonment. By the time the A-10 attack happened, many guys in Bravo felt that the battle was slipping away and they had been left on the sidelines.

The sense that Medusa was off the rails was shared by NATO's Afghanistan headquarters in Kabul. On September 6, 2006, during a reception in the Afghan capital for General Pervez Musharraf, the Pakistani president, ISAF Lieutenant-General David Richards complained openly about how the Canadians performed. The attack across the Arghandab

River had been too timid, he said, and the allied forces had not put enough pressure on the Taliban. The shockwaves of the rebuke were felt all the way back in Ottawa, which dispatched Ambassador David Sproule and his deputy, Richard Colvin, to deliver a message to the NATO general. They met with Richards on September 8, two days after the Musharraf visit, according to classified documents I viewed later in the war.

Richards, a man of uncommon intelligence and blunt words, stuck with his criticism. He said the Taliban in Panjwaii had been squeezed and the Canadians should not have paused after the incident with Charles Company. They needed to keep up the "tempo," he said.

"There is a risk in giving time to the Taliban, who had been running low on ammunition," said an account of the meeting relayed to the Foreign Affairs Department. "The pause allowed them to resupply—'if we'd pressed them resolutely,' we wouldn't have given them the chance."

Richards pulled out a map and laid it on the table for the two diplomats. The attack by Charles Company was made with "regrettably insufficient strength," the general told them. After recounting the battle from his perspective, Richards suggested that Canadian commanders and politicians in Ottawa "had perhaps not fully appreciated the need to push hard at the start of the operation."

NATO wasn't totally heartless, Richards insisted, and was cognizant of the need to minimize casualties.

"But sometimes you have to spend to save," he said.

A renewed offensive was to take place in Panjwaii, one with a greater concentration of force, one that would deliver no mercy to the Taliban. Throwing the right number of troops at the hardened schoolhouse positions meant there would be few casualties, Richards argued.

The incongruity of that kind of statement never ceased to amaze me. More troops; no matter what the problem, more troops was always the answer. It was an automatic reflex that seemed genetically programmed in most generals. Maybe they couldn't help themselves. In past wars, the policy had been applied on an industrial scale, leading to industrial-sized slaughter. Afghanistan was a different war in another time, but I could hear echoes of the Somme and Dieppe in some of Richards's biting analysis. It's hilarious how there are those who insist on telling you that you've needlessly gotten yourself beaten up and killed—something they would have never done.

"The first day or two was not a perfect way of doing it, but that is all history," Richards said.

What was important, he declared, was to keep pushing forward.

It was easier said than done when one of your units has been chewed up and spit out. Regional Command South struggled to rewrite the battle plan. The surviving elements of Charles Company were rolled in with a mobile squadron made of members of the Royal Canadian Dragoons, known as ISTAR (Intelligence Surveillance, Target-Acquisition, Reconnaissance). Together, the Canadians were grouped into Task Force Grizzly under the command of an American, Lieutenant-Colonel Steve Williams, of the 207th U.S. Infantry Brigade. Their job was to hold the southern flank and act as the anvil to Bravo Company's hammer. It was in essence a reversal of the original battle plan. Williams, a hard-charging U.S. Army officer, ordered rock music blasted at the Taliban from speakers set up on the southern bank of the Arghandab River. He used AC/DC's "Back in Black" to not only aggravate the enemy, but also to mask the sound of armoured vehicle movements. Some of the guys told me they loved it.

Bravo Company, under Major Geoff Abthorpe, was deployed south of the newly created Patrol Base Wilson, located on Highway 1. Early in the battle, before Charles Company took its pounding, Bravo had pushed up to a deep irrigation ditch and road network that arched across the blistered landscape from the east to the southwest. From that line Abthorpe's troops patrolled, harassed and generally made life difficult for the Taliban. Anything between the north bank of the river and the south side of the irrigation ditch was effectively no man's land. Over a six-day period, the artillery, the helicopters and the fast jets were let loose on it. Anything that moved was decimated, smashed or burned to the point where some of the guys wondered if anything would ever grow on the land again.

Although they were reluctant to say it, there was something deeply satisfying for them in the terror that rained down on those long, late summer days in the desert. The Canadian army's ammunition usage figures were secret, but it was common knowledge that by halfway through the battle they were running low on 155-mm shells for the big guns. Grape huts and compounds were levelled and the countryside made faceless. It didn't stop even at night.

Four soldiers in Bravo Company were wounded when the Taliban tried to bring an 82-mm recoilless rifle to bear on one of the armoured vehicles. The troops eventually forged across the deep, wide irrigation ditch and pushed south toward Objective Rugby, the White Schoolhouse that had already cost so much blood. To get there, they bore down on the tiny village of Pasab, where a few months before Medusa I'd watched Romanian troops and Canadian army doctors try to win hearts and minds with a portable medical clinic. Many of the young fighting-age males who had loaded their pocket-sized children into wheelbarrows to receive Western care now fought tenaciously to keep the same army out of their fields. How many were willing recruits, how many were coerced and how many died as their world was turned upside down would never be known.

Task Force Grizzly laid it on thick from their side of the Arghandab River throughout those long days of hard heat. By the second week of September, Williams was ready to charge across the thin divide. On September 12, the soldiers of Charles Company once again found themselves being told to move, with little preparation or intelligence on what awaited them. The Canadian officers argued against it and many of the guys I talked with thought Williams believed they were vacillating. But Captain Trevor Norton put any hard feelings down to the fact that the guys in Charles Company were "getting their legs back under them" and to the colonel being a typical American army officer.

"I didn't perceive him being overly risk-taking," Norton said. "He just wanted to advance. That was his thing; there was a little bit of apprehension there [for us], having never worked with Americans before."

After a nighttime reconnaissance patrol gave them the eyes they needed, everyone did go across. They forged at a point farther east than the September 3 assault. They met light resistance, fanned out and rushed westward. The fighting lasted about a day and a half. One of Charles Company's platoons was among the first to reach Objective Rugby and, along the way, they passed the burned out carcass of the LAV that had been abandoned in the earlier fight. It had been pummelled to tinfoil by the heavy guns and bombs.

It was dark by the time they overran the White Schoolhouse, which had been reduced to a bowed, cratered hovel. The roof and back walls were gone. Supporting beams had collapsed on to a pile of jagged rubble. The school that had been built with American money and had cost so much Canadian blood was the very definition of a Pyrrhic victory. When Norton rolled up in his LAV in the faded daylight, he surveyed the ruins with a numb eye.

"All I could think about was how we could have done this better," he said later.

He walked the ground in the following days and inspected every inch of the Taliban's elaborate defence works.

"Some of the bunkers were so well concealed; we only found them because there had been some burning of the underbrush and we could see their entrance," Norton said with a genial, earnest respect.

Norton has reconstructed the September 3 battle in his mind many times, and over the years has made a point of talking to the targeting officer who directed the air strikes, some of the artillery spotters, the commanders who made the decision to charge across the river and even colleagues of the A-10 pilot who strafed him. The question that ate away at him was whether the bombardment should have continued as planned in those first few bloody days.

"You know, I'm not convinced they had the targets that they could have hit that would have changed the course of that day," he said.

"There were so many enemy there it wasn't permissive to put in a ground recce, so we couldn't confirm those positions. So I'm not sure we would have been able to hit the enemy. We could have bombed a lot of compounds. Some would have been the right ones, some would have had nobody in them. So at the end of the day, we didn't know where to bomb; that's probably why we didn't bomb."

Major combat operations ended on September 14, but that didn't stop the bloodshed. The Taliban who had survived the slaughter at Pashmul reverted to guerilla tactics. There would be no more standing, fighting and dying before coalition guns for a long time. Instead, they would battle almost exclusively by remote control and pressure plate, exacting a slow, steady bleed of dead and wounded. By the end of October, another ten soldiers were dead, including four in one day to a suicide bomber. ISAF commanders ordered the construction of a new paved road between Ma'sum Ghar and Patrol Base Wilson and the battle group's focus in the following months was to defend that project. It was called Route Summit. In selling it to embedded reporters, the generals emphasized the economic potential; how it would help farmers get their crops to market more efficiently than the old, winding dirt path. When you talked to guys on the ground, however, there was a slightly more self-interested story. A paved road meant it was harder to bury roadside bombs, and movement for armoured vehicles over a straight run of blacktop meant better mobility for forces running to stamp out insurgent hotspots.

As it turned out, the Taliban found the new road only a minor inconvenience. They took to burying explosives in the gravel along the edge or stuffed them in drainage culverts. The land the Canadians paved over was expropriated, but it took months to sort out. As with everything else in Afghanistan, the land registry system was in shambles. The farmers were paid in Afghanis—the national, nearly worthless currency. I once rode out to Patrol Base Wilson in a Bison armoured vehicle sitting on top of cardboard boxes stuffed with the Afghan cash. The soldiers joked about being "awesomely kitted-out" Brink's guards. If they wanted their money, the farmers had to walk past a security cordon that included tanks.

The army set up three major defensive fortifications—known as strongpoints—along Route Summit. Scraped out of the hard-packed earth, they became the perfect metaphor for the next phase of the campaign. The strongpoints, a mixture of earthen works, reinforced wooden bunkers and trench lines, looked like something out of the First World War. They screamed bloody stalemate. Without enough troops to properly chase the Taliban farther into either Zhari or Panjwaii, the Canadians dug in along the road. The line they carved through those rural districts would, with few exceptions, remain static for the next three years. The western reaches of both unsettled districts became Taliban territory, where insurgents freely rested, resupplied and built their bombs. The line ran roughly north-south. Behind it and running back east toward Kandahar city, there was the occasional pocket of resistance; tough nuts as the military called them. The villages—Senjaray, Sangasar, Salavat and Nakhoney—would become Taliban hotbeds and would be repeatedly swept over the coming years.

Days after the major combat of Medusa ended, Lieutenant-Colonel Williams gave American reporters with the *New York Times* and National Public Radio a tour of the battlefield and invoked comparisons to the bloody hedgerow fighting of the Normandy campaign. He posed over a bunker that the newspaper said had been destroyed by "his" forces. Williams showed them the makeshift hospital where wounded Taliban fighters had been brought at the height of the fighting. The bloody rags, discarded needles and IV bags had been hauled away for further examination. The number of enemy killed by "his" forces amounted to 200, including seven or eight Taliban commanders, Williams said. That "his" forces were mostly Canadian received scant attention in the *Times* story and that rubbed some of the soldiers raw. Whether by design or oversight, the soldiers saw themselves disappear in the shadow of the flashy American colonel, who was later awarded the Canadian military's Meritorious Service Medal.

Some of the Canadian media accounts that followed the battle also irritated soldiers, particularly the guys of Charles Company, who saw themselves displayed as victims. There was something almost pathological about it, from their viewpoint. No matter how many times they said they were okay, the stories about how bad it was for them just kept coming.

"The press has its own view and that's the way the press should be; it sees what it sees and it's supposed to be impartial, but I was frustrated by reading those kind of articles because we got them out in the field," said Norton.

There is an unspoken creed between journalists and soldiers. You never bitch on behalf of the troops, unless they ask. And whatever you do, don't feel sorry for them.

The headline "Charles; A Shattered Company" in one of the major dailies drove most of them around the bend, and for a while they didn't want to talk to any journalists.

"That really angered me because I hadn't seen that; I didn't feel that," said Norton, whose men, along with members of 9 Platoon, stayed in the field throughout the tour. "There was never a point when we became gun shy, scared or shattered."

* * *

Not much changed on the streets of Ottawa during those glorious early autumn days. The bells of the Peace Tower chimed on time. The daily gaggle of tourists hovered over the eternal flame and took pictures. Civil servants and shopkeepers mingled on the Sparks Street Mall, smoking, drinking coffee and enjoying the last gasp of warm sunshine before the long Ottawa winter arrived. Life went on pretty much as it had before.

But if you squinted really hard and gazed between the tall buildings across the Rideau Canal you could see the only visible sign that the country was at war. The flag atop National Defence Headquarters was at half-staff. It stayed like that pretty much throughout September 2006. By halting the practice of lowering Parliament Hill flags, the Conservatives had tried to shove the war off centre stage, but it wasn't so easily boxed away. The flag at DND was like a balefire for anybody who walked along Elgin Street. There were times when I didn't have to look at my BlackBerry to know there were casualties; I just had to glance over and see that flag. Inside the twin office towers, whenever a soldier died, the name was read over the building loudspeaker and a moment of silence observed. There was a lot of silence within those walls that fall.

The Conservative government, which had embraced the war in Kandahar as a manifest sign of the new, harder-edged Canada, was now confronted with what the army refers to as the butcher's bill. Slapped down beside it was a request for reinforcements from Brigadier-General David Fraser.

"This was what some would describe in the vernacular as the Come to Jesus Moment," Peter MacKay recalled.

The events of the summer and autumn of 2006 had a sobering effect on both the politicians and the Ottawa-based military establishment. What the Taliban showed during those critical early months was that they were not the spent force everyone believed. They were determined to retake Kandahar. The full realization of the responsibility that rested on the country's shoulders settled in like a lead weight. The consequences of losing Afghanistan's second largest city—and of having that loss hung around Canada's neck—was enough to make the blood run cold, even among those who already had ice water in their veins. The damage to the country's reputation would be incalculable. Some in the Foreign Affairs Department were stopped dead by the thought of what could or might happen. There was no worse fate for a diplomat than losing face. A seething resentment was born around that time, partly out of the sense that the professional service had been sidelined, its voice muted. The military was running the show and the show was turning into a disaster. Fingers weren't pointed, but they were raised. Those in uniform, whose pride was often as big as their guns, were also determined not to fail. Too many years had been spent being patronized and mocked as blue berets for them to fold now.

That there was no clear, unambiguous endorsement of the war stuck painfully in the side of a lot of Tories, especially in those early days. Victories were supposed to create public momentum, a sense that "our" side was on the march. Instead, what they got out of Medusa was a deepening sense of dismay and disillusionment. And Conservative strategists had been warned the previous spring that when John Q. Public went against the war, he didn't come back. The Battle of Pashmul sent a lot of people that way and the slide accelerated when Jack Layton took the stage at the NDP convention in Quebec City on September 10, 2006.

During the summer, Layton's public statements had called for Canadian troops to be moved out of Kandahar to a more benign region of the wasted country, but as the convention unfolded, he was pushed to toward a harder line. The motion put before the delegates was dubbed the "out now" proposition and demanded the immediate withdrawal of all combat troops. The notion that Canada could walk away from an international commitment in the middle of a shooting war without regard for the consequences appealed to the party's fundamentalist core, the very sort of "loony left" Layton had tried to suppress as he dragged the New Democrats back toward the political mainstream and electability. He had throughout most of his time as leader tried to deliberately cast the party as moderate, responsible and non-threatening. Moving the troops out of combat into what many considered the more traditional role of peacekeeping elsewhere in Afghanistan fit with his vision of responsibility. But the party's anti-war faction wanted none of it. They demanded a clear, dramatic stand against the emerging quagmire. Debate over the issue threatened to divide the caucus when long-time Nova Scotia MP Peter Stoffer described the motion as "premature" and other delegates suggested cross-country consultation.

"We want the troops out of Afghanistan. Okay, fine. They're gone. Then what?" Stoffer told the *Toronto Star*. "What happens in Afghanistan after that? What's our role with NATO? What about our commitment to the Afghan government?"

He was the only MP to speak out against the withdrawal and his objections were slapped down hard by delegates spoiling for a fight. The anti-war sentiment was further whipped up by warnings from Afghan MP Malalai Joya, whose contempt for the government of Hamid Karzai dripped from her fingertips. She said the growing conflict only benefited warlords and drug barons.

In the end, it came down to cold, hard political calculation. Layton and his advisors knew Quebec was fertile ground for the anti-war movement and the NDP, long relegated to the sidelines in the province, had a chance to take centre stage.

Layton's speech was met with thunderous applause. He demanded the Harper government "support the troops by bringing them home." In earlier interviews, the NDP chief had set February 2007 as the deadline, the initial expiry date of the deployment. But delegates even tweaked that by passing a motion that urged the "safe and immediate" withdrawal of the troops.

The furious political-establishment response started with *Globe and Mail* columnist Jeffery Simpson, who thundered: "Spare us the NDP's mistaken moral crusades."

He wasted no words in carving up the party's position, stating that ingrained anti-Americanism was at the heart of the withdrawal demand and ridiculing the NDP as naive.

"The New Democratic Party, largely because it has never known the responsibility and discipline of power, views a frequently immoral world through the prism of moral crusades."

Almost overnight Layton became synonymous with appeasement and retreat. Some postings on the on-line military message boards at the time even equated Layton's position to treason. The nickname Taliban Jack—whether born during the catcalls of Question Period or of a headline in the *Globe and Mail*—emerged and stuck.

When the House of Commons resumed later that month, NDP members walked into a flaming cauldron of rhetoric and taunts. It knocked many of them back on their heels. They had been expecting a backlash, but the fury of the response was unsettling. Layton later described it as a "blast of hate" and tried as best as he could to brush it off. I asked if the Taliban Jack label bothered him.

"No. What it meant was we had touched a nerve and a debate was going to get started," he answered. "I don't mean to sound trite about it, but it makes you stronger when people resort to calling you names instead of having a discussion about the issue. I think our party members, our caucus, became more convinced of the position as a result of the name-calling."

So as the battle lines that would define the next three years in Kandahar were drawn in the sun-baked earth of Panjwaii and Zhari, political trench lines were dug across Parliament Hill. The country's war would play out in two places at once, with one intruding equally on the other.

Years later, Layton would claim to have no regrets, other than the melancholy sense that comes from the country being mired for so many years in a brutal war. He described the political rhetoric in Ottawa throughout as "toxic" and blamed the Harper government for painting every question about the conflict as an attack on the troops.

"That was the biggest problem," he said. "Patriotism involves trying to make sure your country is doing the right thing. I believe what we were doing there was contributing and opening a door to a debate. It was patriotic, not unpatriotic. It fits within the concept of citizenship within a democracy. When you're not allowed to debate, you're drifting away from the fundamental democratic impulse."

He said the polarization in Ottawa made it tough for the public to under-stand what the war was all about, a situation that was compounded by the political spin of the various parties and special interests. He repeatedly returned to the theme that the Conservative government had a civic responsibility to rise above partisanship, especially in the early stages, and to form some kind of ongoing consensus with the Opposition parties about the direction of the conflict. There was little doubt that after his Quebec City speech any such harmony would have been impossible.

"Do you think the position of the NDP contributed to the [political] division?" I asked him.

Surprisingly, Layton didn't seem ready for the question. He set his jaw and looked away for what seemed like a long time.

"I wonder . . ." he said quietly. "Hindsight always gives the benefits. What started out as an attempt to find, search out and destroy al-Qaeda turned out to be a completely different kind of war, one we couldn't support."

* * *

During the fall of 2006, as troops settled in for their first Kandahar winter, something so totally unexpected happened that those of us who heard about it could scarcely believe it. The *Globe and Mail* came close to nailing the story at one point, but it wasn't until years later, when poring through access to information documents obtained by my colleague Stephanie Levitz, that I saw the first tangible proof.

"Efforts are ongoing to explore the possibility of a peace arrangement in Panjwayi and Zharey districts, similar to the one reached in Musa Qala," Canadian diplomats in Kandahar wrote in a weekly summary of Afghan events compiled by the Foreign Affairs Department.

Musa Qala is a district of nineteen villages in northern Helmand province, where in 2006 the British brokered an uncertain ceasefire with the Taliban. Under the terms, NATO forces withdrew from the district centre and handed security over to local village elders. The Americans, and to a lesser extent the Karzai government, were outraged by the arrangement. The British had been under siege in the village throughout much of that summer. Lieutenant-General David Richards saw the deal as a way to empower local authorities. But the net effect, the Americans argued, was to create a safe haven where Taliban fighters could rest, regroup and plan attacks. That the Canadians had attempted to do something similar was nothing short of mind-blowing. It flew in the face of almost every public statement the Conservative government had ever made about dealing with the Taliban. It ran the risk of angering the Americans, who were never in the mood to talk with insurgents under any circumstances. And it was kept secret, so secret, in fact, that officials at the Canadian embassy in Kabul were cut out of the information loop. I showed the document and supporting backgrounders to several former staffers, who were dumbfounded by the news.

"Had the Americans known, they would have flipped out. They hated Musa Qala, hated it," said a former official who spoke on background. "The U.S. perspective was the Brit arrangement was undercutting the central government. They were reducing Afghan sovereignty, removing Kabul's sovereignty over this key district, essentially creating this autonomous enclave where the government's writ didn't apply."

Years later, Omer Lavoie, who'd been promoted to full colonel, told me that he never took the idea of a Musa Qala–type deal in Panjwaii seriously.

"My perspective was, those ceasefire zones, those safe havens had created . . . they worked for the Taliban," he said.

"They would pick and choose when they'd abide by it. Whenever it came up within the confines of RC-South, it was [more] philosophizing than anything else. I told them, all those things do is build up more time for them to get strong."

Yet diplomats on the ground continued to muse about it.

"The overarching goal is to split so-called 'tier 1' hard-core insurgents from so-called 'tier 2' supporters," said the Foreign Affairs documents, dated November 28, 2006. "It is believed the local population is sufficiently weary of the ongoing fighting and that they can be convinced to pressure 'tier 1' militants to leave."

I laughed when I read that paragraph. At the time, it probably reflected an honest assessment, but in hindsight, it represented a stunning ignorance of the tribal dynamic at play in western Kandahar. The premise was that if villagers could be convinced to expel the Taliban, we would leave them alone. It ignored the fact that the Noorzai, who made up the bulk of the population in the troublesome districts, had embraced the insurgents, partly out of fear and partly out of ethnic sympathy. Even if they wanted to kick out the Taliban, they were powerless to defend themselves against the well-armed guerrilla fighters. What eventually sealed the fate of the Canadian initiative

The ghostly ruins of Osama bin Laden's compound at Tarnak Farms, near Kandahar Airfield, February 2007. It was at this al-Qaeda training compound that 9/11 was thought to have been planned. (Murray Brewster)

The view from an observation post of the no man's land of western Panjwaii district in December 2010. (Murray Brewster)

The moon rises over the wasted farmland of Panjwaii district east of Sperwan Ghar in December 2010. The scene is peaceful, but Canadian troops fought repeated battles, including the landmark Operation Medusa in 2006, through the many grape fields and compounds that litter this desolate region. (Murray Brewster)

An old Soviet tank, used by the Taliban in their defence of Kandahar, still sits abandoned along the highway leading to Pakistan in this May 2009 photo. The landscape around the provincial capital is littered with debris of thirty years of war. (Murray Brewster)

Soldiers belonging to Alpha Company, 1st Battalion, Princess Patricia's Canadian Light Infantry assuming a blocking position on a road north of Kandahar city in April 2006. (CP Image/Murray Brewster)

Soldiers belonging to the headquarters element of November Company, 3rd Battalion, Royal Canadian Regiment, sit silently in a Canadian CH-47D Chinook on the way to assault a Taliban command post near Mushan, Kandahar province in March 2009. (Murray Brewster)

Soldiers belonging to the headquarters unit of November Company, 3rd Battalion, Royal Canadian Regiment take up position during a raid on a Taliban command-and-control area near Mushan, Panjwaii district in March 2009. (Murray Brewster)

Capt. Nichola Goddard, the first female soldier to die in combat, relaxes in the back of her LAV at FOB Robinson in Sangin, Helmand province in April 2006. (CP Image/Murray Brewster)

Soldiers of 7 Platoon in Charlie Company, 2nd Battalion, PPCLI, patrol a road in Arghandab district looking for land mines in May 2008. The Arghandab became one of the bloodiest battlegrounds of the war as its thick orchards and winding irrigation canal provided perfect cover for Taliban fighters. (CP Image/Murray Brewster)

An unidentified soldier from 7 Platoon, November Company, 3rd Battalion, Royal Canadian Regiment, guards Afghan villagers near Mushan, Panjwaii district, during a search for Taliban weapons caches in March 2009. (CP Image/Murray Brewster)

An Afghan National Army soldier pets a camel as its owner tries to cross a roadblock in southern Panjwaii district near the village of Khenjakak in March 2010. (Murray Brewster)

Afghan National Army Capt. Rahmatullah, a company commander in the ANA 205 Corps, 2nd Kandak (battalion), plans his next move in an operation in the spring of 2010. As the months passed, the ANA to firmer control of operations. (Murray Brewster)

An unidentified Canadian soldier pauses following the news that four troops were killed in a roadside bombing near the village of Gumbad, north of Kandahar city, in April 2006. (CP Image/Murray Brewster)

was the fact that it was being done without the consent of the Kandahar provincial council.

"The process is to include concurrent political and military pressure," said the Foreign Affairs report. "Unlike Musa Qala, the provincial administration is not currently involved in the engagement process."

What was clear was that the Canadians were attempting to keep the president's half-brother, Ahmed Wali Karzai, on the fringes, especially after he expressed public doubts about the willingness of NATO to fight. He would have been in no mood to talk or deal and understood better than his foreign benefactors that a tribal war with the Noorzai had been layered atop the insurgency. As an elder of the Popalzai, he was determined to fight for the supremacy of his tribe, using international forces. His feud became our war. The smart Canadian officers and diplomats soon figured it out, but by that time, it was too late.

There were uncomfortable moments, moments when you didn't know quite what to say. Most often they came when you were dealing with soldiers whose buddies had been killed or wounded. Some guys let fly with hard anger and a machine-gun staccato of expletives, and you just knew to get out of the way. Other guys cried. There's nothing that can shut you up faster than watching a sweaty, exhausted, hulk-sized soldier break down. The army hated that too. They probably didn't mind as much when it happened in front of print reporters, but it became a national emergency if TV or photographers were around. Soldiers could talk to you as long as they "stayed within their lane" of expertise, the media commandments said. But crying so that the whole country could see wasn't on. This wasn't some petty, macho, bullshit objection; it was a cold calculation of optics. And if the genuine heartbreak and dismay of fresh loss was verboten, then expressing a political opinion, especially to a journalist, was nothing short of radioactive.

"I hold Jack Layton personally responsible for the deaths of my friends," one soldier blurted out during an overnight convoy to Zhari, the heart of darkness itself.

There were six of us packed into the back of a Bison, one of half a dozen vehicles in the convoy bound for Patrol Base Wilson, where Bravo Company of the 1st Battalion, Royal Canadian Regiment had spent most of its war. Two soldiers stood in the air sentry hatches. Two of my colleagues from CTV were in full, open-mouthed sleep. The third soldier, in his late thirties or early forties, tried to doze at first, resting his chin on his rifle butt, but eventually gave up. I didn't even try to sleep. The weather had turned cold with the onset of winter, a fact that always startled people who'd never been to Afghanistan. The Bison, as I recall, had no heat that night, just the occasional blast of warm diesel air that left a sooty aftertaste in your mouth. The Taliban had been hitting convoys all up and down the road. Roaring through in the middle of the night was thought to be safest—the best chance of catching insurgents and their cellphone triggers asleep at the switch. The Afghans always seemed to have trouble staying awake. I'd heard story after story about local cops or soldiers conked out at their posts or in their vehicles. It was thought, by guys paid to know that stuff, that the Taliban were probably no different. Even so, I wasn't about to shut my eyes. The soldier, a former member of the disbanded airborne regiment, tried to be social. We talked about the change in weather and other things that annoyed us, all of it pretty benign until we hit politics.

"I'll never fucking forgive him as long as I live and you tell him that," he said after learning I was based in Ottawa and had regular access to the politicians.

"Every time you guys printed his bullshit bring-home-the-troops crap, the Taliban would hit us harder. I'd like to see him and his wife bicycle into KC and see how long they last. Wonder then if the Taliban would want to talk to him."

He spoke about losing a friend to a roadside bomb and although he didn't name him I realized he was talking about Private Josh Klukie, who was killed at the end of September, as opposition to the war had turned into a full-blown political storm on Parliament Hill.

The idea that the Taliban would try to inflame the peace movement was hardly original. It was a strategy as old as war itself. What's less certain is whether there was a direct cause-and-effect going on in southern Afghanistan. In all my years of covering the war, I never came across a study that linked specific political events and statements in Canada to the timing of attacks in Kandahar. What I did notice was how the English-speaking Pakistani media paid particularly close attention to every burp coming out of Ottawa, especially the political debates about the Afghan deployment. As it was explained to me by a journalist friend in Islamabad, the Pakastanis were intensely interested in whether Canada had the stomach for the fight in Kandahar. As Canada went, they reasoned, so went NATO. It sounded like a benign version of the strongman talk I'd heard from the Taliban.

The only evidence of an actual connection, however, was the raw, blood-spattered gut instincts of the guys on the receiving end of the blows. The notion that they were fighting for democracy and freedom of expression chafed quickly with each bomb and near miss that fall. There was a veneer of skepticism that greeted those from Ottawa who'd stay for forty-eight hours, tour bases by helicopter, champion the "blood, guts and glory" line, and then go home to pronounce themselves experts in all things Kandahar.

"They don't know jack shit about this place," another soldier told me during the same trip. "If this is such a fucking great time, why aren't they here?"

At moments like that I just nodded and smiled. The guys I rode with that fall had spent so much time staring at the beast that any kind of empathy would have sounded stupid, and disagreeing or making excuses would have been ornery.

When the ramp dropped at Patrol Base Wilson, the sky showed only the first hint of dawn. Somewhere in the distance was the sound of gunfire, but the soldiers around us were deaf to it and behaved that way. As long as nobody was shooting at them, everything was cool. We tumbled out the back on to the oversized parkade of rocks and lugged our gear to the shelter of a Hesco bastion. A cold wind blew across the flat mud fields outside the base, leapt the walls and cut across the open spaces. The leeward side of the Hecso provided a bit of relief as we waited for somebody in Bravo Company to take charge of us. Eventually we got tired of waiting and presented ourselves at the company command post (CP), a flat, two-storey whitewash cement building in the centre of the camp. The company 2IC—second in command—was startled to see us, even though we'd been expected. The place was bursting at the seams with troops and they had no tents for us. They parked us in the CP's conference room, and we dragged our gear in amid warnings that there might not be any space for us at all.

The room was a tight, windowless burrow with folding chairs and a lived-in smell of sour sweat that seemed to ooze from the walls. A makeshift plywood table at one end contained chunks of mortars the Taliban routinely lobbed into the base. The broken-off bomb tails, for that was all that was left, were a happy reminder to all of how they had cheated death thus far. The door, with Pashto writing on it, looked as if it had been kicked one too many times. A huge floor-to-ceiling satellite photo of the area surrounding the base was taped to the wall with black electrician's tape, right next to whiteboards with sentry notices and other routine chores that needed delegating. I sat down, put my head on the conference table and promptly fell into an agitated half-sleep, the kind where you knew you really weren't unconscious, just idling in neutral.

Word spread around the camp pretty fast that a trio of journalists had come in with the last convoy and soon a parade of curious and bored guys started wandering past the door. They'd stop, glance at us the way people at the zoo regard animals, and then move on. Too tired to be social, the three of us were content to play monkeys, but soon some of the guys decided to see whether we bit. One by one, they trudged in and sat down.

A part of me was still upset that I'd been in Ottawa at the time of Operation Medusa, but as I came to realize, that was horribly naive. In fact, I didn't miss the biggest battle of the war at all. It was all around me in the pale, exhausted faces and war-wasted expressions of the guys who came through the door, and in others I met over the next few days. In faded, nicked and occasionally stained fatigues, they sat and poured out the horrors of the previous few months as though they were talking to their fathers or brothers. I'd assumed that, as strangers, we'd be kept at a distance, but that didn't seem to matter. They were way past giving a shit what others thought. They just wanted to talk to somebody, to anybody who would listen. It was heartbreaking, listening to the steady beat of anguish, to stories that you could only hear and never really understand or fully appreciate.

There was the convoy driver who'd been blown up thirteen times by either suicide car bombers or roadside bombs. The double layer of ballistic glass that protected him in his armoured patrol vehicle cracked under the weight of one bomb. Afterward, he stared at it and laughed. Home on leave, he found himself driving at Mach speed down Ontario's highways to avoid phantom bombers. He'd check constantly to make sure his rifle was at his feet. His companion would ask what he was looking for and he'd say, "Nothing." All the while he spoke to us, he shuffled a deck of cards. His hands moved in the quick, precise, deliberate motions of a skilled dealer, but he never broke eye contact. It must have been liberating for him to talk about how he'd dodged fate, but after a while, I couldn't look anymore. I just cast my eyes toward the table.

Some guys were in denial; the world was screwed up, not them. This often came out in jokes and off-colour references. Much later in the war, a friend lashed out at somebody who was annoying him: if they didn't shut up, he said, he'd shoot them in the face. He never understood why people back home were horrified.

It was that sort of detachment, that kind of dark humour that spilled all over the CP conference table that day. It continued with guys we met outside.

"I'm told on leave that I look different, act different," Private Jacob Williams said with a perplexed expression. "I can't explain it to you because I have no idea what they're talking about, [but] I'll give it to them. I've seen a lot of weird stuff. Some of the guys have done a lot of weird stuff. I'm sure it's changed us all—who knows what, for . . . better or worse."

He talked about the day a Taliban rocket-propelled grenade came close to ending his life. "I've never had a rocket fly past my head," he said with an uneasy chuckle. He was twenty-one years old, but in his flamed-out condition he looked more like mid-thirties.

"It was a couple of feet away. It was a pretty cool experience. You can hear the whiz, the crack going by you. I could almost feel the heat on it."

Such youth, such enthusiasm; I was almost sucked in to believing that he'd described the latest PlayStation shooter, but then his face went grim and it was almost as if we were in a dream conversation.

Kandahar was "a place of hell," Williams said.

Even though he hadn't been born when the Vietnam War finished, he said he felt as though he'd been there.

"I've seen the pictures."

At one point during the fall campaign, he'd gone fifty-two days without bathing.

Most of the guys smoked constantly, one cigarette after another after another. For those who didn't talk, everything was betrayed in the slight trembling of their hands. I'd never seen guys so exhausted, so wasted. A lot of them looked through you, not at you. Many were too tired to put on their flak vests inside the camp; too worn out to eat; too beat to shave; too whipped to shower. The only thing they had the strength to do was smoke.

Outside the CP, I watched some troops stretched out on the open ramp of their LAVs and would have sworn they were stroke victims. Orders for another patrol and the resulting shot of adrenaline invariably jolted them back to life, but even then it looked like they were stumbling through a bad dream. All of them were running on fumes and they knew it.

That kind of complacency worried Corporal Jordan Woodacre, especially when one foot either way could make the difference between living and dying.

"About two weeks ago, I walked past an anti-personnel mine, like within a foot," he said, holding up his hands to emphasize the distance.

"It's easy to let your guard down because you've seen the area over and over. The area of the mine was one I had walked countless times. These guys are sneaky and you've got to stay sharp."

While we were at Wilson a wave of relief troops from the 2 RCR were about to come in, and word had already passed among the vets that the new guys were under orders to wear their flaks inside the camp. Nobody was going to try and force the boys in Bravo to put their jackets on.

One soldier, who stood outside the CP with a precarious grip on his cigarette, talked about his tour as being "one big spin," a sort of mad kaleidoscope of firefights, seemingly endless stretches of boredom, rocket attacks, unbearable heat, patrols, sweat, food in plastic bags and more patrols. It was all blended together in a grey ooze of memory. He was glad to leave it behind and get back to the real world, whatever real was.

"Good luck to these guys," Corporal Alexander Darroch said of his replacements. "Hopefully they have a better go than we did. Hopefully they stay safe, know what I mean?"

There was a buffed, starched, pink-cheek quality to the replacements who rolled off the U.S. Chinooks over the next few days. They'd hump their gear away from the powerful rotor wash and burning smell of exhaust while the outgoing troops lined up, hooting and hollering with joy. It was when the new guys saw the survivors, those who weren't leaving right away, that the shock set in. They did their best to keep up the poker faces, but you could've written an entire feature piece on the amazement in their eyes. Not even the veterans of multiple peacekeeping tours were immune. They'd watch them depart with a mixture of compassion and dread, as if, in some screwed up way, they'd seen the future.

* * *

"If you want to help our school, just bring one big generator for this building," the Afghan kid said in almost perfect English. I was standing outside a 1960s vintage apartment building whose roof was bowed and partially collapsed. One half of the building was used as a school. They called it Syed Bacha school and it stood in the shadow of Kandahar Airfield.

The block of four buildings had been erected by the Americans almost half a century before, for the workers who'd built the airfield. An ugly mustard colour, three-storeys high and each with its own cement balconies and wire TV antennas, the buildings screamed suburbia. The Soviets had used them as barracks for officers during the occupation and added their own dour, communal touches. After the overthrow of the Taliban, Afghan army officers moved in with their families. Artillery shells and anti-tank rockets had torn huge gashes in each building and partially caved in the roofs on two. They were a structural engineer's worst nightmare, a quivering mass of brick and mortar with bits of concrete dangling on the threads of steel webbing. Yet people still lived there.

There was a big push in the post–Operation Medusa days for us to write about all of the good things happening around Kandahar. In fairness, there were often wonderful stories about heartwarming exchanges with Afghans or people who made a difference, and if you kept the story lens tightly focused that's what you'd see. That's all some wanted us to see. The problem was, no matter where you looked, the bigger picture was brutal, ugly and often infuriating. It was like listening to doctors bragging that they had stopped the bleeding in a long-dead patient.

The apartments, the families and the school in all its squalor had been there for years. The Canadian military started dropping school supplies to Syed Bacha weeks before we showed up. The kids had the routine down pat. They'd see the "deuce-and-a-half" (2.5-tonne truck) pull up in the muddy, garbage-strewn compound, wait for about five minutes and then swarm like angry locusts. The overwhelmed soldier in the back tried to keep order and hand everything out fairly, but the kids crawled over him to get to crates. Unlike the shy, nervous children you found in villages, these kids were savvy, spoke English and had a callousness that would have made street urchins elsewhere blush with amazement.

Seconds after getting out of one of the army's four-by-fours, I felt a tug on my backpack. I swung around to find a kid. He'd been busy. He'd already unzipped one of the pouches and was rifling through the contents, all while the pack was still on my shoulder. I couldn't help but be impressed. If you chatted with these kids, you'd gain a new appreciation for Herbert Spencer's survival of the fittest. Children can be cruel no matter where you go, but there was an unmerciful quality to the way the little ones here would get pounded by the bigger ones for pencils and erasers. They'd beat each other mindless over five-cent packages of lined, unmarked paper. I watched one little guy, with a distended shaved head, sit in a mud puddle and weep after losing one such battle. Ask them what they needed and you'd get a Toys "R" Us extravaganza. They were certainly poor, but they'd had enough exposure to the outside world, having lived elsewhere in the country or in Pakistan, to catch the consumer contagion. Some asked for laptops and cellphones. Others wanted music players. A jungle gym for the rubble-strewn playground was on someone's wish list. One of the bigger kids asked for a Universal weight set by name. Throughout the cacophony one child, who was slight, pale and somewhat Russian looking, kept his silence. His friends snickered, poked him in the back. Finally they shoved so hard that the boy stumbled into the centre of the circle. He was the most serious-looking child I'd ever seen, with dead, centuries-old eyes.

"Our big problem is just electricity," said the boy. His name was Kaleemulah and his friends egged him on in Farsi, the language of Kabul and northern Afghanistan.

"If we don't have electricity, then we don't have water because of the machine for the water.

"You go back and tell NATO that we don't need balls; we don't need swings; we don't need toys, we need water and electricity."

The school's exhausted, no-nonsense head master, Mohammed Isa, agreed, while trying desperately not to sound churlish or ungrateful for what little he'd received. The man looked like he was run off his feet keeping up with the herd of *enfant terrible*. They had only enough electricity for two hours a day, he said, and while the power was off so was the water, because the pump was electric. He didn't know where to begin with the structural problems in the building, or which shoddy electrical sockets had the potential to start a fire if portable heaters were plugged in. The wooden doorframes were rotted and no one had even considered what to do about the artillery-shredded roof, whose cascades of smashed concrete virtually cut the building in half. Taking a wrecking ball to the place would have been my vote, and that sense was only reinforced when I asked a French army engineer, who'd visited and was expected to write a report for NATO's southern Afghan command, about the absence of washrooms in the building.

"Is this place even safe?" I asked.

Captain Pierre Le Prado shrugged.

"If you think of it in European or Western standards, it's not," he said, "but they are used to living in such conditions. They carry on with [classes]."

"Tell them," Kaleemulah insisted. "Go back and tell them what we need."

* * *

The road to Zangabad is lined with graves—hundreds of them. Unable to scratch down into the hard-crust ground, the Afghans have taken to burying their dead in shallow indentations and piling rocks over them in mounds. Withered poles and petrified pieces of wood, some six metres high, are punched into the soil as grave markers. You can often tell the prevailing wind in the area by the direction some of them are bowed. Tattered pieces of white, green and black cloth—prayer flags of the martyred—are fixed to the poles. Occasionally you will catch glimpses of teal and red flags. The colours all have meaning. Khan told me green was meant to symbolize Islam, but I knew in other cultures the colours represented the elements, such as earth, fire, wind and sky. Prayer flags were also meant as symbols of peace, but as with many things in Afghanistan, they had been co-opted by the war.

Kandahar is sympathetic to the Taliban would often come to the graves of al-Qaeda fighters and other militants to pray for miracles. They did it at the Luw-vala cemetery, north of the city. Provincial councillors told me the same thing happened at the cemeteries between Ma'sum Ghar, Sperwan and Zangabad, which were connected by a ratline kind of road, a centuries-old indented trail no more than ten metres wide. The farther along you travelled, the more the road felt like one long graveyard. Many of the Taliban dead from Operation Medusa were buried in those cemeteries. As I and three other colleagues journeyed to Zangabad in the aftermath of the great battle, we witnessed hundreds upon hundreds of fresh graves. It was a breathtaking concentration of death and a mighty testament to the grinding efficiency of NATO's war machine. Some of the locals claimed the dead included hundreds of innocent civilians. That no hamlet was left untouched by the battle is without question, but since the Taliban drew recruits from outraged tribesman, the word "innocent" is elastic. There is no doubt, however, that people throughout that bucolic region saw themselves as victims: first of Karzai's political alienation and second of NATO bombs. The militants fed off of that, and what a banquet it was. The response of the international community was often hollow promises and an atrophied system of aid.

Before the offensive, NATO had warned people throughout Panjwaii and Zhari to get out of the way. The Pashmul area was of particular concern and aircraft dropped leaflets encouraging civilians to flee. Tens of thousands throughout that vast swath of farmland west of Kandahar heeded the call and within days whole villages were turned into ghost towns. The majority fled to the provincial capital, but I know of others who kept going all the way to Pakistan, where they had already spent a good chunk of their lives as refugees. Still others congregated in camps around the city. Some hardy souls, mostly tenant farmers unwilling to part with what meager possessions and land they had, elected to brave the storm.

The swirl of firefights that whipped around Zangabad were nowhere near as intense as what happened in the north, at Bazaar-e-Panjwaii and in Zhari. NATO had deployed a screen of special forces troops to catch militants who tried to flee to the border, and as fall passed into winter the number of short, sharp battles around the community increased. Early in 2007, NATO was confident enough to declare the area pacified and the provincial governor, Asadullah Khalid, made a big show of going to Zangabad to declare that refugees could return to their homes. It would be almost four years before another representative of the Karzai government dared show himself in the community, which was really a collection of nineteen tiny villages. The Taliban chose to draw their line of retreat at Zangabad and in the years following would turn the place into a redoubt whose name elicited groans from Canadian troops.

Eager to chronicle the return of refugees and desperate for a fresh perspective, I piled into an SUV with my colleagues, including Graeme Smith of the *Globe and Mail*, whom I'd met the previous spring. Compared to the rest of us Graeme was young, but the age difference had been eradicated by experience, especially in the interceding months. Graeme radiated a boyish charm and a roguishness you couldn't help but like. He always called you "sir," which made everyone around him feel older. It wasn't the rigid kind of "sir" you'd reserve for a principal, teacher or authority figure; it was the genuine, warm courtesy of good manners from a bygone era. The second time I ran into Graeme, he looked older and a little harder, not necessarily in body

but in the face. He'd survived a suicide bombing and the hell that had been
Operation Medusa. Much of his time was spent travelling unembedded in
Kandahar city, giving voice to the counter-narrative of this war. He had a deep
respect for the Afghans and took care in dressing like them and learning the
cultural nuances. It was remarkable to watch him during his six-to-eight-week
stints. He'd start out looking unremarkably Western, but the longer he stayed,
the more he evolved. The shalwar kameez came out, and even the cadence
of his speech changed. Whether talking on the cellphone or even to us, his
English sounded local, but without the accent. He bled for the Afghans and
understood their pain in a way the rest of us couldn't, or sometimes refused
to do. Although his dispatches likely did more than most to stoke the anti-war
sentiment back home, he agonized about the nightmare of bloodletting and
civil war that would rise in the aftermath of a Western withdrawal.

When we'd said we wanted to go to Zangabad, most of the fixers turned
us down. Only Jojo agreed. In fact, he was eager to make the drive and assured
us it was safe. We dressed as Afghans and, as further insurance, stopped at
the ANP command post in Bazaar-e-Panjwaii, where we paid the local commander for the protection of two officers, who followed us in a separate car.
Despite the blue sky and sunshine, it was terribly cold that day and we kept
the windows rolled up. A camel with a red knitted woolen blanket covering its humps grazed at the brown edge of one wasted field. A rope dangled
from its snout as though its owner had fled in a panic upon our approach. The
animal looked up only long enough to watch our mini-convoy pass. There
were very few signs of life, save for a group of people who held close to a
half-completed, domed mosque, which Jojo said had been used as a Taliban
command post during the great retreat after Medusa.

We stopped just outside of Zangabad where I marvelled at one of the
vast cemeteries. The road where we posed for pictures was scattered with
dead grape leaves blown over from nearby fields. Many of the compounds
had been bombed and were collapsed in on themselves. Others were pitted
with bullet fragments. It was a remarkable scene of desolation, made even
more stark by the backdrop of winter-scorched fields. A white Toyota minivan,
with an overburdened roof rack of household items, and two adults and at
least half a dozen children stuffed in the back, pulled up behind us. It was
a family going home after months in the city. They were anxious to know if
there was anything left of their home and said they had been promised tents
and food to get them through the readjustment.

"The government said they were going to help us, now we are going home," the man driving the van told us.

We arrived in Zangabad to find literally hundreds of men—young and old—huddled by the roadside with thin woolen blankets wrapped around their shoulders. We were an instant curiosity. Some of the kids, who noted our Afghan clothes, pointed and laughed. The older men sat on their haunches and looked up from underneath the brims of their turbans with a weary tolerance that made us apprehensive. A village elder, Abdul Hai, emerged from the cluster with a catalogue of complaints. Roughly 400 families had returned to the area, he said, mostly because of the promise of government relief. Some had waited by the roadside or in their bombed-out homes for days. He had initially mistaken us for Western aid workers, but the perception vanished when the TV camera came out.

"When are they going to help?" Hai asked. "What we're looking for are tents and food items."

The complaint was the same as we moved through the village. Some people had been back in their homes for two weeks with no sign of aid. We sat cross-legged on a rug in the front yard of a farmer's compound as he delivered his own stream of grievances.

"The Afghan army and foreign troops promised to help us so we could feed our families," said Mohammed Najeem as his sprawling extended family buzzed around us.

The Canadian government set aside $4.9 million in emergency food aid specifically to feed those displaced by the fighting, but the cash was handed over to the United Nations World Food Programme, which required villagers to trek as much as twenty kilometres to register with them. Many of the people in Zangabad had no transportation. As much as 4,400 tonnes of food sat in warehouses around Kandahar city, waiting to be delivered.

Afghan soldiers occupied the sector, their presence meant to discourage the Taliban from returning. They showed us the sum total of assistance the region had received: two sea containers full of reconstruction supplies. The giant cans had been delivered by the Canadian military within days of the announcement that the refugees could go home. The delivery was called a "CIMIC bomb"— CIMIC stood for civil-military co-operation—and was meant as a quick goodwill gesture. Later, a couple of us got a hold of the manifest. The containers were loaded with paint for mud-walled homes, lumber, light bulbs for a village free of electricity, seed and some cooking oil. The Afghans didn't quite know what to make of it. Neither did we.

A few weeks later I went with the military into Pasab, a village in Zhari district that had been ground to dust under the weight of the Medusa offensive. The complaint was the same.

"We need everything [because] we moved with our families to escape to the city, but the robbers, the thieves came into our house and stole everything," said a wheat farmer by the name of Ataullah, who like many Afghans went by only one name. "Now we need tents, food and water."

If the situation in the villages was uncomfortable, it was downright desperate in some of the refugee camps near the city. The Afghan government banned the distribution of food aid in those places during the early winter of 2007 as a way of starving people into going home. Some groups, including the European-based Senlis Council, defied the edict and quickly became harsh critics of the Canadian International Development Agency (CIDA). Graeme Smith and other journalists would join Senlis on its frequent visits to the camps, which would set off a frenzy as hungry Afghans clawed for a limited supply of packages. The group knew how to use the media and soon it delivered repeated siren-like warnings directly to Ottawa about Afghans starving in the desert. They were shrill and over the top, but that's exactly what was needed in the face of bureaucratic indifference. The previously unknown think-tank rocketed to superstar status among Opposition politicians, but was greeted with frost by the Conservative government and with outright derision among the diplomatic and development community, which hated having its feathers ruffled.

When I talked to development officers on the ground, they would often ask you to call Ottawa for official comment. When they did speak in the early days, it was a big deal. I vividly remember one young official sweating up a storm before the interview. The institutional message on aid and development was: You couldn't rush into a war zone and start throwing dollars or food around; corruption among local Afghans demanded accountability. However, a few brave souls did acknowledge that things needed to get done more quickly. They faced a lot of questions that first winter. When I asked about Zangabad and Pasab, the only thing CIDA representative Adrian Walraven could say was: "We're monitoring what's going on."

It wasn't the greatest of the war's contradictions, but it certainly instilled an unbelievable sense of shame. There were millions of dollars available and warehouses stuffed with food, but we were being asked to stand idly by as people went hungry. The diplomats, development workers and political spinners I dealt with were always full of an optimism that no amount of misery could undo. Whether they realized the Afghans could see through every contradiction and obfuscation was never apparent. In the end, it didn't matter. People in Kandahar had long been filled with a gnawing cynicism that good deeds alone could not erase.

Years later when I sat down with Peter MacKay, he said the great battles of 2006 convinced senior members of cabinet that the war the Liberals had signed up for—a short, sharp counterterrorism fight with some aid thrown in—had morphed into a protracted, bloody counter-insurgency. The rapid delivery of aid and development, even while bullets were flying, was key to winning over the population. Yet it would be almost two years before Ottawa embarked on a surge of civilian staff. MacKay acknowledged the "lag," but characterized it as due diligence.

During that time "there was a great deal of information gathering," he said. "They were there trying to get a sense of what projects would have a quick impact. What do the people need? And this is a classic Canadian approach; consultation, showing compassion for the local needs as opposed to going in and saying these are things we're going to do for you."

It was a ponderous, glacial exercise that spoke volumes about how ill-prepared the country's civilian agencies were for their role in the war. Around meeting tables in Ottawa, diplomats, officials and mandarins demanded to be included in decisions and bristled at how the military sucked the oxygen out of the room, yet in all of the people I spoke with and interviewed I never felt a vibe of urgency or the sense that what was unfolding in Kandahar was anything more than a bureaucratic exercise.

In fairness, part of the problem was that there weren't enough diplomats and aid workers on the ground. And those who were there found themselves restricted to the fortified compounds of the provincial reconstruction base and KAF. Getting out to meet locals, arrange projects and generally do their jobs was an arduous affair made cumbersome by the heavy hand of the federal bureaucracy. An ugly, dark humour arose in those days when helicopter space was taken up by civilian staff. Soldiers joked how their lives were considered less valuable because they still travelled by ground, with all of the threats that entailed. It wasn't as if the diplomats were deaf to the wisecracks. I remember one senior official who referred to Ottawa's attitude as "The Nanny Factor."

The reluctance to expose staff to the hazards of the mean streets of Kandahar was the direct result of the assassination of Glyn Berry in January 2006. Ottawa wasn't prepared to lose any other attachés and brought everyone home in spring of 2006 while it figured out what to do. And finding anybody in either Foreign Affairs or international development to volunteer for a Kandahar posting was a nightmare. It took almost until the spring of 2008 for the institutional panic to subside.

"In a perfect world, of course, I'd love to be out there on a bicycle, walking down a street, talking to people in the market," Gavin Buchan, the diplomat who replaced Berry, said at the time.

"That is how the most effective diplomacy gets conducted. But you can't do that in the current environment. That's simply the reality. We work as effectively as we can given the security constraints."

For the two most critical years of the war in southern Afghanistan, the Canadian military was largely on its own and restricted in how much cash it could spend to tame the insurgency.

In relatively peaceful eastern Afghanistan, on the other hand, U.S. commanders were flush. They had access to a huge pot of money called the Commander's Emergency Response Program (CERP). Tens of millions of dollars were at their fingertips to build bridges, repair roads and buy goodwill. The poor Canadian cousins started the war with something called the Commander's Contingency Fund, roughly $1.3 million in pocket change. And the political hand-wringing that went on when the fund was doubled was enough to make you weep. It was like reluctant parents giving their teenager a bigger allowance.

Throughout that time and beyond, a huge academic debate raged about the appropriateness of the military delivering aid. The development community, both in Afghanistan and elsewhere, screamed blue, bloody murder at the thought. Food, blankets and immediate relief coming from the hands of soldiers tainted the process, a UN staffer told me once. Such staples needed to come from neutral hands, from people with no stake in the conflict. The staffer described it as the militarization of aid, which endangered development workers. Yet these very same people would declare regions unsafe and not only refuse to help, but also kick up a fuss if the army lifted a finger for those in need. The hypocrisy blew your mind.

The other part of the problem was that nobody—neither the military nor the diplomats—knew at the beginning who they were fighting in Panjwaii and Zhari.

"We had no clue," a senior intelligence officer, who was still serving, told me near the end of the war. Over a number of years, I interviewed nearly a dozen current and former spooks, both civilian and military. All were required to speak off the record, but the story was the same.

The nexus between tribal rivalries, the burgeoning illegal drug trade and the conservative Islamist leanings of most people in southern Afghanistan was only vaguely understood.

"Intelligence was very weak back then, very weak. The intelligence effort was under-resourced."

The military intelligence effort in 2006 was almost exclusively geared toward the counterterrorism—finding bad guys and whacking them. There was a small stable of intelligence officers at Kandahar Airfield. Despite that, the NATO establishment missed the initial Taliban buildup west of the city. There was modest civilian effort in the form of Canadian Security Intelligence Service (CSIS) spies, but they took their cue from the army and often worked with the ultra-secret Joint Task Force Two (JTF2) commandos. There were no analysts to decipher the tribal and political dynamics. In fact, the provincial reconstruction base in 2006 had only one soldier—a reservist corporal— dedicated to putting those pieces of the puzzle together.

"It was a lack of resources, a lack of prioritization, a lack of will," a former intelligence officer said. "Nobody asked big questions or looked at the big picture."

And yet, when they were presented with an opportunity to understand what was unfolding before their eyes, nobody seemed to want to listen. Talatbek Masadykov was head of the Kandahar office of the United Nations Assistance Mission in Afghanistan. He was an extremely bright man who'd been in the country since the 1980s and had even completed a doctorate on Pashto literature. Masadykov tried on a couple of occasions to offer an assessment: NATO was up against not only a hardline Islamist insurgency but also a drug war between rival tribes.

"They didn't want to talk to someone like Talatbek," said the still-serving intelligence officer. "They found him too negative. So they just shut him out."

* * *

One day in the early winter of 2007, my CTV colleagues and I sat with a group of soldiers at one of the fortified strongpoints that overlooked Route Summit. The guys were veterans of Medusa, but still fascinated and a little horrified by our tales of travelling without them into Kandahar city and places like Zangabad. Some looked at us as though we were insane.

"Do you guys carry guns? Are any of your fixers armed?"

Nope.

"That's fucked, man. You guys are fucked in the head. I'd never step outside the wire in this shit-hole country without a weapon."

One soldier, who sat hunched over a tan-coloured plastic ration bag, looked up and asked a question so innocent, so unexpected that it momentarily rendered me speechless.

"So, what do they think of us? What do the Afghans *really* think of us being here?"

This was a guy who'd earned his cynicism the hard way, yet he was earnest in his bewilderment. Even though he'd walked among the villagers and probably chatted with them through interpreters, he had no real sense of who they were. It wasn't like I had any particular insight; the Afghans were often just as stone-faced and enigmatic with us as they were with the military.

"They say they're happy," I told him, hoping it would be enough of an answer.

"Yeah? Then why do they keep shooting at us?"

I often think about all the unsavoury characters I ran across in Kandahar. Even some of the self-proclaimed do-gooders had a taint, an unmistakable whiff of corruption that made the hair on the back of your neck stand up. Most of them were harmless. Many were hapless; just desperate people trying to hustle a few bucks. They possessed none of the smooth, calculated grease or schmooze you'd see back home. There was no finesse or subtlety. It was in your face and you learned to expect it and deal with it.

"Everything has a cost in Afghanistan, even good deeds," a senior military officer joked one day.

A colleague of mine, Alex Panetta, one of the most gifted writers and political reporters I know, once remarked that he loved Kandahar because it was an entrepreneurial heaven. Everybody was trying to sell something to somebody. He found exhilaration and hope amid the racket. At times, it was hard not to agree with his enthusiasm, but the line between good-hearted free marketing and larceny was crossed swiftly and unmercifully in such a place. Altruism was spoken about, but often it was nothing more than an echo that bounced off walls and never settled on any particular deed or event. There were exceptions, naturally, but most dealings with Afghans inevitably came down to the bottom line.

The only arguments I had with Khan were over money. That's not to say he was unsavoury. He could be grasping, covetous and had a tendency to inflate prices, but he was generally harmless. The more I got to know him early in 2007, the more I realized he could be a hustler in fancy linen. All of the fixers were the same, though. They treated westerners as flesh-coloured ATMs. Jojo was perhaps the most notorious. He always had some scheme at play. One venture saw him wanting to import armoured SUVs from Dubai to rent out to the media for unembedded travel. Another time he invested money belonging to a local drug lord in a Nigerian Internet pyramid scheme. He lost tens of thousands of dollars. The only thing that saved his skin was the fact that he earned a huge living, by Afghan standards, and could repay the debt.

On one occasion, while trying to trace people who'd been tortured by the Afghan intelligence service, I was linked up with a shadowy pair of men who passed themselves off as researchers. They met with me on the mistaken assumption that I represented human rights groups in Canada and the U.S. that had allegedly contracted them to find and document the cases of abuse victims. The meeting, in the dim back room of a Kandahar guest house, was only a few minutes old when they demanded U.S. $40,000 in cash and claimed to have made an agreement, through an intermediary, with someone named Paul—or maybe it was Peter. The research was already underway; they had incurred expenses and were determined to extract some kind of payment before the day was out. Khan, who had reluctantly driven me to the meeting, exploded in a stream of Pashtu admonishment. The wretched . pair immediately lost interest when they realized we were journalists with no connections to the cash cow they sought. The victims, if they knew of any, were commodities; their misery and indignity were to be bought and sold like so many cases of soda pop in the nearby market.

I confess my stream of sanctimony has its limits. If the truth is to be told, everyone fed off guys like that. The army, civilian staff, the media—we were all so desperate to find out what was going, so eager to solve the riddles of the place and so sure in our condescension that we encouraged their behaviour. We paid because it was easy. The longer I stayed in Afghanistan, the more I realized that everything had its price because we were willing to buy—or willing to tolerate those who did. It was the free market gone utterly mad, capitalism without limits, business with an AK-47 as the calling card.

Even with this degree of hustle, there were those who would stop you cold, the ones you knew were dangerous just by the vibe in the room. Asadullah Khalid, the notorious governor of Kandahar early in the war, was one such character. He was smooth, charming and somewhat oily, but he gave you the sense that a lot went unsaid. He spoke, at times, with an awful urgency, especially when the topic was the Taliban. You left thinking that a powder keg lurked somewhere just below the surface, that he had the ability to reach out and kill someone just with the touch of his finger.

Canadians knew very little about Khalid when they moved into Kandahar in late 2005 and early 2006. The Americans liked him, so naturally we did too. He was a zealot when it came to fighting the Taliban, and he wasn't afraid to get his hands dirty by picking up a gun. His hatred of the Taliban came honestly and went back to his days as a political science student in Kabul when the hardline Islamists swept through almost the entire country. Khalid fled the capital and eventually became close with some of the key figures in the Northern Alliance. As soon as Hamid Karzai came to power, the university dropout was appointed governor of Ghazni province in the central southeast portion of the country.

By the time Khalid arrived in Kandahar in 2005 he'd gained a reputation for brutality, but he was also fanatically loyal to Karzai. He replaced Gul Agha Sherzai, a hardened mujahideen commander who captured Kandahar city from the Taliban in 2001, but whose influence the president sought to limit. It wasn't long before the streets of the city buzzed with rumours about Khalid's militia, which he'd brought with him from Ghazni. The group of thugs became known as Brigade 888 and were notorious for shooting first and not asking questions later. Gossip spread about how the governor fancied himself a lady's man and allegedly had his mistress, a French aid worker, murdered in 2003 when she reportedly let slip about their affair. Separating fact from fiction in Afghanistan was a monumental task. The rumour lingered even though the Taliban publicly claimed for her killing. Two assailants were captured within minutes of the woman's shooting and tried in an Afghan court. Supporters of Khalid, including his most powerful patron, the president's half-brother Ahmed Wali Karzai, blamed the character assassination on Sherzai's defenders. Yet the governor never did much to scrub away his sleazy image. Later in the war, when Canada appointed an artful, pleasant-looking young woman to head its civilian mission in Kandahar, Khalid would confide to provincial councillors and even interpreters the kind of things he wanted to do alone with her.

Despite his insolence, Khalid was at first rewarded with unqualified Canadian support. Both the British and Dutch, when they moved into southern Afghanistan, asked for the governors in their respective provinces to be replaced. They got their wish. According to secret diplomatic cables I viewed later in the war, Karzai asked Canada in July 2006 if it wanted a change in provincial leadership. Brigadier-General David Fraser declined. It was a fateful decision.

"Karzai quite liked us back then because we asked him for so little," a senior Canadian diplomat in Kabul told me in 2009. "We just sort of trudged along in a sort of myopic kind of way without looking at the big picture."

Records obtained under access to information laws show that the military considered Khalid a governance work-in-progress, something Fraser later confirmed when he said that by the end of his stint as NATO's southern commander, the governor was more inclined to "pick up the phone rather than a gun" to solve his problems. It wasn't as if Fraser was insensible to what was going on, but the consensus among the military and even the diplomats, who grew evermore alarmed, seemed to be that Kandahar was safer with the devil they knew.

It was late 2006 when the Conservative government sat up and took notice of Asadullah Khalid. Chilling reports circulated within the human rights community that the governor operated a series of "black sites," secret detention facilities not open to the inspection of the International Red Cross. In early December, the mounting pile of allegations, rumours and frustrations were put on the table for a meeting involving the prime minister's national security advisor, Margaret Bloodworth, as well as senior bureaucrats and military officers. Once again, the consensus was to let sleeping dogs lie. There had been no verified reports.

"There was no policy for dealing with something like this, something sensitive," said one senior government source. "Nobody quite knew what to do."

* * *

The winter of 2007 was miserable in Kandahar. It rained an awful lot and the only thing more miserable than Afghanistan in the piercing sunshine at 55°C was Afghanistan in a grey, cold, bruising rain at 5°C. Our tents flooded and the roads turned to chocolate pudding. Vehicles skidded as though on cooking sheets of grease. Boots got sucked down into the mud and ripped off your feet if you ventured more than twenty metres outside a strongpoint.

The cold had a tendency to keep everybody on edge, more so than the hard summer heat. In July you're too exhausted to be pissed off about anything. Those from a northern climate have genetic expectation that cold somehow means fresh, but Kandahar still smelled like a sewer.

It was in February 2007 that an extraordinary meeting took place. At the table were a senior Afghan government official, Khalid, a collection of diplomats, and the senior officer in charge of civilian police mentoring, RCMP superintendent Dave Fudge.

One of the first items on the agenda was an update on the year-old investigation into the assassination of diplomat Glyn Berry. The main suspect in the case, Pir Mohammed, had been released from custody after the intervention of tribal elders. The case had gone cold.

Despite that, Fudge said he was pleased with Kandahar's police chief, Esmatullah Alizai, who was in "Canada's view doing a good job," said a classified summary of the meeting I uncovered later in the war.

The chief had recently sacked two corrupt district governors and arrested crooked cops whose territory overlapped with Highway 4, the main north-south all-weather road that connected Kandahar city with Quetta, Pakistan. It also happened to be the main transport and smuggling route out of the province. Khalid excused himself from the meeting and the Afghan government official listened patiently. When it was his turn, the official spoke softly, but his words landed like a bolt of lightning. Both Hamid Karzai and one of his senior ministers had called that very morning to demand Alizai be removed. The official pointed to the empty chair where Khalid had sat.

"This man wants him fired."

The district officials whom the police chief had taken down were involved in the drug trade, Fudge said.

"This man is involved in drugs," said the official, who again pointed at the empty chair. "All drug dealers like him."

There was an uncomfortable silence. By virtue of doing his job, Alizai had made himself a marked man and the realization hung heavy in the room. Fudge noted that if the chief didn't go, he'd likely be assassinated.

"This man will kill him," said the Afghan official, motioning once more toward the empty chair.

He appealed to the Canadians. He said he would try to protect Alizai, but confessed there was "no system." What was needed was political support and intervention directly with the president.

"I am here alone," the official lamented.

For years to come, historians will debate the moment when the light bulb went on; the moment we realized what we were up against in Kandahar; the time, some would suggest, when we should have run screaming from the room; or the time when we should have gotten tough. If I had a vote, I would say it was this moment, which only came to light in classified Foreign Affairs reports I read later in the war.

Who knows? Maybe it was all over for us in Kandahar before the first tents went up at the PRT base in 2005. We could fight all we wanted and batter the Taliban into a bloody stupor; we could shower the place with cash and build, build and keep building; we could write reports and press releases about all of the good deeds—and there were many. Yet for all of the talk, for all of the good intentions, one simple, cold reality set in that winter day: Yes, we could win the war, but what about the peace?

"Without changes in governance" in Kandahar, said the official, "it will be very hard to control society."

We need a "clean, professional administration" that can "fill the gap between the government and the nation."

A summary of the meeting was sent up the line to Ottawa, but qualified by the notation that nothing said at the meeting was "shocking" to those on the ground. The report tried to paint a balanced picture, but the inevitable question was asked: If the governor had to go, who would replace him?

"In Asadullah's favour, it can be said that some other individual might be worse; that Khalid is responsive to international [including Canadian] requests/pressure; and that he is loyal, and energetic in fighting the Taliban," the summary read.

"Discredited with the population, not respected by tribal elders, corrupt and dissolute, dangerous and self-serving, Asadullah discredits us through association, undermining our efforts to build public support for the Karzai government and NATO's presence in the south."

Two months later, the situation took on a new urgency when a prisoner handed over to Afghan authorities by the Canadian army alleged Khalid had personally tortured him in a detention facility next to the governor's palace. The report, by the political director of the provincial reconstruction base, was sent up the line on April 25, 2007, right at the height of the prisoner abuse scandal.

The detainee "claimed to have been beaten and electrocuted by the governor himself," Gavin Buchan wrote in a memo distributed widely within the Canadian government and NATO.

Around the same time, we started to hear reports bubbling up from the street that Khalid was selling government jobs. For a bribe of U.S. $150,000 some lucky candidate could become a police chief or a district head. Appointees who refused to pay the "tax" were tossed in jail. Even prisoners captured by coalition forces were turned into a source of income. There is a long tradition in Afghan justice of buying your way to freedom and it was said Khalid took a cut of the payment. Those who were reluctant to cough up, either too poor or maybe relying on the fresh Western ideals of fairness and rule of law, were slapped around until they came up with the cash. There were other schemes too. Cash coming from the government in Kabul was siphoned off, as were compensation payments for families bombed out of their homes. All imported and exported goods, including illegal narcotics, became the target of a 20 per cent "shadow tax." Khalid and Colonel Raziq, the border police commander, allegedly made millions. So did others around them. The machinery of government in Kandahar became one giant, churning cash machine that seemed to have no off button. It sickened and angered ordinary people—labourers, tailors, street vendors—many of whom existed on one dollar a day. Even the so-called middle class—the doctors, police officers and government officials who earned U.S. $50 per month—watched with a seething anger as grand houses, many shaped like wedding cakes, were erected behind high walls and armed guards.

"Afghans are not stupid," one provincial councillor told me at the time. "We have eyes. We have ears."

Khan would make snide remarks to Khalid's face during news conferences at the governor's palace. He would tuck them into the preamble of his questions and smile as he spoke. He never got over Khalid robbing the victims of the Tulakan bombings of their land compensation and took every opportunity to verbally stick the knife into the governor. It was so bad sometimes I winced.

"Are you trying to get us killed?" I asked him one day.

"Everything is perfectly all right, sir. He is not scared of the Canadians and he is not scared of us. The day he becomes scared is the day we should hide ourselves."

"When is that day?"

Khan smiled. "I will let you know, sir, if I am not already dead."

My colleague Stephanie Levitz had more guts than the rest of us. She directly confronted Khalid about the prison-torture allegations. It was about a year after the government first received warnings and the scandal over detainee treatment burned red hot, so hot that most were content to lie low and let the secret history of Kandahar stay secret. Not Stephanie. She had a tough-as-nails quality that hid itself behind a mane of brown hair and a serene, blue-eyed expression. There were times I was convinced that what Stephanie saw in the streets of Kandahar haunted her and that gave her the courage to lob the tough question. She was probably the perfect person to ask and get away with it, not only because she was a woman, but because she had the gift of timing and the ability to surprise you.

"I'm the governor of Kandahar, I am not an investigator," Khalid snarled at her.

He claimed never to have visited a prison, except in the company of Canadian diplomats, and said he wouldn't have been in the room with a detainee.

"Never, never, never," he said, and then added that some people in prison will say anything to get their freedom. "I think this is clear for everyone that if you have some prisoner in the jail they will accuse everyone."

But there were too many whispers to ignore. An Afghan, serving with the Canadians, once told me of a picture booklet Khalid kept in the armrest of his armoured SUV. It was the cheap, plastic kind, the ones most of us use to show our friends snaps of the vacation or the kids. In his, however, the governor kept photos of dead Taliban in all states of bloody disrepair. Whether he killed them himself or not didn't seem to matter. They were his enemies. They were trophies, part of the bragging rights in his vicious, deeply personal war. He would take them out, not to share with anyone, but rather to thumb through when he was bored. Some of the photos were apparently of Mullah Dadullah, the Taliban's notorious, one-legged military commander who was killed in 2007. Khalid paraded his body before the Kandahar media to prove to the world that the bloodthirsty commander, who'd pioneered suicide bombing as a strategy, was really dead. It was an act that so outraged the Quetta shura that the insurgents launched a deadly wave of bombings to punish the city.

It was around the same time that staff working for the Afghanistan Independent Human Rights Commission uncovered the fact Khalid maintained a private jail, a so-called black site. There had been rumours of such a chamber in the basement of the governor's palace. Now, however, the agency documented how Khalid showed up one day at Sarpoza Prison and demanded custody of five Taliban prisoners. A doctor and the staff at a local health centre had been captured by insurgents and threatened with death. Khalid wanted the men as bargaining chips and he got them. He made it known that if the hostages were harmed in any way he'd kill—in the most brutal way possible—each of the captured Taliban. The threat worked. What happened to the prisoners was anybody's guess.

By the summer of 2007, Khalid was entrenched as an institution and the warnings going to Ottawa had taken on the quality of a broken record—the grainy, scratchy kind that just kept playing over and over.

The governor had "lost the support of even pro-government tribal leaders," said Richard Colvin in a July 17, 2007, memo I saw later in the war. He "has no genuine interest in governance or security in Kandahar but cares only about his own advancement."

Even Canadian military officers, some of whom had been quick to make excuses for Khalid in private, grew impatient and frustrated. The governor was spending more and more time out of the country attending to "business matters," according to access to information documents. Campaign assessments prepared for commanders noted that major decisions were held up and district leaders were left with very little guidance. It pissed off the soldiers and they had no qualms about putting it on paper.

So much dirt built up that it was hard to contain. Journalists in Kandahar were warned off pursuing stories about Khalid with dark tales of people who'd been skinned alive in his cells. Whether it was true or not, nobody ever knew, but the caution was repeated often enough to leave a layer of frost over the mention of the governor's name. Most of the warnings my colleagues and I received came not from Afghans but from Canadian officers, including some army spooks. That just fed the paranoia every time we stepped outside the wire on our own.

When Maxime Bernier, the beefcake who replaced Peter MacKay at Foreign Affairs, blurted out in the spring of 2008 that Canada wanted Khalid replaced, he opened the door just enough for some of the filth to slide out. Colleagues who were in Kandahar at the time told me you could almost hear the relieved sighs from those who felt they could now legitimately pursue the governor. But it was way, way too late. And the political feeding frenzy that followed missed the point. It focused on Bernier speaking out of turn and embarrassing the Afghans rather than on the more serious questions of what the government knew about Khalid and when.

It wasn't until very late in the war when the most senior civil servant in charge of the file was called to account. I remember sitting under the bright lights and high ceilings of a House of Commons committee room and listening to David Mulroney, the former deputy minister of the government's Afghanistan task force, answer questions.

He acknowledged claims that the governor tortured prisoners were "widespread in Afghanistan."

By that time, Khalid was long gone, appointed minister of tribal affairs in Karzai's government. Nobody cared anymore. The war had passed along. He rated only a few questions. Mulroney himself had moved on from managing the civilian side of the commitment to become ambassador to China. Most MPs who heard his testimony that day just shrugged and carried on with their prepared set of questions or bombastic rants.

The federal government had asked the provincial reconstruction base to investigate the allegations against Khalid, including the rumoured torture chamber in the basement of the governor's palace.

"We could not find any evidence that we could bring to the Afghan government about this," said Mulroney. "We visited his residence, we didn't see any facility. We spoke to people at a very high level in Kabul to express our concerns, but we never had any item that we could specifically point to."

It all sounded so clinical and academic when you sat in Parliament's stiff-backed, green leather chairs and rested your elbows on the paper-scattered, polished wooden tables. The temperature of the room barely lifted when considering the thousands of people who'd been ground under for lack of "hard" evidence. It was as though we weren't even talking about real people, who bruised and bled, but rather some vague abstraction. And Khalid? He was some kind of comic book villain. Somehow, there had been a common failure of imagination and empathy, made worse by the poisoned politics that surrounded everything Afghanistan in Ottawa.

What was widely known in those early days, but not easily recognized or appreciated, was that the country had no policy in Kandahar on a wide range of issues, even critical ones like a brutal governor who was often out of control.

"We were completely passive," a senior diplomat in Kabul later told me. "This helped our relationship with Karzai because we never asked him for anything, but then we just kind of sat back and let things unfold, which was kind of an irresponsible attitude when things are going downhill. We were just sort of watching the thing deteriorate."

* * *

It was early February 2007, around the time of the fateful meeting over Khalid, when military columnist Scott Taylor rolled through Kandahar Airfield. We stood outside the media tents on a bright sunny day. Dressed in a light blue shalwar kameez and a grey vest, he looked tired after being on the road with the Senlis Council. They'd gone to Arghandab, the lush fruit-growing region north of the provincial capital, to visit police chief Abdul Hakim Jan. Karzai had only recently appointed the former warlord to the post. He was notorious, and Taylor, a blunt-talking, hard-charging former soldier, urged me to check him out.

"You won't believe it, man. The warlords are back and Commander Blue [Jan's nickname] is one of the biggest," he said.

As Scott later reported, Jan was loathed and feared by the people of Arghandab. He controlled the police and a local water supply, the latter through a series of underground wells on his property. Over the years, he'd fought the Soviets and the Afghan communists, and was one of the warlords the Taliban rebelled against. Driven into exile with the Northern Alliance, Jan returned with the fall of the Taliban and set up an opulent, exotic menagerie at his compound. NATO liked him because of his zeal in fighting the Taliban. The overlord of the area, the largely respected ex-mujahideen commander Mullah Naqib, had made it clear to insurgent leaders that he wanted them to steer clear of the prosperous area and for the most part they obeyed. That left Jan free to prey on the local population. He amassed an even greater plunder than before the Taliban rule and strolled around the region carrying an AK-47 with a gold-plated stock. I met Jan only once, briefly, on the grounds of the governor's palace. Jojo introduced me and the name didn't register. It only clicked when he smiled and I saw the gold-plated front teeth Scott had mentioned. He was an imposing figure and better groomed than most Afghans I'd known up until then. You knew he carried some kind of heavy authority by the way his entourage jumped when he spoke and were so eager to show their devotion. When Jan and his group took their leave, Jojo looked at me.

"He is a very important man that you don't want to make angry," he said.

The warlords were cropping up all over the place, or so it seemed during that time. Outside of the PRT base, there were shabby-looking guys with the AK-47s. The first couple of times I spotted them, they kept a respectful distance and in my innocence I thought that maybe they were Taliban. Eventually, it became evident they were part of the security screen. It would be years before I was able to confirm the men belonged to a Kandahar warlord by the name of Haji Toorjan, who'd been contracted to provide extra security around the base. It smelled like a protection racket and cost taxpayers at least CDN $2.5 million throughout the war.

* * *

Mullah Abdul Salam Rocketi plopped himself down in the chair with an expressionless stare. It was hard to know what he was thinking. He was a member of the Afghan Parliament representing Zabul, the province next door to Kandahar. He was advertised as a former Taliban commander who knew the whereabouts of Stinger missiles left over from the anti-Soviet jihad. During those years, Kandahar was awash in rumours that the Taliban had the ability to shoot down U.S. helicopters and coalition aircraft. Jojo had promised me for months that he would land that story. Within the first few minutes of the interview, however, it became clear that Rocketi knew nothing current. I lost interest and politely sipped tea as he talked about how he had held on to some Stingers from his days of fighting the Russians, but the Pakistanis had confiscated them.

"I made them pay," he said through Jojo. He never explained how, but I read later that he kidnapped a local official and several Pakistani soldiers.

The more I listened, the weaker his Taliban credentials seemed. He'd fought for them in 2001 against the U.S. invasion, but surrendered to the Americans in his home province within weeks. He joined the democratic system and was elected to Parliament in 2005.

Like most Afghans, he was disillusioned. Like most Afghans, he'd played both sides and had now come to regret his surrender.

"The government is weak and corrupt," he said. "Things do not get better and the people blame the foreigners for supporting this government. Soon the foreigners will see how angry they are."

There was no ring of doom in his voice, but he looked stern and convinced of his own wisdom.

I closed my notebook, thanked him and left with Jojo. The notes and quotes were stuffed into my backpack and almost immediately forgotten—just one more bellyaching opposition politician who didn't have the story I wanted that day. I should have listened more closely.

What struck me on the ride home, in the late winter afternoon sunshine, was the number of guns on the street. We passed a guest house where guards armed with AK-47s walked the pavement. There were government buildings with armed men outside. Even one of the bigger mosques had a Kalashnikov-touting man on the sidewalk. Even God, it seemed, needed protection here.

Worst Days 12

Gordon O'Connor snores. I'm not sure if the former defence minister snores all the time, but he sure did the night we flew to Riga, Latvia, in November 2006, for the NATO leaders' summit. He was plopped in the back of the prime minister's Airbus among PMO staff and the media. General Rick Hillier, the chief of defence staff, would later join us. O'Connor sat across from me in the middle row of seats, where he was able to stretch out for the red-eye jaunt. I think we exchanged fewer than half a dozen words during the seven-hour flight, which was delayed at the start because he and the prime minister had taken part in the quasi-historic vote on the motion that recognized Quebec as a nation within Canada. The politicians and officials were pretty chuffed when they hit the tarmac.

O'Connor, the former brigadier-general described within the Forces as a frosty Cold Warrior, rarely talked with journalists on a social basis. Contrary to his grumpy public persona, I always found him pleasant and astute in interviews. A military man to the core, he always struck me as politically tone deaf, which is the kiss of death in Ottawa and was pretty much his undoing. Yet what he lacked in political finesse, he made up with a deep understanding of the military and the byzantine defence bureaucracy.

A lot happened under Gordon O'Connor's watch, stuff that never made the headlines. Grievances that mattered to a great many old soldiers, some dating back to the Second World War, were quietly and respectfully settled. Still, he made a lot of enemies and frustrated a lot of people, including Hillier.

"Gordon seemed to forget he was no longer in uniform," one senior officer confided during that time.

Rumours that the two of them hated one another were legion and whenever they appeared together at events the media would pay special attention to how they interacted. O'Connor had been Hillier's brigade commander in Germany.

"I have no idea what Gordon O'Connor did to Rick Hillier in Germany, but it must have been bad," a Tory spin doctor moaned at the height of a public disagreement between the two over Afghan army training.

Hillier, after he retired, denied there was a rift, but conceded their partnership, although fruitful in terms of delivering equipment to the Forces, had been strained. What angered Hillier the most was O'Connor's habit of going around him and seeking advice on policy from subordinates. Whether it was an intentional slap or hapless due diligence was never clear. The more the tension between them spilled over in public, the more those around O'Connor lashed out against Hillier in private. I recall one long, wine-fuelled lunch with a Conservative staffer, who was not in O'Connor's office in those days but still a defender of the minister. If the Liberals wanted to hang Hillier out to dry for convincing Paul Martin to go to Kandahar, the Conservatives wanted to lynch him for not staying on message. The bad blood had started with the military's refusal to provide Taliban body counts, and Hillier's personal veto on closing ramp ceremonies to the media only escalated things.

No wonder it was a quiet flight.

The NATO summit was a quasi-annual event that hadn't meant much in the Canadian context, at least since the fall of the Berlin Wall. The possible exception was during the Kosovo crisis and the bombing campaign against the Serbs. Even during the early years of Afghanistan, the summits retained a sleepwalking quality. I attended one in Brussels in 2005, where the story that made the biggest splash was *The Economist* magazine hanging the label "Mr. Dithers" on Prime Minister Paul Martin. The real news that time around was that Ottawa had decided not to participate in the Bush administration's ballistic missile defence, but that had been cooked up before we even left Canada. Riga was to be NATO's first honest-to-goodness wartime summit.

The war—as wars have a tendency to do—was not going according to plan. The Taliban had not been lying down and playing dead, nor had they bowed to NATO's superior weapons, which laid waste to entire insurgent cells in the blink of an eye.

There was a sense of naive optimism on the part of the Canadian delegation going into the summit. Even though other nations had publicly rejected the notion of sending more troops, there remained a stubborn flicker of hope that NATO would recognize the blood being spilled in southern Afghanistan and find some way to deliver reinforcements. The alliance was, after all, founded on the notion of one for all and all for one. It had a standing army—among twenty-six countries at that time—of nearly two million men and women. In theory, it could have flooded Kandahar, Helmand, Uruzgan and Zabul provinces with troops. It was just a theory, though. Many nations had entered Afghanistan—NATO's first out-of-Europe combat mission—with caveats and qualifications on their armies' use. The Germans, for example, couldn't go out after dark. They had to be rolled up tight and tucked into their forward bases by sunset, making them effectively useless as a combat force. The Spanish and Italians had similar restrictions. Even the Dutch, who'd agreed to come south, made their forces on patrol ask permission of local Afghans before entering villages. Their iron-fist-in-a-velvet-glove approach irked the Americans, who like the Canadians saw the mission more in terms of whacking a few bad guys than in being nice to the people. Being nice came much later in the war, when people were so pissed off it almost didn't matter any more. I heard more than one U.S. soldier refer to the Dutch as "wooden shoes; wouldn't shoot." Getting countries to remove the shackles on existing forces, increasing the overall troop commitment and delivering more helicopters—tactical lift in military-speak—was the intent at Riga.

Peter MacKay worked the phones from Foreign Affairs ahead of the summit.

"We had discussions most notably with the Americans and the Brits," MacKay recalled in a 2010 interview.

The long-distance Anglo–American huddle resulted in an unusual behind-the-scenes shaming. It was nothing to hear the Americans complain about allies, but when mild-mannered Canada started to grouse it was an event not to be missed. Lieutenant-Colonel Ian Hope served at CENTCOM, the U.S. central command for the Middle East, after his tour as battle group commander. He was there when the Americans, tired of unfulfilled promises to backfill in Regional Command South, threatened to withdraw their medical support helicopters and reconnaissance drones. The move would have not only punished recalcitrant Europeans, but Canadians too. Hope made a personal appeal to a U.S. three-star general not to leave them high and dry. In the end, the Americans kept everything in place, but it spoke volumes about the bitterness behind-the-scenes. NATO's affable secretary-general, Jaap de Hoop Scheffer, didn't need to be told he had a problem.

Unfortunately, the extension to the Canadian deployment had taken away any real leverage the country might have had with NATO. And those in the diplomatic community thought it was a bit rich that Canada, long considered a slacker within NATO, had the temerity to make demands of its allies. It seemed the path back to respectability was paved with blood— something MacKay became more and more cognizant of with each fresh round of casualties.

"I felt I had to communicate that to other countries," he said in a later interview. "If we didn't succeed in RC-South the whole mission was doomed."

The military had sounded the alarm at the time of Operation Medusa, warning that Kandahar was in danger of being overrun by the Taliban. Despite the public declarations, however, MacKay said he never got "the sense that Kandahar would fall."

Still, the Conservative cabinet was consumed by the steady stream of caskets returning from overseas, and by the perception they created. There was nothing more embarrassing for a nation than to be seen screwing up a war.

"I remember there was some reticence on the part of a few that we were sustaining losses and the fear was almost more of the public impression of the job we were doing," MacKay said.

"I don't think there was any doubt everyone understood the gravity. People felt shaken to be more alert, more mindful of the soldiers, of their families. You have to be pretty unemotional, pretty disconnected not to be moved by what happened."

The intense violence of Kandahar had driven a wedge between allies, and de Hoop Scheffer wanted to prevent the crack from becoming a canyon. Every year a mixture of government and opposition MPs with an interest in defence from all member countries get together before the leaders' summit to sip wine and discuss the state of the world. The 2006 meeting was held in the historic Citadel district of Quebec City about two weeks before the trip to Riga. The reception at the Chateau Frontenac was like something straight out of James Bond. Strolling dimly lit, dark-wood-panelled rooms, you found small klatches of old and older Europe nattering away and eyeing each other with barely disguised suspicion. The Americans mingled the most and the Brits generally stuck to themselves, but seemed to drink an awful lot. Most of the Canadians hung around the hors d'oeuvre table. A thick, humid sense of intrigue hung in the air.

"NATO is about solidarity and sharing burdens and risks," the secretary-general said in his precise, clipped English, addressing the meeting via video conference.

Many delegates stared at the screens with the hollow emotion of hyp-notized chickens.

"National caveats reflect genuine and understandable concerns of governments and parliaments for their soldiers. Apart from restricting the ability of our military commanders to fulfil their mission, they—that is those caveats—can also be perceived as divisive."

Some watching the speech were not convinced that the political situation, or even the war itself, was as bad as the secretary-general made it out to be. There were all sorts of excuses to look the other way. The French grumbled about having troops tied down in peacekeeping commitments elsewhere in the world. Others declared that their role in Afghanistan was not combat, as though this grand military alliance was some kind of à la carte buffet. They said they preferred to help rebuild the country, as if what was happening in the south wasn't really war.

"When I go to discussions in my country, of course people have hesitation about a mission in Afghanistan," said Bert Koenders, a Dutch parliamentarian. "I have them and I'm still looking [with] a very critical idea at what we're doing there."

Still others were downright passive-aggressive, especially after Gordon O'Connor made a direct pitch for more help in Kandahar. A Portuguese delegate stuck up his hand in the question-and-answer session.

"Public opinion is very important, we know," Júlio Miranda Calha said. "What is your government doing to get [the] message out to the Canadian public about Canada's important role in Afghanistan?"

The question was delivered with the kind of dripping sarcasm you sometimes get on the continent. The delegate had no doubt heard some of the bellicose rhetoric coming out of Ottawa. The "cut and run" speech was infamous among some European parliamentarians and they were determined to mock it. Maybe it would have been funny had not so many been dying. But the Portuguese weren't the only ones who viewed such bombast with jaundiced eyes. The Germans and the French, still bruised and smarting over their fight with the Americans about the invasion of Iraq, saw the Canadian Conservatives as watered-down U.S. Republicans and were not ashamed to say so in private. There was almost a whiff of betrayal in some of the cutting remarks and snide asides.

"I have never seen so many people so anxious to have German troops on foreign soil," a member of the Bundestag sniffed into his wine.

When the plane finally touched down in Riga, O'Connor brushed himself off and nodded curtly to me before going to the front of the plane. I was trolling through BlackBerry messages while waiting to exit when one note stopped me in my tracks. Mary Ann Peace was the widow of a peacekeeper whom I'd written about years before. We'd stayed in touch and she'd sent me a note overnight to say that her husband's best friend, Chief Warrant Officer Robert "Bobby" Girouard, had been killed along with Corporal Albert Storm by a suicide bomber in Kandahar. Girouard was the regimental sergeant-major (RSM) for the battle group that had just come through Operation Medusa. RSMs are the hearts and souls of their regiments, setting the standard the troops are expected to meet. Most of the ones I knew were father figures, tough-as-nails veterans who carried themselves with a leathery indifference, but had hearts of gold. I didn't know Girouard, but judging by the heartbreak in Mary Ann's note he was cut from the same cloth.

It seemed perfectly fitting for us to step off the plane that morning into the teeth of a heavy, cold rain. The conference was held in Old Riga, a part of the city on the right bank of the Daugava River that dated from the thirteenth century. The footprints of history—both recent and long-dead— were everywhere. Out of the Canadian media centre windows you could see the spire of St. Peter's Cathedral in all of its middle-aged grandeur. But just before entering the close, ancient streets you passed cement, block-style apartments, dreary monuments to Latvia's long Soviet occupation. The end of the Cold War had brought a revival of the merchant society that had sustained Riga for centuries. On the left bank of the river, toward the airport, shiny new Western car dealerships had sprouted amid the crumbling, salt-sprayed neighbourhoods closest to the Baltic Sea.

There was a genuine eagerness on the part of NATO's new East European members to talk about Afghanistan. The founding members of the Alliance were preoccupied with the U.S. ballistic missile program and picking and choosing which former East Bloc countries would be allowed to join the club next.

Poland eventually stepped forward with an offer of 900 troops. The Slovaks said they were willing to send helicopters. The old East Bloc was in and ready to fight. Yet when it came time for the big European powers to speak, you could practically hear the crickets chirping.

Sitting in the row behind Stephen Harper, Peter MacKay looked around the summit table and tried to appreciate the political straitjackets binding other members.

"A lot of those countries were in either coalition governments or in countries where support for the mission was well below fifty per cent, even in the early days," he said later.

Some of the other foreign affairs ministers had been privately open to Canada's appeals for help, but "their political realities were such that they felt quite limited in the contributions they were going to be able to make."

Leaders are kept calmly sequestered at these summits, well away from the baying of protesters and the media. Photographers and camera operators get close during photo ops. Journalists, many of whom have travelled halfway around the world to cover the meetings, often end up congregated around giant television screens for photo ops and public speeches. These events are piped into the media centre via house feed like oxygen or stale air, depending on what's said and who's talking. You're showered with paper and smiles from an army of cheery, uniformed volunteers. The media overseers crammed so much useless information, so much abortive data into our hands and laptops that our arms literally strained under the weight. A summit had so many moving parts it gave the illusion of some great, enormous machine grinding forward. Where it was going and why were almost irrelevant.

An Italian journalist with a mane of chestnut hair slipped up beside me and placed her recorder on the speaker next to a big screen TV. She smiled and we struck up a conversation. Full of praise for Canadian, British and Dutch troops, she wondered how long the war would last. The Italians had a provincial reconstruction base in Herat, near the Iranian border, and nearly

1,000 combat troops in the region. Aware of the Canadian preoccupation, she declared that we wouldn't want Italian troops serving in the south.

"We dress up great, but we don't know how to fight," she said in heavily accented but perfect English. "The English, the Americans; all of you are tough. You know how to fight. You beat us in the war."

The leaders got the same message, but in a different vein. Behind the scenes, American officials scoffed at the combat effectiveness of the European armies. One particularly chatty U.S. officer wondered if some of the allies—he didn't say which—were fit for anything beyond garrison duty. At the heart of the criticism was the fact the Germans, the Greeks, the Danes, the Turks and the Norwegians all maintained conscripted armies, which some said made them less effective and more likely to get slaughtered in places like Kandahar. The Italians had only recently ended mandatory military service. The allies were armed and dangerous, just not as dangerous as everyone wanted them to be.

What irritated the Americans about Ottawa's plea for reinforcements was the perception that despite the tiny size of its army, the Canadians themselves could do more. I recall having coffee with one colonel, who noted that Canadians had fielded 4,300 troops for peacekeeping missions in the Balkans—not quite double the commitment in Kandahar. An increased Canadian contribution was possible, he argued, if Ottawa adopted year-long rotations instead of six-month deployments, which had been the hallmark of the peacekeeping years. The Canadian delegation just nodded and smiled.

"I don't think they fully appreciated the toll it was taking on public opinion here . . . just the grind, the wear and tear Canada was enduring," MacKay said when he looked back years later. "I got the sense the Americans, even with their own presence, their own intelligence, perhaps didn't quite grasp how difficult it was going to be to establish the security level we were all seeking to achieve."

When the cameras finally left the room and the doors closed at Riga, MacKay said there was an uncomfortable hush. The smarter nations saw it coming. They knew what Stephen Harper was going to say. They knew the complexion of the mission in southern Afghanistan had changed dramatically. The nation-building exercise NATO had embraced only months before had slid into a dirty little war.

"I remember the prime minister's submission and you could almost see some shifting of the chairs and eyes on the floor," MacKay said. "Nobody wanted to lock eyes with some of the [leaders of] countries in RC-South."

George Bush and Tony Blair made their submissions, as did Dutch Prime Minister Jan Pieter Balkenende.

Jaap de Hoop Scheffer followed up with a clever, understated warning that NATO was becoming a two-tier alliance. He also cautioned the allies about publicly blaming and shaming other nations. He must have been looking straight at the Canadian delegation when he said it. Days before the summit, Harper and Balkenende took out full-page ads in major newspapers to make their pitch directly to a skeptical European public. German chancellor Angela Merkel countered that a military solution wasn't the only solution in Afghanistan. It was like nails on a chalkboard to the Americans and even the Canadians, who privately chafed at Germany's demand for a say in the overall war strategy, despite the fact that it had no troops doing any real fighting. At the time, however, the Germans were—on paper, at least—the third-largest troop-contributing country.

By the time of the final statements, the Germans, the French, the Italians and the Spanish had agreed to allow their troops to be used in the south on a short-term basis, if there was an emergency. Afterward, de Hoop Scheffer spoke with an optimism and enthusiasm that made many of us in the cheap seats wonder whether we'd witnessed the same summit.

The decision to help out was "the most fundamental demonstration of NATO's solidarity," he said with a straight face.

"There was a clear commitment by all twenty-six NATO allies that in an emergency . . . they will support each other."

One of the Brit journalists, sitting next to me on the camera riser at the news conference, plucked out the translator earpiece and looked toward the brightly lit podium.

"Well, that's bloody reassuring. I know I'll sleep better tonight, mate. How about you?" I don't think I've ever heard a sentence so lathered in sarcasm.

A U.S. officer pulled journalists aside and noted in quiet, confidential tones that NATO's existing rules stipulated that in emergencies, restrictions would be lifted regardless of national considerations. It was an utterly hollow gesture delivered with thundering gravity, as though it really mattered.

The meeting broke up and the leaders held separate, often concurrent news conferences. Stephen Harper did little to hide his irritation at the thought the cavalry would come only if southern Afghanistan were falling down around NATO's ears.

"Obviously we don't intend to be in an emergency," he said. "Look, we're not going to kid you, the security situation remains a challenge in the south. We still believe we are under-manned, but we're getting more forces all of the time, we're getting more flexibility from our NATO partners."

MacKay tried to take the long view and said the spadework done by each country following the summit lay the foundation for the massive surge of forces years later. He refused to characterize Riga as an "abject failure."

Yet I recall it was a quiet plane ride home.

The American editorial pages were quick to pick up on Ottawa's discomfort and, while sympathetic, questioned whether Canada would stick around. MacKay said he never got the sense from the Bush Administration, either privately or publicly, that it was worried Canada would bolt. The message he took home from the country's two most important military partners was unspoken, yet pretty clear.

"I think they had modest expectations . . . that we would hold the fort. I think we matched—even surpassed—expectations with everybody, but the Brits and Americans in particular."

The U.S. had the ability to flood southern Afghanistan with troops and turn it into a smouldering parking lot, but in the fall of 2006 Iraq was at the height of its bloody nervous breakdown and the Pentagon said it had no troops to spare. Besides, the argument went, NATO's European members needed to step up. Some Europeans privately used Iraq as a justification for their own inaction. They argued that Washington had the ability to straighten out Kandahar and would have done so, had it not been for that "other" unnecessary war.

"It's easy to say in retrospect," MacKay said. "I'm not sure I necessarily agree with the fact that they could have turned the tide so much earlier had they focused on Afghanistan and not Iraq."

* * *

The time following Riga was a head snap. Within weeks I went from sitting alongside powerful men who spoke ferocious words but killed no one to riding with bloody-minded men who spoke little and killed when the opportunity presented itself. It was like being rocketed from one pole to the other without taking a breath. The longer I spent back on the ground in Kandahar, the more I realized Riga didn't matter. Let the politicians talk. They had their maps, PowerPoints, memos and backgrounders, all of which were ground up and sliced into bite-sized thoughts and slogans for the cameras. Feeding the beast was all that seemed to matter. As long as they got past the latest news cycle everything was cool, nobody got hurt. The real war—the one everyone wanted to reach out and touch in those days; the one where everybody got hurt—could be found in the devoured expressions of the soldiers I followed on patrol and in the circumspect eyes of the Afghans we passed along the way. Never would the two worlds collide. Nobody at Riga really wanted to understand what Kandahar was all about and nobody in Kandahar cared much about what was said at Riga. It was one of those icy contradictions you had to wrestle with and pin to the ground. If you didn't get past it, the cynicism was painful enough to eat you alive.

It was a cool, breezy winter day in the desert and I sat at one of the strongpoints that overlooked Route Summit. A column of LAVs pulled up and when the ramps dropped, fresh troops tumbled out. Master Corporal Colin Chabassol was among them, although I didn't know it at the time. We met later in the war, and talked about his first impressions that day. In front of him was a maze of sandbagged fortifications built around baked mud walls and thatch-covered grape huts. Cases of water were scattered across the vehicle marshalling yard and barrels of burning shit created a lazy, inky black stain in the sky. Chabassol looked out from underneath his helmet.

"I gotta live here?" the Pictou County, Nova Scotia, native asked out loud.

Other troops had the same reaction, even the veterans who'd been in-country before. Master Corporal Russell Moquin had done a tour in Kabul in the early 2000s, but couldn't get over the winter-wasted desolation of Zhari and the hollow stillness of the rippled farmland around him. It was like something unspoken and heavy was in the air.

"Everything was dead," said Moquin. The son of a career soldier, he was used to the hard living of army life. "When we got there in February there wasn't any green. Everything was brown or grey and empty."

Easter Sunday—April 8, 2007—dawned like most days in Afghanistan, with a hazy, grey repetitiveness that made it indistinguishable from the days on either side. The rhythm of life is totally different in this part of the world. Friday is the Muslim holy day of rest. Holidays, festivals, even the New Year are celebrated at different times. The net effect can throw you off; you were never quite sure what the date might be. But some days are so terrible they sear themselves into your memory, and no matter where you are in the world, you have to stop and pay respect. A number of us who followed the war closely were home for the holiday then, yet we were still numbed by the news that day.

Ever since Canadian boots had touched the ground, a quiet smugness about the invisibility of their light armoured vehicles had been in the air. Taliban rocket-propelled grenades and machine gun fire just skipped off the reinforced armour. Casualties happened mostly in G-Wagon jeeps. The LAVs had been impenetrable to roadside bombs. The Taliban tried. There had been blown tires, wrecked drive shafts and some guys knocked about in what the soldiers referred to as M-kills—mobility kills. But there had never been a K-kill—a catastrophic kill. The Taliban hadn't been able to build and bury anything big enough.

Both Colin Chabassol and Corporal Joel Trickey were on a foot patrol along an empty pathway when they heard the explosion. It was about 11 a.m., when the sun was almost at its blinding best. They were dozens of kilometres away from the dull crack, but it made the patrol stop and look around.

"It was a huge hit," Trickey recalled later. "I think everybody in the battle group heard the explosion. I just had that gut feeling that you knew something went wrong."

The sound of an explosion, nearby or distant, does things to your head, nasty things. The mind starts racing. Hunkered down inside a patrol base or observation post, you try to figure out what's happened, but it's like solving a mystery with no clues. One of the guys put it this way: "You hear a bang and you think three things: Who's hurt? Where's it at? And how bad?" The radio is the only window on the world.

About half an hour after they heard the blast, Trickey and the rest of his section set up a patrol base in one of the many pulverized compounds that dot the Zhari landscape. Then they sat and waited.

The war had settled into a stalemate. The Taliban hit and ran. Trickey said he knew that every time they stepped outside a fortification or base they would be shot at. Consequently, every move became very deliberate. Convoys and patrols were planned with maniacal precision. The one small bit of comfort was that the Taliban, at that time, were lousy shots.

"We'd have rockets shot at us [but] the guys didn't arm them properly so they wouldn't go off," he said.

But it was the random, unmerciful nature of the roadside bombs and booby traps that terrified them the most. Soldiers can be obscenely blunt, but their dread of improvised explosive devices (IEDs) rarely articulated

itself directly. Some joked about it. Others immersed themselves in technical explanations, as though understanding the inner workings of the devices
somehow made them immune to both fear and the flesh-tearing results of the
blasts. You learned a lot about dread—how to master it, how to ignore it and
how to let it go—by watching these guys step off on foot patrol or button
up inside a patrol vehicle day in and day out. At first, they flew on autopilot
and with each encounter came the ecstasy of survival, but the weight of
the unknown ground against them with a relentless attrition. Some had the
courage to know when they had their fill.

"The first ambush was kind of surreal because you didn't know what was
going on," said Master Corporal Ryan Hawkyard, of Bravo Company, 1 Royal
Canadian Regiment. He saw combat for four straight months at one point.
"When a buddy of mine lost both of his legs [to a mine], I said: 'Okay, that's
it. It's fucked. Enough of this shit; let's just fucking go home.'"

On that Easter Sunday, a platoon of infantry from Hotel Company, 2
RCR was tasked with pushing west through Zhari district and out toward
the border with Helmand province. The Canadian battle group was supporting American operations. Elements of the entire company were scattered to
the west and north of the district, but they had radio problems. The platoon
was dispatched in their LAVs to a hill about two kilometres from the company's main position, to act as a rebroadcast site. To get to the high feature,
the column of three armoured vehicles followed a dry riverbed down into
a spidery series of emaciated irrigations canals and wells known as a *kareez*.
It was massive—dozens of kilometres long, by some estimates. Before the
Soviet's scorched-earth policy, it would have sustained the whole western
half of the district.

The explosion was massive too.

"That is a day I will never forget," said Sergeant Scott Seeley. His eyes
were fixed on the mess hall table as he later described the day.

The bomb, planted in one of the wells, was powerful—so powerful that
a 136-kilogram tire from the stricken LAV landed almost half a kilometre
away. The armoured vehicle's back ramp, which required a chain-linked
hydraulic lift to open and close, was sheered off.

"It split the LAV open like a tin can. Massive, just massive . . ." Seeley
said, his voice trailing off.

The attack instantly killed all six soldiers in the LAV, including Seeley's best
friend, Sergeant Donald (Donny) Lucas—a Newfoundlander, a wise-cracker

and a real character. The two had met in the late 1990s, when they were posted into the battalion at the same time, and were often inseparable. The other soldiers who died that day were Corporal Christopher Paul Stannix, Corporal Aaron Williams, Private Kevin Kennedy, Private David Greenslade and Corporal Brent Poland.

The word went over the radio that there were six VSAs—short for "vital signs absent." The platoon had lost a third of its fighting strength in one stroke. In the immediate aftermath, soldiers in the two remaining LAVs wondered whether the bomb strike was going to be followed by an ambush. The surviving troops, about twenty guys, formed a security screen around the mutilated vehicle and searched with futility for signs of life amid the smoking, bloody ruins. They cleared a landing zone for the medevac helicopters. Talking with Seeley months afterward, you could tell there was a heartbreaking stoicism, an almost dream-like quality to the routine they performed.

"I think about that day," he said. "It was something that happened and I can't erase it from my memory."

There were days in Afghanistan that you just couldn't wait to end. Those were the worst days. And there were more ahead that Easter weekend. Three days after the bombing, on April 11, 2007, two members of the Royal Canadian Dragoons were killed in an ambush. And so it went for much of the 2nd battalion's tour. The Taliban had figured out how much powder it took to destroy a LAV and they soon struck again, killing six soldiers on July 4, 2007. Guys died or were wounded so often throughout that tour you found yourself wondering how long it could go on. Because Operation Medusa received so much attention there is a mistaken impression that it was the apex of the bloodletting. But if you parse the statistics, the period between February and August 2007, when the campaign settled into a raw standoff, was the worst. The steady stream of casualties caused even the spiritually fortified to bow under the strain. I attended the internment of a soldier at Beechwood National Cemetery in Ottawa that summer. The padre looked exhausted, but recognized me from other military funerals I'd covered.

"This is too much," he murmured as we watched the family lingering over the grave. "We've done this far too many times."

I read later in access to information documents that the worst cases of non-combat burnout were suffered among the military chaplain service, especially the padres working at CFB Trenton, where the repatriations happened. It said something when even God was getting tired.

Back in Kandahar province, the troops sprinkled hither and yon increasingly referred to their job as a "whack-a-mole" exercise.

Master Corporal Joshua Graham remembers little about 2007. His time with Charlie Company, 2 PPCLI was spent sitting in the back of a LAV, always on the way to somewhere.

"You'd drive hours to get to a village, walk around and you'd get blown up on your way back," said Graham. "You'd go here and drive there. That's all it ever was. Something would come up, you'd drive forever and you'd walk around someplace where you'd have no clue who the leaders of the village are; you'd have no clue who the people in the village are."

The completion of Route Summit saw the battle group push westward into Taliban territory along both sides of the Arghandab River. It was a grind.

"Pretty much every thirty-six hours you were getting into a fight," said Sergeant Eric Coupal, who was with India Company of the Royal Canadian Regiment. "That's all it was. You fight, pull back, regroup, get new orders, walk right back in and fight. That pretty much went on right to the last week we were there."

They laid on the artillery. They laid on the air strikes, but every time they pulled back Coupal saw it in the eyes of villagers. Because the Canadians weren't staying, the Taliban had won.

It wasn't until the summer and a particularly fierce multi-day battle for the town of Sangasar that the troops actually felt like they were holding ground. Shortly after the 2 RCR battle group was relieved by the Royal 22e Régiment, the famed "Van Doos" out of Valcartier, Quebec, who immediately found themselves drawn into a protracted, bloody fight in Zhari around Gundy Ghar, an area south of Ma'sum Ghar. In the fall, as the Van Doos battled to retake Arghandab district, Zhari slipped back out of control and went straight to hell. And so it would go for the next two years. There weren't enough Afghan troops to hold the areas that had been cleared and the local cops were a corrupt, menacing joke.

"That is the only thing that bothered me that whole tour," said Coupal. "All that ground we fought for, when the Van Doos stepped in it was lost. Everyone we lost, that was for nothing. I think that's the only thing that bothered me . . . because all of the hard work we did was for nothing."

Yet the troops kept going, exhibiting a restless energy that defied survival instinct and outstripped purpose. Joel Trickey recalled patrols going out every day over a small walking bridge in Panjwaii, not far from the main base in Ma'sum Ghar. The bomb-sniffing dogs arrived one day to discover that the tiny span had been wired with up to ninety mortars and old Russian 105-mm shells. They had been there a while, just waiting for someone to pull the trigger. The engineers got rid of them in a controlled explosion that had the force of 1,000-pound bomb blast. I looked at him in horror.

"You guys walked that thing every day?"

"Yup. Roll of the dice, man. We just got lucky. It's the way she goes sometimes."

* * *

It was around this time that I began to hear the war described with gravity-defying optimism by the officialdom in Ottawa. As I watched the daily Question Period in the House of Commons, it seemed as though everyone on the government benches had been infected. They smiled through the havoc and insisted all was well. But away from the political circus there was heart-rending reflection.

Halfway through 2007, Peter MacKay was called to one of the semi-regular NATO ministerial meetings in Brussels. Just before going, he attended a repatriation ceremony at CFB Trenton. He hopped a transatlantic flight immediately afterward and stewed all of the way to NATO headquarters. When the conference room doors closed, MacKay unloaded on his startled colleagues. He talked about the dead soldiers and the grieving families he'd left behind. You could "hear the wringing of the hands and the sucking of teeth," he said.

Later, he was pulled aside by one of the other ministers. "I don't know if we really want to hear that," he was told, "because it makes it very personal."

The room was flooded with weak winter sunshine. Smudged windows framed all sides of the office and I wondered how often they had to be replaced. Kandahar was very hard on glass. Despite the chill outside, the office was warm and comfortable and radiated a calm efficiency rarely seen in the city. Two staffers greeted Khan and me as we were ushered through the door. Their handshakes and smiles were genuine and a lucid contrast to the stiff, tolerant greetings you often got elsewhere.

"Welcome," a voice said.

We turned. An older man stood up from behind a spindle-legged desk. He had the weathered charm and lined face of a grandfather. Maybe it was the sweater vest. I'd never seen anyone wear a knitted sweater vest over a shalwar kameez. The man's grey-wool sports coat cemented my paternal impression, although I wouldn't have bet money on his age. You never knew how old Afghans might be; someone who was thirty could easily be mistaken for fifty. Kandahar was as hard on the faces of its people as it was on windows.

We had been called to the local office of the Afghanistan Independent Human Rights Commission in late February 2007. Khan counted the executive director, Abdul Qadar Noorzai, among his best contacts, and judging by the conquering-hero greeting, I assumed something important was about to be revealed. We were shown to a pair of cozy sofas in a brightly lit sitting room beside Qadar Noorzai's desk. The man was an engineer by training, and he moved like one. His motions were precise and sparing. He spoke a little carefully considered English with a tinge of a German accent, which seemed very strange until Khan explained that the man had spent most of the Soviet occupation in Germany.

That's the way it was with much of the professional class in Afghanistan. The doctors, the teachers, the lawyers, the engineers, the bureaucrats—basically anyone with any amount of education—had gotten the hell out of the country during the 1980s. Those who stuck it out were rewarded with the insanity of the mujahideen years and an unending, bloody civil war. We won't even talk about the Taliban. It made you wonder how much a guy like Qadar Noorzai, with so many years spent in exile, had in common with the granite-eyed, illiterate farmers with their mud-spattered sandals.

"I am very pleased you have come to see us," he said as his staff placed crystal dishes of nuts and dates on the glass-topped coffee table. They served green tea and placed the glass mugs on white paper doilies.

"I have a story for you; a good story. This is very good news." He leaned forward and looked me straight in the eye. "Khan says you are trustworthy. So I trust you, and I trust you will understand the importance of what I am going to tell you."

The old man had my attention. He leaned even closer.

His office, he said, had agreed to act as a watchdog for the Canadian military and to check on the condition of prisoners turned over to local authorities, including Afghanistan's intelligence service, the notorious, Soviet-trained National Directorate of Security. He leaned back and spread his arms, almost as if to say "ta-dah." The old man folded his hands on his stomach, obviously pleased with himself. It took me a moment to process. I glanced at Khan, who, seeing Qadar Noorzai pleased, was beaming.

The Canadians military had, out of the blue, approached Qadar Noorzai's group to monitor the prisoners. It was strange. Everything we'd heard to that point suggested that Ottawa trusted the Afghan jailers. As part of the nation-building exercise, Foreign Affairs diplomats had been establishing contact with the nascent AIHRC, but that was a long way from giving it responsibility over something that had international legal implications. Canada was bound by convention not to hand over prisoners to an authority that practised torture. It was a war crime.

"Canadians respect human rights very well," said Qadar Noorzai, who couldn't hide his delight at being taken seriously. The money that Ottawa promised to throw at the agency only added to the sense of celebration. I'm sure if they had been allowed to drink, champagne corks would have been popping at the commission.

The agreement had been signed the previous week—on February 20, 2007—with the commander of Canadian troops in Afghanistan, who at the time was Brigadier-General Tim Grant. The commission would receive a list of suspected Taliban who'd been captured and turned over to the intelligence service. It would check on them, report back on their condition and most importantly notify the Canadians as to whether there had been any abuse. The commission was expected to conduct a brutality reconstruction, which struck me as odd and almost useless. It made about as much sense as asking a guy who's had his teeth punched out to put them back in his mouth. The Afghan commissioner gushed and treated the news like the manna it was for the agency.

The agreement with the Karzai government, which laid out the transfer arrangement, was tenuous, whether anyone in power wanted to admit it or not. It hung on the slender threads of honesty, goodwill and humanity. How anyone in their right mind could have thought the Afghans were capable of setting aside thirty years of blood feuds and homicidal tribal rivalries is beyond me. Still, the American excesses at Guantanamo Bay and Abu Ghraib had made it politically impossible for countries like Canada to hand over war prisoners to the U.S. The alternative was for NATO to build its own detention centre, but that was nixed over concerns about cost and manpower. The last option, the one everyone professed not to like but still chose, was to transfer prisoners to the Afghan authorities. Behind the scenes, Amnesty International gave NATO a fourth, unconsidered option of embedding soldiers or military police in Afghan prisons to monitor for human rights abuses.

An entire bureaucratic cottage industry had sprung up over the years to justify the transfer decision, but no matter how many numbers they crunched or excuses they massaged, there was simply no escaping a basic fact: in all likelihood, people were going to get ripped up in the worst ways after being handed over to their fellow countrymen. The entire issue had come into sharp focus the previous spring, with Captain Jon Snyder's riveting tale of having to stare down an ANA lynch mob.

Qadar Noorzai had little doubt that he would be busy. He sat in his easy chair, amid the warming sunshine and beside a pinwheel arrangement of fake roses, and described some of their early investigations in vivid, unflinching detail. One almost made me throw up. He said he expected many new, horrific cases to investigate.

My mind reeling, I went back to KAF and started asking questions. Silence. It was uncanny; I'd figured the government would be tripping over itself to talk. The Conservatives, who'd been taking a hammering for months over Afghanistan, would normally have seized any opportunity to make themselves look good, or to throw on the cape of human rights defender. The news would, if anything, have blunted the criticism on the floor of the House of Commons.

The baffling silence about the AIHRC went on for a couple of days, and Foreign Affairs didn't respond to my request until I threatened to write the piece without government comment. I was in Dubai and about to start vacation when the e-mail arrived. Yes, the deal existed. That was a no-brainer; Qadar Noorzai had shown me the written agreement. What I wanted—and what they weren't prepared to give up—was why the arrangement was necessary. If everything was as hunky-dory as O'Connor had claimed, why was it necessary to engage the commission?

"It's simply an added layer of protection," Marc Raider of Foreign Affairs wrote.

Raider did his best to paint the arrangement as a faceless bureaucratic exercise and said the Canadian agreement recognized the human rights group, but had previously given it no role. Now they had one.

Much later in the war, I found out the British had laughed at the arrangement. They put no stock in the watchdog group and called it "two men and a dog." They believed it lacked the capacity to monitor effectively, according to an April 2007 briefing note.

My colleague Graeme Smith and I spent a few days in Dubai that winter. We lounged by the pool, took a desert safari and talked about what we'd seen in Afghanistan. We shook our heads and laughed a lot but couldn't seem to shake the dust off our boots. Graeme was particularly consumed. Before we'd left, Graeme had started to track down some of the prisoners who'd been captured by Canadians, turned over to Afghan intelligence and tortured. He was about to light the war on fire.

Watching everything unfold over the next few months was like witnessing a slow-motion car wreck. The reaction of the uniforms, politicos and
bureaucrats to my questions about Qadar Noorzai had been instructive. It
seemed that I had a piece of the puzzle, but not the whole thing, and what
I sensed was a cold kind of fear. I didn't see that very often. Their reaction
contained none of the usual political kinetics either, where the reflex was
to stamp out a bad story like it was a tiny brush fire. This time, they closed
their eyes and hoped it would burn itself out. Without realizing it, Qadar
Noorzai had peeled back the curtain on the Canadian government's worst
nightmare. This wasn't going away.

In the winter of 2007, the Canadian military recognized it had a problem, although this only became evident much later, when access to information documents and other records were tabled publicly. Perhaps reports
from the field tipped them off; tales like Jon Snyder's were not state secrets
and what most people don't realize is that many soldiers gossip like old
women. Word had gotten around. In addition to Snyder's story, there was
the one about a platoon that had to rescue a prisoner from a beating just
moments after they'd turned him over to Afghan cops. That happened in
June 2006.

Precisely when the light went on in Ottawa isn't entirely clear, but by
late 2006 or early 2007, General Rick Hillier had proposed a more diligent
system of monitoring Afghan prisoners. He drafted what's known as a tasking order, instructing the army to "proactively engage Afghan authorities" in
order to "confirm acceptable detainee handling procedures and practices"
were in place. Hidden under the bureaucratic language was a stunning fact:
unlike almost all statements by the Harper government and the military,
this one recognized that abuse was likely taking place in Afghan jails. The
defence chief's instructions seemed aimed at laying a foundation to deal
with torture claims.

"This direction is issued despite the fact that allegations of mistreatment of such detainees have not been supported by specific facts and remain
unsubstantiated," Hillier wrote.

The task order instructed senior commanders to compel Afghan authorities
to meet with Qadar Noorzai's human rights commission and the International
Committee of the Red Cross. Hillier evidently didn't trust the Afghans to
handle the issue on their own: "Canadian officials [should be] present to deal
with any allegations of mistreatment."

The proposal was a key step toward the prison-monitoring system that Ottawa was eventually dragged—kicking and screaming in the aftermath of Graeme's stories—in to implementing. Yet Hillier's tasking order was never implemented. It became trapped in an even bigger quagmire than Kandahar. It was sucked into the Ottawa bureaucracy, specifically the vortex between the Defence and Foreign Affairs departments known as "whole-of-government." Some referred to it as "whole-of-government." Some at DND referred to it as "hole-in-government," a place that sucked up ideas, never to be seen again. Years later Gabrielle Duschner, a civilian defence policy advisor, told a public inquiry that the tasking order was put on hold while other departments considered its impact. This bureaucratic foot-dragging went on throughout the spring of 2007. Around that time, the Harper government appointed seasoned mandarin David Mulroney as a deputy minister in charge of an interdepartmental task force that would oversee all the moving parts of the war.

Not long after my story on Qadar Noorzai appeared, Richard Colvin arrived in Ottawa for consultation. The previous spring, his opaque warnings about torture in Afghan prisons had seemingly gone over everyone's head. This time, however, there could be no mistaking his siren call. In closed-door meetings, he stated clearly and without reservation that prisoners handed over to the NDS faced torture. Duschner, who spent two years working at Canadian Expeditionary Force Command, the country's Ottawa-based overseas head-quarters, was present at one of those meetings. She dismissed what she heard.

"Looking at it from a contextual perspective, it was an isolated comment, which I gathered to be opinion," she later told an inquiry by the Military Police Complaints Commission.

Whether her indifference was to the message or the messenger isn't entirely clear from the public record. By that point in the war, Colvin's name was poison around the Defence Department. Angry defence bureaucrats and officers wanted him reined in—or fired from his post in Kabul. One toughly worded memo, dated May 7, 2007, painted Colvin as a troublemaker "with a pattern of questionable reporting decisions." It warned he "could become a liability to the Government of Canada's interests if left unchecked." The memo, which circulated around CEFCOM as the interdepartmental meetings took place, recommended that Colvin be reminded of responsibilities as a diplomat and "boundaries as a reporter." If he was not checked, it said, "his contribution to the Embassy in Kabul should be re-evaluated." Colvin's reports from the field had clearly gotten under the skin of a lot of people

THE SAVAGE WAR 177

at the Defence Department, who openly accused him of reporting "highly sensitive" operational details in his dispatches to Ottawa. They didn't like the fact he expressed personal opinion "without prior consultation" and offered "unqualified criticism of Canadian Forces leadership decisions."

Throughout the war, a lot of people tried to doodle happy faces over the rocky relationship between Defence, Foreign Affairs and CIDA. Much ink was spilled trying to convince the media, and by extension the public, that the three very distinct bureaucratic cultures had joined hands and were singing "Kumbaya" over Afghanistan. Individuals often got along; the institutions did not.

"It was bad. There was a lot of bad blood," one still-serving diplomat told me in a background interview. "There was always this kind of attitude at DND: We know what we're doing and you guys don't. There was a determination to call the shots. At the same time, I don't think they realized how little they knew [about what was really going on in Afghanistan]. They didn't like the civilians telling them what they saw as their business."

There were times when the relationship became downright petty. One smouldering Foreign Affairs staffer told me about how Ambassador David Sproule showed up in Kandahar in late 2006 and wanted to attend a ramp ceremony for soldiers who'd been killed in a roadside bombing. He was relegated to the back ranks; the front was reserved for senior army officers.

"This is a military ceremony," he was informed.

The staffer was irate that a senior diplomat, who'd made a point of going to Kandahar out of sympathy, was treated so shabbily.

"He was the ambassador," said the staffer. "It was unbelievable. It was that kind of stupidity that went on."

Other times it was just plain brutal. Diplomats would offer advice only to be told that until they got outside the wire and actually sat with Afghans and drank tea the way soldiers did their thoughts weren't welcome. I saw it happen once and I felt sorry for the poor guy. In the early days, when a journalist showed up, especially a familiar face, we were greeted by the Foreign Affairs folk like long-lost cousins. There was, at times, nothing like the misery-loves-company situation of being a civilian among uniforms. Some soldiers tried to pull the you-don't-get-outside-the-wire crap with a few of the journalists too, although that lasted about as long as it took for you to tell them you travelled Kandahar city unarmed and dressed as an Afghan. The diplomats didn't have that defence. Glyn Berry's assassination had prompted Foreign Affairs to restrict staff to bases. It was infuriating for them.

"It was like we were cowards, cowering in our little tents afraid to leave. They knew the restrictions that had been imposed on us," a diplomat later confided. "It was kind of cheap."

* * *

If the relationship between civilians and the military was corrosive, the political atmosphere became downright toxic in the spring of 2007. I arrived back in Ottawa just in time to hear Gordon O'Connor apologize for telling the House of Commons that the International Red Cross was solely responsible for monitoring Canadian-captured prisoners when it wasn't. The Red Cross knew it. The Harper government knew it. But saying it got the government through a couple of news cycles. The humanitarian agency, which rarely speaks openly, took the step of contradicting O'Connor in public. The debates and catcalls in the Commons were ugly. MPs aren't choir members on the best of days, but there was a lip-curling, vile tone that made even the most stout-hearted politico wince. By early spring, Stephen Harper had had enough.

"I can understand the passion that the leader of the Opposition and members of his party feel for the Taliban prisoners . . . I just wish occasionally they would show the same passion for Canadian soldiers," the prime minister said on March 21, 2007, in answer to a question by Liberal Leader Stéphane Dion.

I literally dropped my pen.

Maybe it was meant to be glib—at least that was my first thought as I quickly retrieved the pen from the floor. But the notion evaporated when those words became a refrain for the Tories, a grim chant that was almost tribal in its rhythm. The underlying message was unmistakable: they were out for blood. Hearing them, I became convinced that these were the kind of people who got their war on television and in movies. No amount of violence, no amount of horror could satisfy the screeching demand. Maybe it could have been forgiven had the words slipped from the mouths of the soldiers, who were entitled, some would say, to preach bloody murder. But to hear it from those whose greatest threat was a paper cut struck me as obscene. Even the most hardened soldiers would have been cool to condemn anyone to suffer. They would rather have put a round through the poor bastard's head and be done with it. Yet the Tories had tapped into a simmering wellspring of public anger. This was especially evident after I appeared on the CBC to talk about the prisoner controversy. I'd barely gotten the earpiece out and the makeup off before my phone rang. It was a caller who didn't want to give his name. How he got my number, I'm not sure.

"Why did you defend the Taliban?"

"I didn't," I answered, somewhat startled. "I just tried to point out there are other considerations and responsibilities, like maybe international law for starters."

"You know what, mister? Nobody cares about the Taliban. They're killing our soldiers. People back here don't care what happens to them. People care about their jobs, health care, whether their kids are in a decent school. Who cares what happens to those bastards?"

"Funny. I thought we were supposed to be better than them. At least that's what we tell ourselves."

It was his turn to be startled.

"Huh?"

"We say we're there to protect human rights, make sure little girls can go to school and all that. If we're no better than them, if we can't hold ourselves up as an example, if we've stopped caring about doing the right thing, then it's time to pack it up and come home."

My anonymous friend and I agreed to disagree, and he never called me again, yet throughout that spring I heard his refrain over and over again. What was even more disgusting was the blinding ignorance it represented. I can remember watching junior cabinet minister Helena Guergis stand up in the Commons and answer for the foreign affairs minister one day. With beauty-queen poise she spewed such ugliness it made you cringe. The point that really hadn't sunk in with most in Ottawa was that the Taliban was largely a mercenary force, offering enticing rewards for service. Other times they appealed to the sense of injustice many Muslims felt. When that didn't work they simply pointed a gun. Commanders usually didn't get caught; they were too smart for that. No, it was the farmers and the labourers who ended up zap-strapped by soldiers and handed over to the clutches of the Afghan intelligence service. Oftentimes the NDS realized these guys were useless from an information point of view and dumped them into Sarpoza Prison, where the corrupt Afghan justice system expected them to buy their way out of jail. The bribe could be as little as U.S. $10 or as much as $500. When the prisoners didn't have the cash, the guards would beat them until the family raised the money. The intelligence service would ultimately release the prisoners and complain to the Canadians there was no evidence to retain them. It was a vicious circle that made us more enemies than friends.

Soldiers had a simple answer for the conundrum: Don't pick up a gun. But that's easy to say when your family is secure and fed. The expectation that grungy, desperate people should behave with some sort of angelic dignity was least of this war's contradictions. The military as an institution recognized that putting shovels and tools into the hands of these people made it less likely that they would pick up AK-47s and bombs. In fact, by the time the off-with-their-heads mentality had gripped Ottawa, the army had started laying out a whole series of small cash-for-work programs. The people whom we would condemn to torture, either through indifference or septic bile, were the same ones we wanted to bring in from the cold with cash. There are times when Canadians have a particular gift for not realizing they're being ridiculous.

* * *

By mid-April 2007 the military and the diplomatic community knew Graeme Smith had a story coming. They didn't know the details, but it caused enough consternation to prompt e-mail traffic. Foreign Affairs documents also showed that the recent arrangement with the AIHRC was in trouble. The country's intelligence service has refused to grant inspectors access to their prisons, said an April 10, 2007, message from the embassy in Kabul.

The stories and the questions slowly forced the Canadian government to focus on Afghan prisoners. The further you went into April, the more institutions began to take a hard look at what was perhaps going on.

"The Afghan justice system was viewed as unpalatable. There are three categories of detainees: the destitute (unable to buy their way out), the insignificant (no political or tribal connections) and the stupid (who admitted they're guilty)," said the April 20 note.

"Any Talb can buy his freedom for $10. The NDS system is somewhat less corrupt."

All hell broke loose on April 23, 2007. Graeme's horrific story of torture and misery shrieked from the front page of the *Globe and Mail*. He wrote with an intensity that made you feel you were listening to cries of the abused themselves. It took my breath away, and I wasn't alone. The horror and the shame over the fact that could have been associated with such gross brutality, even by extension, set off political convulsions the likes of which I'd never seen. The allegations bulldozed everything—and I mean everything—off the political agenda.

Politicians do righteous indignation at the drop of a hat, but what spewed forth in those days was beyond the experience of even the most hardened Hill climber. There was a manic verve, a quake in the voices that separated it from the usual bile. Every Opposition question for two weeks after the story related to Afghan prisoners; it was an unrelenting, almost unprecedented fury.

If you sat in the public gallery of the Commons during those days, you would have noticed the government benches were uncharacteristically cold and silent. Through all of the screaming, shouting, lecturing, pontificating and rhetoric, they seemed to hang their heads. Gone were the partisan bravado and the swagger of spit-balling the Liberals, NDP and Bloc Québécois. I could never figure out whether the reaction stemmed from mortification or contempt. The angrier and the longer the debate became, the more the Conservatives fell back on what the Press Gallery called the "Taliban lover" defence. The government didn't answer questions; it accused the other parties of supporting an enemy that didn't deserve to be treated as human.

"These people have no compunction about machine-gunning, mowing down little children; they have no compunction about decapitating or hanging elderly women; they have no compunction about the most vicious types of torture you can imagine," said Stockwell Day, the public safety minister at the time.

It took a few days for the government, the Defence Department and Foreign Affairs to get their act together. When they did, a lawyerly language took over in public. The screams of Canadian prisoners were to be given more credence than those of anyone else.

"We have yet to see one specific allegation of torture . . . If [Opposition members] have a specific name, we'd be happy to have it investigated and chased down, but they continue to repeat the baseless accusations made by those who wish to undermine our forces there," said government house leader Peter Van Loan.

At one point, the spin became even more precise. Specific allegations would have to have been heard by "Canadian officials." As if that really mattered. How such horror and misery could be parsed and dissected with a straight face and without overwhelming shame is something that amazes me to this day. There was a malignant cynicism at the heart of the defence and it stuck around as long as the issued remained before the public. However, the notion that Canadian officials had no direct reports of alleged torture unravelled quickly. Within forty-eight hours of Graeme's story, the new political director of the provincial reconstruction base, Gavin Buchan, and a Corrections Canada officer who was mentoring Afghan justice officials were inside Sarpoza Prison and heard abuse claims from two inmates. Eventually Canadian diplomats, with the help of Afghan intelligence, identified three of the four prisoners quoted in the *Globe and Mail*.

Privately, the head of the NDS was furious. The suave, articulate, well-mannered Amrullah Saleh threatened to arrest the patrician Abdul Qadar Noorzai, and accused him of being the source of Graeme's story and "an Iranian spy." Canadian diplomats had to talk him down from the ceiling.

The Karzai government put its hand over its heart and promised a thorough investigation within days of the story. The news release from the Afghan embassy made all the right noises and the Ottawa press corps duly noted it. What wasn't apparent at the time was how mystified Kabul was over the uproar. Their silent composure belied a layer of recalcitrance, which hid an amiable savagery. A secret Foreign Affairs note, which surfaced later in the war, told of an April 25 meeting involving diplomats and Hamid Karzai's chief of staff. The Canadians were there to deliver a démarche, a formal representation. Omar Daoudzai evidently hadn't read the papers.

"Daoudzai was not aware of the issue. Nor was he seemingly especially concerned," said the note.

He gazed at the diplomats in amazement and noted that "this wasn't the first time" the NDS had been accused of torture.

"According to Daoudzai, for Afghans, this is not an issue—they are more worried about getting blown up in a suicide bombing."

He looked the diplomats straight in the eye: "If a Taliban is tortured . . ." Daoudzai's voice trailed off and he shrugged.

If the Afghans were sanguine, NATO was losing its mind. The story sent the acting civilian head of the mission rocketing over to the country's deputy minister of justice. He was met with the same blasé haze and empty smiles.

"There is great concern within NATO about this issue, which could have 'enormous political implications' across the alliance," the April 25 report continued. "The US ambassador among others has expressed concern. NATO would therefore like to see Karzai very speedily announce an impartial investigation."

The allies grumbled to one another that "an internal NDS whitewash" would simply not do. But then there was the burning question: Did they really want to know what had happened?

The moment Graeme's story appeared, Richard Colvin hammered Ottawa to rewrite the arrangement that prevented Canadians from following up with their own prison inspections. He wrote a forceful memo to Foreign Affairs headquarters, telling his superiors that without close monitoring by Canada, "efforts to prevent abuse of detainees were not likely to be successful." Colvin argued that the Red Cross was not permitted to report directly to Canada and that the AIHRC lacked the capacity to do the job.

"In our view, the only practical and sustainable solution is for Canada to take responsibility for the well being of Canadian detainees in [Government of Afghanistan] custody," said a memo dated April 25, 2007.

It was the last thing senior officials in Ottawa wanted to hear. Colvin received a telephone call from the assistant deputy minister of Foreign Affairs, Colleen Swords. She told him not to put stuff in writing and to use the telephone. Conducting business verbally was a well-known practice in Ottawa, meant to get around the access-to-information system through which long-forgotten memos often came back to bite officials in the arse. Swords later told a special House of Commons committee investigation that her intent wasn't nefarious; she simply wanted to talk things out before anything was committed to paper.

The veteran bureaucrat denied she was trying to silence Colvin, but suggested she did want more rigourous analysis of what Canadian diplomats were hearing. "I welcomed and expected factual reporting from the field," said Swords, who went on to be the associate deputy minister in the Department of Indian Affairs and Northern Development. Colvin scoffed at the explanation.

"Her message to me was that I should use the phone instead of writing," he said in 2009. "I had never met or even spoken to Ms. Swords before her phone call, and did not do so again until after I had left Afghanistan."

By the time of the *Globe* story, bureaucrats had developed something called a Detainee Diplomatic Contingency Plan. It was one of those break-glass-in-case-of-fire measures, although nowhere did it mention that Canada should rewrite its prisoner-transfer arrangement with Kabul. Regardless, with the House of Commons burning out of control over the torture allegations, it was time to break the glass. The Kabul embassy, in an analysis separate from Colvin's note, weighed in with three additions to the contingency plan: negotiating a new deal, setting up a system to monitor prisoners and asking the military to capture fewer people. Within hours, David Mulroney had vetoed the recommendations in a blistering e-mail. He told Colvin to implement the contingency plan as written. Mulroney was never one to tolerate dissent once a decision had been made, but within hours, the war inside the war took a dramatic turn.

It was standing room only at the Commons foreign affairs committee when Gordon O'Connor made his appearance. He looked tired and grumpy as MPs squeezed into Parliament's West Block hearing room. The only thing anybody wanted to talk about was Afghan prisoners and O'Connor pretty much shut them down. He blurted out that an agreement had been reached with Kabul for Canadian officials to check on the prisoners they'd captured "any time they want." He refused to lay out details. He left the hearing enveloped by journalists, a prickly mass of microphones, camera lenses and lights that moved with him to the elevator. He remained stone-faced at the cacophony of questions. The next day, however, the prime minister rose in the Commons and contradicted him. No, he said, there wasn't a deal. Stockwell Day tried to douse the flames. His correctional service officers had had access all along, he said; there was nothing to worry about. He was quickly shut down by the Afghan ambassador, Omar Samad, who said no such access was ever granted.

A rewritten transfer arrangement was signed on May 3, 2007, but not before the issue had reduced the Harper government to a babbling, incoherent mess.

I ran in to Jack Layton shortly afterward coming out of the elevator near his sixth-floor office in the Centre Block of Parliament. He just looked at me and shook his head.

"This is chaos," he said.

Earlier, in the Commons, Stéphane Dion had looked around at the confusion and marvelled at the government's inability to keep its story straight.

"We would laugh, Mr. Speaker, if . . . human being's lives were [not] at stake."

Jojo had been warned several times not to come back to Kandahar Airfield. And when dudes from the U.S. Special Forces are issuing the warnings, it's more than just a friendly suggestion. The warning and a lot of what happened to Jojo really didn't make much sense at the time, and it makes even less sense when you look back on it.

Jojo had started working for the Special Forces soon after the 2001 invasion, and had then moved on to private security contractors. He was in with them. He was cool. When he started shooting and fixing for CTV following the Canadian move to Kandahar, Jojo was one of the only Afghans given a camp pass, which basically got him on the airfield with few restrictions. It was nothing to turn around in the media tent and see him coming through the door, carrying a tripod, with one of the reporters or cameramen in tow.

Other Afghans, the folk who came to clean toilets and mop floors, got the full once-over from security. Not Jojo. He breezed through the gate with his oversized shades and rock-star demeanour. I remember one of the Romanian guards cracking up over the country music that blared from Jojo's car. He ate in the mess tent, bought coffee at the Green Bean alongside the soldiers, picked up a few trinkets for his family on the ever-expanding boardwalk, and left the Saturday market outside the gate with an arm full of action-flick DVDs. He was so accepted he was part of the wallpaper.

The threats started in the summer of 2007 and by fall his access to the base had inexplicably dried up. That was when he was warned to stay away. I'm not quite sure when his break with the Americans started, but it was pretty clear that the Canadian military hated his guts right from the beginning. I remember one officer, early in the mission, warning all of us not to go out with him; they were fairly confident he'd "end up dead in a ditch somewhere." The officer never said who would do the shooting. We all took it with a grain of salt. The footage Jojo shot of suicide bombings and the interviews he conducted with ordinary Afghans often contradicted the official line, something that was deeply embarrassing and frustrating to a government and military that was already hopelessly inarticulate. They had plenty of reasons not to like Jojo.

One day in late October, Jojo got a cellphone call, straight out of the blue, from a guy who passed himself off as a U.S. Army public affairs officer. The man invited Jojo out to KAF in order to have a chat and fill out a survey that all local journalists were required to complete. Later, in e-mails, Graeme Smith and Al Stephens filled in the rest of the story.

Jojo and CTV reporter Steve Chao had been at the gate when an Afghan family arrived with a bloodied, injured child. The family begged for help and claimed the young boy had been shot by the Canadians. It was chaos. There was crying and screaming and no one except Jojo spoke Pashtu. The sentries called an ambulance from the multinational hospital at the base, known as the Role 3, and when it arrived, Jojo jumped in the back and went with the family in order to translate.

Sometime later, as both Jojo and Chao left the plywood-and-tent complex, a group of U.S. military police officers slammed them up against a chain-link fence with guns drawn.

"Don't move!" they screamed.

Jojo was wrestled face down into the dirt. It took a few minutes of talking before the military cops realized Chao was a Canadian citizen. He was let go, warned and shoved on his way. Jojo, however, was taken to "the round house," KAF's prisoner detention facility. His brother, who had been waiting in the car outside of the gate, was also briefly detained as MPs searched the vehicle and seized almost everything in it, including $17,000 worth of camera equipment belonging to CTV. The material was never returned, despite repeated pleas to the Pentagon, which assured the television network after every letter that it "was looking into the matter." They also took the cash Jojo had set aside to buy a plot of land outside of Kandahar.

When we spoke much later in the war, Jojo said he was held in Kandahar for nine days before being sent to the U.S. prison facility at Bagram Airfield. His head was shaved, he said, and he was put in an orange jumpsuit. He claims not to have been allowed to sleep and he refused to eat. He said he was told he was going to Guantanamo Bay and had been accused of providing weapons to the Taliban as well as having contact with senior leaders of the insurgency in Kandahar. Military cops said they found insurgent cellphone numbers in his address book. Of that there was no doubt. Everyone knew Jojo had outstanding access to the Taliban, the results of which were splashed all over Canadian television screens and newspapers. It was in the interest of the insurgents to cultivate an ambitious, young Afghan journalist, rather than chop his head off for co-operating with infidels.

When we learned of it, the weapons accusation left everyone gobsmacked. Canadian officers privately added a heavy heaping of smear by suggesting the Taliban tipped off Jojo to suicide bombings. That, in their estimation, was what allowed him to get such great, exclusive footage. It was an utterly ridiculous assertion and spoke loudly about the ignorance of some in uniform as to how journalists did their jobs in war zones. For the accusation to be true, I pointed out to an intelligence officer one evening over a cigar, Jojo would have had to know what the vehicle looked like ahead of time. He would have had to chase it through the streets as it searched for targets of opportunity. As anyone who's driven in a private car in that city would know, trying to keep up with normal traffic, let alone a jihad-crazed bomber seeking his reward, is next to impossible. Besides, I knew from my own experience that Jojo did what every other Afghan journalist, including Khan, did. He heard the explosion, saw the smoke plume and drove toward it.

What never seemed to enter the minds of his critics, both inside and outside the military, was the guts it took to run toward an explosion armed only with a camera. Another fact they carelessly disregarded was that if Jojo had truly been what they claimed, he would have at one point or another been able to sell one of us to the Taliban and possibly even al-Qaeda. He could have slipped away and lived like a king for the rest of his life. It never happened.

Throughout his ordeal, Jojo protested his innocence, but never denied his contacts with the Taliban. It was, he claimed, his job as a journalist to seek them out and include their voices in his reporting. He told me much later in an e-mail that one of his guards stopped him as he was clapped in irons and led away to Bagram.

"He told me: 'Journalists have no rights in this war,'" he wrote in February 2009. "Remember that, bro."

In the winter of 2008, a secret military review board at the detention centre declared Jojo an unlawful enemy combatant and claimed there was "credible information" to support the charge. Naturally, nobody outside the base ever saw the evidence.

The International Justice Network and the Committee to Protect Journalists took up his cause. Legal challenges were mounted in the U.S. because human rights groups saw the detention as part of a wider tactic by the military in both Afghanistan and Iraq to intimidate the media.

Jojo spent eleven months in Bagram, where he claimed he was interrogated repeatedly and made to stand barefoot in the snow for hours on end. He said he was sent to solitary confinement after the New York Times published an article about his plight. There are tales of chains and being forced to stand in the stress position. He compared his treatment and that of his fellow captives to the treatment of animals. After his release, the U.S. military denied his claims and said "there was no evidence of mistreatment."

It would be a cliché to say Jojo was changed by his time in detention and leave it at that. When we spoke in the winter of 2009, I hardly recognized him. The scruff on his cheeks had grown into a thin, wispy beard and his shrewd, brown eyes had hardened to the point where they looked as though they'd crack. But it was his voice that freaked me out the most. It had this disembodied, almost maniacal chime that was both chilling and heartbreaking. There wasn't much left of the slick entrepreneur who had seemed endlessly enthralled with all things Western. That man had been ground to dust between the stones of the two worlds. Jojo had reached out and embraced with moxie the Western ideals of wealth and getting ahead at all costs. In the end, it was both his religion and his undoing.

I remember reading an e-mail from him one day and gasping at the signature line: Javed Ahmed Kakar/Jojo. The Miracle and The Killing Machine.

It's funny the things you remember about certain days. It rained really hard in Ottawa the morning John Manley was appointed to review the war in Afghanistan—one of those cold, hard, autumn rains that chips away at your cheeks. It had eased by the time the bus arrived downtown. It was heavily overcast on the walk to the World Exchange Plaza, but by the time I emerged, coffee in hand, the sky had begun to clear and shafts of sunlight cut between the squat, concrete buildings. It turned into one of those fresh, cool, glorious October days, the kind where you just want to breathe in the air.

Nobody saw Manley coming, or at least very few outside of the PMO did. A source who often had his finger on the pulse of the war during that time said he was startled. One day, he looked through an open doorway in the brownstone fortress of the Langevin Block and there was Manley, waiting to see Stephen Harper. Initially, the source didn't make the connection and thought it was some unscheduled session with the former Liberal deputy prime minister. That Manley would be consulted on Afghanistan seemed the furthest thing from everyone's mind.

Staff close to the prime minister looked at the calendar in the spring of 2007 and came to a few conclusions: Canada was stuck; we simply couldn't walk away from Kandahar; and the Parliamentary mandate had to be renewed. Insiders said senior policy advisor Mark Cameron pressed Harper's chief of staff, Ian Brodie, to recommend a blue-ribbon panel with Manley as its head. At the same time, Clerk of the Privy Council Kevin Lynch, the most senior federal civil servant, and Susan Cartwright, the deputy secretary to cabinet and a senior foreign policy advisor, came to the same conclusion, only they called it a "red-ribbon" panel.

It took until fall to put all of the pieces in place. There were a number of moving parts, not the least of which were the allies, whom PMO staff considered "frozen" and waiting for a new U.S. administration. Domestically, the aim was to galvanize the civilian side of the mission.

"Foreign Affairs and CIDA were plainly not putting the same effort into the ground effort as the CF were, and that had to change," said a senior Conservative source.

Word of the independent commission filtered out in a friendly leak to CTV a couple of hours before Harper and Manley strolled into Parliament's Centre Block. In theory, the arrangement looked a lot like the commission George W. Bush had assembled to chart a way out of Iraq. Some PMO staffers detested that comparison. The Press Gallery gleefully made repeated references to it.

"Our government wants a full, open and informed debate about our options," Harper said in the House of Commons foyer. "Given what's at stake . . . we are prepared to announce today an independent panel to study our options."

Much later in the war, it became clear that the media, the Opposition and the general public weren't the only ones shocked by the decision. Conservatives were too, including senior members of the government and key decision makers.

"It wasn't discussed with the broader cabinet, no," Defence Minister Peter MacKay said in a 2010 interview.

I put down my pen. "Did you know?" I asked.

"I didn't know all of the specifics," he said quietly, his voice trailing off uncomfortably.

The two of us sat in half-embarrassed silence for a minute. The natural thing would have been to ask how he felt about it, but I hardly needed to. His reticence said it all.

The recruiting of Manley was a stroke of political brilliance, something the Conservative spin doctors happily underlined with their repeated use of the phrase "eminent Canadians" to describe the panel. It was hard to disagree. The panel consisted of Pamela Wallin, a former journalist and president of the Americas Society and the Council of the Americas in New York; former U.S. ambassador Derek Burney; former Canadian National Rail president Paul Tellier, who'd also served as clerk of the Privy Council under Brian Mulroney; and former Mulroney-era health minister Jake Epp. It was an impressive array of very smart people, but Manley was certainly the prize. The business community adored him and Conservatives respected him. MacKay noted with a smirk that some on the government benches considered Manley "one of them."

"I would characterize him as small 'c' on a number of philosophical issues, especially when it came to support for the military," he said.

The lovefest harkened back to Manley's famous comment while serving as foreign affairs minister under Jean Chrétien: "You can't just sit at the G8 table [the group of leading Western economies] and then, when the bill comes, go to the washroom."

Not surprisingly, much of the coverage on the day the commission was announced focused on the finger in the eye it presented to then-Liberal leader Stéphane Dion. Manley looked almost sheepish answering questions. He said he'd called Dion the night before and explained that he believed Canada's future in Afghanistan transcended partisan politics. He emphasized he was still a Liberal.

When chased down by reporters that day, Dion said the panel would be useful, but that it shouldn't be used as a cover to extend the end of the combat mission, which at the time was slated for February 2009. Bob Rae, the Liberal foreign affairs critic who had yet to win a seat in a by-election, welcomed the panel. It was precisely the sort of division that all of us covering the story expected to see and were eager to trumpet. But what we saw and portrayed as an attempt to further undermine Dion was, according to MacKay, a conscientious overture to work with Liberals who knew that Canada could not simply walk away.

The "coup" of recruiting Manley "allowed us to reach across the aisle and build a pedway for some rebels to walk across," he said. "They weren't comfortable coming out at that point and saying we need to support an extension of the mission. Although many of them would have private, in-the-hallway conversations with you, they would not agree to state their opinions publicly. Bob Rae was one of those."

By the fall of 2007 Afghanistan had become "a political, partisan morass," MacKay said. "We couldn't get past the daily to-ing and fro-ing of Question Period and say, 'What is the right thing for us to do here?'"

The skulking, official paralysis had also gripped the civilian administration at the National Defence. No one can understate the traumatic effect the 1990s had on the Canadian military establishment. The results of years of budget restraint, cancelled programs and used, fire-prone submarines could be found in the wavering that accompanied the purchase of battlefield helicopters, something each field commander saw as an imperative. Lieutenant-Colonel Ian Hope, the first battle group commander in 2006, had made an impassioned plea. Airlift was essential for getting soldiers off Kandahar's bloody, booby-trapped laneways, he said. Seeing the need, the U.S. Army, in the spring of 2006, offered the Canadians six used CH-47D Chinook helicopters through a military hardware resale program. At any other time, the whole helicopter fiasco would have been funny. It was one of those comic, bureaucratic operas—complete with gravity and heavy, pondering music—but in the end it was just plain sad.

Despite Washington's offer, a source in the PMO said that at no point before the Manley Commission did the Defence Department "come to cabinet with an urgent request to buy helicopters." The Conservatives planned in the summer of 2006 to buy a fleet of CH-47Fs—the latest, greatest version of the helicopter. By the fall of 2006, with soldiers dying in droves, the air force was still dickering with Boeing about the specs and the improvements they wanted to see to make the chopper more Canadian. The auditor general would later take a flame-thrower to defence bureaucrats over the program, which at the time of writing still hadn't gotten a single CH-47F on to the tarmac.

MacKay tried to explain the hesitation. The U.S. Army's offer for the six used helicopters was there, he confirmed, but officials who pulled the strings at National Defence were suffering "shell shock" and were worried that somehow the politicians would pull the rug out from underneath them.

"They didn't turn them down. They deferred the decision until they could get the funding in place," MacKay said.

By the time of the Manley panel, that deferral had been going on for eighteen months. That should have been plenty of time to shake the loose change from between the cushions at the federal Treasury Board. No one who'd followed the Afghan war closely could ever understand why an independent panel was needed to push through equipment that was so clearly required and necessary to save lives. MacKay stuck to the political.

"The Armed Forces had the guts ripped out of it for a long, long time and to be completely fair by the end of Paul Martin's tenure some of these procurements had begun, but there was still a feeling in the upper echelon of the DND building that they were going to be able to secure the type of funding needed to get major equipment," he said in 2010.

"There was disbelief that they could move that quickly. The cabinet and the prime minister were very receptive to these requests."

There was another unspoken fear among bureaucrats at National Defence, who often get their backs up when the Chinook fiasco is mentioned. I lost count of the number of conversations I had with project officers, staff or public affairs officers who would mumble into their beer mugs or oversized café-latte bowls that they were petrified about starting some projects for fear the Harper Conservatives would fall and be replaced with the Dion Liberals, who would cancel whatever it was they intended to buy. The 2009 pull-out date was also an obstacle, they argued. Why spend hundreds of millions of dollars on helicopters and other shiny objects when the troops were coming home soon? Listening to it, you didn't know whether to laugh or cry.

Derek Burney put his finger on it in a much more procedural way when he noted the existence of three separate Afghanistan task forces within the federal government, one each in Foreign Affairs, Defence and CIDA.

After the Manley panel's report was released, Burney told *Maclean's* magazine that decision-making needed to be streamlined and that Stephen Harper should have demanded it.

"If the prime minister was in charge, you know what, I think the old creaky Ottawa bureaucracy would respond a little more quickly," Burney said.

The mechanical management of the war would eventually be centralized out of the Privy Council Office, the bureaucratic arm of the PMO. A special committee within the federal cabinet was also created to give greater oversight, as was a special House of Commons committee. It became bureaucratic overkill—death by committee and deliberation. Why the prime minister had not taken charge during his two years in office was a question many were too embarrassed to ask.

The panel spent time in Afghanistan, meeting with senior commanders and officials, and they got an unvarnished look at what a mess everything had become. You got the sense that no one tried to feed them the blind jargon of "progress," or that if someone did they weren't buying. In the same *Maclean's* article, Manley sounded startled and troubled by what he'd seen.

"What surprised us most in our visit was what we saw as a lack of coordination among the various groups and agencies that are there," he said. "You've got a Broadway musical with no choreographer. I mean, they're bumping into each other on the stage. They're not getting anything done. This is of critical importance."

The fact that other NATO countries were avoiding joining the fight alarmed Manley perhaps the most, and there was no mistaking how he felt when he and Burney testified before a Parliamentary committee following the release of the panel's report.

Unless NATO comes up with more troops and equipment, "Afghanistan could be lost—again," he said.

The final report, released January 22, 2008, recommended that Canada accept an indefinite extension to the combat mission, but on the condition the allies deliver a thousand extra combat troops to Kandahar. If they failed to do so, the panel suggested Ottawa should withdraw its troops on schedule in February 2009. Some of us who lined up at the microphone in the basement of the Ottawa hotel where the report was released likened the strategy to playing chicken with NATO. Manley and soon-to-be-senator Pamela Wallin preferred to use a more polite description: "leverage." They sat at a table in front of a series of giant screens checkerboarded with images of the war, including the perennial political favourite, Afghan children. It struck me as a startling contrast to have these highly starched and manicured people against the backdrop of bedraggled children—two worlds that rarely if ever met. But what made the biggest imprint was how free they were to speak their minds. Some of the words coming out of their mouths had already been uttered by Conservatives, or were things you knew they'd been tearing at themselves to say. Yet coming from Manley and the others it was somehow more credible, more believable, even more soothing, as though we were listening to a familiar CD.

If you closed your eyes for a moment and tried to imagine Stephen Harper mouthing those words, the effect just wasn't the same. The air had been made so noxious, so unbreathable by rhetoric that it was sad.

The nation was at war, and the words of its leader either couldn't be trusted or were dismissed as mindless politicking. The Conservatives under Harper were often hostages to their own dogma and practiced a narrow-eyed, ungenerous style of politics. While they were usually the authors of their own misfortune, most days they faced a shrill Opposition, whose shrieking accusations leaned more toward ranting than thoughtful research. That the Manley Commission had to be created at all said something so profound about the country that fair-minded people should have recoiled in horror. Finally, the war had been given to the adults to figure out.

Although he naturally disagreed with that kind of harsh assessment, MacKay acknowledged that the desire to extend the combat deployment was firmly established among cabinet before Harper assembled the panel. How to get the Opposition and the Canadian public to accept the inevitable was another matter. Hearing it from someone else was pretty much the only alternative.

"It was political cover as much as it was a practical contribution to what we were already attempting to do as a government," he said. "Without diminishing their advice, everything they recommended [on the equipment side] was in the pipeline and was either on the verge of being announced or was essentially already in place."

There were some elements of the final report that did catch the government by surprise. The offbeat idea of putting a dedicated political stamp on Kandahar reconstruction projects, for example, caused people in the development community to light their hair on fire. So-called signature projects, the idea of taking domestic credit for something as fundamentally altruistic as rebuilding a shattered country, was an offence to their sensibilities. The thought that the public needed to see something—anything—to justify the enormous expenditure of blood and treasure was so outside their realm of comprehension that it might as well have come from another planet. There were also some who saw it as pandering to criticism from the military and outside groups like the Senlis Council, which had savaged CIDA by calling for it to be removed from managing what was at that time $1.2 billion in projects. For the most part, staff at CIDA had successfully plugged their ears to the demands that development had to be delivered right away.

"Bullshit," thundered Graham Lowe, whom I met at the army staff college in Kingston, Ontario, around the time the Manley report came out. He was the former head of the UN Habitat program in Afghanistan.

By cleaning irrigation canals and sponsoring entrepreneurs, the way CIDA had, he said, Canada encouraged stable, long-term development and that was in everybody's interest.

"You go in and do something quickly," Lowe said. "It's visible. The only reason you want something visible is you want people to say how wonderful Canada is. If we're not noticed, then we're probably doing a better job."

He warned about the paternalistic bias in Western countries.

"We go into development thinking we have all the answers," he said. Lowe had spent the better part of two years in Afghanistan. "There is expertise in how to get things done and that expertise comes from the locals. If you're smart, you tap into it. We're so busy showing the 'darkies' what to do . . . instead of listening to what their problems are and reaching out to create that marriage of [our] experience and their expertise."

Nipa Banerjee, who at one point ran Canada's aid programs for CIDA in Afghanistan, was equally horrified. Singling out Kandahar created a special enchantment for the people there, a sense that they were being chosen, that they were special and somehow separate from the rest of the country, which was equally and perhaps even more deserving.

"Canada as a troop-contributing country should never have focused its aid predominantly in the province that houses its [provincial reconstruction team]," Banerjee said in an interview later in the war. "Such a strategy is vulnerable to criticism that aid is politicized and militarized."

Five months or so after the Manley report, the Harper government settled on three signature projects and a number of priorities, all bundled up in a tidy bureaucratic phrase: "benchmarks." What the government did—and this is something politicians are loath to do on most occasions—was set out a scorecard by which Canadians could measure progress in the war. The Prime Minister's Office may not have gotten the Taliban body count in 2006, but it did get this kinder, gentler report card, which it could enthusiastically wave in the public's face.

The quarterly reports delivered to Parliament were at first treated with the fanfare and preparation of a Hollywood blockbuster. Multiple cabinet ministers were paraded before the lights and cameras to solemnly reflect on the sacrifices while waxing poetic about the advances. To be sure, there were small victories at the time, but like everything else in Afghanistan they were isolated and incremental. Obscure factoids like the Canadian technical advisor in the Afghan Ministry of Education launching a round of teacher competency examinations became fodder for celebration. The relentless, grinding nature of the insurgency was—to the government's credit—borne out in the swath of pages that flooded into Parliament with machine-like efficiency. But the longer the stalemate dragged on, the more the show was scaled back. It dwindled to just one cabinet minister at a news conference in the basement of Parliament and then eventually to no media availability and nobody to answer questions. The report would just get tabled, sometimes on Friday afternoon, when everyone was getting ready to go home.

Canada set out to rebuild the Dahla dam, a creaky irrigation works north of Kandahar city; eliminate polio in the region through inoculation; and build or refurbish fifty schools in the province. It also set goals for training Afghan troops and cops, as well as improving the delivery of services such as health and education. There was an undeniable nobility to what was laid out on paper in front us. It all looked so good, so elegant, and those of us who'd been there since the bad old days of no plan whatsoever wanted to kiss the first development officer we saw. The full weight of the federal government's spin-machine was put behind the good works program. There were websites, testimonials, speaking tours and I'm sure there would have been a tickertape parade had the budget allowed. And that was before anything kicked into gear.

I remember being invited to talk with David Mulroney after the Manley panel reported and just before I went back to Kandahar in the spring of 2008. Mulroney, with salt-and-pepper hair and small, intense eyes, was perhaps one of the sharpest minds I'd met covering the war, but he was clearly uncomfortable acting as pitchman. He took time to talk to not only me but also to other Ottawa media colleagues about the good works that were at hand with the impending civilian surge. Kandahar was going to be flooded, for the first time, with enough diplomats and development officers to do the job properly.

When I hit the ground, some of the fine things he'd laid on the table were evident, but actually getting any of his people to talk about them was another matter. Some accuse the military of being a closed institution, but if you ask any journalist who covered Kandahar they will tell you they faced the most hostility, indifference, paranoia and vilification from the civilian side. They wanted your questions before you asked them and routinely ditched interviews with journalists on the ground in order to be the mar-quee speaker—via teleconference—at Foreign Affairs media briefings in Ottawa, where the great, insatiable beast known as the National Press Gallery would get its vicarious dose of war for a couple of hours a week. There was a deeply ingrained institutional cynicism that was unavoidable as much as it was impossible to comprehend. They were sometimes eager to showcase what they were doing, but they wanted the story told their way, without interruption. Most times, the stories they offered were window dressing, or carefully orchestrated photo-ops. I cannot begin to describe the dismay within the confines of the media tent when we would be would offered a chance to risk our lives to cover a ribbon-cutting somewhere. What wasn't cool, in most instances, was asking tough, uncomfortable questions about how money was being spent. They made it so tough to cover real news, real issues, that often journalists just gave up. The Manley panel had ordered the government to be more open, but we quickly found out that this didn't mean more articulate.

* * *

Stephen Harper's government accepted the panel's report and recommendations almost immediately in the winter of 2008, but in order to ram an extension through, the Conservatives needed the Liberals. Using John Manley as the bridge was brilliant, but it did not guarantee success. The one who really needed to be won over was Stéphane Dion, who went on the record during his 2006 leadership bid as opposing extension. Publicly, the Liberal leader was committed to ending the military deployment in February 2009—or before if possible—and repeatedly called in the Commons for Harper to issue a withdrawal notice to NATO. He was resentful that the prime minister had "blackmailed" Parliament in 2006 by threatening to unilaterally extend the combat mission and possibly call an election. Dion's stand was popular among the quasi–New Democrats who inhabited certain quarters of the Liberal caucus, but forces, both public and private, chipped away at his resolve. At a town hall meeting in Halifax in early 2007, the father of a soldier who'd been killed early in the mission implored him to reconsider. Dion refused to budge.

The real turning point came in December, when Dion and deputy leader Michael Ignatieff undertook a secret trip to Kabul and Kandahar, where they caught a first-hand glimpse of the war. They met with Hamid Karzai and senior officials around the Afghan president as well as military commanders. Ignatieff, who'd visited Afghanistan under the Taliban as an academic, was strongly in favour of some sort of extended commitment.

The Liberals, in their submission to the Manley Commission, stuck with Dion's line of seeing Canada out of Afghanistan by February 2009, but it was clear they were caving by the time the report came out. The panel's recommendation for an open-ended extension, as long as NATO anted up more troops, pretty much sealed their co-operation. Two weeks passed between the report and the government's official response of a proposed continuation until the end of 2011. The motion the Conservatives put before Parliament said the government "does not believe that Canada should simply abandon the people of Afghanistan after February 2009." The Conservative war machine was likely itching to paint Dion as someone who "abandoned" the Afghans. The motion made all of the right noises about more troops, extra equipment and development, yet Dion remained defiant. He said his party would propose amendments to the plan but stressed the combat part of the mission had to end on schedule.

"If we are ambiguous . . . it will be a never-ending mission," he told Vancouver's CKNW radio.

Ignatieff, who would say he didn't want to contradict his leader but then proceed to do so, pointed to the wording of the motion, which talked about a reduction in Canada's combat role. He suggested this could form the basis of a compromise. Twisting themselves into pretzel shapes had become a Liberal speciality on a whole host of issues, but the mother of them all had to be Afghanistan. They had gotten the country into this chaotic mess and while they scrambled to disavow, disown and disperse that legacy they still wanted to appear committed. They knew full well that if they ever formed a government, they would be staring into the hard eyes of their allies, including expectant Afghans. They proposed that the thousand reinforcements Manley had suggested should do the bulk of the fighting, while Canadians took up the more politically acceptable task of reconstruction. You could almost hear the shrieks of laughter coming from Kandahar, in between the concussion of roadside bombs. The proposal, however, did form the basis of a compromise and it allowed the Liberals to close their eyes and vote on March 13, 2008, to extend Canada's involvement, if not with a clean conscience, at least with the sense that they had put some kind of leash on the dogs of war.

The wording of the motion itself was tweaked and sugar-coated so the Liberals could swallow it without gagging. References to abandoning the Afghan people were replaced with "remaining committed to the people of

Afghanistan." It set out a very specific timeline that in and of itself laid seeds of political and public expectation—seeds that would be stomped on two-and-a-half years later.

The motion committed "the government of Canada [to] notify NATO that Canada will end its presence in Kandahar as of July 2011, and, as of that date, the redeployment of Canadian Forces troops out of Kandahar and their replacement by Afghan forces start as soon as possible, so that it will have been completed by December 2011."

The motion's nuances were lost on most commentators and on the public. They read it to mean that Canada would be out of Afghanistan entirely in three years, when in fact the door was left wide open for the army to go somewhere other than Kandahar. Yet six months after the motion passed, and at the beginning of the 2008 election, Stephen Harper slammed that door shut. He declared Canada would be out of Afghanistan entirely, leaving behind only a few soldiers to guard the embassy. The statement solidified an assumption in the minds of the public, the media, the Ottawa bureaucracy and Canada's allies. And as almost everyone knows, assumptions are harder to kill than facts.

A little more than three weeks later, there was an undeniable gravity in the room as the prime minister formally announced the 2011 extension. The Canadian delegation at the NATO leaders' summit in Bucharest, Romania, commandeered a room in Nicolae Ceauşescu's cold, gaudy marble palace. With its imperial columns, wide-sweeping staircases, red carpets and gleaming crystal chandeliers, the place breathed history. Unfortunately, it was a septic, brutal, self-indulgent kind of tale. Most Romanians looked at the palace as a symbol of the delusions of a mad dictator, who'd hoarded all of the country's marble over the course of decade in order to build a gross monument to himself. Some were convinced Ceauşescu's ghost wandered the empty corridors where the country's Parliament now chose to sit. It was a remarkable backdrop from which to tell Canadians there would be three more years of war.

The French immediately agreed to supply more troops for eastern Afghanistan, a deal brokered among the linen napkins and clinking silverware at the perfunctory leaders' dinner. The moment President Nicolas Sarkozy made it known, George W. Bush completed the domino effect by telling Stephen Harper that the Americans were finally able to free up fresh boots for Kandahar.

"There wasn't any rock-solid assurances going in to the summit that anything was going to fall into place," Peter MacKay said later, "but there was a feeling of confidence going into Bucharest that we had plowed the ground and done all of the back-channelling . . . that would allow us to piece together what was needed to create a better scenario for us in Kandahar."

Yet when the heavy wooden door closed and the Canadian delegation shut out the rest of the allies to announce it was staying in Afghanistan, something felt amiss. I looked up from my notepad and tape recorder. Harper, MacKay and Foreign Affairs Minister Maxime Bernier were on the platform, and all of the familiar staff faces had assembled in the wings. Then it struck me. General Rick Hillier, the man whose fingerprints were all over this war, was nowhere to be seen. In fact, throughout the summit, we hadn't heard a peep from him and the only sighting had been a passing glimpse in the hallway. His absence from such an historic, if somewhat anti-climactic event, resonated like thunder and would only make sense a few weeks later, when he announced his retirement.

One of the other things that struck me about the statement and the summit overall was how the prime minister had moderated his language around the war. Gone was the old rhetoric about the fight against the Taliban being a blow against terrorism.

"What we've actually found is: when you argue our self-interest, that's actually less appealing to Canadian public opinion than the argument that we are actually concretely helping the Afghan people with their lives," Harper said, sitting next to Hamid Karzai at a panel discussion.

It was a profound shift and not all of it related to Manley's finding that the government had been hopelessly inarticulate about Afghanistan. It was evident that Harper had done a lot of thinking. Only a few months before Bucharest, I'd been part of a tag team of CP reporters who'd interviewed him in the living room of 24 Sussex Drive. I'd asked why, in his opinion, the public didn't seem to appreciate what was at stake in Afghanistan.

"I don't know, the short answer is I don't know," he said with a slight sense of amazement and maybe even irritation.

For a moment, it looked like he was going straight to the on-message track, but then the answer became more thoughtful: "The government understands we took on an important international commitment for important reasons of international security that in the long run impact directly on our country.

"So I don't know whether Canadians do—or don't—understand. I think Canadians are deeply troubled by the casualties."

Afterward, I slipped on my coat and thumbed my cellphone for a cab pickup. My colleagues and I were standing in the basement of the drafty, old Victorian mansion.

"Can I have a cab for 24 Sussex Drive?" I said when the dispatcher picked up.

"Sure. Is that an apartment or a house?"

I just looked at the cellphone and then gawked at my colleague Bruce Cheadle.

We had talked and talked so much about Afghanistan. Maybe it wasn't that people misunderstood. Maybe they were just completely unplugged.

An Epitaph to Good Intentions 16

My stomach always twisted into knots during a lockdown. It didn't matter whether I was in Kandahar or someplace else. Knowing there were casualties had a way of focusing one's attention like nothing else I'd experienced in journalism. The military's self-imposed silence following a battle gave all of us the chance to reflect on how we'd be writing a terrible story that day and how somewhere out there someone's life had been ruined or irrevocably changed. While we waited for the army to notify those families, it was hard not think about how intimate this war had become. You'd sit there wondering if you'd known, interviewed or run across the person who'd been hurt or killed. The longer the war went on, the more likely that was.

It was eerie how the word "lockdown" could halt all of the nervous, bored, incoherent talk in the media tent. Nobody seemed interested in going to Green Bean for coffee or the U.S. Post-Exchange (PX), if you happened to be at KAF. Out at the forward bases, you'd sit in the mess tent and stare at the big screen, though you weren't really watching it. You knew you might be writing someone's obituary that day, and the thought sobered you up pretty quickly. Our words often ended up being the first and last written about many of these people—at least in national publications—and that carried a certain weight, a burden of conscience that got heavier each time it happened.

It was worse not being in Kandahar, as screwed up as that sounds. On the one hand, you were relieved of the responsibility of writing the story; on the other hand, you felt sidelined. News of the lockdown would percolate up from the foreign desk in a tightly held "FYI"—just in case there was anything to contribute as the story unfolded. But essentially, you were cut off and blind. The worst aspect was that you were surrounded by well-meaning colleagues or politicos who would talk nonchalantly about the horror and fear of Afghanistan without ever having been. Most wouldn't even know a lockdown was underway. It could make the casual, sometimes awful things they'd say about the war, about what we were doing there or not doing there, sound so callous and ugly.

I learned about Sergeant Jason Boyes on a day like that. He was killed on March 16, 2008. I was in Ottawa, still in the throes of covering the Commons debate that would lead to the final, three-year extension of the mission. It was one of those fresh, bright days, the kind that contained the promise of spring. Only a few weeks before, Boyes and I had been thrown together for an interview. Both Jason and Jay Adair, newly promoted to major, were offered up as subjects for a piece about the burdens and strains of multiple tours. We reminisced about the spring of 2006 and each of them talked about the battle of Bayanzi, where Nichola Goddard had been killed. It was a touchstone event for both men, a moment seared into their memories. Jason had been a heavy weapons commander during the first tour and went back as a platoon sergeant.

We talked little about the travails of Afghanistan, and more about family and life. Guys usually loved to chat about weapons, bad food, hot chicks, uncomfortable boots, sports and politics—in that order. Jason was different. He tried to come off gruff and unsentimental, but it was an act. He lit up whenever he mentioned his wife, Alison, and their two-year-old daughter, Mackenzie. Between pre-deployment training, the rotation in 2006, more training and the latest mission, Jason had been away for most of her short life. Even still, there was a bond. Father and daughter shared the same birthday and whenever Alison would walk past his picture on the shelf, she'd point at it and say, "Daddy." Mackenzie would notice and whenever he came home, Jason said she knew who Daddy was.

Never one for writing letters, Jason said he kept in touch with Alison through e-mail and the ten-minute satellite phone calls each of the guys was allotted every couple of days. He said Alison understood that soldiering was what he did and realized "that's probably never going to change." She accepted that there were things he had to do that he didn't want to do.

"At the end of the day, I think, she's very proud of what I do," he said.

Asking somebody if they have "reservations" is code for "are you afraid?" You didn't ask that too often. Years of experience taught me never to ask it bluntly, even though soldiers usually relished frankness. Jason paused for what seemed to be a long time. Sure. He had reservations. But he'd done the math and figured the odds were in his favour.

"I'm a black-and-white person," he said. "Math doesn't really lie, [but] any sane, rational person has that little voice in their head that says, yeah, well, guess what . . ."

Jason said he extinguished his doubts by thinking about what he saw on the streets of Kandahar. He brought to mind images of barefoot, dust-coated Afghan children, begging along the roadside for pens and paper by making scribbling motions on the palms of their hands. I'd seen it myself.

"When I listen to some of the more intelligent people speak, I know that these people are ready for a change; I'm more than willing to go and help; me and my platoon mates."

Many guys I knew who'd been there had fallen into positions of rocklike cynicism and irony over what the war was all about. Their compassion had been scrubbed raw by the Judas kiss of Afghan ways or their own disillusionment. Few would tell you that there was much about the place or the people that was worth their life. If they were going to die, it was usually for their buddies. Guys who were forced to pick bits of flesh off the sides of their armoured vehicles were rightly given an exemption from spouting noble ideals, but there were always exceptions.

"At the end of the day, I'm extraordinarily proud to be a Canadian," Jason told me. "I love my country. I believe in what we're doing there and what Canada is trying to do is the right thing."

Jason died going through the door of a booby-trapped compound in Panjwaii.

When the lockdown ended in Kandahar that day and his name was flashed across the computer screen, I pushed back from my keyboard with a startled, involuntary jerk. I went and stood in the hallway outside the Ottawa bureau and stared at the pictures that lined the corridor, snapshots of history and important people. The elevator opened. Some of my fellow reporters stepped out and wondered what was wrong. I took the stairs down from our eighth-floor perch and stood outside without a jacket. It was freezing and the sunshine was blinding. The smokers huddled nearby in the alcoves of the government buildings. Bored civil servants wandered the pedestrian mall. Some had iPod buds shoved in their ears to block out the world and their own thoughts. Others hurried over the slick granite stones, preoccupied with getting out of the cold and around the snow banks that had accumulated during the brutal winter. I wandered up the street, not quite sure what I was looking for or where I was going. The cold finally drove me back inside. I stood in the Press Gallery building's glass enclosure and marvelled at how everyone just kept walking past, heads down. No one even looked up.

* * *

The stalemate had been going on in Kandahar for a year when the first whispers of compromise were finally heard. They were subtle, almost imperceptible, except to those who'd been around for the bad old days of "save the planet, whack a terrorist." Patrols would step off in Panjwaii and Zhari in the spring of 2008 to wind their way through Bronze Age villages. The sprinkling of development workers who now joined them would sit down in cross-legged shuras with phlegmatic elders. By that point, it had become an almost ritual dance: the same words and the same old promises of co-operation were exchanged in the same tiresome steps until one side or the other waltzed out the door. It had happened so often that some of the soldiers doing force protection on the meetings could predict to the minute how long they would last.

But that spring, someone switched the tune. The dance steps shifted and the conversation underwent a subtle but significant change. "Tell us where the Taliban might be so we can 'get' them and help you" became "tell the Taliban that they aren't going to win and if they come in, we are willing to talk and maybe find them jobs." If there was a moment when counter-insurgency (the winning of hearts and minds) asserted itself over counterterrorism (taking out bad guys) it came during those months. The idea that we would consider talking to low-level Taliban drew an incendiary reaction from the defence minister's office and culminated in a call to my cellphone in Kandahar from Peter MacKay. He had agreed to an interview from Halifax to "set the record straight" on what was happening in the fields west of Kandahar city. The political trench lines in Ottawa were deeper and the positions more hardened than the bunkers outside my tent. It was all part of the zero-sum politics that drove this war off the cliff. The army, bloodied by almost two years of combat, adapted to the reality on the ground. Yet the government wasn't prepared to cede one centimetre. It had massaged its post-Bucharest message to refocus the war aims on helping the Afghans, but to concede that negotiation could play any sort of role in stopping the bloodletting was simply a bridge too far. MacKay said it was up to the Afghans to seek reconciliation, but if you talked to people in President Hamid Karzai's circle, they got virtually no support from the international community for peace bids. One of the president's aides laughed when I read back the official Canadian position, as articulated by MacKay. He literally howled. It would be another two years before allied nations would grudgingly promise cash so Karzai could try to buy off what everyone knew was a largely mercenary army. They promised $500 million in the winter of 2010, but prying the cash out of everyone's hands proved to be a gruelling exercise. Months after the trust fund was established, it had collected only a fraction of the committed funds.

There had always been clear divisions among the allies, stretching back almost to the beginning of the war. The British and the Dutch both favoured talking, but were shouted down by the Americans and, to a lesser extent, the Canadians. You got the sense in those days that there were some who just wanted to blast away and turn the whole country into a parking lot. They would have been happy to bomb and keep bombing until all 804 kilometres of the Hindu Kush were squashed flat. There was an almost impotent rage to some of the comments—a cry in the night, a rage against the storm, a tacit acknowledgement that the country couldn't be won, just obliterated.

If we needed any more proof that something had to give, all you had to do was to follow my colleague Doug Schmidt from the *Windsor Star* to a shura in one of the hotly contested villages in Panjwaii. The date and the actual village escape me now, but I recall him coming back from the patrol in mid-2008 with a befuddled expression. Doug had a round, happy face and a lilting voice. He found everything fascinating and dealt with the ugliness, grinding poverty and uncertainty of Kandahar with a gentle good nature, even when confronted with bullies. He'd sat quietly at the back of a shura that day and was allowed to ask a few questions at the end. Naturally he asked about the Taliban. The elders looked startled.

"We are the Taliban," one of them declared.

I guess you could have heard a pin drop. I'm not sure if any of the soldiers tightened the grip on their guns, but the villagers didn't flinch.

"The Taliban are our local people. We speak their language, we can work with them," one elder mumbled into his beard.

The meeting broke up and everybody went on his way.

Around the same time, Canadian Major-General Marc Lessard walked into a provincial shura. The gathering of up to fifty tribal elders happened every few months in Kandahar and many of the grizzled, bearded chieftains had seen a parade of officers come and go. But as the newly appointed commander of NATO troops in southern Afghanistan, Lessard admitted later on to exhibiting a certain swagger.

"It was in the first month I was COM RC-South and I thought I was a saviour," said Lessard, who went on to command all of Canada's overseas operations.

He was infused with the mantra, the new way of thinking, which said that the allies were there to help, protect and rebuild shattered lives and land. Lessard and other NATO commanders outlined their plans for the coming months and waited for the wave of approval. It never occurred to him that the Afghans would be anything less than grateful. What he got was a rude shock.

"They appreciated and accepted a little of what we were doing, but then said, 'You're foreigners,'" he recalled.

And then there was the crowning touch, delivered with no amount of subtlety, grace or apology.

"You're non-Muslim."

Lessard, a tall, quiet soldier with large brown eyes, was utterly amazed.

"Ooookay then," he told them.

These people were poor; they were desperate; they'd been slaughtering each other for decades, yet for pride or misplaced moral superiority they were unwilling to accept the help and guidance of so-called infidels. I'm not sure if that said more about our nature or theirs.

The meeting made a lasting impression on Lessard. In a later conversation, he offered what could be called an epitaph to good intentions. "We had their support, we had their approval, but I don't think we had their full commitment in terms of what could they do for us."

* * *

It was late one evening and I was alone in the media tent, trying to watch a movie on my laptop, which was always a weird experience. It was even more surreal if you were at a forward base in the middle of nowhere. Movies immersed you in the familiar, the comfortable and the safe. You could watch your favourite TV shows with the crash of artillery outside the tent or hard-topped shelter. Places, people, things that you'd recognize, feelings that reminded you of home—no matter how contrived—were supposed to lighten the burden. But I knew guys who couldn't watch a full DVD in one shot. They'd have to pause it, remind themselves of where they were and then restart the movie.

"It's fucked, I know," a soldier once said to me, "but you gotta stay real, man."

The problem that night was that I couldn't find the pause button for real life. Khan and I had roamed the roads that day in a futile attempt to track down some sketchy information about Jojo's imprisonment. We knew the Americans had tossed him in a cage at Bagram. That fact was never in doubt; hadn't been for months. But we'd been hearing things about his treatment. Some of the employees at the local human rights commission office talked darkly about what they'd heard, but were too petrified to verify it or go on the record. The volcanic anger of the country's intelligence director over the prisoner torture scandal in Canada had them running scared whenever a Western reporter showed his or her face.

Very little could distract me that evening. A photographer from a small French wire service had embedded with Canadians after spending weeks with the U.S. Marines in Helmand province. He'd been in the tent earlier and had chatted up a storm. He was a character. Most of us were amazed that he hadn't been summarily shot by some annoyed leatherneck. There are times when you run across people who embody all of their national stereotypes. "Le petit froggy," as he'd christened himself, was one of those people. He was short, dark-haired, slightly built and fond of sandals and cursing exclusively in French, even when he was speaking English. He'd been everywhere and covered everything—life experiences that only reinforced the notion that the French were the most culturally evolved creatures on the planet. He would sigh at the slightest inconvenience, especially if a computer was involved. It was annoying at first, but there was a genuine, manic life-at-the-edge quality that made him oddly endearing. He'd just left the tent when there were two business like knocks on the steel door. The task force public affairs officer stepped in. Major Jay Janzen was tall with a broad handshake that had a tendency to swallow your hand like a baseball mitt. He had a booming voice, but was a good listener and sincere.

We were under lockdown, he told us, but it would be the next morning before the general could say anything. I closed my laptop. Screw it, I thought.

People get torn up in different ways by Kandahar, some obvious, some not so obvious. The dead you can see. You know they're there, along with the wounded. It's evident. It's real, sometimes a little too real. Talk to any of the guys who washed blood out of the back of a LAV or picked up pieces of a friend after a bombing and you encounter a whole different kind of real. It didn't even have to be a friend; it could be an enemy. I once watched soldiers pick up bits of a suicide bomber who'd blown up himself up at the gates of a forward operating base. The attack had happened a day or so before, but the first cleanup had been a rush job and the guys were sent back out. They collected the chunks in plastic garbage bags and brought them back in to be burned. The effects may have been harder to see, but you knew what that kind of real did to people. Kandahar was the kind of unsparing, remorseless place that wasn't satisfied just to steal body and mind. It clawed at you in ways you'd never expect.

It was the next day before they told us who was dead. I still wish they hadn't. We gathered solemnly underneath the shade of a wilted tree behind the headquarters, a jumble of microphones, cameras and notepads with legs.

Captain Jonathan Snyder.

I dropped my digital recorder. For a second, I wasn't certain I'd heard right. Maybe there was another Snyder in the army. It was Brigadier-General Denis Thompson's first casualty announcement. He seemed a bit a nervous, but when he recited Jon's history, I knew it was my Jon. We'd kept in touch only occasionally since Sangin, the odd e-mail exchange. I knew he'd worked with my colleague Chris Wattie of the *National Post* on a book about the first battle group tour, but I had no idea he'd been in theatre with the mentoring team that was training the ANA.

Jon died leading one of the night ambush patrols that had become common and seemed routine. He'd been crossing a field with his section when he fell in an open *kareez*, one of the many unmarked wells that dot the countryside. In full body armour, he tumbled dozens of metres down the long, dark hole, which was linked to the ancient system of underground irrigation canals.

The wells in Afghan fields have no barriers around them. They're just big, friggin' holes that appear out of nowhere and are hard to spot even in daylight. The soldiers who were with him said Jon was there one minute and gone the next. Some of the guys later said he'd survived the fall, and there were even suggestions that he'd managed to eject his flak jacket, but they couldn't get a rope to him in time. An engineer reportedly slid down the clammy mud-sided pit to retrieve him.

In the end, there are no good ways to die, but you have certain expectations about fate. There are people who deserve better than they get. Jon was one of them. You'd have thought a guy like him—someone who faced down the Taliban and Afghan soldiers who wanted to execute a prisoner—deserved to go with better dignity, or at least in a manner of his choosing. You'd expect a guy like him would have wanted to exit in a haze of lead, not as a millstone at the bottom of well. The thought made me physically ill.

Thompson's praise of Jon, although well-meaning, was full of the same hollow, mechanical phrases that headquarters used for everyone. One line, however, stood out. The general talked about how Jon had saved a joint Canadian Afghan patrol a few days before. He offered no details, no qualification, no explanation. The sentence just hung there awkwardly, like an unpruned branch in a tidy laneway. I didn't grab on to it until after the ramp ceremony that sent Jon home.

The deputy commander of the mentoring team talked to us, albeit reluctantly. But he opened up when, as the last question, I asked about the ambush. He spun the most spellbinding narrative about how the Taliban, lying in wait in a small gully, hit the patrol from three sides. The five Canadians and dozens of Afghan soldiers were pinned down in a hail of brutal fire. The Afghans were terrified, but Jon rallied them to fight back. There were wounded and he reportedly yelled to them.

"Nobody gets left behind!"

Corporal James Ball doubled back across broken ground with one Afghan soldier to open up an escape route.

Captain Robert Peel, Corporal Steve Bancarz and Corporal Cary Baker organized the fighting retreat. With bullets whizzing past and kicking up dust fountains, the tattered patrol slowly, painfully backed out of the trap. No one died that day and it was a miracle.

Jon was posthumously awarded the Star of Military Valour, the country's second-highest combat decoration before the Canadian Victoria Cross.

For his exposed run through enemy fire, Ball received the same decoration. Peel, Bancarz and Baker were each given the Medal of Military Valour.

What struck me at the time was the army's deep reluctance to talk about the ambush. For an institution that complained its soldiers and their heroic actions were not getting enough ink, the recalcitrance was stunning. The account we received on the tarmac was thin, but it was enough to at least wedge into that day's story as an illustration of the kind of guy Jon was. But whatever sense we tried to make of Jon's insensible death was trumped by his father. A heart-stricken, angry David Snyder spoke out in an interview. "War is stupid," he said. "Everybody knows that. Everybody knows that. Well, no they don't. The politicians don't know that." His words, naturally, became the story.

It wasn't until I opened up the medal citation from the governor general months later that I read the first complete account of the firefight. Why I had to read about it in a press release from Rideau Hall when I, and others, had stood there asking questions was impossible to explain. The excuses were varied and sometimes pathetic. One officer later had the audacity to tell me, with a straight face and yet mumbling in to his brass buttons, that making a big deal out Jon's heroism elevated him above other guys in his outfit and that wasn't fair to them. As it turned out, the thing they were most afraid of was having to explain the terrified stampede of Afghan soldiers from the battlefield.

"The *kandak* [Afghan battalion] basically collapsed that day," one officer declared to me a few years later.

"Almost Normal, But Not Quite" 17

The words "peaceful" and "Kandahar" usually don't belong in the same sentence, but there was definitely a new vibe on the street in the spring of 2008. The place was still screwed. The people were still muted, stone-faced and closed off to outsiders. The same old rubble piles were still in the same old spots. Villages in the desert and farmland to the west of the city were still being turned to icy dust. The city seemed to be the only place that was alive.

As I drove around with Khan during those breezy spring days, before the really hard heat of summer set in, it was impossible not to catch a whiff of optimism along with the various other scents. It was one of the few times I was able to put the threat of roadside bombs and suicide cars packed with explosives out of my mind. Maybe people in the city had grown used to the military stalemate. The fighting was in Zhari, Panjwaii and Arghandab. The Taliban weren't clawing at the gates, the way they had in the past. Maybe, just maybe, Kandaharis could begin to have a life.

Hundreds of ramshackle shops were open in the Rangrazal market, hocking everything from live chickens and rancid-looking goat carcasses to cases of soda and anorexic vegetables. The smell was toxic. At a nearby traffic circle, a new financial exchange building with an escalator had been constructed. The Afghans were fascinated; many had never seen an escalator before. Khan was the tour guide that day, as he loved to be, and pointed out a new billiard hall where literally hundreds of entertainment-starved Kandaharis spent evenings watching matches with bated breath, as though it were the World Cup. Television was a luxury few could afford.

We drove to a shop in the commercial district where I bought a cheap, green, Chinese-manufactured bike for pedalling around the air base. I'd purchased another one along with some colleagues at CTV only to have the wheels fall off. The new one wasn't much better. On one shabby street corner, there was a rundown gymnasium, complete with a Mr. Atlas sign outside. The thought of scrawny Afghans pumping iron struck me as hilarious until an indignant Khan pointed out that that there was quite a bodybuilding culture among the warrior Pashtun.

The cab eventually dropped us off in a covered alcove outside the hotel that housed Khan's office, where prying eyes on the street couldn't see that a foreigner was in the building. We were carefree, but not stupid. The three-storey hotel in downtown Kandahar, with its filthy stairwell, dingy concrete hallways, well-worn rugs and crooked wooden doors, was just as I remembered. The smell of roasted meat and spices wafted through the hallways. The Noor Jahan Hotel was still the hangout for local Afghan journalists and fixers, the place where they ate, drank, slept and argued about the ills of their country. Khan's cramped, poorly lit office/apartment, with its thin woolen blankets hanging over the window, also seemed frozen in time, with the exception of a television. He was one of the fortunate few. It was a useful convenience, he explained. In order to build up contacts in the restive regions west of the city, Khan had taken to hosting small parties for district council members. His television was an enticement, though it quickly turned into a drawback when he discovered the councillors were more interested in watching Indian soap operas than in giving him story tips.

Soon after seating ourselves on thin, multicoloured floor mattresses, a young boy arrived with a carafe of tea, followed quickly by plates of lamb skewers, rice and flatbread. We ate mostly with our hands and spent the time catching up. It was the first chance we'd had to really talk since I had returned.

"Do you want to see my pictures, sir?"

I froze. For the life of me I couldn't imagine what he was talking about. What flashed through my mind were the grisly trophy shots of Taliban dead that circulated every once in a while in Kandahar.

"Pictures?" I choked.

"Yes, I've been doing modelling in Pakistan."

"You've been doing what?"

"Modelling, sir; to earn extra money."

"You get paid for it?" The question, I realized in hindsight, was somewhat rude, but Khan either didn't notice or was too gracious to respond.

Khan pulled out a portfolio of his glamour shots. There he was—my friend, my trusted confidant, the man skilled at steering us through sticky situations on the mean streets of Kandahar—sleeveless and preening before the camera. I was amazed.

The first photo looked as though it belonged in a teen magazine, and the thought of Khan setting the hearts of young Pakistani girls afire left me further dumbstruck. He had a whole folder full of glossies. There were nice, artsy, black-and-white studio shots, where a stubble-chinned Khan stared pensively into the camera. And then there was the smiling Khan; the carefree Khan; the serious Khan; and my personal favourite, the thoughtful Khan.

My shock shouldn't suggest that my friend was ugly. In fact, I'd always thought Khan had a pleasant face, one that lit up whenever he smiled. But every time we worked together he always had a befuddled, just-rolled-out-of-bed quality, not the chiselled-jaw intensity of a male model. Rarely did he shave the patchy scruff from his cheeks, and his hair always stood at awkward right angles, tousled as if just removed from a toque. He was not standard *GQ* material. Yet he earned money from this work, which said a lot on its own. Later, he would even parlay the modelling gig into a brief but memorable career as an actor on the Pakistani nighttime TV soap *Shela Bagh*. He played a bad guy and revelled in it. His stories of how the show's producers fawned over him and his performance almost caused me to bust a gut. With all of the attention, he took to wearing Paris Hilton–sized sunglasses and often demanded I take his picture.

"Why should I take your picture?" I would ask.

"Because I am here," he would answer.

That Khan and I had been able to enjoy a relatively carefree, uninter-rupted lunch in the confines of his office was nothing short of a miracle, and a lucid demonstration that life in Kandahar had improved. We would have never have attempted such a thing a year or two before. But when I climbed into the cab for the return trip to KAF that afternoon, I was gloomy. The peaceful verve wasn't going to last. We all knew it.

It turns out the halcyon days were over within hours of Khan dropping me at the airfield gate. A rash of booby-trapped bicycles exploded in the southwestern district of the city. They were followed over the next few days by a pair of suicide car bombings. Explosions happened so often over the next week I was convinced poor Khan had gone bomb-happy. One early morning after having slept at his uncle's house in a gated, exclusive district of Kandahar, he awoke to the loud concussion of what he thought was an explosion. Dazed but determined, he rolled out of bed, got dressed, jumped in his car and then telephoned me about the attack. He said he was going to check out the blast site and would report on casualties. But as Khan peeled through the hazy, early morning streets, there was no familiar column of black smoke to beckon him. What he had heard from his bedroom window was a tire blowout reverberating through the mud-walled alleyways. After about two weeks of steady bomb-chasing, Khan told me he needed a vacation. I agreed.

* * *

It was a Friday morning in mid-May when Malim Akbar Khakrezwal stepped out of his compound into the ascending sunshine. He was on his way to mosque. The fifty-five-year-old outspoken former government intelligence officer and revered mujahideen fighter lived in the relatively peaceful village of Lowall, a community in the lush fruit-growing region just outside the city. Khakrezwal had taken only a couple of paces when a motorcycle whizzed along the street and slowed just long enough for a passenger on the back to spray him with gunfire. Khakrezwal shook like a rag doll and toppled back into his doorway. He was dead before he hit the ground. The bike roared off up the street.

I had never seen Khan as distraught as when he recounted the story to me later that day while we drove to town. Instead of lathering me with platitudes and joking in his normal fashion, my friend somberly looked at the road ahead and clutched his *misbaha*—or prayer beads. Khakrezwal had been a friend, someone Khan had respected not only for his plucky nature but also for his knowledge of the Koran and his ability to win debates with local mullahs.

Soldiers carry the casket of Capt. Richard (Steve) Leary, who was killed in an ambush while leading a patrol near Zangabad, Panjwaii district in May 2008. The ramp ceremony and flag-draped casket became one of the most enduring symbols of the war for Canadians. (CP Image/Murray Brewster)

Master Warrant Officer Albert Boucher, the Canadian camp sergeant major at KAF in the spring of 2008, salutes at the sunset ramp ceremony for Capt. Richard (Steve) Leary in May 2008. (CP Image/Murray Brewster)

The author, dressed in Afghan garb, in the winter of 2007, in the village of Zangabad. NATO and the Afghan government allowed people displaced from their villages by heavy fighting to return to their mostly ruined homes. (Graeme Smith/author photo)

An unidentified Afghan elder in the village of Zangabad in December 2010. The area was a notorious hotbed of Taliban activity throughout the war. Many of the local Noorzai tribesmen openly supported the insurgency. (Murray Brewster)

An Afghan boy stands watching Canadian and Afghan soldiers as they conduct a security operation before the opening of a school in Bazaar-e-Panjwall In February 2009. (Murray Brewster)

A Canadian army deuce-and-a-half (2.5 tonne) truck delivers school supplies to children of Afghan National Army soldiers at Camp Sherzai in February 2007. The school, located in the ruins of a bombed-out apartment complex, was a squalid mess with electricity and running water for only two hours a day. (CP Image/Murray Brewster)

Afghan workers harvesting poppies in the spring of 2008 just outside Kandahar. The end of the harvest and the resulting unemployment usually signalled the beginning of fighting season in southern Afghanistan. The attacks on security forces would last until October each year. (CP Image/Murray Brewster)

Ahmed Wali Karzai, the half-brother of President Hamid Karzai and the kingpin of Kandahar tribal politics. His influence was felt far and wide during the Canadian mission, and his attitude toward governance sometimes contributed to the instability. (CP Image/Murray Brewster)

Haji Agha Lalai, the head of the Kandahar Peace and Reconciliation office. He spent years trying to convince Taliban fighters to lay down their weapons with promises of cash and amnesty. His efforts were largely ignored by NATO and the Afghan government until later in the war. (Murray Brewster)

Abdul Qadar Noorzai, the head of the Kandahar office of the Afghanistan Human Rights Commission, along with A.R. Khan, CP's fixer. The head of Afghan intelligence blamed Qadar Noorzai for the fiasco over alleged prison torture and wanted him arrested as an Iranian spy. (CP Image/Murray Brewster)

Graeme Smith, of the *Globe and Mail*, poses along with two unidentified Afghan army soldiers. The photo was taken in late 2005. (Private Collection)

Louie Palu, former *Globe and Mail* photographer who now works for Zuma Press out of Washington. The picture was taken in the summer of 2010 as he covered the U.S. Black Hawk teams who evacuate casualties from the battlefield. (Private Collection)

The CBC's Laurie Graham and Khan at Osama bin Laden's compound in Tarnak Farms in March 2010. (Murray Brewster)

An unidentified Afghan boy, the child of a tenant farmer, picks weeds out of a field within sight of the ruins of Tarnak Farms. The land was reclaimed thanks in part to Canadian irrigation projects. (CP Image/Murray Brewster)

As former head of the government's intelligence arm in Kandahar, Khakrezwal had a list of enemies as long as your arm. After retiring, he spoke out forcefully against the Taliban and government corruption, which he said sucked as much life out of the country as the insurgency. He was a particularly staunch critic of Governor Asadullah Khalid, who enjoyed the unqualified support of Ahmed Wali Karzai. Khakrezwal was a prominent member of the Alokozai tribe and an advisor to the young Kalimullah Naqib, who'd been appointed as tribal leader the previous fall by the president. The Alokozai presented an obstacle to AWK's attempts to consolidate power in Kandahar. Khakrezwal had made his reservations about Khalid and corruption public earlier in the spring. The grizzled warrior was the only person among dozens interviewed who was willing to be directly quoted as critical of the governor. It was a story Khan had helped to arrange.

Afghan police were quick to blame the Taliban for the "assassination." Khakrezwal's murder was an attempt to sow fear and weaken the government, argued senior officers. Being the bodacious sort, Khan picked up the satellite phone and called the Taliban's principal spokesman in the southern region. The Taliban are often quick to claim credit for any mayhem or murder in Kandahar. They are happy to be the poster boys for brutal, nefarious and horrific acts of violence. If it makes the government look bad, the police look like idiots and the Afghan army appear hapless, you usually don't have to ask if they were behind it. But this time was different. Khakrezwal was grudgingly respected for his days in the anti-Soviet jihad and his status as a former intelligence officer made him nothing more than a mouthy, cranky old man. No, they were not responsible for his murder, the Taliban told a speechless Khan; they had more important targets. General Sayed Saqib, Kandahar's rotund and greying provincial police chief, didn't believe them. His investigation was focused on known militants and their sympathizers, he said.

No one was ever arrested for the killing.

Khan blamed himself for Khakrezwal's murder. Rightly or wrongly, he believed that the story months earlier had angered someone powerful. He didn't have any evidence, only well-honed suspicions built up over years of survival on the brutal streets of Kandahar and Quetta. It didn't matter that the Taliban could have been lying. It didn't matter that the power struggle between the Karzais and the Alokozai was indiscriminant. It didn't matter that his friend had made many enemies over the years while doing the unsavoury bidding of questionable governments. The way Khan saw it, he was responsible for the interview. He had urged Khakrezwal to speak out and now his friend and mentor was dead. That was all the proof he needed.

"As journalists, sir, we are supposed to help the people, not get them killed," he said wistfully as our car finally arrived at its destination.

Within a day or so, Khan left for Quetta to check on his pregnant wife and their three children. He took some gifts I'd brought, which made him somewhat more cheerful. He often told me, even when Kandahar was quiet, that moving his family back to the city was out of the question; it wasn't safe. As it turned out, the relative serenity of Quetta, with its pillared, blue and white mosque, was just as easily disturbed. Later that summer, another story Khan helped facilitate—on the porous border between Pakistan and Afghanistan—prompted the notorious Inter-Services Intelligence agency to begin sniffing around his family. The piece, which received wide play in both Canada and the U.S., made Pakistani officials look stupid and corrupt, and it came at a delicate time, when border-trade talks between the two countries were in their infancy. Soon, Khan spotted someone keeping an eye on his house and tailing the car that drove his children to school. They packed up and moved in the middle of the night to an apartment.

* * *

Khan's absence coincided with the need to finish a story on the end of the annual poppy harvest in Kandahar. A rough draft was already on my laptop when Khan's cousin, Noor, offered to take me out to observe the cropping. The fields were almost picked clean and the season would soon be over, he declared. My television colleagues wanted pictures for their own piece and Noor, who was also the Associated Press reporter in Kandahar, intended to take them the following Friday. Did I want go?

There was no better day. Friday is mosque day. The typical crush of cars, trucks, donkey carts and livestock was always reduced by half, sometimes two-thirds. It was the safest time to visit a poppy field—if there was ever a safe time to observe people engaged in the multi-billion-dollar illegal narcotics industry.

Just after sunrise, three of us slipped into the back of Noor's Toyota at the front gate of the airfield. As in months past, my partners in crime were Paul Workman and Al "Big Daddy" Stephens from CTV—both were excellent company for tricky assignments. Urbane, sophisticated and cool, Paul always projected a sense a confidence that had a calming effect on those around him. Whether he was as pacific on the inside I never knew. With his sharp blue eyes, he kept a steady watch out the right side of the car for guns or any sign that we were being followed. Big Daddy, famous for sleeping through rocket attacks, was also placid. He sat with the bulky camera straddling his lap and watched the oncoming traffic. Occasionally, he'd lift the camera and roll some footage of the countryside. Minding the left side of the vehicle was my responsibility.

Both of them had chosen not to wrap themselves in Afghan clothes, the way we had on other occasions. I expected them to get a lecture from Noor, because most fixers were nervous about travelling with westerners who looked like westerners. Instead, it was I, the one who had dressed in a shalwar kameez, who received the rebuke for forgetting to ditch my sunglasses. Shades automatically gave you away.

Our car whipped past wheat fields where turbaned scarecrows kept pests away from the grain. There were few vehicles on the road at that hour and the temperature was comfortable enough to allow us to drive with the windows cracked open. A handful of the city's corrugated-tin shops were open and offered their potpourri of slaughtered goats and vegetables. Little heed was paid to us as we rolled through the sun-bleached streets and made a brief stop to pick up the local Al Jazeera reporter. He had been to the poppy field the day before to do a story. We knew he would be valuable in providing introductions to the field hands, as well as in watching our backs.

Our destination was a plot of land on the northwestern outskirts of the city, just beyond Loya Wyala—the roughest district in town and the place where the Taliban did most of their recruiting. They would troll the tightly packed compounds and teeming laneways looking for young men eager enough, poor enough or desperate enough to carry a gun for them. The cemetery within the district contained the bodies of seventy al-Qaeda Arabs killed in the Taliban last stand of December 2001. With their fluttering green flags of martyrdom, the graves served as a shrine.

The district, with virtually no running water or sewers, rose around us like an ancient apparition. Hundreds of mud-walled homes were carved into the ground on either side of the highway. Except for the sprinkling of satellite dishes pointed at the faultless sky, one could have been fooled into thinking that the homes had lain untouched for centuries. As we passed into the countryside and crested a small hill, I glanced back and realized how vast the northern slum was. Some compounds stretched halfway up a mountain face in what looked from a distance like some crazy biblical maze.

We pulled off of the highway and slowly drove up a long, rutted driveway that was partially sheltered by some withered trees. The car halted at the wooden gate of a seemingly empty compound. The field was not visible from the road, for obvious reasons. It was set back behind a tree line a half-kilometre from the highway, which connected Kandahar city with the even wider swath of parched farmland in the Panjwaii and Zhari districts to the west. Even still, the poppy field was hiding in plain sight.

"Somebody must be getting paid off if this is still here," one of our group observed as we hopped a drainage ditch.

"Of course," replied Noor, with a slightly puzzled look. His matter-of-fact tone contained no trace of irony.

We skirted the edge of a grain field near the highway, crossed a dirt road and slipped into the poppy field along a small path between two trees. Before us—spread over land the size of three football fields—was one tiny vein in the corrupt, polluted, poisonous lifeblood of this country: an oasis of green, bulbous plants, sprinkled with scarlet flowers and set against a dismal background of desert and volcanic mountains.

The facts and figures slammed into you with the weight of a freight train. The export value of the opium and heroin produced by fields like this was U.S. $3.1 billion in 2007, or about one-third of Afghanistan's entire gross domestic product. The Taliban, in co-operation with local drug lords, converted the cash into weapons and explosives, which they then turned on Afghan security forces and NATO troops. Of course, corrupt local officials also took their cut. Some became obscenely and unapologetically wealthy. They breathed in the misery of others like some sick, intoxicating smoke. Despite its proximity to the provincial capital, this field had been spared the Afghan government's high-profile eradication program. It was one of many. Only 8,000 hectares out of a potential 193,000 hectares of opium-producing poppy were eliminated by forced eradication in 2007, according the country's opium survey.

As we trudged down the path, the hair on the back on my neck stood up. Over the previous year, the Taliban had made the kidnapping and murder of foreigners a cottage industry. Being seen on the streets of Kandahar was always a dodgy prospect, but willingly walking into their arms—or at least into the arms of their surrogates—seemed in that moment a tad insane. It was, however, too late for second thoughts. Despite my galloping paranoia, we were received warmly by three farm workers with smiles, rough hand-shakes and the traditional "peace be with you" greeting of "salam aleikum."

The trio of sun-baked Afghans stood around a brand new steel tub that contained a sticky, dark resin—their black gold. They pointed at it almost gleefully. It was evidently a good harvest.

In the field directly before us, half a dozen stooping harvesters slowly stood up, more curious than alarmed by our presence. Noor told our apparently benevolent hosts that we were only there to observe and wouldn't interfere. Happily, the three Afghan farmers urged us into the field, as though we were witnessing something as benign as the corn harvest back home. There wasn't an AK-47 in sight, a further sign these farmers knew they had nothing to fear, from either local authorities or Western journalists.

I almost fell into an irrigation ditch as we hopscotched our way to the poppy pickers. By the time we got there they had resumed their tedious task. Hour upon hour, day upon day, they cut open and pinched poppy bulbs, squeezing the resin into thin plastic cups. It takes about half an hour of gently pinching a number of different plants to fill one plastic cup. The resin got everywhere and on everything   under their nails, up their forearms; it stained their clothes.

As we silently watched and took our pictures, one of the workers began singing; his quavering, rich voice carried across the entire field and enter-tained his fellow pickers. Noor told us the tune was popular on Kandahar radio, but the refrain was so solemn it was easily mistaken by my tone-deaf ears as one of the hymns that come from the loudspeaker of a mosque. In this largely illiterate country, where traditional propaganda is next to impossible, the Taliban were known to distribute their message through songs and even cellphone ring tones. I wondered if that's what I was hearing.

One of the pickers stopped to talk. His eyes sparkled with amusement and he looked us up and down. There was no hesitation, no self-conscious air about him even though his trade was ostensibly illegal. He spoke casually about his burden in the same unaffected manner as any worker back home. He shrugged; it was a job. I'd seen the same sort of weary, unruffled ambience on hundreds of assembly lines. The farmhand told us his name was Sha Wali, which may or may not have been true. His fingers and white, full-length shirt were stained with gooey black opium resin. He was paid about U.S. $10 per day.

"It's a good business," he said.

The work, however, lasted only for the spring and he said he had to find other work in Kandahar city to fill up the rest of his time. Men like Sha Wali—poor migrant workers on the edge—were targeted by the Taliban in their enlistment campaigns each spring. Once the poppy harvest was done, thousands of young men of fighting age—eighteen to twenty-five—were available for hire.

The more we talked, the more it became clear that it was a matter of benign indifference to Sha Wali what happened to the resin he squeezed from the poppies. The fact that it ended up as a potent narcotic in the veins of addicts all over the world elicited nothing more than a polite shrug. It was of even less concern that the drug trafficking cash bought guns and bombs used to kill other Afghans and foreign troops. What happened after he did his job was of no consequence, he declared.

"We are just trying to fill these cups and earn money," he said with a deadpan expression, wiping more resin on his shirt. "Each day it's hard to find work and I don't care what's going on elsewhere."

His ambiguity was like a splash of cold water, but then the Afghans were like that. On the one hand, they loved you. They'd do anything for you and some would die to protect you. But then there was a dark, grasping, covetous streak—a part of them that really didn't care. We hadn't given a damn about them as they bled and tore themselves to shreds and now many of them didn't give a damn that we were bleeding to help them.

For a moment, Sha Wali stood silently while the camera and tape recorder continued to roll. The glint of humour was gone from his eye. He wasn't uncomfortable with the questions, just puzzled that we would ask him to consider the consequences of his actions. We never asked Sha Wali about his politics, whether he supported the Taliban or fought for them. It seemed better to stick to simple, un-provocative questions.

Nearby, a small boy about five years old played with a broken poppy stem, using it as a rake in the mud, laughing and showing off. Another boy—older, maybe about ten—carried away a heavy load of cut and harvested stems. Unlike some of the other children playing on the edge of the field, this child didn't look up or smile. His face was burdened by the weight on his back. I had never seen such a desolate, hopeless expression on a child's face. It stopped me cold on the muddy pathway. This boy was not yet old enough or tall enough to do the harvesting work, but soon he would graduate into the same life as Sha Wali.

I'm not sure who was the first to look up across the field and notice that a car had blocked our vehicle. All I remember is Paul Workman's calm, steady voice saying it was time to get out of there, if we could. Noor took a deep breath and nervously thumbed a number into his cellphone. I also went for my phone, straining to see how many people were in the other vehicle and whether they were armed. Reaching for the phone was a reflex. None of us were under the illusion that the cavalry could arrive in time to make a difference.

We were on our own and it was one of those moments of sheer terror, the kind that usually hammered your feet to the floor. You know you have to move, but your legs feel like they're made of lead. I'm not sure how Paul or Big Daddy felt, but I was stunned and numb. We gathered our gear and made our way quickly back along the dusty pathway in between the trees without so much as a goodbye to the poppy farmers.

I felt cornered as we walked toward Noor's sedan. On assignments like this, you never stopped imagining different scenarios. I'd always wondered how I'd behave in a kidnap situation. The training I'd taken back in Virginia flashed into my head. Be the grey man, our Royal Marine trainers had told us. Don't stand out. Don't show much emotion. Don't try to be intimidating. Just blend in with background. The only thing I could think of as I hopped over the irrigation ditch near the driveway was how much I'd hated having a bag over my head. I felt stupid. Our instinct had been to run for the car, as though we could stage a getaway. But the possibility crossed my mind that we had just calmly walked into our own captivity. There was only one man standing beside the car that blocked ours. I looked around to see if others had formed a security perimeter, but there was no sign of anyone else and no movement among the emaciated trees and low-lying shrubs. I glanced at the mud-walled compound to see if anyone was on the roof, but the sun blinded me.

In a stern, hoarse whisper, Noor told us to get into the car. He turned and spoke to the man. The Al Jazeera reporter, who'd been with us the whole time, joined the conversation. Pashtuns always sounded angry when they talked, but this exchange seemed almost insane. I watched from the back seat. Noor had parked almost right up against the compound's wooden gate. The man, who was slightly built and dressed professionally with a black satin vest over his shalwar kameez, stormed off to his car, jumped in and threw it into reverse with a spray of gravel. Noor leapt in to his driver's seat and the other reporter tumbled into the back with us. A quick three-point turn and we roared up the driveway and back out on to the highway. We held our breath as the car rocketed back toward the city. In turn, each of us checked to see if we were being followed. Noor looked worried and so did the Al Jazeera reporter, but there was no one behind us. The farther we went, the more air returned to the stifling cabin and finally Noor spewed one long breath, as though he'd sprung a leak. We turned right on to one of the main boulevards and found ourselves back within the confines of the city.

Noor looked back at us and laughed. It was one of those tight-lipped, crazy kinds of cackles, like he didn't believe we'd actually gotten away. There was more nervous laughter as we passed pickup trucks stacked with farmhands returning from other fields. They rode on the lips of the open flatbeds; there were so many that it just looked like a tangle of brown arms and legs.

Big Daddy stared at the overrun streets and smiled.

"I never thought I'd be so happy to see Kandahar city," he said quietly from the front seat.

"I never thought I'd hear anyone say that," I replied.

"Feel Free to Exit at Your Leisure" *18*

They were called CLPs—combat logistics patrols. In the old days, we would have called them supply convoys. But a new war, one run by professionals, required new jargon. Early one morning, a very earnest young soldier explained it to me like this: in the age of the "asymmetrical operating environment," the enemy places a high value on "hunting" logistics. Translation: the Taliban liked to ambush and blow up resupply convoys, in very much the same way U.S. Army wagon trains were attacked in the Old West. When I put it in those terms for my serious young corporal, he looked at me as if I'd farted in church. It wasn't the same thing, he insisted. It was much more sophisticated. CLPs were planned with the same "fidelity" and attention to detail as full-fledged combat operations. It wasn't just a bunch of guys throwing crap on the back of a deuce-and-a-half and going for a drive in the countryside, he insisted, still eyeing me as though I were a heathen.

We could agree on one point. A CLP certainly wasn't an ordinary drive. If I were going for a ride in the country, I wouldn't show up four hours ahead of time, usually in the middle of the night, all for what under normal circumstances would be a thirty-minute point-to-point excursion.

The briefings given by convoy commanders were the most humourless exercises I'd ever witnessed. That's not meant to be flippant, or to take away from the obvious gravity of the threats they faced. Humour does have a tendency to wash away after guys get their vehicles blown up a dozen or more times during a tour. But I'd taken part in combat operations where the air was less oppressive than during briefings for a logistics patrol.

That's why it was such a treat to arrive just after dawn one summer morning at the KAF marshalling yard to find a stand-up comedian in the ranks. The place bustled with guys who'd been up all night and whose every stagnant movement screamed exhaustion. Most were reservists near the end of their tours and all were long past the point of being ready to go home. The convoy commander was from New Brunswick. His layout of the timings and threats was rock solid, but since another reporter, the padre and I were riding with him, he gave us a little extra attention. We got the what-to-do-in-an-emergency speech as well as the tactics and procedures for if the vehicle was disabled.

"Wait for my instructions before dismounting from the Bison; however, if your vehicle is hit and on fire, please feel to exit at your leisure." He delivered it so dryly it almost came out like dust.

It had been so long since somebody made a joke on one of those trips that it took me by surprise. I immediately howled, though I noticed that neither the other reporter nor the Cape Breton padre was laughing.

* * *

As time marched on in that spring of 2008, and we along with it, there was a growing sense that the Arghandab region was about to explode—again. It wasn't quite clear when. It wasn't quite clear how. It was just there, like a sick feeling in the pit of your stomach. It was present every time soldiers stepped off on a patrol through lush, interwoven orchards; constricted, uneven mud paths; and low-lying shrubs. On foot patrols, there was an urgency to the questioning of villagers. It was as if the army were desperate for some actionable intelligence, although no one would come out and say that.

Despite being considered pro-government—or maybe semi-government—the Alokozai of Arghandab were as tongueless as their brothers elsewhere. The Taliban were firmly entrenched in Khakrez, the district immediately to the north. They had slipped into that region from Shah Wali Kot, the area where Canadian troops first deployed way back in 2006, but left when Zhari and Panjwaii went up in flames. The only thing that had held the Taliban back from the northern gates of Kandahar was Alokozai militia under Mullah Naqib.

Naqib's death in October 2007 and his son's installation as tribal leader set in motion a cascading series of events that climaxed in a bloody assault involving several hundred Taliban. They captured most of the north bank of the river. The ANA eventually beat them back, but the Alokozai militia was smashed and many people, including prominent families, fled the region for the relative safety of Kandahar city. Throughout the long winter, the Taliban carried out selective assassinations and even overran the occasional police outpost and murdered the cops. As I trudged the laneways and fields with patrols that spring—places that had been soaked with so much blood over the years—it was hard not to feel like we were being followed by ghosts. Arghandab's shady groves, checkerboard shadows and twisted overhanging trees seemed perfectly haunted.

Not helping matters was the impending end of the poppy harvest in mid-2008. At one shura in a nondescript village along the south bank of the river, Captain Jeff Thebo sized up a group of tough-looking teenagers at the back of the room. Fighting-age males, with their determined jaws and bitter eyes, always stood out and made everyone nervous. Thebo, the commander of 7 Platoon, Bravo Company, 2 PPCLI looked them up and down. In just a few weeks, these young men would be Taliban recruits and on the wrong side of a gun barrel. A whole range of emotions coloured moments like that, even for those of us who stood back and watched. Brutality. Disgust. Pity. Indifference. No one escaped the feelings, no matter how hard they tried. Thebo told me how he quietly implored the village elders to counsel their young men.

"You guys don't want to do this. You don't want to take us on," he would say. "There's no reason for this to happen, guys; please let's find a better way."

In the end, it got harder that spring to weep for some of the Afghans.

* * *

The patrol base was so close to the mountainside you could have leaned over the cement wall and kissed the rock face. Mountains were like that in northern Kandahar. They had a tendency to appear out of nowhere in the desert, seemingly thrust straight up from the centre of the earth like a set of giant, Precambrian incisors. Nothing grew on the sides of those mountains. The soil had long eroded to the point where only scorched rock was left. Greenery, vegetation and life in general clung to the base of each peak. The mountains gave the Arghandab an isolated feeling. The world could have long blown itself up, but no one in the valley would have known or likely cared. If you looked out from the patrol base toward the river, which was stitched with reeds and tall grass, it wasn't hard to imagine what it would have been like at the dawn of time. One of the guys on guard duty in the plywood tower marvelled as the sun set to the right of us. The river cut a diagonal path away from us toward the receding western horizon.

"So cool, man," he said as he lowered his binoculars and rested them in his gloved hands. "I'm waiting for T. Rex to come stompin' through the grass at the river edge. The land that time forgot."

"In more ways than one," I answered.

The moon poked its face over the mountain into the cobalt-coloured eastern sky. I watched from the foundation of the guard tower as soldiers switched on their red headlamps and pin lights and went about their business. The patrol base was nothing more than a half-completed concrete shell that would eventually serve as the joint district coordination centre in the village. There were no windows, or even wooden frames. The place was wired, but there were no fixtures or switches, just cables sticking out of the wall.

"Do you snore?" one of the guys asked me.

"A little," I said.

"I bayonet guys who snore and keep me up." He laughed and I laughed, but I wasn't sure he was kidding.

My snoring ended up being the least offensive of the crowd.

* * *

Giving interpreters a hard time was pretty much standard operating procedure. Some were just as rough-and-tumble as the soldiers, and gave as good as they got. I remember one terp with the Quebec-based Van Doos who could swear up a storm in English better than the guys he worked with. Some of the Afghan terps tried hard to fit in, sometimes too hard. Although they were often mute and inscrutable, I always found there was a quiet dignity to most ordinary Afghans—Pashtun, Hazara or Tajik. Hearing terps try to intimate Western manners, phrases and vulgarities, however, always felt a touch obscene. There were others who didn't try to fit in, who seemed more like apparitions than real people. They huddled over their hand-held radios and listened for Taliban communications chatter. Only occasionally would they look up, usually with wide, frightened eyes.

The guy attached to my section in Arghandab was named Sharif, but the guys called him Shakira. He didn't help his cause any when he acknowledged that he knew who Shakira was and was happy with the nickname because she is "beautiful." For the record, there wasn't even the remotest resemblance between Sharif and the Colombian bombshell, even though the terp was twiggy and effeminate. There were always tonnes of rumours about the sexual orientation of some of the terps. The army kept many of them strictly segregated at forward operating bases, giving them their own showers and bathing times. Many I ran across had one thing in common: a healthy curiosity about the sex habits of westerners, both male and female. I fielded a lot of strange questions through the years and I know the soldiers did too.

The one thing that used to drive many of the guys nuts was the way the terps and even some of the villagers gawked at Western women. It's not that the troops were prudes, but some of the Afghans were uncomfortably creepy in the way they'd stare at a woman or make excuses to fawn over her, especially the civilian diplomats or journalists. (The terps seemed to know they'd get a punch in the head if they bothered one of the female soldiers.)

Inside the wire, the interpreters could be chased away, but villagers were handled with kid gloves. Those that fluttered around and stared were tolerated because patrols were only there for a short time. In the villages, though, you'd sometimes encounter the opposite end of the spectrum: the old granite faces that couldn't hide their contempt, especially if they caught a glimpse of a woman with her head uncovered. Going between the two extremes induced a jarring form of social whiplash. There seemed to be no middle ground, and after a while you just learned to live with the twisted, pungent sexual repression that coursed beneath the surface of many conversations.

One Sunday on the base I awoke to the sound of nearby gunfire. My eyes cracked open. I recognized the belch, like ripping Velcro, of AK-47s. It was followed by the steady, even pop-pop of an M-16—or the Canadian equivalent C-8 rifle. I was too startled to be scared and lay hammered down on top of my sleeping bag. A throbbing .50-calibre machine gun opened up somewhere in the distance. Two nearby mortar blasts dislodged some dust, which hung in the shafts of blinding sunlight that streamed through the incomplete windows. The soldiers lying on either side of me, who had pulled guard duty overnight, snored blissfully. The firefight went on for a short while, yet no one around me moved. I could hear squawking from someone's radio outside. And then, from over and above the mountain, I heard what can only be described as a freight train descending on our position. I closed my eyes. The ground quivered and I realized immediately that the artillery strike had happened down the road. All firing stopped and everything went quiet. I rolled over to see my two minders still sleeping peacefully. The shadow of someone in full body armour and helmet appeared in the doorway and told us to get up. We'd been given a ten-minute warning order to move. My comatose companions were instantly awake, as though someone had flipped a switch. It was weird how they could wheeze through an attack, but sit bolt upright at the sound of the warrant officer's voice.

The Taliban had attacked and tried to overrun a U.S. Special Forces compound nearby and were beaten back with artillery and an air strike. They were seen loading their wounded into a white van and hightailing it toward the highway. The guys in 7 Platoon were told to stand by to intercept the vehicle if it turned south. If it went north on the highway and headed to Khakrez, the job belonged to 9 Platoon.

A UAV, buzzing unseen in the blue sky above us, reported that the vehicle was headed to a flat, deserted stretch away from our position. We huddled around the open hatch and listened to the chase unfold over the radio. The 9 Platoon LAVs scrambled to get in to position. The faces of the guys around me were impassive but I could see by their eyes that they followed each move, each turn, each drill as though they were doing the takedown themselves. It reminded me of watching a prizefighter wince and flinch when someone else was in the ring.

A disturbed patch of earth was spotted and for a second everyone held his breath at the thought of a roadside bomb. The radio crackled. A white van appeared. I sat on the steel ramp of the LAV and leaned in further. The troops blocked the road and dismounted. Silence. All of us looked at each other. They got them. There were two Afghans seated in the front and three lying down in the back. One was bleeding. We hung on every word until the sergeant in charge of our section ordered the radio turned off.

"What the fuck?" someone whispered.

A couple of the guys looked at me, as if seeing me for the first time. The edict about keeping reporters in the dark over prisoners, momentarily forgotten, was about to be strictly enforced.

It wasn't until I got back to KAF some days later that I was able to ask around. My questions about what happened on the road that day prompted one intelligence officer to gulp as though he'd swallowed a rock. His eyes narrowed.

"How do you know about that?" he asked.

"I was there, sort of . . ."

My official queries to headquarters were met with polite, dumbfounded expressions; the public affairs officer would just shrug innocently. There were all sorts of things that could have happened to the prisoners. Imagination can run wild at times like that and the longer I went without answers, the more paranoid I became. The high of witnessing something exclusive had a way of evaporating swiftly and the feeling could become downright chilling when you found out Special Forces were involved. Out in the Arghandab, one of the guys had warned me that some of the American Special Forces operators in the area were badasses. Because I kept asking and not going away and maybe because I looked a little crazed, another officer finally pulled me aside near the white, aluminium-sided Canadian headquarters.

"We let them go."

"You did what?"

"We wanted to see where they'd go. You know, follow them back to the nest."

"You mean those guys risked their lives to . . ."

"Those guys risked their lives to get eyes on and verify who we were dealing with. You know how this is done. There was a bigger payoff doing it that way."

I stared at him for a moment, at a loss for words. Men were risking their lives for a game of hide-and-seek that nobody quite understood—for some unseen, unspoken, ill-defined payoff somewhere down the road. Maybe there was something wrong with me, but I found the explanation sickening.

* * *

Kandahar Airfield was rocketed like clockwork in the spring of 2008. It happened almost every night in late May and early June. Everyone in the media tent had gotten used to the distant thumps and ensuing sirens, but this whole "up-close-and-personal" practice became quite menacing. Gone were the days when rocket attacks were a spicy but harmless diversion from the mind-numbing sameness of KAF. In those days, thankfully, the Taliban rarely hit anything. It wasn't until 2009 that people started dying, when the population at KAF became so big they couldn't help but make contact with something or someone.

The rockets, usually Chinese-made 107-mms, would land in pairs, sometimes in threes and always at the same time of the evening. We knew to take cover at 9 p.m. You could set your watch by them. We all took to calling it the bewitching hour—a magical time of day when the army made everyone don his or her flak vests and helmets, no matter how far inside the wire you worked. We'd all hurry to get our work done, or our meals eaten; we knew we'd be sitting in a bunker at the appointed hour. The longer the attacks went on, the closer it seemed each volley came to the centre of the airfield.

One night, I was talking with Paul and Big Daddy about what I'd seen in Arghandab when there was a familiar whoosh and whistle directly over the tent. I stopped in mid-sentence and we all went for the floor. On my way down, I smacked my jaw on the desk and blood squirted from my mouth. The tent shook with the concussion of the blast and then the second rocket roared in. By the time it exploded, the air-raid siren had already started to wail. We crawled out from under cover and Big Daddy looked at the time. It was only 8:45 p.m. Not to disappoint, the Taliban unleashed another volley precisely at 9 p.m.

One night, all of us were invited over to the DFS Middle East compound for a little thank-you-for-your-business barbecue. DFS, which stood for Diplomatic Freight Service, was the charter airline that flew most civilians directly in and out of Kandahar and they had their own cordoned-off area on the base. There were no uniforms. In fact, shorts and loud, flowered vacation shirts seemed to be the order of the night. There was steak, salad, refreshments and—best of all—music. About halfway through the evening, the sky over the Hesco bastions lit up with the white flashes of two nearby rocket hits. The air-raid sirens moaned. Someone stopped the music. We all looked at each other and waited for about three minutes. When it was clear there were no more rockets coming, the music went back on and the party continued. Nobody went to the bunkers. Crazy.

* * *

On an unusually cloudy Saturday morning in mid-June, Khan and I slipped out of a car and into the doorway of a compound that overlooked the city's District 9 and the sprawling Loya Wyala slum. Freshly back from Quetta, Khan seemed rested and somewhat giddy. He was still in vacation mode. We climbed a set of steep, dark stairs. The air was moist and humid and smelled as though someone had been boiling rotten cabbage. We passed through a series of corridors lit by shafts of grey light that jabbed at the darkness through holes in the mud walls.

Haji Mohammad Qasim, a provincial councillor and member of the Kandahar Industrial Association, greeted us in his sitting room with tea and cans of Pepsi. We were there to talk about economic development and the city's non-existent electricity grid. He spoke English with a raspy, high-pitched voice. When the interview ended, Qasim had a strange, almost amused look on his face.

"I am surprised you chose to be in town today," he said.

"Why?"

"Because we hear that the Taliban have gathered two hundred fighters in the next district, with small arms and bombs." Qasim's reply contained no more urgency than a discussion of the weather. "We are told they intend to attack government offices and foreigners."

I looked at Khan, who sipped his Pepsi and seemed only mildly perturbed. Qasim didn't take his eyes off of me.

"Would you like a guard to accompany you?"

"No, that would just draw more attention to us," I said with a polite wave. "But we should go. Thank you for your time."

We tumbled back in to the car and Khan looked at me over his shoulder from the front seat. He motioned for the driver to go.

"So, where are we going for lunch, sir?" he chirped happily.

*　*　*

You had to hope that somewhere, somehow the really smart ones saw it coming, but evidently not. Within days of Qasim's warning, a truck laden with explosives blew through the front gates of Sarpoza Prison on the city's western outskirts. The blast was so big it flattened a series of ramshackle shops across the road. Taliban fighters on motorcycles streamed through the breech, mowing down guards. Buses pulled up on the shoulder of the narrow, paved road that ran past the notorious detention facility. The iron gates that separated the political and criminal wings were blown open and freed prisoners picked their way over the rubble and dodged bullets to get away. The ordinary criminals scattered to nearby fields, as did some of the Taliban. They were hunted down and killed almost immediately by U.S. Special Forces. In the smoke and confusion, others slipped away aboard the buses or in private vehicles.

Everything unfolded in real time before the eyes of helpless Canadian commanders who watched over a UAV video feed. A Quick Reaction Force of less than a company of soldiers deployed from the provincial reconstruction base, but they approached cautiously, wary of causing civilian casualties. The main Canadian battle group was locked down almost twenty-five kilometres to the west and southwest, sprinkled over southern Zhari and northern Panjwaii. It was late evening when Major-General Marc Lessard was informed of the breakout. At first, he was told that only a few hundred prisoners had gotten away.

"It was about half an hour, forty-five minutes later I was basically told they were all gone," he recalled later.

Lessard spent the better part of the night of June 13, 2008, on the phone with ISAF commander U.S. General David McKiernan.

"By the time we were doing things the next morning, it was already too late. They were going in all directions. In fact, we could follow them through the use of their cellphones and we could see they were going left and right."

The absence of a competent Afghan security force hurt more than the breakout itself, Lessard said. The disaster smashed what little semblance of trust the people had in their local government.

At the precise moment the gates were kicked down at Sarpoza, Bravo Company was clawing its way into the dirt a couple of kilometres south of FOB Wilson. The Taliban had laid down a thick blanket of small arms fire on their trenches and scrapes.

"We were taking a shitload of fire when I heard about the prison," Master Corporal Jim Collins would later say.

Within hours, Bravo was pulled out of the tangled fields and propelled upriver into Arghandab with most of the battle group, in anticipation of hunting down escapees.

Two days after the prison break, the Taliban launched a second offensive to seize the Arghandab district. Within hours of swarming into the area, insurgents captured most of the north bank of the river, as they had the previous fall.

Lessard was startled.

"Oh my God," he said, reflecting back. "Bridges started blowing up and villages falling."

The ANA immediately rushed an additional 1,500 troops to the province. In a meeting that went late in to the night on June 16, Lessard, Canadian task force commander Brigadier-General Denis Thompson, the chief of staff for the ANA and the regional chief of police tried to decide what to do. They had intelligence reports of tanker trucks filled with explosives that were about to descend on the city for follow-up attacks.

"It was when things were bad," said Lessard.

The first priority wasn't to retake Arghandab, they decided; it was to reinforce Kandahar city. Within two days, 1,300 additional ANA troops were rushed to the province. The 3rd Battalion of the British Parachute Regiment—the 3 Para—was dropped into city by RAF Chinooks that thundered in low across the desert to let everyone know they were coming. The choppers skimmed the rooftops and landed close to government buildings and the city's soccer stadium. Lessard said it was exactly the show of force needed to stiffen spines. Afghan government officials and bureaucrats had stopped going to work and the city was almost at a standstill. The United Nations was getting ready to pull out of Kandahar and had chartered a plane for that purpose.

With the British patrolling the streets of the city, the Canadians positioned themselves alongside the Afghans and launched a bloody four-day operation to retake the north bank of the Arghandab.

I was in Paris to cover the long-planned international donors conference, where countries involved in Afghanistan passed the hat for cash to prop up the Karzai government. They got U.S. $21 billion in pledges. I sat with a drink in my hand and watched television coverage of the bloodletting in the Arghandab. Amid the jumble of images—troops, frightened civilians, the rubble of Sarpoza, the bodies—I caught sight of the road outside of the district centre, where I had been only a few days before. I sat on the edge of my hotel bed and started at the screen.

Losing Hearts and Minds 19

Kandahar city became a stark, frightening place in the aftermath of the Sarpoza Prison break. Not that it had been a model of calm and civility prior to that, but the city never seemed to fully recover from the attack and the lingering aftertaste of fear it deposited in the mouths of most people. The Taliban, on the other hand, seemed invigorated, even though Canadian and Afghan troops mowed them down like so much curbside grass. They died by the hundreds, maybe even the thousands, yet they didn't seem to go away. They kept coming back, setting ambushes and laying bombs in what seemed like a long, head spinning nightmare. What was worse, they didn't seem to tire of it.

Officials in Ottawa and some officers on the ground took pains to emphasize that the city was under control, but much depended on your definition of control. In a span of three weeks during the early winter of 2009, the bomb disposal team at the provincial reconstruction base was called out to defuse more than 100 roadside bombs and booby traps. They found them everywhere: slipped into culverts; dug into walls; loaded on wheelbarrows; in bicycle seats; strapped to donkeys. You name it, the Taliban hid a bomb in it. And of course, nobody ever saw them do it. A few of the explosives went off, killing and maiming locals unfortunate enough to be nearby. Yet the nervous exhaustion that gripped the streets in those days had more to do with a sense that the Taliban were everywhere, watching everything. They were an intangible, malevolent presence.

On the way to an interview one day, Khan, his cousin and I hit a police roadblock. Yellow crime tape had been strung across the main boulevard and an out-of-shape Afghan cop ambled in front of the barricade. Khan rolled down the window and hollered to him. A 100-kilogram bomb had been found strapped to the support casing of the bridge ahead. The cop directed us on to a secondary road. We turned left with the rest of the traffic and within minutes it was total gridlock.

We were on the border of a barren, penniless neighbourhood teeming with people, ramshackle shops and the smell of raw sewage. It took twenty minutes to advance twenty paces, and our snail-like progress was accompanied by a loud chorus of car horns. We only needed to travel a few blocks. Ahead was a traffic circle and when Khan stepped out of the car to look, he reported that it was crowded, but moving freely.

I'm not sure when I spotted the two men. They had a hard look about them, even when compared with the other stony faces in the vicinity. The pair sat outside one of the shops on plastic chairs. Around them were piled cases of soda, motor oil and bicycle tires. "Convenience store" was an eclectic term in Kandahar. The men were dressed in dark, knee-length Afghan shirts and balloon pants. One wore an outfit dyed emerald; the other's was ruby. Both had jet-black turbans and beards as thick as steel wool. The baneful pair watched everything and everyone around them, and passersby went out of their way to avoid eye contact. It was as if they expected the men to suddenly explode—not that such a thing was uncommon in this place. The body language of the people on the street displayed a shrinking deference. I felt my skin go cold.

The car became very quite. Khan's cousin, who was introduced as Agha and seemed like a chatterbox, went stony and silent. He gripped the steering wheel and stared straight ahead. Khan lit a cigarette and cracked a window ever so slightly. He tried to behave casually. A kid came up to the window, stared into the back and pointed at me. Although I was dressed in Afghan clothes, my white skin no doubt had a neon effect, even through the smudged, dust-coated windows.

"Who is he?" asked the boy, who was about ten.

"He's your father's brother, now get lost," Khan told him, translating for me as the kid wandered to the curb. The boy looked back over his shoulder and continued to stare. He hovered there for a long time.

I hadn't taken my eyes off the two men. Khan leaned back in the passenger seat and spoke in a hushed, confidential tone.

"Sir, do you see those two tough-looking guys over there?" he asked with wide, pleading eyes. "I think they are Taliban. Actually, they are Taliban. That is what they look like."

Agha glanced over.

"Yes. And they are looking straight at us."

We sat there for what seemed an eternity, just staring at each other. The guy in red said something to his companion out of the corner of his mouth, but never broke eye contact. The one in green slipped a cellphone out of his pocket and switched it on. None of us even needed to look around: there was no place to run. The shops were packed so tight there was no room between them, no alleys for an avenue of escape. In one sense that was good: if we couldn't get out, they couldn't get reinforcements in. But what if they or somebody around them was armed?

You learned a lot about fear in a moment like that. The thought of being kidnapped and then beheaded while being filmed on the Internet was always there, but it was usually a hazy intangible. The soldiers marvelled at how most journalists travelled unarmed, stubbornly adhering to the deeply held principle that we were observers, not combatants. Some called us stupid and grumbled about how they'd have to risk their lives to either rescue us or collect our remains. I knew some journalists who'd given in and did pack weapons. If you knew you were going someplace dodgy, you brought along somebody with a gun—a cop or private security. Most times, you relied on stealth and speed to get you through, but it was easy to make mistakes. When face to face with one of those mistakes, however, telling the difference between stupidity and courage was almost impossible.

The longer our stalemate dragged on, the more Khan panicked. He insisted we get out of the car and walk to the traffic circle. From there, he reasoned, we could catch a cab and disappear into the masses while Agha patiently waited for the traffic to subside. I told him we would stay put and that if somebody were coming for us they would have to tear us out of the vehicle. We were not going to leave his cousin to an uncertain fate, nor give anyone the chance to snatch us off the street. Agha looked back with an indebted expression as our tormentors leaned in to one another and chatted feverishly. They did everything they could to suppress the instinct to point or gesture toward us. The cellphone belonging to the one in the green went off. He answered and nodded. And then, as if by divine intervention—if there was such a thing in Kandahar—the vehicle in front of us moved. We advanced with an energy bordering on ecstasy. A cop at the traffic circle had finally gotten off his wooden chair to untangle the diesel-clouded strands knotted around him.

"Bastard," Khan mumbled to the closed window as we passed.

* * *

The face of the war throughout southern Afghanistan became more menacing and sinister after Sarpoza. In some respects, NATO had only itself to blame. Since late 2006, it had conducted a very successful Special Forces campaign to assassinate mid-level and top-tier Taliban commanders. In fact, they had been so good that by spring 2008 a power vacuum had developed to the point where the Quetta Shura, the nominal moniker for the exiled Taliban leadership, was not able to replace commanders as quickly as it was losing them.

What is not widely understood among the public is that the insurgency in Afghanistan is actually a constellation of badasses. There is the Quetta Shura, made up of Mullah Omar and the remnants of the hardline Islamist regime chased from power in 2001. They take their name from the northern Pakistani city where they are said to be based. This is the face that most people see, but the term "Taliban" has become a virtual spittoon for every radical, nutbar and narco-drug lord with a gun in Afghanistan. It gets even more complicated when you consider that "Taliban" is also used to describe the moral conservatism of people in rural areas.

The other two branches of the insurgency have a hardened radicalism that can make the Taliban look like pikers. There is Hezb-e-Islami, a violent fundamentalist group that traces its roots back to the anti-Soviet jihad. It is headed by Gulbuddin Hekmatyar, who is best described as the Don Corleone of the insurgency set. Some analysts say he's in bed with al-Qaeda, but his orthodoxy appears more flexible than that. Yes, he's a hardline Islamist, but he's more for Gulbuddin Hekmatyar than anything else. He did offer to shelter Osama bin Laden while serving briefly as Afghanistan's prime minister in the 1990s, but was toppled after two months and disarmed by the Taliban. He led one of the most disciplined groups of mujahideen fighters during the 1980s and, at one point during the civil war, slaughtered the residents of Kabul with an artillery barrage. U.S. arms and cash fed the Hezb-e-Islami movement in the 1980s, but Hekmatyar was virulently anti-American. The 2001 invasion brought him out of retirement in Iran.

The third group, perhaps the most sinister, is the Haqqani Network. It is cozy with al-Qaeda. The elderly Maulavi Jalaluddin Haqqani, another former favourite of the CIA, heads the organization, but is too old and frail to be of much use humping around the mountains. His son, Sirajuddin Haqqani, pretty much runs everything. He's burnished his terror credentials enough for the U.S. to put a $200,000 bounty on his head. He controls most of the insurgent combat elements in the corrugated mountain passes of eastern Afghanistan, along the Pakistani border. The Haqqanis are highly trained and truly make your blood run cold. Their techniques are more precise, their ambushes more deadly, their bombings bigger than anyone else's. Unlike the Taliban, they don't care if they kill civilians. The Taliban in southern Afghanistan would often express regret at the shedding of innocent blood, recognizing that they had to live among the population and it wasn't necessarily a good idea to go around killing them. The Haqqanis didn't care. They'd spray acid in the face of schoolgirls or set villages on fire just to watch them burn. Their motto could very well be: The More Mayhem the Better. They've targeted innocent people with the rationalization that killing them undermines confidence in the government. More like traditional terrorists than insurgents, they carried out a 2008 bombing campaign in Kabul that included an attempted assassination of President Hamid Karzai.

The power vacuum created by NATO's off-with-their-heads campaign against Taliban leaders afforded the Haqqanis a golden opportunity to exert influence in southern Afghanistan, a place where normally they had little. Sirajuddin Haqqani sent fighters to train the local Taliban in bomb-making and ambushes. Special cells adept at the assassination of government officials were also dispatched to bolster the fight. There was friction between the two groups and by the late winter of 2009 the entire underworld grid in Kandahar was buzzing. My window on that world was often the director of the local peace and reconciliation office.

"We have been told the Haqqanis are here and al-Qaeda is with them," Haji Agha Lalai warned one day.

He was in constant contact with Taliban fighters and tried to convince them to turn themselves in for a shot at money, a house and land. There was almost a comic operatic quality about him. He was constantly on the cellphone, wheeling and dealing, but he carried himself with a gravity that suggested it was life and death every moment. He made a lot of promises that he knew he couldn't keep to shifty men who made promises they couldn't keep either.

It was the Haqqanis who were responsible for putting intimidation teams on the street, like the ones we ran across, experts later told me. The idea was to create a virtual presence that would contribute to a sense of insecurity and feed the panic. Lalai told me you could find thugs like that all over the city. A pair of them walked into the newly constructed financial exchange one day and within an hour had virtually cleared the place. Rarely did they hurt anybody, but they did act as spotters looking for foreigners to kidnap, Lalai added with a guffaw into his beard. NATO knew the Haqqanis were around. Canadian officers refused to talk about it, but some Americans at Regional Command South admitted to being worried and even called it the biggest threat they faced. The one thing in the coalition's favour was that Kandahar was a long a way for Haqqani fighters to travel from their sanctuaries in northern Pakistan.

Canadian military documents I obtained under access to information laws showed the army knew something was up in the spring of 2008 when the ambushes became more sophisticated. The first indication came in the attack that killed Trooper Michael Yuki Hayakaze; the fighting quality of the new militants shocked soldiers. Canadians were used to battling a tough but ragtag band of undisciplined Taliban. All of a sudden they were up against seasoned fighters who knew most of the ambush tricks and didn't flinch in a firefight. Lalai knew things had changed because the number of fighters looking to retire through him dropped considerably in the latter half of 2008. One explanation was that the success of the prison break had put more steel in the Taliban's spine. They looked and felt like winners at that point in the war. Sipping some green tea and munching on dates, Lalai sighed and offered a more basic explanation.

"They're scared if they get caught in the reconciliation program that they'll be killed," he said.

* * *

There are times when stuff just leaps off the page and hits you square in the face, so hard it makes you shudder. I'm not talking about gruesome or graphic accounts of the misery that went on outside of our gates. A lot of that didn't get written down. No, oftentimes it was numbers that had a unique way of making your skin tingle.

I happened to be going through a batch of academic reports on-line in the media tent one day when I had to stop, slide my chair back and pay tribute to the trepidation on my screen. In mid-2009, the Washington-based Open Source Center painted a statistical portrait of the Afghan insurgency that should have made the skin of every intelligence officer crawl. The analysis showed that between 2004 and 2008, ethnic Pashtun Taliban were responsible—or most likely responsible—for 97 per cent of the bombings, ambushes and kidnappings in the country. Foreigners such as al-Qaeda could account for only a tiny fraction of the misery. That meant the violence was a bottom-up exercise, not something driven from the top down or outside. Like some crazy, insidious monster from a bad horror movie, the insurgency had exploded into tiny fragments, sprinkled everywhere and infected everything. The report told me that the people whom we claimed to be trying to help had turned on us.

That night, I showed an intelligence officer with whom I occasionally shared my secret stash of cigars the report. He took a long slow drag on his Cohiba and gave a tight-lipped smile.

"Yup. We're fucked."

His assessment was more than just a reflex. The Canadian military had its own data. It suggested that the goodwill of our hosts, what little there was of it, was sliding into history. The army had commissioned public opinion research through an Afghan firm in Kabul. The war was being fought with bombs, bullets, pens and now polls. It was a novel idea to try and crack the mute enigma that many Afghans presented.

The data, which I caught snippets of in 2009, provided a fascinating look at the disenchantment of ordinary people in Kandahar. It took another year and an access to information request by Roland Paris, of the University of Ottawa, to get a look at the full breadth of the research the military had conducted to understand what kind of mess it was in. What the polling told them at the beginning of the first surge of U.S. troops in 2009 was that support for the Taliban was at "an all-time" high. A full 25 per cent of the population in the province either had a "favourable" or "very favourable" view of them. If Afghanistan were Canada, the Taliban would be pulling the same numbers as the Liberal Party, a comparison that blew my mind. The numbers simply added sauce to an already rotten dish, but friends in Afghan civil society, what little of it there was, found my bewilderment hilarious. Ajmal Samadi headed up a human rights group called Afghanistan Rights Monitor. He said foreigners laboured under the notion that just because they hated the Taliban, everyone else hated them too.

"People look at it as though the Taliban—and even al-Qaeda—did not harm them, even though they were harsh," he said with a hint of mirth in his voice.

Kandahar was the "birthplace of the Taliban." It was one of those throwaway lines that everyone would repeat with little thought or consideration. Maybe it was meant to qualify the risk to soldiers and even excuse how little had been accomplished to that point. That it could have real relevance or weight in the face of our overwhelming firepower, pipelines of cash and wellspring of good intentions just seemed absurd, especially to those watching comfortably from the sofa back home or from their perch in the House of Commons.

"The Taliban is still a political force in Kandahar. It is the reality," Samadi said.

When Hamid Karzai started making noises in the spring of 2009 about talking peace with the Taliban, many Canadian and U.S. government types labelled him as loony. You'd bring up the subject and invariably the conversation would end with your companion circling a finger around an ear and making whistling sounds. You'd hear diplomats moan about Karzai's "erratic" behaviour; sometimes they'd lay it on thick, mocking the president for crying in public. In his book *Obama's Wars*, Bob Woodward speculated that Karzai suffered from manic depression.

I'm not sure about you, but if I was president of a country that had been ground to dust and was having the crap kicked out of it every day, I'd be crying and depressed too. The fact that Karzai was playing to a constituency—one that many of his countrymen saw as legitimate and one that would be around long after we'd slapped ourselves on the back and gone home—received only an honourable mention in a lot of the nasty things that got said. None of that is an excuse for the mafioso way in which Karzai ran the country, but there was a certain stunning ignorance and blinding self-absorption to the way we dealt with him and Afghans in general.

* * *

We rolled almost right up to the door of the Kandahar electric utility headquarters. I don't think Mirwais, another Khan cousin, could have parked
any closer. If he could have driven through the front entrance, I'm sure he
would have. Neither he nor Khan liked being seen with me on the street,
despite my underrated Afghan fashion sense and attempts to blend in. Khan
turned around with a weary glance. He was so tired and worn out by stress
that most of the colour had drained from his brown skin.

"Sir, we cannot stay very long. It is perfectly all right for the moment,
but it is not safe here."

The utility building was tucked up against the city's walled-off government district. There were local cops everywhere and even a couple of ANA.
Khan kept his eye on the swirl of people, turbans and livestock across the
boulevard as we slipped through the front door of the shattered building.
The entire ground floor was nothing but hollow rubble and motorcycles. The
workers parked the bikes over scattered chunks of masonry. The far wall was
a gaping hole that looked out across the side alleyway. We walked up a long,
narrow, irregular flight of concrete steps. The building smelled of roasted
lamb, stale cigarettes and sewer.

Hadagatullah Tokhi, the director of Kandahar's power supply, met us at
the top of the stairs, just outside his office. He was a young, tiny man with
sharp, sad eyes. His staff, who milled about as though they'd just rolled out
of bed, stopped dead in their tracks when we showed up. Tokhi waved them
back to work, closed the door to his office and pulled the shade on the window that looked out over the boulevard. Photos of towers and power lines
were taped onto the whitewashed concrete wall. There was a new ViewSonic
computer screen on his tidy desk—a heavy, 1950s relic made of battleship
linoleum. On one corner was an oversized bouquet of plastic flowers—red,
white and pink—in a vase. It was a curiously feminine touch, one you saw
in many offices around Kandahar, and it seemed so out of place that it fairly
screamed at you.

A man waiting in the office greeted Khan like a long lost friend. The two
shook hands and embraced. The stranger was the only Afghan I'd ever met with
an Afro. He had delicate features, neatly trimmed chin stubble and generally
took care of himself. I was about to ask if he like Khan was a male model in
Pakistan, but I didn't get the chance. Turns out he was a local singer, someone
whom Khan insisted we had to profile in a story some day. I just nodded and
smiled. There were a lot of moments like that in Afghanistan. Why not have a

lounge singer in the utility office? It was like having a cowboy in the control room at NASA—so random it was almost hilarious. But then, that was Khan. He had a motley parade of friends, associates and hangers-on who trailed him wherever he went. Whether the singer had come hoping to audition for a story, I wasn't sure, and didn't much care. It had taken us a while to set up the interview with Tokhi.

Beneath the bustle of Kandahar there was a fragile, crumbling infrastructure. Rolling electrical blackouts were the norm. Throughout the city and in some outlying districts, power was on for only two hours a day. We'd spent the better part of the previous week talking with business leaders, who said the absence of stable electricity forced many of them to keep shops and small factories idle. Reopening just the existing businesses with a supply of uninterrupted power would have put 6,500 men back to work right away, according to statistics gathered by the city's industrial commission. How they came up with the number, I have no idea. But whether the number was 6,500, 4,000, 2,500 or 10, the gist of what they were saying was true. There were thousands of fighting-age males just looking for an excuse not to carry a gun for the Taliban.

Tokhi walked me through the power grid requirements and expectations. What they were waiting for was to be hooked up to the Kajaki hydro dam, in Helmand province. The allies had made refurbishing it a major priority and naturally the Taliban did everything they could to screw it up. Putting in diesel generators, even temporarily, to meet the Kandahar's power demand was ruled out; the international community didn't want to foot the ongoing fuel bill.

"You are spending millions of dollars a day on war planes and tanks, yet diesel for lights is too much money," said Tokhi, who at first had bought in to the wisdom of waiting for clean hydro power, but had given up after three years.

"There are almost forty factories that I know of that are shut down because of no electricity. We often can't have water because of no power. We need power to run in pumps. We could provide many business to the people with electricity."

His building, perhaps one of the more strategic offices in the city, was a festering, hollowed wreck. Broken transformer boxes were littered on the back patio. On one wall hung thousands of key rings to the individual neighbourhood lock boxes and substations. There were no markings, and how they kept them straight was a mystery. One properly timed suicide car bomber could have brought down the place and thrown the city into even more chaos.

It was the same all over southern Afghanistan. The new governor of Kandahar, Tooryalai Wesa, told me later about a visit he made to the western province of Herat, where staff in the agriculture ministry office showed off ten motorcycles donated by the French government. The bikes were still wrapped in their shipping plastic. Wesa didn't understand why they weren't being used.

"Because we don't have fuel for that," he was told. "The donor gives us ten motorcycles and we have to provide the fuel and spare parts, but we have none."

At the Mirwais Hospital in Kandahar, life-saving equipment sat in storage closets because there was no one trained to operate it and the international community couldn't agree on a program to educate staff. It was mind-boggling to Wesa, a stout, low-talking professor who'd spent his exile years at the University of British Columbia teaching agriculture. "Afghanistan is a poor country, it's a war-torn country," he said. "It's easy to bring stuff here, but to perpetuate that, to take advantage of that, we have to have the infrastructure."

The war had become death by bureaucracy. We were literally killing people with our good intentions. The development brains were maniacal about not wanting to create an economic dependency among the Afghans, but there is a point when even tough love becomes sadistic. You could probably absolve everything if you thought for one minute that we didn't know what we were doing, that somehow we were blithely running between disasters, just trying to make everything better. But among those same public opinion polls that told us the Taliban was becoming more popular was research that showed a wide gulf between what people in Kandahar wanted and what the world, including Canada, delivered.

Late one night, I thumbed through a campaign assessment, written for the Canadian overseas command in the spring of 2009. I lingered on the conclusion page.

"We are visible, but not meeting perceived needs," read the report.

In others words, the Afghans saw us but didn't quite know what we were doing for them. In fact, when you drilled down into the numbers you saw that almost everything we were doing for them was tailored to our tastes. In surveys stretching back to 2007, Afghans clearly listed their biggest concerns as unemployment, an absence of stable electricity and high prices.

"One half of Kandaharis view unemployment and electricity as the greatest challenges in their community," said the survey.

Yet what did we give them? Schools, polio vaccinations and the restoration of agriculture through the Dahla dam project. Coincidentally, education and health care are two gifts that Canadians hold close to their own hearts. The issues were easily understandable by people back home and, most importantly, politically sellable to a public that had already turned away from the war in droves. Our solutions to the Afghan problem were elegant, thoughtful and well-crafted, but so ill-timed for a society in survival mode that it made you want to weep. The schools were great, as long as the Taliban stopped blowing them up or killing teachers. Getting rid of polio was noble, as long as you got into the districts without being gunned down and stuck the required number of needles into the proper arms. Clearing irrigation ditches and putting a rickety dam back into use was terrific and would eventually contribute greatly to the region's long-term economy, but did nothing in the immediate term to convince young men to stop fighting.

Ben Rowswell, the government's civilian representative in Kandahar, tried to convince me the choices were made by Afghans, but then noted wryly that Ottawa's plans and a host of other "priorities" were calculated with both the 2011 end-date and the blatant political need to show progress in mind.

Although it might have taken some of the sting out of the insurgency, the electricity problem was a massive undertaking.

"We were not as confident we could have tangible progress in that area by 2011 and . . . the entire idea behind focusing was to demonstrate to Canadians that their investments would make a concrete difference on the ground," Rowswell said.

Canada and the U.S. eventually bought a handful of diesel generators for Kandahar in late 2009 and early 2010.

* * *

Not long after the Rowswell interview, I was crouched in a poppy field with a group of soldiers listening to an explosion bounce off nearby mud walls. The smoke plume from a Taliban weapons cache rose high into the air in a mini-mushroom cloud. Later that day, a compound was searched. Troops had marched male villagers out of their homes, near a place in Panjwaii district called Mushan. The women and children were segregated in another part of the village. The men were lined up against a wall and made to sit in the blinding sun. An Afghan intelligence officer in a black leather jacket and with his face obscured by a sweat cloth went along and picked those he deemed suspicious. There was no rhyme or reason to the choices, at least none that I could see. The soldiers with test kits dutifully swiped the hands of the chosen, looking for gunshot residue.

A small Afghan boy, in a compound that had yet to be searched, yanked aside a worn woolen blanket that served as a door. He looked around with a fierce expression that belonged on a much older face. He moulded his forefinger and thumb into the shape of a gun, aimed it at us and pretended to shoot. One of the soldiers made as though he was going after him and the boy bolted back into the compound with the flourish of a startled bird. The other guys laughed.

"Kids. What are you gonna do?"

The Devil's Workshop 20

The gentlemen from rural Kandahar came bearing a gift for their esteemed and powerful host. I was told they were businessmen, but my inquiry as to what "business" they were in was met with a polite, vacant smile. Something strange was going on. The businessmen I knew usually exchange trinkets—cardholders, watches and pens—and while I'm sure bigger bounty often changes hands in the world of high finance and power politics, the gift presented that day in the spring of 2008 was in a different category altogether.

Maybe I shouldn't have been surprised. It was, after all, Afghanistan. And to pay homage to this particular man—arguably one of the most influential in the country—an ordinary gift wouldn't do. It had to be unique, extraordinary. The turbaned men, whose leathery hands and faces suggested that they were farmers, graciously handed over an AK-74 assault rifle—the more muscular version of the AK-47. This was no ordinary Kalashnikov. It was a folding stock rifle, the kind favoured by the Spetznaz, the Soviet Special Forces during the occupation of the 1980s. It was still in excellent working condition. The shoulder strap was somewhat worn, but the rifle smelled freshly oiled.

Ahmed Wali Karzai examined it with obvious pleasure. There was a wide grin across his chubby, stubble-strewn face. It was when he smiled that he looked most like his half-brother. He handled the weapon gingerly and took care not to get grease or dirt on his neatly pressed white shalwar kameez. Wali Karzai was a man who seemed to take care of his appearance, although the same couldn't be said of his associates. They were rough-looking characters, even by Afghan standards. One repeatedly glanced over his shoulder, looking through me with a set of dead eyes—although there were flashes of curiosity in his gaze. He undoubtedly wondered what business I had with the great man.

Karzai thanked the men for their generosity. Khan said they were farmers. Whenever someone in southern Afghanistan told you they were a farmer—or that they own a few *jeribs* of land—there was a knowing smile and maybe even a wink or two. It was an inside joke that even foreigners eventually understood. The biggest cash crop coming out of the region was opium poppies. The men shook hands warmly with their host, clasped their chests with open palms in traditional Pashtun fashion, muttered into their scruffy beards and backed out of the room, as though they were leaving the presence of royalty. In some respects they were. Karzai's family was affiliated with the Durrani monarchy, which had ruled Afghanistan for nearly 200 years.

After the door was closed, Karzai turned his attention to me.

"Those two gentlemen who just left, that's their gift to me," he explained proudly and held up the rifle.

When Karzai sat down, he placed the AK-74 on a coffee table between us. The sight of Kalashnikovs was really nothing new to me; I'd just never had anyone bring one to an interview. Needless to say, with the muzzle pointing in my general direction, I was determined to choose my questions carefully and ask them as sweetly as possible. Karzai must have noticed my unease, for he eventually picked up the weapon and leaned it against the couch.

We met in the third-floor sitting room of his heavily fortified home in downtown Kandahar. It was a small L-shaped space where thin blinds waged a futile struggle to beat back the stifling springtime heat. The air in the room was heavy and for a few a moments after the farmers left, the only sound was the whirl of a single window-mounted air conditioner. Khan had arranged the interview on the pretense of discussing the most recent assassination attempt on Hamid Karzai. It was an emotional issue for Wali Karzai, one he was eager to talk about. His father had been assassinated by the Taliban and now his brother, who had already survived three previous attempts on his life, was also marked. There were many other things to talk about, but that's what got us through the door.

At that point, two years into our partnership, Khan had cultivated a great many contacts among the Kandahar elite and was eager to demonstrate his new clout. This was my first interview since being back on the ground and the speed with which it came together impressed me. When I turned to compliment him, I found my sidekick mulling over the controls of the video camera I had given him to record the interview. His tongue was clenched between his teeth as he thumbed through the different settings. This was the man to whom I had entrusted my life. I sighed and tried not laugh.

Karzai assessed both of us with dark, inquisitive eyes. Although he was plump when compared to his half-brother and nowhere near as grey, the two shared many facial expressions and mannerisms. He spoke almost flawless English from the nearly ten years he'd spent in exile in Chicago, running that end of the family's restaurant business. There was a relaxed earnestness to his manner, as though he was determined to make a good impression.

The Afghan custom of sitting on a pillow-strewn floor was abandoned here. Instead, we were seated across from one another on plush, patterned, hopelessly outdated sofas, furniture that looked as if it had been rescued years ago from someone's basement rec room. With everything I'd heard about Wali Karzai, I'd expected his house to be flashy—maybe some paintings and perhaps even some imported furniture—but it was understated and unpretentious to the point of being rundown. Unlike the Kandahar governor's palace a few blocks away, there wasn't a fleck of marble in sight. The floors were cement. The carpets looked as though they needed a good sweeping and the glass dishes that served our dates and chai could have come from my grandmother's house. The only photograph in the room was of the president, who stared benignly at the three of us in a manner that seemed more befitting of Soviet-era portraits.

And then there was the Kalashnikov. In retrospect that's all that really needed to be said. There we were, six years after the fall of the Taliban, hundreds of lives and billions of dollars spent, yet legitimate power in this country was still derived from the barrel of a gun. Maybe it was naive to expect it any other way.

Karzai waxed on about the Afghan love affair with the AK-47 and I was loath to interrupt. Apparently, every household had one. North Americans had toasters and microwave ovens; Afghans had automatic weapons. No matter how much the spinners tried to dress up the idea of nation-building, you couldn't run from how coarse and violent these people were. By Karzai's estimation, 90 per cent of Afghans owned an assault rifle and knew how to use it.

"When they're hungry—or their children go hungry—they will take a weapon to rob and to fight," Karzai said. There was a touch of whimsy in his tone. "That unfortunately is how we solve problems."

It made you wonder what happened to the estimated U.S. $200 million the international community had contributed toward Afghan disarmament and demobilization after the fall of the Taliban. Like so many other good intentions in this mixed-up land, it ended up everywhere and nowhere at the same time. The country was awash in guns. I remembered talking to a tribal elder from Maruf, the province's easternmost district, who declared the disarmament program a failure. People would hand in their rifles and use the money to buy new ones. He said the only way to pry a gun out of the hands of an Afghan was to stick a gun to their head and force them to give it up.

AWK had a reputation that was well known to me by the time we landed in his sitting room. The Americans and, to a lesser extent the British, hated the guy. The Canadians tolerated him in the way a renter tolerates an oafish landlord. Unlike their allies, the Canadians in Kandahar suffered in silence. As head of the provincial shura, AWK was someone they had to deal with, whether they wanted to or not. He was an elder of the Popalzai clan of the Durrani, one of the most populous tribes in the region.

According to British and U.S. diplomats, AWK was more interested in manipulating coalition countries for his own and his family's interest than in repelling the Taliban. They claimed he was a drug smuggler—or at least a facilitator. On two occasions, the diplomats claimed, he had intervened to liberate seized heroin shipments bound for Pakistan. They said he used his inconspicuous interests to poison legitimate government institutions. He posed as the champion of the tribes and hand-picked people for public office who had no money or influence. They came to rely on his patronage.

Wali Karzai scoffed at the bureaucracy-based institutions that Canada and the West tried to establish, believing instead in the traditional Afghan way of conducting politics—balancing off competing tribal interests. He allowed his allies to reward their friends, a situation that led to the provincial administration initially being filled with members of the Barakzai tribe. Karzai's alienation of the Noorzai, who later welcomed the Taliban into Zhari and Panjwaii, as well as the Alizai and Ishaqzai tribes, did more to stoke the fires of rebellion in the province than just about any other political act of the last decade.

The Western allies were desperate to get rid of him. A group of diplomats and spooks, calling themselves the Tea Group, met regularly in Kabul and lamented about the burgeoning corruption within Afghanistan. Its members were consumed even early on with what to do with Wali Karzai. Later in the war, I got a long, exclusive look at Canadian diplomatic traffic related to him.

"U.S. (deputy head of mission) suggested that, if people are to be got rid of, we start with Kandahar kingpin (and the president's brother) AWK," said one cable from the summer 2006. "The U.S. has already told AWK that he needs to go—for example, as ambassador to Dushanbe (comment: Tajikistan is a major drugs transit route, so perhaps this suggestion was not as nasty as it sounds)."

That the Americans would deal so bluntly and so directly with Wali Karzai suggested to me they had a deeper relationship. If you listened to the rumour mill on the streets of Kandahar, the president's half-brother worked for the CIA. The city and its ashen, airless cafés were always hotbeds of gossip and intrigue, but the notion later came out in print in the New York Times, sourced to anonymous U.S. officials. Karzai naturally denied it, but not too hard. What was suggested to me was that there was a power struggle going on between the State Department, which was committed to long-term good governance and stabilization in Afghanistan, and the CIA and to a lesser extent the Pentagon, which saw AWK as a key asset in the war against extremism. One group in Washington wanted him ejected from Kandahar, while another allegedly paid to keep him there. The allies bought into the State Department line and wondered how to deal with the troublesome wheeler-dealer.

"UK ambassador asked what our next steps should be," said minutes from a meeting in Kabul among senior diplomats in early September 2006. "Raise the issue with President Karzai? How can Karzai be persuaded to i) focus on the problem and ii) that the growth of corruption is jeopardizing his presidency? [Canadian head of mission] suggested that the Tea Group develop a one-page action plan setting out options."

Later on, there was evidence that the allies did confront the president, who at a meeting of tribal elders in Kabul fumed at Wali Karzai and accused him of making "a mess of Kandahar." Deeply offended, AWK accused his brother of making a mess of the whole country. One of the tribal elders who was there told me later he was shocked and worried, especially when AWK stormed out slinging a stream of abuse. Time magazine reported that the president eventually summoned both the CIA and MI-6 station chiefs in Kabul and demanded to see evidence of wrongdoing. They said they couldn't produce it, but if AWK was on the intelligence payroll, you had to wonder how eager they were to actually dig up dirt. Even still, the president appeared to listen.

"We have heard rumours that AWK may be appointed as an ambassador, possibly to China," said a leaked September 29, 2006, Canadian diplomatic report.

"U.S. certainly has been trying to have AWK pushed out of Afghanistan. Given fraternal relationships, this issue would obviously need to be handled very delicately. President Karzai's reaction in the past has been to demand proof of his brother's misbehaviour, but even U.S. seems to lack hard evidence."

The two brothers had been particularly close throughout the years, my Afghan sources told me. They said AWK essentially supported Hamid Karzai, who was heavily engaged in organizing anti-Taliban resistance, when they lived in Quetta prior to 2001. The tenderness was evident when I interviewed him. In the end, that's what may have saved him and sealed the fate for governance in Kandahar.

Six months before I sat down with Wali Karzai, he had been instrumental in one of the most notorious political events in the besieged province since the fall of the Taliban. The Alokozai tribe, which dominated the Arghandab district, had long been a thorn in his side. The tribe, led by a respected former mujahideen commander, was viewed as neutral. Mullah Naqib, a former governor of Kandahar, resisted both the Taliban and the Karzai influence in the prosperous farming region. When Mullah Naqib died suddenly of a heart attack in October 2007, AWK saw it as an opportunity to bring a rival tribe to heel. He reportedly instructed the president to anoint Naqib's twenty-six-year-old, politically inexperienced son as the new head of the tribe.

Some of the Alokozai elders I spoke with said it resulted in chaos. Kalimullah Naqib was not his father and he struggled to hold his own against more wily rivals. The Taliban saw the upheaval as an opportunity and pounced on the district with a major offensive in the fall of 2007. The area, which had experienced an almost Shangri-La existence to that point in the war, degenerated into wretched killing fields. It never recovered. Canadian and eventually U.S. troops would fight there for years to come.

* * *

A few months after my spring 2008 interview came one of the most naked examples of Wali Karzai's determination to torque the politics of Kandahar in favour of the "family." Canadian military sources said he was behind the firing of the newly appointed governor Rahmatullah Raufi. A former Afghan army commander, popular with the troops and an often fickle public, Raufi was sacked only four months into the job. He had replaced the notorious Asadullah Khalid, who throughout his reign did AWK's bidding without question.

Governors throughout Afghanistan's thirty-four provinces serve at the pleasure of the president. It is an appointed position that carries public responsibility but very little power. The real authority was with the provincial council, which Wali Karzai ruled with an iron fist. Canadian officers said that Raufi got it into his mind that village councils should report to him, a notion that many ordinary Afghans embraced, at least those who believed Western promises of democracy and justice. AWK got wind of Raufi's attempts to organize the councils along more democratic lines, as opposed to tribal lines, and promptly had him dispatched. The startled former general even called Canadian commanders the day he was fired and pleaded for intervention. There was nothing they could do.

Raufi was replaced almost immediately by Tooryalai Wesa, but Raufi's dismissal touched off a backlash in the villages and among civil society in Kandahar. In the months and years afterward, the event was cited by a number of elders as proof that the province was being run mafioso style. Beyond public perception there was a deeper, more troubling result. The uproar led to political turmoil throughout the winter and spring of 2009, something the Taliban moved swiftly to capitalize on with a more focused, determined campaign of assassinations.

"The removal of Governor Raufi and subsequent replacement with Governor Wesa lends itself to political instability at the provincial level," said a June 2009 briefing document prepared for the general in charge of Canada's overseas command.

"Politically, many Raufi supporters have called for his reinstatement, demonstrating general displeasure with the amount of power held by a few individuals in the province."

The same report noted that Wesa faced resistance from Raufi's supporters and that progress toward good governance was "frustratingly slow."

Later in the war, Wali Karzai would be accused of helping rig the 2009 presidential election in the province in favour of his brother. Opposition politicians in Kabul spoke about ballot boxes in some districts stuffed with more votes than there were people.

The references to AWK sprinkled throughout Canadian military reports were all opaque, but there was no escaping his malevolent influence, or the disastrous impact he had on attempts to stabilize Kandahar. Yet he was tolerated.

Part of the reason was probably his alleged CIA connection, but military commanders in both NATO and with Operation Enduring Freedom were dependent on his intelligence and the security muscle he provided through private militias. In some respects, all we could do was stand by impotently and watch.

Even as Canadian involvement in Kandahar was winding down, diplomats seemed almost afraid to challenge him. The country's ambassador in Kabul, William Crosbie, told me in a 2010 interview that Wali Karzai "exercises authorities that are beyond" the scope of his office.

"I think the way I would characterize it is that we—along with the rest of the international community—are willing to work with Ahmed Wali Karzai and with others who will support the establishment of representative, responsive government in Kandahar."

The problem was that AWK had no interest in building a representative government and dramatically demonstrated that fact with the firing of Governor Raufi. I'm not sure how much more proof Ottawa needed that he wasn't with the program. Part of the problem was there was really no alternative. Just the mention of the president's brother was enough to make some in the Conservative government chippy.

"The concerns about his brother—well documented. [Just] because we haven't publicly commented doesn't mean we haven't made our views known at various governmental levels," said Defence Minister Peter MacKay in a spring 2010 interview.

Crosbie sounded almost apologetic when he talked about how Canada justified talking out of both sides of its mouth.

"Whenever I speak publicly to Afghans, I start with saying two things: The first is, Canadians recognize we're here as guests. We're guests of the Afghan government and the Afghan people. Secondly, we're here to support Afghans. In both those cases that does not mean we're here to support specific individuals—or their personal views—on how governance should be in this province. What we want to see is that Kandaharis have the opportunity, free of pressure from any source—from the insurgents, or from powerbrokers—to make up their own minds about what kind of government they want to have; how they wish to be represented."

It was a lovely sentiment, the kind Canadians are famous for expressing.

During our interview, AWK pleaded for Canada to establish giant public works projects as a way to put the legions of unemployed—those most vulnerable to the Taliban—to work.

"What is the phrase your people use?" Karzai asked.

"Idle hands are the devil's workshop," I answered.

He nodded approvingly.

It took a while, but I screwed up the courage to ask him about the corruption allegations. Karzai clasped his hands together and looked at the ceiling, as if to collect his thoughts. For a very long moment, the only sound in the room was the whirl of the air conditioner. Khan gave me an apprehensive look from behind the video camera.

Like many Afghans, the president's half-brother presented nuanced arguments about corruption. He acknowledged it existed, but then went on to add that, "in the last six years, enough people, lots of people, made more than enough money." He contended that it was time for leaders to start putting back into the community because they—whoever they might be—had "made millions and millions of dollars." Anyone who spent any amount of time in Afghanistan understood that the country's accounting standards and practices, much like its traffic rules, were not laws; they were merely suggestions. Karzai praised Canada's contribution to the National Solidarity Programme, which helped create the community development councils that oversee reconstruction and help direct how international funds are spent. He was no doubt happy because he oversaw those councils.

"This is the most important project," he said. "Even, even if the money has been stolen, it has been stolen in the community; it ends up in the community."

As I scribbled down the quote, I imagined the bureaucrats in charge of the program reading it and having a stroke.

It was clear by that point that our interview was over. Karzai gave me a beefy handshake and agreed to pose for pictures outside. We made our way downstairs, where the second floor was teeming with barefoot visitors who chatted while waiting patiently for just a few minutes with the influential elder. Everyone stopped talking when Karzai appeared. He quietly issued a few instructions in Pashtu and continued down the cement steps to the outside, where we passed a mound of sandals piled at the front door.

The compound was ringed by two sets of high walls, both topped with razor wire. Karzai stood in front of the white and blue trimmed inner wall, near a set of rose bushes and a flagpole where the Afghan standard drifted in the blazing sun. On the curb beside us was a brand new white Toyota RAV4. Although hardly media-savvy, Karzai had obviously done photo-ops before. As I looked at him through the lens, he stiffened into the expressionless, almost angry pose most Afghans strike when you want to take their picture. Gone was the congenial air of the moment before. There was no elegance to the transformation; it just happened. It was the sort of gaze that cemented you in place.

The more we had talked that day, the more I realized I had arrived at the end of a long dark river. Months and months of clawing my way through the opaque Kandahar landscape had brought me to this place. The journey to truly understand the shaded heart of Afghanistan began and ended with Wali Karzai. The man and the place reeked with power, the slow, deliberate kind that turned your insides cold. It's impossible to convey in words the epiphany of that moment. Politics was always about power, but as we sat and discussed the naked brutality of the country, it struck me that I was in the presence of one of its more artful practitioners.

Ahmed Wali Karzai met his end in July 2011, gunned down by an assassin in the very house, if not the very room, where we had met. The shooter was Sardar Mohammed—one of AWK's closest confidants, and a man so trusted over eight years in the employ of the Karzai family that he was one of the few allowed to be armed in the inner compound.

Mirwais, Khan's younger cousin, came to pick me and two others up at the gate the day of the funeral. He was relieved that a member of the inner circle was being blamed. Had it been the Taliban or a member of a rival tribe, he said, the streets would have been filled with blood. The Taliban tripped over themselves to claim responsibility and one of the elder Karzai brothers lent them some credibility by accusing them, but Sardar Mohammed's links to the insurgency were tenuous at best. Some on the provincial council felt AWK's death was the result of a personal dispute.

His murder left a gaping power vacuum in Kandahar and weakened Hamid Karzai's already fragile grip on the region.

As we drove down the highway into the city, I couldn't help but think of how he had been swallowed by the casual savagery of his own people and tried hard not to taste the bitter irony of it all. Friends of mine compared the murder to a mafia hit and invoked Mario Puzo's name, but I found the allusion to the *Godfather* saga to be so pop culture it was almost obscene. Khan used to shake his head whenever I told him about comments like that.

"Sir, why does everyone think this place is a movie?" he asked. "Do they not know that when you're dead here, you don't get up afterwards?"

There was a delicious little story that got served up regularly around the media mess table in Kandahar. It went something like this: An army public affairs officer watched a battle unfold up the road from his position. Amid bursting shells and the whoosh of rockets, his phone went off. It was a request from Ottawa to get embedded reporters to write a few reconstruction and development stories because there was too much war news in the papers back home. Incredulous, the spokesman held the phone up to the sound of the fighting, then took it back and said: "Yeah, I'll get right on that." The story was told and retold early in the war to the point where some dismissed it as urban legend. Thing was, it was true.

And this wasn't the only story like that. Later in the war, a seasoned correspondent—a guy who was perhaps the best soldier-slice-of-life storyteller in Afghanistan—got upbraided by a newly minted public affairs officer. The young officer, straight out of school, stuck his nose into the interviews to the point where the reporter told him to butt out and let the soldiers speak for themselves. The spokesman went off like a flare. Journalists were civilians, he said. They were "nothing" and the embeds wrote for a public with a Grade 8 education. He sneered: If you wanted the "keys to the kingdom" with the battle group, in terms of access and interviews, then he'd better see some "positive stories," otherwise the reporter's request would get "lost."

The "message" was usually not in your face to quite that extent, but by that point both the government and the army had stopped trying to sell the war and were eager, each for its own reasons, to get the hell out of Kandahar. The relationship between military and media was always strained, but in the end it was headed toward an ugly divorce.

We were, in the eyes of the military, an unruly, unkempt, sometimes unmanageable lot. The media tent was often full of misfits, characters and outright lunatics. There were guys who spent so much time chained to their laptops that they ended up living beside them. Others were happy to file one story a week and spend the rest of their time playing war tourist. One guy came back from a firefight and thanked the public affairs officer for letting him out. There was a French photographer who walked around KAF in his Speedo underwear, a TV reporter who didn't draw the curtain when she changed, and a journalist who declared publicly that she wasn't leaving the theatre until she got laid by a soldier.

Whenever journalists showed up in the field attached to a combat unit, we were initially treated as a curiosity, something the soldiers could look at but not get too close to. That residual suspicion hung on with a lot of guys. Others would behave as though they'd never seen a correspondent before. Some made up their minds to dismiss you even before you'd showed up and would either sit with their backs to you or behave as though you didn't exist. A few would talk, but you could see the wheels turning as they tried to figure you out. There was a whole rite of passage each of us had to go through, protocol and customs that had to be strictly observed. Once the proper rituals were satisfied you were granted observer status, but you were never truly allowed inside their circle.

This arm's-length posture wasn't borne of shyness. I don't think I ever met a soldier who was truly shy. The first ones to warm up to you were usually the guys tasked with protecting your life, soldiers who were supposed to take the bullet for you and tried hard not to resent it. You could talk, but not too much. You could ask questions, but not too many. Invariably you heard every horror story about every journalist who'd screwed them in one way, shape or form. More than anything else, you had to share their burden without reservation or complaint.

One time north of Kandahar, in the late spring of 2008, a presence patrol went out in the mid-afternoon heat. Since life came to a standstill at 55° C, it was considered a good time to catch the Taliban napping. The guys took bets on who would carry me out of the brush. We made our way through the tangled undergrowth and past low-hanging mulberry trees, where the fruit would be sheared off by the scrape of passing helmets. We marched through the pallid green fields that clung to the banks of the weedy Arghandab River. I made it through, with over forty pounds of gear on my back, without passing out or crying like a child. The guys appreciated that. And in time, some came to appreciate the fact that I didn't have to be there, and neither did the other journalists who stepped off—unarmed—into the unknown with them. We were volunteers and many of us walked in without the training and financial incentives that the troops took for granted.

If the journalist in the field happened to be a woman, the road to consent was a bit easier. The guys always wanted to see a pretty face and openly told public affairs officers to send them "hot" reporters. Richard Fitoussi, the documentary filmmaker who survived the roadside bombing in Gumbad, came roaring through the tent door one day after fruitless attempted interviews. He pointed at me and then at himself.

"Dude, when we come back in the next life, we gotta make sure we have boobs; only way we can do this job," he said.

Everybody had an opinion about the media, just like everybody has an opinion about the weather. I was constantly amazed at the number of people—great and small—who with the straightest of faces would tell me and my colleagues how to do our job, as though journalism was somehow akin to ditchdigging and something any idiot could do. The easiest way for a public affairs officer to make an enemy in the media tent was for them to tell us what the story might be on any given day, as though they were dictating a press release. The smart ones didn't do it. One time, a senior officer complained I spent too much time travelling unembedded and interviewing Afghans, and not enough time out in the field with the troops.

"Sir, do I tell you how to plan a battle?" I asked. The officer shook his head, a little startled at the impertinence. "Then please don't tell me how to cover a war."

Early in the war the army had a deep, vested interest in keeping the spotlight squarely and tightly focused on itself. The embedding program was weighted toward telling individual soldier stories, not exploring the bigger picture. The attitude that the public wasn't getting the *real* story on Afghanistan was set right at the top and almost right at the beginning. On the fifth anniversary of 9/11, the prime minister gathered around him in Parliament's Hall of Honour the families of soldiers serving in Kandahar. It was just weeks after that first bloody summer.

"There are Canadian heroes being made every day in the desert and the mountains of southern Afghanistan," Stephen Harper said in the nationally televised address.

"These are the stories we don't hear—the countless acts of courage and sacrifice that occur every day on the battlefield and in the towns and villages where Canadians are reconstructing the basic infrastructure of a shattered nation. Because of their efforts, the Taliban is on the run, not the charge."

I watched the speech on the internal Parliamentary feed. Everyone, at that point, was straining so hard to hear some good news that we almost fell out of our chairs. What we heard that night was more than cheerleading. It was cold political calculation, and it was also completely, utterly untrue. Never mind that the newspapers and airwaves were, at that time, full of the harrowing stories of the soldiers who'd fought and won Operation Medusa. Never mind that there were, at the time, virtually no civilians on the ground organizing reconstruction. Never mind that, at the time, the Canadian military was begging both the Foreign Affairs Department and the country's international development agency to spend money on projects that had already been approved, projects intended to win over local Afghans.

Beyond that, dealing with the military as an institution and trying to get them to tell their story was painful. There's no other way to describe it. Individual soldiers were poets, but the great monolithic beast, the establishment, was bound up with talking points, communication strategies, political considerations and that catch-all blanket for sins, operational security. It was a babbling incoherent mess. The fact was, if you weren't around to see those hundreds of individual acts of heroism that Stephen Harper had referenced, nobody would tell you about them. And if by chance you did get wind of one, the institution usually did everything in its power to obstruct you. My personal experience with the circumstances surrounding the death of Captain Jon Synder spoke volumes on this topic.

A few months after the prime minister's speech, at a university conference in Kingston, Ontario, I was asked at the last minute to sit on a panel with two academics to talk about perceptions of the war. When the doors closed I realized to my horror I was the only journalist in the room. For two hours I was the designated media piñata for Canadian and American military officers, diplomats and development staff. If they could have fashioned the curtain ties into a noose, they would have. What was painfully obvious was that for all the brainpower in that room, for all the collective wisdom of years of government service, everyone had an opinion about coverage of the war, but no one had the first clue about how the modern television-centric, image-driven media worked. Someone in the audience, a senior public affairs officer, asked whether journalists should be given uniforms and swear an oath to the Queen, as had been the case in the Second World War. It was a school of thought that believed good coverage could be ordered, just like bombs and bullets. I was pilloried at one point for referring to Afghanistan as "the war you're trying to fight." It was "our war," the nation's war, a development officer huffed. The very same people who demanded objectivity and balance in reporting all of sudden screamed for us to take sides.

Even as late as 2010, when the military had all but given up on selling the mission, a bipartisan tagteam of senators lit into what they considered to be the public's skewed view of the war and accused journalists of confining themselves to Kandahar Airfield and not reporting the successes.

"We haven't necessarily been getting the A-team war correspondents out in the field," said Liberal senator Roméo Dallaire, a former major-general and a peacekeeping icon for his work during the Rwandan genocide.

"The media organizations in regard to security concerns, insurance concerns, has restricted, in my opinion, the availability of some good, solid, consistent reporting in the field as war correspondents should be."

Tory senator Pamela Wallin, a former journalist and interviewer, supported him. I sat in my usual seat at the National Press Theatre and gawked at them. They'd held hearings in the airtight, brightly lit Senate committee rooms on Wellington Street across from Parliament Hill that spring. And as the senators listened to a parade of witnesses and stuffed shirts, I and a handful of colleagues had leapt out the back of Chinooks into the powdery crud of rural Panjwaii and slept in the desert trenches alongside soldiers. That they chose to say such a thing less than six months after journalist Michelle Lang was killed in a roadside bombing spoke volumes about the mindless pabulum that was spoon-fed around Ottawa. There was nothing more embarrassing for a country than when a war went wrong.

What no one in power seemed to realize until very late in the war was that the battle to win over the public was actually lost very early in the game. Some would even say it was lost before troops ever set foot in Kandahar. If you asked most journalists to pick the point when they believed the wheels really came off the bus, it would be that awful first spring and summer of 2006, when what had been sold as a peacemaking mission on steroids devolved into an ugly guerrilla war. The political spinners and legions of communications staff were all walking dead after that; they just didn't realize it. They organized speaking tours for soldiers and officials, they wrote talking points and created fancy travelling displays, but public opinion swung decidedly against the war that summer and pretty much stayed there for the next five years. People watched the steady stream of casualties return from overseas and freaked out. The country, which had developed a strong pacifist streak, was in the middle of its first shooting war in almost half a century.

Over the years the media and the public, thanks to the Internet, were buried under a mountain of reports, backgrounders, speeches and testimony, all of it well-meaning but most of it blindingly optimistic. But the elephant in the room, the question no wanted to answer—or at least couldn't answer convincingly—was: Why were we there? The first argument was that it was about fighting terrorism, something that rang hollow with many Canadians, even after a homegrown plot was uncovered in Toronto. The fact was, most people in the country didn't feel threatened. They were too busy with their own lives and latest gadgets to feel endangered. Then there was the appeal to altruism. But over time even that argument was shredded. If we were there to help the Afghans, why did a vast swath of them continue to help the Taliban to blow us up? If this was about social liberation and clearing the way for young girls to go to school, why did the Karzai government pass a law that legalized rape within a Shiite marriage and turn a blind eye to the exploitation of children? If this was about being a good ally and helping out the United States, then why did no one else want to set foot in Kandahar?

Beyond the Liberal and the Conservative inability to articulate a coherent case for war, very few seemed willing to deal with the national trauma that unfolded that summer. There was nobody to hold the public's hand. There wasn't even an official recognition that a country that hadn't been at war in a generation needed comforting. The government went into bunker and it was left to the Canadian military to explain what was going on. I stayed up late one night in Bucharest during the 2008 NATO summit and debated that point with a senior official in the PMO. After much back and forth she conceded that they were at loss.

"We were a new government and we were still feeling our way around," she said.

It was a bitter irony. The government was often pleased to work with the mile-wide and inch-deep perspective of television, where the vast majority of people got their news. The Liberals were bad in that respect, but the Conservatives were by far the worst. If a cabinet minister had a choice between doing an interview with a television or print reporter, television won almost every time. The message lines were simple, clean and bite-size. The Conservatives obsessed about television; they catered to television. Yet the war, and by extension their policy of wrapping themselves and the military in the flag, was being done in by the powerful, moving and uncontrollable images of ramp ceremonies and firefights. The puzzle of it all even made some in the media tent queasy. As the number of dead climbed into the dozens, the *Globe and Mail* stopped writing about ramp ceremonies, although critics didn't seem to notice. Matthew Fisher, the rock of CanWest's news coverage in Kandahar, opined in a 2010 speech at Carleton University that emphasis on casualties meant an individual soldier died as many as five times in the media, from the initial report to the funeral. Not long after the speech, I heard retired general Lewis MacKenzie repeat the same thing, verbatim, to the Commons defence committee. What no one in the government, or outside for that matter, seemed willing to acknowledge was that the decision to open up ramp ceremonies and keep them open was a conscious choice of the military, made right at the top.

* * *

I never met a war correspondent in all my time in Kandahar who was insensible to their duty to the public and didn't do their level best to honestly convey what they saw. We usually travelled in a loose professional gaggle, whether it was going to the mess tent for dinner, heading outside the wire with the troops or moving about independently with our fixers. We always felt outnumbered, outgunned and under-represented. If there was a major failing of the media during the war, it was that there wasn't enough of us.

In the early sledding, the eleven to fifteen embed bunks were filled. But as the war settled in for the long haul, only a few news organizations stuck around to cover it. That fewer and fewer reporters got outside of the wire became a reality only late in the war and it was something that crept up on almost everyone. The 2008 kidnapping of a CBC journalist and the December 2009 death of Michelle Lang prompted some editors to shackle their teams to the base. By the end, only The Canadian Press allowed its journalists to travel unrestricted with both the troops and fixers. But by that late point, nobody in the government or the military seemed to care whether the story was told.

There were days when you felt like driving your head through the nearest solid wall when dealing with the legion of "experts" who spun their way into and out of this conflict like dizzy tornados. During a lull in the bloodshed of early 2006, I sought refuge at the provincial reconstruction base. I was happy to retreat and tell a few nice, quiet stories. The problem was, when any of us asked to talk to somebody on the civilian side about those glorious development and good-deed projects, we were told there was no one available, even though they were standing right in front of us. Not that there was much more than fighting happening at that time. There was only one aid and development officer at the base that spring and he told me that I'd have to call Ottawa if I wanted to interview anyone about what was going on in Kandahar.

Two years later, as I was about to leave for my third tour, I was urged by the assistant deputy minister in charge of the Afghanistan file to seek out the recently appointed Canadian civilian representative in Kandahar. I put in an interview request the day I arrived. It took three weeks. The first week I was told the Representative of Canada in Kandahar (the RoCK— they love their acronyms) was going to speak by teleconference to a weekly gathering of reporters in Ottawa and that nobody wanted to "trounce on the message." The following week the excuse was that Ambassador Lalani was to deliver a similar address to the same crowd and nobody—whoever nobody was— wanted "conflicting messages out there." By the third week, the RoCK was on vacation and unavailable. If you asked for lists of development projects so you could travel independently to view them, some of the development people would stare as though you'd spoken in a foreign, incomprehensible language. If you wanted lists, some of my colleagues were told, you should go through the access to information process.

There were few cracks in the official façade, so when they happened you appreciated them all the more. The most heartfelt and honest break I witnessed came in the spring of 2009 as Brigadier-General Denis Thompson relinquished command in Kandahar. He called all of the journalists together in the wood-panelled, second-floor conference room of the Canadian head-quarters. It had been a rough tour for Thompson, who'd endured the Sarpoza Prison break and a surprisingly savage nine months of fighting.

"People's sense of security has absolutely plummeted," Thompson told us in the most frank assessment and analysis I'd heard about the war to that date.

Ordinary residents of Kandahar felt dramatically less safe than when the mission had begun, he said.

His realistic, clear-eyed tone would be carried on, for the most part, by Brigadier-General Jon Vance, who succeeded him. But that didn't stop the baying in Ottawa. It only served to underline the disconnect.

That Kandahar was teetering on the edge came crashing home a few days after Thompson's departure with a call that caused my *Globe and Mail* colleague Gloria Galloway to shriek into her cellphone.

Jojo was dead. He'd been gunned down at a traffic stop in one of the most heavily fortified and guarded sections of the city. Someone had driven up to his vehicle and pumped between three and six shots into his chest through the passenger window, according to his brother. Jojo had been alone at the time.

I remember being in a state of absolute disbelief; a cold, grey funk that for months was impossible to shake. Just days before, Jojo had pitched me on a story about the alleged dirty dealings of private security contractors, including the Watan Group, a company owned by a cousin of Hamid Karzai. He didn't say what information he might have had and with Jojo you always had to be careful about the promises he made. The local police chief blamed the Taliban for the murder, as he always did, but it was very instructive to see local journalists assemble outside the United Nations compound the day after Jojo's death, pleading for protection from "corrupt government officials." No one was ever caught for the killing.

A lot of people I'd liked and respected had died in this war, but for one reason or another Jojo's death hit me more than most. There were those I knew who celebrated his demise, as awful as that may sound. Much as I understood that Jojo's life had been lived far too close to the razor's edge,

I couldn't help but feel that some of the spirit of what we were trying to accomplish in Afghanistan perished with him. He hustled to get ahead and it took him to some very dark places—places from which there was no return. His story was very much our story, as loath as we were to admit it.

Khan went into hiding. He locked himself in his office for days after the murder and refused to come out. He would call at all hours, sobbing into the cellphone and pleading for some kind of deliverance. When he did emerge, he wrapped his head in a desert scarf and concealed everything except his eyes. How he drove like that, I was never sure.

"You realize, you are probably the only one on the street who is hiding their face," I told him. "It's not a very effective disguise."

"I know, sir. It just makes me feel better."

It was a non-smoking hotel room, but my source didn't seem worried. He slid back the blinds and cracked the patio door open. The cone of smoke around his finger was instantly mashed by an icy breeze. It took a moment for the room pressure to equalize and begin to draw the hazy trail outside. He leaned against the doorframe and looked out at a leaden winter sky that warned of snow. I sat on an uncomfortable, stiff-backed sofa with my woolen overcoat still on, holding a pair of thin leather gloves. Through the open door I could hear the sound of traffic and the splash of tires rolling through the slush. My contact blinked through the smoke and looked at me. It was one of those assessing kind of gazes, as if he hadn't made up his mind to trust me. A drop of sweat took a long time to run down the back of my neck. I was grateful to have the door open. The cool air felt good. It was fresh and vital, and seemed to bleed some of the pressure from the room.

Most of us covering the war approached it with the intention of getting as close as we could without getting burned. That was the whole point, right? To bear witness; to understand what the soldiers knew; to see it the way the Afghans did; and to communicate it all, however inarticulately and imperfectly, back home. Some treated it as a duty and an obligation. Others got lost in it and flew way too close to the sun. You couldn't blame them. They wanted so badly for all of this madness to have some kind of meaning, some kind of purpose, that they "went AWOL" from the media tent. Some went so far into the army's corner that they either literally or figuratively put on uniforms. Others went in the opposite direction and found nothing redeeming or honest in what the military did or said. The farther away from the killing fields of Kandahar you got, the more clear and powerful those distinctions became to point. They were almost like forces of nature, ready to tear you apart.

What I discussed with my contact in the hotel room that day was probably the closest I'd come to being burned by Afghanistan. That afternoon we picked through the pieces of a puzzle together, asking many of the same questions, both out loud and silently, about what we had seen and experienced. Although we'd come at the issue from wildly different directions, we'd both been on the same path. No matter how we put the disparate pieces together, the puzzle looked pretty much the same—varying shades of one horrifying picture. We were like two scientists running the same formula over and over in our minds, hoping for a different answer.

* * *

Through all of the heat of the Afghan prisoner scandal there was always an assumption that incompetence, naivety and even stubbornness were at play. You just assumed the country didn't know what it was doing when it signed the transfer deal with Kabul, the one that precluded us from checking on the welfare of those we captured. Or maybe it was just that Canadians trusted the Afghans not to beat or butcher their own. Even when it was clear that something very bad could happen, the refusal to change the agreement had more to do with mindset than malice, at least that's what you told yourself. It was totally unthinkable that all of this had been anything more than a clumsy, blubbering accident or outright neglect.

The thought that there could have been anything willful going on seemed absurd—at least to most of us who'd spent a lot of time there. It wasn't that we were naive. Afghanistan, and Kandahar in particular, has a brutal way of robbing your innocence. Maybe we just didn't want to believe that we were knowingly handing people over to torture. Was it the ultimate act of self-delusion? Had we become so steeped in the myths of our own good nature that we were blind to the obvious? By the time I hit that hotel room I wasn't sure anymore. It was the end of a very long trail, one I'd started walking months before, in September 2009.

An investigation by the Military Police Complaints Commission, a watch-dog born out of the Somalia scandal, had been grinding on for two and a half years by the fall of 2009. Like many federal panels, it gave off a "daycare for lawyers" vibe. Hardly anything seemed to be going on and when something significant did happen it was usually of more interest to the chin-scratching set than to a public that already looked at the treatment of Taliban prisoners with ice chips in their eyes. As presentations droned on during one particular hearing, a fellow scribe sighed and remarked how this wasn't great TV. No kidding.

The MPCC had been asked by Amnesty International and the B.C. Civil Liberties Association to investigate the military police's handing of suspected Taliban prisoners. It was one of several concurrent court actions fought with the aim of halting Canada's handover of prisoners to Afghan authorities. It was being driven in large part by Amir Attaran, a University of Ottawa law professor whose passion spoke with an acid tongue. The harder the government and the Forces pushed back, the more siren-like Attaran became. I got the sense that he revelled in the fight. Sitting beside him was Paul Champ, a well-known Ottawa human rights lawyer. Champ was sharp and articulate, but cloaked his determination in a less inflammatory style.

The pair had appealed to the Federal Court to stop the transfer of prisoners. They sought an injunction and even tried to have Charter of Rights' protections extended to those in Canadian custody overseas. The court battles failed and, by late 2009, the last best avenue open to them was the police complaints commission, which had called a public hearing. But even there the Harper government brought out the legal hammer. It forced the watchdog into court and narrowed the scope of the investigation into matters related strictly to the military police. There would be no prisoner circus and no questioning of government policy.

Cabinet ministers in the Commons put their hands on their hearts and swore they were just as determined as everyone else to get to the truth and that the watchdog would not be obstructed. Yet when the commission asked for documents to help build the case, federal lawyers got a pained, uncomfortable look on their faces, as though suffering from a bad bout of gas. There were national security issues at play, we heard. They'd have to think about the request.

Although the Defence Department was often cast as the creepy, paranoid bad guy, Foreign Affairs actually kicked up the most fuss about handing over records. The commission lawyer at the time, Freya Kristjanson, was incredulous. Journalists who'd dealt with the department, and tried to get answers for even some of the most basic questions about Afghanistan, just chuckled.

The commission issued subpoenas in early September 2009 for the public hearing later in the fall. I flipped through the witness list with only passing interest. The military names were the ones that leapt out. They were generals and task force commanders mostly, some of whom I'd known and interviewed. My finger lingered over one name, and it took a moment to recall the face. Richard Colvin was at Foreign Affairs. We'd met in passing in 2006 in Kandahar. He'd arrived to take over as political director of the provincial reconstruction base as I had been on my way out. Kristjanson told me in September 2009 that commission investigators had tried to do a preliminary interview with Colvin, who indicated he was willing, but had been blocked by his bosses. My radar snapped to life. Why would a government institution with nothing to hide want to stop Colvin from speaking? I put the question to those I knew at both Defence and Foreign Affairs and was met with only gurgling sounds.

At the end of September, a loaded motion hit the bench in Federal Court with a thud. Justice Department lawyers demanded the removal of Colvin and twenty-two other senior government officials and military officers from the list of subpoenaed witnesses. They also let it be known that those witnesses who did show up would be subject to Section 38 of the Canada Evidence Act, a national security clause that had been injected with steroids in the aftermath of 9/11. Those whom the commission wanted to question could sit, but they were not permitted to speak. When I started inquiring about the usefulness of a hearing where witnesses couldn't answer questions, many people I'd known and respected turned to Jell-O. These were not meek, shallow or stupid people, yet they would have had all of us believe that muted witnesses somehow represented co-operation and openness. Others looked at me with straight faces and unloaded the most incredible explanations.

"Based on the information to date, the Crown is of the view that Mr. Colvin does not possess information relevant to the [commission's] limited mandate. As a result, the Crown has moved to set aside the [commission] summons requiring Mr. Colvin to appear," I was told.

My e-mail inbox overflowed with all manner of notices, missives, tips and junk. Keeping it clear was a full-time job in and of itself, and some days I deleted whole pages of useless stuff. One afternoon, my finger hovered over the left-click button when something caught my attention. I opened it and found a letter to the Military Police Complaints Commission from Lori Bokenfohr, Colvin's lawyer.

"For greater clarity, Mr. Colvin does have personal knowledge of what the military police subjects knew or had the means of knowing," she wrote.

She told the commission that Colvin had documents that related "to the risk of torture resulting from the transfer of detainees to Afghan authorities."

The next day when my piece appeared, the Opposition hammered Defence Minister Peter MacKay during Question Period. He stuck to the line that Colvin had nothing of substance to add to the investigation. The spittle-flinging had barely subsided when my e-mail chimed again. This time, the letter was from the lead Justice Department lawyer on the case, Alain Prefontaine, asking Colvin's lawyer for "clarification." Exactly what did her client know and whom had he talked with among military cops? It was clear they had no idea what Richard Colvin was going to say and it terrified them.

Spin, especially political spin, is an art form. When it's done well, the object doesn't realize until afterward that they've been fleeced; it sort of moves over them like a grey fog so that no facts or cynicism can cut through. Done poorly, however, spin can look like a slow-motion car wreck. But the spin around Colvin and the Military Police Complaints Commission was different. It was a tsunami—a sheer, cold fury surrounded by a halo of panic that was so evident you could see it in some of the faces. It wasn't only the Press Gallery that caught whiff of the fear, the Opposition parties did too, and it was strange to see to how routine charges of obstruction suddenly had more vigour and greater impact. And the government's usual defence tactic of getting past the news cycle didn't work; the revelations just kept coming. There were leaks about how Foreign Affairs had stopped paying the bills of Colvin's lawyer, whom he hired after refusing Justice Department representation the previous summer. Contacts within the department pointed out that he had hired Bokenfohr, an ex-girlfriend, and was trying to line her pockets. It was just another layer of smear. The truth was that Bokenfohr had a small Calgary practice and took the case out of respect for her former boyfriend. She was eager to hand it over to a bigger firm, which she quickly did, but not before Richard Colvin became a household name.

The tipping point came in early October. It was clear something was up when Ujjal Dosanjh, the affable NDP-premier-turned-Liberal MP, was the one asking questions of me and a couple of colleagues outside the Commons one day. He was curious about our perceptions of what was going on with the police commission, whether we thought it would get anywhere. You could see the wheels turning. And the calculation was more than just whether the Liberals could embarrass the government. They sensed a genuine vulnerability, an opportunity to make the Conservatives, and Stephen Harper in particular, bleed—and bleed badly. It wasn't one of those "wound them for the sake of wounding them" conversations. It was gut level. Yet I don't think any of us got the sense the Liberals had thought through where they wanted to go with this. And that was a huge departure. Like most political parties, the Liberals put on a good show. They say the right things at the right time, but they were always circumspect when the camera lights went off. There was usually a calculation in their gaze about whether the brush with which they were tarring the Conservatives could some how be turned back on them. But there was none of that here, just the icy calm of waiting for the right moment.

It didn't take long for the moment to arrive. The police commission was forced to push back the opening of its public hearings by two days in early October after Justice Department lawyers papered the place with motions and objections. It looked bad, but you got the sense the government team didn't care.

It was left to Peter MacKay to explain the government's motivations. All three Opposition parties tagteamed him during Question Period.

"What are they trying to cover up?" Quebec Liberal Marlene Jennings repeated over and over again.

"This is not politically motivated," MacKay thundered in response to taunts by the NDP's Jack Layton.

Justice Department lawyers had to have been taking their instructions from someplace, I pointed out to a member of MacKay's entourage one day. The staffer, whom I'd known for a long time and trusted, swore no one in National Defence was giving the marching orders. I was later told by a senior official in the Privy Council Office that the legal pit bulls took their direction from senior levels inside the civil service. It became abundantly clear around that time that this ran much deeper than flash-in-the-pan politics and the revelation stopped me dead in my tracks. It was one thing for politicians to run interference to avoid looking stupid. It was entirely different when the institutions of government lined up shoulder to shoulder.

The raw power of the state can be an awfully chilling sight, and that's exactly what we saw in the fall of 2009. Sure, it was a Conservative secrecy thing—a desire to manage the message so tightly that it squeaked. But this was history with fangs, an issue that just wouldn't die. In fact, it had been around for years, since the day in 2002 when badly burned Liberal defence minister Art Eggleton was dragged before Commons committee for his lapses in memory over Afghan prisoners. Culpability extended beyond political lines. It was the Liberals who pulled the trigger first. They called on the House of Commons Defence Committee to investigate the treatment of Afghan prisoners. But the NDP's aim was closer to the mark. They slapped a motion down before the special Commons committee on Afghanistan, demanding that both Richard Colvin and Peter Tinsley be called to testify. Parliament recessed for Thanksgiving, leaving behind a virtual train wreck of investigations and potential hearings.

Break weeks on Parliament Hill, of which there are several, have a tendency to take some of the steam out of arguments and issues. When MPs return they usually possess a little less bile; sometimes they even look cheerful. Not this time. Even though the politicians were gone, the backbiting over the commission and flood of leaks continued unabated. A letter from Bokenfohr to the police commission accused the lead federal lawyer of trying to bully government witnesses into remaining silent. She referenced a July 28, 2009, letter to all witnesses who had been subpoenaed by the watchdog. It opaquely warned that reputations were on the line and proceeded to outline "what is at stake for you." Prefontaine wrote that military officers risked becoming "collateral casualties" of the hearings and that the purpose of pre-hearing interviews was to catch witnesses in lies. He even described the military commission's lawyer as an "interrogator." The letter convinced Colvin to get his own lawyer.

"I suspected—correctly as it turned out—that the government's lawyers would place the government's interests in front of my own and I didn't want to be in a position where I would be disadvantaged," Colvin said in a later interview.

Prefontaine, in his submission to the military commission, claimed that none of his clients had "seen fit to accept the commission's offer" to be interviewed ahead of time and that they felt it was not "in their best interest to participate." When the Opposition politicians came storming back through the door in late October, they were more convinced than ever that the matter belonged before Parliament. When I asked Prefontaine about his warning, he denied the letter was an attempt to bully witnesses. He said all of the witnesses were smart, articulate people and to say his letter was intimidating would have been "overstating" the case.

"Would they be frightened by the expression 'collateral damage'? It depends on the context, I would assume," Prefontaine said.

Other lawyers at the commission claimed Prefontaine was furious when I published the letter. He certainly seemed angry with Bokenfohr upon the resumption of the hearing, on the assumption she had been the source of the leak. She wasn't.

Everything came to a boil when Richard Colvin filed an affidavit with the police commission. It spelled out in no uncertain terms that he'd warned the Foreign Affairs Department as early as spring 2006 that prisoners faced possible torture in Afghan jails. On the surface, it was the perfect contradiction to the assurances the Harper government had been giving for three years. Everyone went screaming to the rooftops. What didn't get tabled that day were the actual reports themselves. They were part of a trove of documents that Foreign Affairs, National Defence and the Privy Council Office had thrown under the blanket of national security, citing that beefed-up section of the Canada Evidence Act. What made it all particularly embarrassing was that nobody at the hearing knew the documents existed. The federal government hadn't handed them over as part of its disclosure.

The words "cover-up" tumble way too easily from the lips and I often counsel friends not to look for a conspiracy when simple incompetence will do. If there was any sympathy for the government's arguments, however, it evaporated right around this point. I was inundated—and would continue to be for months—by e-mail, phone calls and letters that tried to convince me and any other journalist who would listen that Colvin's reports contained nothing that even remotely resembled a warning. Yet they refused to share the proof, even after the documents were put through "the wash" of national security. It was blood-boiling. They pleaded for pity, thoughtfulness and restraint, but behaved with an undisguised brutality when asked to stand by their words. The attitude was neatly summed up by Prefontaine much later in the public hearing, when he was asked why it was taking so long for the government to produce documents for the commission.

"The documents will be given to your counsel when they are good and ready," he said in April 2010.

His tone was met with utter astonishment from Glenn Stannard, who had replaced Tinsley as head of the military watchdog.

"I find that to be close to offensive, not only to this panel but also to the public. The government of Canada can't tell us how long it's going to take to get the documents?"

Before Richard Colvin came to testify, he was told the Commons committee wanted whatever documents he'd referenced in his affidavit. I'm sure veins started popping in heads throughout government, in particular at Foreign Affairs. Within days Colvin was warned in writing that everything he had was covered by national security and that Members of Parliament had no right to see it. It was one thing to tell the MPCC to go stuff it; it was entirely different to say it to Parliament.

If there was a line to be crossed between the absurd and the truly dangerous, we'd reached it and roared right on over. That sense of exhilaration one feels when chasing a good political story simply evaporated. It was replaced with a dry-mouth gulp, a mind-blowing realization that somebody out there was playing for keeps and that the normal rules of engagement no longer applied. Up until that point, this had been about Afghan prisoners, respect for human rights and even the scoring of political points. But the refusal to produce the documents was much more profound. It had implications for the very democratic system we claim to value, though this fact was lost on most people. The Conservatives were so successful in stoking the fires of blind prejudice, at blaming everything on the Taliban, that they lay an effective smokescreen over one of the most naked displays of power I'd witnessed in years of covering government. It was hard to say what was more chilling: the fact that the full weight of the institution of government was behind the filibuster, or the idea that one of the most basic principles of our system was being set on fire and thrown in the trash can.

Parliament is the supreme authority in this country, or at least it's supposed to be. Cabinet makes decisions, but it is ultimately the representatives of the people who are supposed to act as a check on the abuse of authority. In reality, it hadn't been that way for years. Every prime minister since Pierre Trudeau had chipped away at the power of the House of Commons. All governments keep secrets—some more than others—and MPs don't have the right to see every state secret. There were some politicians I wouldn't trust to carry my lunch tray, let alone the Canadian military's launch codes. But that does not mean Parliament should be denied a fulsome explanation on behalf of all of us. The fact that the Harper government was going to such lengths to not only shut down Colvin but also keep Parliament at bay appeared to signal to everyone that something dark and very bad had happened, something so terrible it went beyond the usual covering of behinds.

The stonewalling over documents would lead the Liberals to introduce an historic motion in Parliament in December 2009, which ordered the government to open its filing cabinets. At the time, nobody expected the government to comply, and that would have resulted in a second even more historic motion—contempt of Parliament. Some claimed the battle over documents forced Stephen Harper to prorogue Parliament just after Christmas. The fighting over those reports would continue for years and remained unfinished when Parliament was finally dissolved for the spring 2011 election, ironically enough after a contempt of Parliament motion over government spending was passed by the Liberals. But by that time, nobody cared anymore.

* * *

The sky over Ottawa was a lead colour the day that Richard Colvin testified. He and Bokenfohr arrived in Parliament's chipped and aging West Block and were shown up to a cramped committee room where they were greeted by a wall of television camera lights. After setting his briefcase on the table in front of the paper card with his name on it, Colvin breathed in the moment.

"There were things I wanted to say and I was pleased to testify," he later told me.

The journey to that point had been long and uncertain, though just how long and how uncertain wasn't clear at the time. We later found out through the MPCC that Colvin's name was poison within the Defence Department and certain branches of the Privy Council Office—the result of all the nagging he'd done over prisoners and other aspects of Canadian involvement in Afghanistan. I noticed as he stood there that he seemed to take a degree of comfort from being in the spotlight. It wasn't the potential adulation or the fact that the hearing was covered live. The public has a tendency to be fickle, but the institution of government has a very long memory and scores are sometimes settled over years and even decades. There was a look of calm on his face and his tone remained steady throughout the presentation and during the questions afterward. There was safety within the white-hot glare of publicity and when he sat down, Colvin looked relieved, like a man who had unburdened himself.

"I disagreed with our policy on detainees. I actually wanted to testify," he recalled later. "There was a framework—a perfect framework where my testimony was being sought. And the government's own position was that they were co-operating fully with the [military police complaints commission]. I thought that's great; you're co-operating and I am too."

His testimony shook the Harper government to its foundations with sweeping allegations that "all" prisoners handed over to the Afghans were tortured and that Ottawa was at best indifferent and at worst trying to cover it up. Everything was perfectly still when he spoke. You couldn't even hear the shuffling of feet during his seven-minute opening statement. Some MPs sat staring open-mouthed at what they heard. The precise recitation, in his clipped English accent, directly contradicted nearly everything the government had been saying for three years, notably that no credible evidence of prison torture existed. He told MPs that captives taken by Canadian troops and handed over to the Afghans were subjected to beatings and electric shocks in 2006 and early 2007. He said the sweeping roundups of prisoners by the military and the subsequent alleged abuse had driven a wedge between Canada and the people of Kandahar, and destroyed much of the goodwill soldiers had fought and died to achieve.

"In my judgment, some of our actions in Kandahar, including complicity in torture, turned local people against us," he said. "Instead of winning hearts and minds, we caused Kandaharis to fear the foreigners."

Colvin claimed most Afghans taken into custody were innocent, and warned ominously that "Canada's detainee practices alienated us from the population and strengthened the insurgency."

He painted a dramatic picture of institutional indifference that morphed into an exercise in damage control once allegations of abuse became public in April 2007. He claimed he was ordered not to write about prisoners, and soon afterward reports from the field began to be "censored" and revised to the point where diplomats could "no longer write that the security situation in Afghanistan was deteriorating."

The reaction among the Opposition, human rights groups and the media was electric. Colvin was lauded as a whistle-blower, a description that irked him because although he was eager to tell his story when summoned, he claimed it wasn't a battle he would have chosen.

"I was testifying within a judicial framework," Colvin said in an interview. "I was being subpoenaed and once I'm subpoenaed my testimony is required. I was obligated legally to provide truth in testimony.

"Whistle-blowing is when you leak documents to the media, you call a press conference and operate outside of any acceptable law and legal framework; you put yourself forward and go beyond what you're committed to do.

"In my case I was acting within a framework and that was deliberate. I expected the government to try and block me. The subpoena was protection against retaliation and against repercussions."

Even before the committee hearing was over, Conservative MP Cheryl Gallant accused Colvin of being a Taliban dupe.

"They know how to take and plant false stories, how to push stories out," said Gallant, who read from a transcript of previous testimony given by a military officer. "It's called information operations."

Others, such as junior defence minister Laurie Hawn, were more cautious but still dismissive. The former air force colonel described what he'd heard from Colvin as hearsay and unsubstantiated by any reasonable measure of evidence. Hawn must have felt safe in making that assertion. After all, no one outside government had seen the documents and nobody expected to, given the legal knots tied by Justice Department lawyers. But then the most bizarre and unexpected thing happened. Little bits of paper, snippets of internal reports, started showing up in my e-mail. It was like witnessing flurries before a storm. The first batch of documents was prison visit reports that suggested cases of torture came to light in mid-2007, after the *Globe and Mail* had published its articles. They further contradicted the government's line and had the effect of bolstering Colvin's arguments.

It took a week for the government to drag out the heavy artillery, in the form of retired Chief of Defence Staff General Rick Hillier. Accompanying him was former Lieutenant-General Michel Gauthier, who'd been directly in charge of the war, and Major-General David Fraser, the first Kandahar task force commander. They appeared before the same Commons committee and, while it was officially a joint presentation, the weight of Hillier's personality left a huge imprint. He bristled with a combination of indignation and folksy charm in one of the most curious yet compelling displays I'd seen before a Parliamentary committee.

Colvin's allegations were "ludicrous," Hillier thundered.

He'd never seen Colvin's reports, never been warned of torture. And had there been any credible allegations, he would have been briefed. To make sure he hadn't missed anything, he'd reread all of the documents before testifying. You could see the ears of Opposition members perk up. Gauthier testified that reports in 2006 and early 2007 never used the word "torture," except in one isolated incidence. Fraser was quiet for much of the hearing and looked horribly out of place compared with Gauthier and Hillier, who were used to dealing with the *Gong Show* qualities of Parliamentary life. But together they delivered precisely the kind of first-hand, blistering defence that the Conservative government had been aching to unleash.

Gauthier, who was responsible for the overall conduct of the war, said he was briefed on detainees every day, but also painted Canada's policy toward prisoners as a work-in-progress. He testified that the first he'd heard of torture allegations was in the *Globe and Mail* in April 2007. MPs led the generals to several international reports that had been published before that, including a U.S. State Department document that specifically warned of torture. Hillier dismissed it and the other piles of paper as unsubstantiated "the sky is falling" reports.

It was Colvin's assertion that the army had rounded up innocent people that really seemed to dig into Hillier.

"Nothing could be farther from the truth. We detained, under violent actions, people trying to kill our sons and daughters who had, in some cases, been successful at it."

The fact that the three generals had been able to review the very documents the MPs sought but were not allowed to read was treated as just another not-so-amusing absurdity. It was like the politicians were blindfolded and whacking away with sticks at a piñata without ever breaking the belly of the beast and getting the prize. You could tell how much it burned them that they knew so little. I can remember watching Liberal Ujjal Dosanjh unconsciously tapping his pen on the table and alternating his glance between his papers and the ceiling. It was as if he was so pissed off he couldn't look at the generals.

The dust hadn't even settled from the generals' testimony before contradictions started to emerge. Uncensored versions of Colvin's reports circulated among the Press Gallery that night. The blind-source e-mail that arrived in my inbox laid out the "alarm" the International Committee of the Red Cross had expressed in 2006 about Ottawa's tardiness in reporting the capture of prisoners and the conditions inside Afghan jails, verifying one aspect of what Colvin had said. It was followed by calls and voice messages from contacts and sources. One of them, who'd seen Colvin's e-mailed reports, conceded the Red Cross was "really pissed off," but for procedural reasons.

It takes a lot of guts for someone to become a confidential source. I respected and came to admire each of the people who put their careers on the line and ran the risk of being charged with leaking state secrets during that time. The sense of urgency was underlined by some of the elaborate ways we devised to get in touch and pass information. One source preferred to deal with me through a girlfriend, a part-time exotic dancer. Others, after the initial meeting, would only do e-mail drops. Nobody used the traditional brown envelope any more. Before long a small web of sources was established. Each made it clear in their own way that they were angry about Canada's involvement in Afghanistan, and that fury manifested itself in a disdain for Hillier. His autobiography had come out earlier that fall and had eviscerated the federal bureaucrats and mandarins who'd stood in his way. It was deeply personal. What we witnessed in the early leaks that supported Colvin's testimony was, in my estimation, the ultimate settling of scores by an establishment that not only blamed him for getting Canada into the quagmire of Kandahar but also resented the media and public adoration of the man. A couple were somewhat more altruistic and spoke about how they disagreed with policy and felt that the country was doing the wrong thing, but by and large they were driven in a fit of pique to discredit Hillier and to a lesser extent the military. Sometimes they didn't even use his name, referring to him only as "that man."

The campaign to smear Colvin captured the attention of both the public and the Press Gallery. We piled on the story because it was the easy, most obvious avenue. But what was really going on during that time was a climactic battle between cultures within the federal government. It was the war within the war and when it was over everyone walked away feeling burned, empty and old.

David Mulroney, who led the Privy Council's Afghanistan task force within the federal government for two years, testified a week after the generals and stunned the committee. Rather than condemning Colvin and throwing him to the wolves, Mulroney expressed appreciation and sympathy for the intelligence officer, who'd gone into Afghanistan when no one else within

Foreign Affairs had volunteered. He supported some of what Colvin had said, but qualified important points with a more nuanced perspective. The Conservatives defended themselves with blanket denials and argued there was no credible evidence of torture until 2007. But Mulroney, who by that time had been appointed ambassador to China, suggested there was indeed evidence of torture—just not involving Canadian transferees.

"The fact that there were allegations of mistreatment in Afghan prisons was known to us," said Mulroney. "There was no mention specifically of Canadian-transferred prisoners. That was a deficiency that we later cleared up."

Mulroney had ordered Colvin to stop putting things in writing, but he denied it was a cover-up. Policy was debated internally and when a decision was made, he demanded members of his team support the consensus. It was, Mulroney insisted, his management style. He believed that ongoing debates just eroded morale.

His most fascinating comment was a narrative on why it had taken so long for Ottawa to revise what was clearly a flawed arrangement with the Afghan government. In 2006, Mulroney said, Canadian troops faced heavy fighting and a situation so "chaotic" that it took until 2007 to put a new prisoner transfer protocol in place. In his words, you could catch a whiff of the panic that must have gripped official Ottawa during that period, especially at Foreign Affairs. At that time, the fear that Canada could lose the war in Kandahar was something you'd hear discussed in hoarse whispers among federal officials. Militarily, the Taliban would never have been able to take and hold the city, but the threat of some kind of sustained terror—or temporary occupation—and the loss of face that would have gone with it gave some in the diplomatic community night sweats. What made it even worse was the recognition that the country was blind on the ground, with very little intelligence or cultural understanding. Mulroney's testimony brought back all of those conversations and framed them in a way that made you lean back and gulp. How far would we have gone as a nation to prevent that kind of nightmare, and what sort of hideous secrets would we have been prepared to keep? The human rights community began to ask themselves the same questions in the aftermath of those hearings, especially since the leaks and revelations kept coming.

Contacts, individually and sometimes together, dumped a veritable truckload of secret documents that kept me writing until Christmas. I was under strict instructions from my editors to verify and transcribe what

I saw, but told to never hold on to the reports for fear of being charged with possession of stolen property. It became a case of fitting pieces of the puzzle together, and in some instances I was able to cross-reference the documents with censored records that had been released or against copies other sources possessed. It was a cool time, where my colleagues and I felt very cloak-and-dagger—although we were never as dangerous as we seemed in our own minds. The stories, however, were pure gold. They laid out how Ottawa had been secretive with both NATO and the Red Cross about prisoners captured by Canadians; how the federal government had turned down the chance to build a prison with allies rather than hand them over; and how there was tonnes of dirt on how much Ottawa knew about former Kandahar governor Asadullah Khalid and his abuses.

The document trail led straight to that hotel room on that grey winter's day, where I sat uncomfortably in front of a contact whom I'd never met. He smoked as we chatted and went over the evidence. Everything I and others had written over the previous months was laid out and summed up. He missed nothing. Yet despite the compelling political tapestry, the mystery felt unresolved. The government had fought so hard to deny and deflect the issue—going way beyond anything you would have expected— that the ache somewhere deep in my bones said there had to be something more at stake. That was when my contact laid the last piece of the puzzle on the table: officers belonging to the Canadian Security Intelligence Service had taken part in the interrogation of Afghan prisoners.

It was the sort of statement that spoke to the deepest, darkest depths of conspiracy, yet it was almost impossible to fathom, coming from a Canadian. The very thought was incendiary.

Wesley Wark, one of the sharpest minds in the country's intelligence community, scoffed, chortled and was appalled all at once when I asked him to comment. He suggested the spy agency would have been even more clueless than the army in trying to extract useful intelligence from Afghans. CSIS rarely operated overseas, had few Pashtun linguistics and wasn't skilled in interrogation. But people within the human rights community, who'd seen monsters everywhere since Guantanamo Bay and Abu Ghraib, detected a pattern and it frightened them. They were convinced that, faced with the prospect of losing the war in 2006–07, Canada allowed for the outsourcing of torture to find something—anything—that could protect the troops and turn the tide. However, Wark was deeply skeptical and dismissed the notion.

And as the months passed I came to share his reservation, even though I'd witnessed first-hand the government's almost maniacal desire to bury the controversy and anyone associated with it.

My sense that much of this had been inflamed by a hyper-sensitive, über-secret government and bureaucracy gone wild was only reinforced by the release of 4,000 pages of detainee documents in June 2011.

"A challenge will be managing the suggestion that the content of material released is inconsistent with government of Canada messaging," said a November 14, 2007, memo tabled in Parliament.

"Cumulatively the documents leave one with the impression of (redacted) flawed Afghan judicial system and of detention facilities that fall well below UN standards," the memo stated.

"In addition, the assembled material may seem to suggest that government of Canada messaging on the detainees issues for the last twelve months has been out of sync with reporting from the field . . . This will present significant political and communications challenges."

Officials felt some materials, had they been released earlier, would have left the impression that Canada should have known "there was the potential for mistreatment of detainees."

Never mind that people may have been tortured. Never mind that the country had been put through an ugly, rending debate that had sullied and even eviscerated several careers. Spin and optics trumped all.

"I wasn't surprised at the lengths to which they went. I thought going in it would be a bloodbath," Colvin said, looking back afterwards.

* * *

The director of CSIS seemed startled by the story when it ran in March 2010. It was penned in conjunction with my colleague Jim Bronskill, one of the most savvy individuals I know and a walking encyclopedia on security and terrorism. A review of the spy agency's activities was ordered and it came back months later saying CSIS's actions had been above reproach.

Colvin suffered no repercussions after his testimony, but his career within the foreign service was put on ice. Prior to appearing before the Commons committee, he had been in line for a promotion, but all of the noise he had made behind the scenes in Afghanistan apparently cost him. There were "pre-emptive" repurcussions to his co-operation, he said.

"Two months before I was subpoenaed I had a promotion that was blocked by people who told me it was essentially over detainees. They've backed off now. They've completely backed off."

Colvin sat on a brown suede sofa during the interview. His posture was slightly hunched, but he nevertheless looked relieved, as if some of the demons that crowd the conscience of anyone who's lived through Afghanistan had been set free.

"Are you happy you did it?" I asked.

He took a long time to answer and looked out through a set of white sheer curtains into the gathering dark of the winter's night.

"Yes. Yes, it felt good."

The Green Hell 23

There were days in Kandahar when you got so tired it was impossible to recall where you were or what time it might be. Still, the first sound of gunfire or the distant muffle of an explosion would snap you back to attention. Instantly, you'd be hyper alert a rush of adrenaline at record speed. Most times you were too far away to see what was going on and during the lulls you'd strain for every little sound, every little inflection. It was the silences after the first volley that killed me. The more extended the quiet, the more I ached to know and the more I almost wished somebody would just start shooting again, if only to relieve the tension. War abhors silence just as much as nature abhors a vacuum.

On a spring day in 2010, we heard the clatter of AK-47s as we strapped on our body armour in preparation for a trip into Zhari.

"Where do you think it's coming from?" I asked. A couple of the soldiers nearby snorted without answering. One of the guys in my vehicle stood on the open ramp and laughed.

"It's coming from where we're going," he said dryly. A part of me admired his calm.

Our column of armoured vehicles was tucked behind two neat, high rows of Hesco bastions at Ma'sum Ghar. There was no seeing what was going on, but the safe bet was that the action was up the road and across the river. The day before I'd looked out from the rocky slopes and ledges across the eviscerated Arghandab River at southern Zhari district. U.S. troops now occupied much of the old Operation Medusa battlefield and the river was the dividing line between them and the Canadians. It seemed as though something was always blowing up in Zhari with the Americans around. Arghandab, the other district where the U.S. had poured in troops, was the same. Not that it was quiet where the Canadians were totally in charge, but you did notice a difference. It was like the river was a curtain. You could hear noises from the other side, but you really didn't want to know what was going on.

As I mounted the back of the LAV, I could hear the click of rifle bolts as air sentries readied their weapons. After some crisp chatter on the radio, the hydraulic lift hummed and the hatch closed with an air-sucking thump. We rolled out the gate and headed toward the gunfire: LAVs had a way of making you feel smothered in fume-soaked darkness. At least outside you could breathe and move around—and run if you needed to.

There was another burst of gunfire, followed by the high-pitched whine of the LAV turret as it swung around and pointed in the general direction of the shooting. It was hard to tell above the growl of the engine whether the gunfire was ours or theirs. An LCD monitor in the cabin was toggled to the LAV's gun camera, but you really couldn't see much. Looking at the display was like viewing a panoramic vista through a straw. The rippled grape fields rolled past like hard black and white waves. Soldiers sitting across from me stared vacantly at the screen until the mud walls, razor wire and iron traffic gate of the combat outpost appeared. Everything went quiet as we drove on to the tiny base. The sight of LAVs did that to the Taliban. They'd be ripping in to a place one minute, but when the armour showed up, they went to ground.

We'd stopped at a combat outpost south of the village of Pashmul, creatively named Pashmul South. It was only after we got out that I heard the U.S. troops refer to the dusty burrow as JFM—an amalgamated acronym of the first letters of the last names of three soldiers killed in action the previous summer.

"It was better than callin' it 'We're fucked,'" an American soldier, a private first-class, deadpanned as we stood in one of the plywood and sandbagged watchtowers.

The troops belonged to Charlie Company, 1ˢᵗ Battalion, 12ᵗʰ Infantry Regiment (1-12), a unit with a long, storied history with the 4ᵗʰ Infantry Division. Most recently the battalion had seen combat in Iraq, but it could trace its roots back through D-Day to the opening days of the U.S. Civil War. By the time I got to them, the guys of the 1-12 had been in Zhari district under Canadian command for ten months. They'd been part of the first wave of American reinforcements ordered by the Obama administration in the spring of 2009.

It was tough to look at a lot of those guys. They'd seen things I really didn't want to know about; things I'm certain they were trying hard to forget. There was a consumed horror in some of their expressions, one that I'd come to recognize. They didn't say much. Most of them huddled around the hardened sea containers that doubled as hooches, smoking cigarettes and cleaning their weapons. The week before, a *Wall Street Journal* reporter had quoted one of them as saying Command had "left them out there to die" and the blowback had turned them off all journalists. Once they saw their commander talking to me they eased up ever so slightly.

The guys of the 1-12 called Zhari "The Green Hell." Not coincidentally, that's how the Russians had described it too. Somebody had been reading his military history, and the irony wasn't lost. In all the time I spent with Canadians I'm not sure I'd ever heard them give the place a nickname. Perhaps they hadn't had time to develop a loathing for one particular district. As far as they were concerned, the whole province was screwed. The 1-12 had been the first U.S. battalion to go into the district in any force and "they had been bloodied pretty good," one American officer told me. Between December 2009 and April 2010, the Americans lost nineteen dead and fifty-one wounded in Kandahar. The numbers were even more eye-popping if you considered the entire year.

The deaths occurred under the command of a Canadian, Brigadier-General Dan Ménard. They'd received virtually no mention in the Canadian media and were conveniently ignored by official Ottawa, which by that point in the war was doing everything it could to forget it was in Kandahar. Ménard tried to make amends by including American names, faces and granite plates on the cenotaph behind the Canadian headquarters, but that didn't change the fact most of the U.S. troops hated him. When the general was brought up on discipline related to an accidental weapons discharge that spring, the story I'd written was plastered all over FOB Wilson, along with occasionally unflattering graffiti.

"When you talk about the raw casualty numbers, they're alarming," one American officer told me at the time.

The perception among the U.S. troops and their generals who ran the war from Kabul was that the Americans had been dropped into the toughest neighbourhoods in Kandahar and left there. As the spring unfolded they started asking a lot of hard questions, most related to why the Canadians stuck to their sector and what kind of resources Task Force Kandahar headquarters dedicated to support both the 1-12 Infantry and the 2nd Battalion, 508 Infantry Regiment—the 82nd Airborne soldiers who patrolled Arghandab district. Did they need more intelligence drones; more bomb-detection and disposal teams; more bomb-sniffing dogs?

"Are we sending any more troops there? How about some Canadian troops? You talk about U.S. sensitivity to casualties? Yeah, it's real high," said the officer. "We've given U.S. battalions to a Canadian general. We've given our blood, we've given our treasure, our national treasure, in what are arguably the two hardest areas."

That the region had been soaked in Canadian blood for three years prior to the American surge seemed forgotten. That was old news. That was yesterday's war, run by another president, one who'd seen a different fight as more important. As much as I really liked some of the officers who made those comments, I couldn't help but feel incredulous. Washington cared, so therefore we had to care. If Canadians had trouble figuring out when they were being ridiculous, Americans sometimes didn't recognize when they were being shameless. I had been there in the bad old days, when the warnings of Canadian commanders about a resurgent Taliban were treated with the same gravity as tears from a hysterical teenager. I'd attended the NATO meetings where the Harper government had to blackmail its allies with threats to leave Kandahar unless there were reinforcements. But it was the grim-faced analysts in Washington and some of the American military bloggers who really made me laugh that spring. They predicted, with straight faces and solemn tones, that the restive province would need about 20,000 troops in order to be properly pacified. That was ten times the number of combat soldiers Canada had on the ground throughout the war.

"They should be throwing a parade down here for you guys for what you've done," Thomas Hammes, a retired Marine Corps colonel in Washington, later told me. "I'm not sure why they don't."

Every time the soldiers of the 1-12 set foot outside of the outpost, the Taliban tried to kick the crap out of them. It was like they'd stored up an extra bit of hate for the Americans. The U.S. troops found bombs sown everywhere: grape fields; laneways; manure piles at the edge of irrigation ditches; and, worst of all, hanging in trees, where they could decapitate unsuspecting souls who were more focused on where they stepped. Anti-personnel mines were among the favourite hanging bombs, and some guys referred to them as ornaments. A lot of them went off with really ugly results.

Depending on the time year, most of the troops couldn't get more than 500 metres outside of the bases without getting hit. When the area was alive in spring, summer and fall, the Taliban were able to wiggle through the brush with little fear of being spotted. Winter gave them less coverage and consequently the attacks were not so up close and personal. The troops marvelled at the bigger bombs too. Not far from Charlie Company's outpost, the militants patiently dug a tunnel in a compound near Highway 1. They burrowed under the road, packed it with high explosives and waited for a passing convoy. It probably took months. When finally lit, the explosion blew the front end off an armoured patrol vehicle, but didn't kill anyone.

"They're determined. Very determined," Charlie Company's commander, Captain Duke Reim, said.

What the Americans didn't count on, or so it seemed from talking with the guys, was that the Taliban in Zhari district, a stiff-necked little nook of "nowhere" Kandahar, were "crazy." That said something when it came from the mouths of battle-scared Iraq veterans who believed the legions belonging to cleric Muqtada al-Sadr had already set the lunacy bar pretty high.

"In Iraq, it was more money- and power-based and here it's more of a religious war, maybe even fanatical, [but] I hate to use the word fanatical," Reim said as we looked out of the guard towers toward compounds flattened years earlier by Canadian artillery.

The Taliban lobbed mortars and RPGs at Reim's base on an almost daily basis. Charlie Company had suffered the highest casualties in the battalion to that point.

"A lot of the training here is a lot of old-school fighters and there's a lot of older Taliban commanders here that fought against the Russians."

It was the same all over the theatre for the surge troops. This wasn't the war they'd expected.

It wasn't like Canadians were unaware of the ground-level complaints. They lived side by side with Americans at FOB Wilson. The tension about casualties was never raised specifically with Ménard, but it was all over Regional Command South and ISAF headquarters.

"No U.S. general has called him and asked, 'What the fuck?'" said one officer.

Why they hadn't remained a mystery to me, but it was clearly one of the reasons Ménard had a big bull's-eye painted on his backside by American military blogger Michael Yon. His on-line rants about the Van Doos general had more in common with flame-throwers than facts. What Yon, a former U.S. special forces operator, failed to recognize was that some of the incoming forces didn't fully buy in to General Stanley McChrystal's recently anointed "population-centric" counter-insurgency strategy. There were some troops who preferred blowing stuff up to patiently negotiating and empathizing. They also hadn't learned to be deliberate in their movements. Some U.S. soldiers would go on patrol because they were bored, something that left their Canadian comrades utterly insensible. They also ignored advice to bring tanks, which had proven useful in keeping Taliban heads down at critical moments.

Some of the units that were part of the second surge ordered by Obama understood what it was all about. The 1st Squadron, 71st U.S. Cavalry Regiment (1-71) slipped into Dand district, south and west of Kandahar city, in the spring of 2010. Their operations officer, a baby-faced, gregarious lug named Major Todd Clark, was brimming with ideas. We met on Friday, the day when the 1-71 wear the Calvary Stetsons and spurs. He was eager to share his ideas and soaked up new counter-insurgency notions like a sponge. He looked everywhere for scraps of information that would help unravel the puzzle that was Kandahar. He'd even read *Three Cups of Tea*, Greg Mortenson's heartwarming if now somewhat controversial appeal for peace in this broken land. He was convinced the only way to win the war in the coming months was to fight smarter.

"It's all about developing cultural intelligence," Clark said. We sat in the mess tent of the base for the interview, a country music CD blaring in the background. Clark had to holler at the soldier tending the mess to turn it down so he could make his point, but he did so respectfully, not with bruising authority.

He was a nice guy and truly wanted to fight a different kind of war. A few weeks after the conversation, Clark was carrying water to his troops in the middle of a sweltering firefight. He stepped on a booby trap amid the tangled underbrush and the blast caught him in the face and the neck. His Afghan war was over before it started. He survived and spent many months recuperating at Walter Reed Army Medical Center in Washington. I never forgot how generous he was with his time and how bitter I was upon learning his fate.

* * *

The spring of 2010 was a tense time around Regional Command South and among the ISAF in general. American, British and Afghan troops stormed the Taliban redoubt of Marjah in neighbouring Helmand province during the late winter. It was the biggest operation to that date in the war, involving 15,000 soldiers, and had been conducted with all the attention and expectation of the Normandy landings. There was a not-so-subtle anticipation that Operation Moshtarak would turn the tide.

The initial waves swept through the area but the follow-up plan, General McChrystal's so-called government in the box, was vague at best. The man the U.S. chose to lead the district and bring good governance to the region, Abdul Zahir, turned out to have a criminal record in Germany, the result of stabbing his own son. He didn't last long in the job.

McChrystal turned his attention to Kandahar as the spring unfolded. He flew with Hamid Karzai to the provincial capital where they tried to convince tribal elders to support the next offensive. Memory, like the water in Kandahar, runs deep. Many of the enigmatic elders remembered Operation Medusa and wanted no part of it.

Khan was at the meeting, where he was allowed to sit bare foot and cross-legged on the carpets amid the tribesmen. We got together later outside the provincial reconstruction base. Amid the honking of traffic and washed-out sunshine, he ran his hand through his tussled mop of hair.

"This is such bullshit, sir." His vocabulary of curse words had multiplied over the years. "None of the elders want the operation. It will kill so many people, just like before."

Karzai promised the elders the planned offensive wouldn't go forward without the consent of the people, which I found politically outrageous. NATO was going to sweep through Kandahar with or without anyone's consent. American commanders had grown increasingly worried about the Taliban strength in and around the city and some blamed General Ménard's strategy. When Ménard took over, he pretty much tore up his predecessor's campaign plan. Brigadier-General Jon Vance had focused on a careful, deliberate counter-insurgency strategy in the rural area. He built a model village in Dand district and counted on the grasping, covetous nature of the Afghans to take over; once villagers elsewhere saw what Deh-e Bagh had, they would want it too. But when the region was handed over to U.S. troops, even though they remained under Canadian command, Ménard felt less inclined to follow the vision. Instead, he proposed something called a "Ring of Stability," where troops screened Kandahar city to prevent Taliban from getting in. It was sort of what McChrystal preached. The American general wanted to spend less time chasing insurgents in rural areas and more time protecting population centres. Yet there were few coalition troops based in the city itself. Later, senior NATO commanders came to believe that Ménard's strategy had the effect of creating a safe haven for the Taliban within the provincial capital—a pocket that had to be cleared in the same manner as when U.S. forces swept through some Iraqi cities, such as Fallujah. That raised the spectre of bloody, house-to-house fighting, something that made almost everyone's blood freeze.

Everybody, it seemed, was focused on the city. The day I arrived that spring a trio of car bombs went off in different locations, killing thirty-one people. The deputy mayor was murdered while praying one evening in his neighbourhood mosque. The spate of violence signalled an early end to the quiet season and left many people I knew in Kandahar more strung out than normal. They'd been through four years of bombings, shootings and "suiciders," and felt collateral damage all over the place. The tiniest rumour or engine backfire was cause for near hysteria. They'd had enough and just wanted everyone—NATO and the Taliban—to go home.

"Why is it that I read all the time that Kandahar city is on fire when it's not?" a member of General Ménard's staff asked me one day. We were having dinner at the mess hall in Ma'sum Ghar.

"I think the Afghans would disagree with that assessment. It all depends on your point of view," I answered.

She wasn't the only one who tried to convince me that black was white and up was down. Another senior officer, who had done a 2008 tour, declared he felt safer in the city than at any other point in the war. I just nodded and smiled and wondered if any of them had a clue.

* * *

You could feel the weight of the second American surge by the middle of spring. It cast a long shadow over everything. It wasn't only in the number of pale green uniforms that seemed to multiply daily around KAF, or in the almost non-stop buzz of helicopters. To truly appreciate what was happening you had to drive to the other side of the airfield, where a former minefield had been cleared and gravelled over in the space of a few weeks. It was the size of about two football fields and the Americans had turned it into a parking lot, literally. Set almost tire to tire was row upon row of mine-resistant patrol vehicles, or MRAPs—a Frankenstein-size SUV. I was bored one afternoon waiting for a helicopter and decided to count them. I lost track at 200. That was at least 200 MRAPs at U.S. $1 million per pop. I shuddered at the enormity.

"This is no longer the Sleepy Hollow," said one U.S. Army officer with a slap on the back. "What the Canadians have done here is great. And I know they're getting their feelings hurt, but I've been telling them, Big Army and Big Government is coming."

There was clearly a sense of loss throughout the Canadian task force by that time. It had run the show for so long but now looked slightly overwhelmed, a bit giddy and a touch envious all at the same time. Some of the diplomats and development staff had a hard time hiding their disappointment. To them Kandahar was the big project, a chance to demonstrate Canadian values and ideals on a grand stage. It was sort of like watching Miss Congeniality take a step back while the surgically enhanced beauty queen with the filthy rich parents claims top prize.

The Americans, at almost every level, were not shy about expressing their dismay at the Harper government's July 2011 combat cut-off date. The official Canadian position was that the country would "transition" to a civilian-focused enterprise. Problem was, nobody knew what that meant. To carry on work in Kandahar the nearly 100 civilians would need some form of protection. That meant one of three things: the Canadian military would have to stay in some numbers; the Americans would have to fill in; or there would need to be some form of private security. Many of the signature projects and priorities would be tough to complete within the deadline. The diplomats would develop a nervous tick or slightly out-of-character giggle if you asked them what was going to happen after 2011.

Defence Minister Peter MacKay had tried to convince the Americans to guard the Canadian civilians. The effort went nowhere. A WikiLeaks cable that came across my desk in late 2010 showed that the Obama administration, the previous year, had tried to convince both Canada and the Dutch to remain involved in southern Afghanistan. The State Department wanted Ottawa to keep running the provincial reconstruction base, but Ottawa was having none of it. When the announcement came in late March that the Americans would take joint ownership of the PRT, it was like a bell started tolling somewhere. The place had been the source of so much political pride. You'd talk to the people in Ottawa about the stream of bad news from the battlefield and they'd pause, look at you and say, "Yeah, but how about that PRT." Soon they wouldn't have that any more.

* * *

The reorganization happened quietly on a Sunday morning, presumably while everyone was still asleep. An American was taking over the deputy director's slot, giving them an equal role in the decision-making process. The civilian head of the mission just shrugged his shoulders when asked what would happen to the Canadian programs into which so much faith and cash had been invested.

"We're awaiting direction from our ministers in Ottawa," Ben Rowswell said diplomatically. "We know that we're committed to delivering development projects beyond 2011, but there are many ways you can deliver development projects, depending on how you do it. You either have civilians on the ground—or you don't.

"We know we'll be conducting development, but what that means in terms of the presence of Canada's civilians in Kandahar post-2011 is a decision that's yet to be taken."

I was thunderstruck and so was Laurie Graham from the CBC. We'd interviewed Rowswell together that morning and ended up just staring at each other as he walked away. It was unbelievable that a bureaucracy that lived to plan, consult and consider had no idea where it was going with a little over a year left in what the Harper government described as its most important foreign policy file.

The Americans and British behaved as though we were nuts and their soldiers in particular looked at us like we were leaving a great party just as it was getting started. The vibe you got from almost every Canadian was that Ottawa was determined to tiptoe out of the room without anybody noticing. The idealism and buoyancy that had sustained many people I knew in Kandahar through some really awful times seemed crushed that day. They still had their PowerPoints and their jargon, but there was no denying that the dream was slipping away. It was sad to witness.

A knock came on the media tent door not long after Rowswell left and a public affairs officer stepped in. My story on the change of authority had already been filed.

"Um, the boss wanted me to remind you"—the boss being General Ménard—"that it's still a Canadian camp, no matter what Ben said. Camp Nathan Smith is a Canadian camp, guarded by Canadian soldiers."

I sat there in utter disbelief. The story had been properly framed around the civilian aspect, but the fact that it exclusively quoted Rowswell had gotten under the general's skin. It was a peek behind the curtain at what most of us came to see as an absolutely poisonous relationship. Ménard's staff made it painfully obvious that their boss had no time for Rowswell and the feeling looked to be mutual. It was hilarious watching the two of them on stage at an ANP graduation that spring. Aside from being awkward in each other's company, the staff members standing near me struck up a petulant narration, complete with cultured French accent for Ménard. That the general took himself seriously was evident, though I don't think anyone realized how seriously until he was relieved of command, accused of having an affair with a subordinate and charged with obstruction of justice. He later resigned in disgrace.

Ménard's dismissal as task force commander was greeted with a mixture of relief and panic by the officers I knew at ISAF. They were happy to have his replacement, Brigadier-General Jon Vance, back in charge, but edgy because the great offensive to sweep Kandahar was about to get underway.

The influx of more U.S. troops during those months saw the Canadians eventually cede responsibility for almost the entire province, except for Daman, Dand and Panjwaii districts. The cavalry had arrived and it was out in Panjwaii that spring when I first caught the faintest, tiniest whiff of optimism. The district government had started to vaguely resemble something we might recognize. Even the corrupt, mercurial, Taliban-dealing district leader seemed to have gotten with the program.

Haji Shah Baran was one of those larger-than-life characters you can only meet in a war zone. Illiterate, barrel-chested and temperamental, he led you to seriously wonder how anything got done with him around. In his trademark flowing white robes and black turban, he was a divisive figure who inspired loathing among some military officers and a few of the Canadian journalists who listened to them. But there were those who were willing to forgive or at least close their eyes to his faults—and to the fact that he could break a tea cup over the head of an intelligence officer and even allow his militia to get into a gunfight with other security forces. What he had going for him was an uncanny ability to connect with local villagers, even if the effect was only transitory. He got up in front of a crowd one day in Adamzai, a well-known Taliban transit point, with tears in his eyes.

"It's so nice to see you guys. It has been too long since I've seen you. I miss you, my brothers."

It was first-rate political theatre that left the officer I was standing with simultaneously amazed and horrified.

"The guy's brilliant," one officer said. "He'll have these old stone faces eating out of his hand."

And he did. Not that it lasted very long. The Taliban still used the area as a ratline to get into Kandahar city, but the villagers were actually listening and there was someone arguing the government's case, no matter how incoherently. Bit by bit, Baran was helping stitch the district back together. Part of his local credibility stemmed from the fact he was Noorzai, the tribe from which the Taliban drew its greatest strength.

"The district leader can understand their pain and suffering. And they throw their full support behind me. I'm happy to be what I am." Baran said in one interview.

Getting the toxic mix of tribal rivalries and politics just right was something Canadians struggled with throughout the war. The Canadian army eventually soured on Baran and late in the war campaigned behind the scenes to have him replaced. His temper was annoying, but it was his attempt to line his pockets with various schemes that did him in. Baran's appointment was a concession on the part of the Karzai government, an acknowledgement that they had to do something to paper over the deep divisions among the tribes. The Noorzai had been virtually shut out of decision-making and were among the first to welcome Taliban fighters and give them sanctuary.

But Baran's soft-soap didn't work with everyone, especially not with rival tribes.

"He is not a sincere person," said Haji Azim, an Achakzai elder from Salavat, one of the most troublesome villages in the region. "He just focuses on his tribe and among his tribe he focuses on those people who can help Haji Baran."

Khan shared the assessment, but my impression of Baran as a politician in training was sealed after a village meeting one day. I was waiting to interview the Canadian commander when I felt a tap on my shoulder. I turned to find Baran and one of the interpreters staring me in the face.

"Do you want to ask me any questions? I'm happy to be interviewed," Baran said through the terp.

I burst out laughing. He reminded me of so many of the politicians I knew on Parliament Hill, it was scary.

All forward operating bases had at least one, sometimes two, big-screen televisions in the mess hall. It was the ultimate man cave. A satellite hook-up beamed a steady stream of sports, news and home improvement programs. There were sweaty guys with guns and snacks. The only thing missing was beer. The longer the base had been around, the more elaborate the set-up. I used to like to write in the mess hall at night. It was quiet. It was better than sitting on the ground in my tent or on the cot. I'd sit there with an open laptop as soldiers breezed in and out, which happened a lot during hockey season. Most would stay only a few minutes before rattling back out the plywood doors, long enough to yell at the television for some sloppy pass or missed opportunity. Television evoked a visceral response. It was like a tiny peephole that cut through the stark, jagged mountains, the dust and the cotton-mouthed heat and offered a glimpse into the world we'd all left behind. It was a world we all missed and there was an unquestionable compulsion about checking in, even for a short time, to get a fix of familiar images, scenes and sounds. Sometimes you just wanted to make sure the place you called home was still there.

Some bases employed Afghan mess stewards, young men either hired locally or brought along with Afghan army units. They kept the place tidy, but spent a lot of downtime watching television. They got an eyeful of our world. I often wondered what these grungy, implacable characters who swept our floors thought of the half-naked dancing girls in the beer commercials, or of the celebrity-obsessed hyperkinetic way our media presented everything. I'm sure it was a head spin. It was about as far removed from their biblical, light bulb–free world as you could possibly get while still remaining on the same planet. They must have thought we were all truly and utterly mad.

The full-on voyeurism we all practised in the mess tents rarely made a lasting impression. Events back home, no matter how big or bizarre, didn't intrude on the war all that often. Guys may have been vaguely aware of things, but unless it was shooting at them they didn't pay much attention. I can remember talking to soldiers about to go home in 2009. They had no idea that the economy had collapsed the previous fall.

One of the times the world did register, I was sitting with some soldiers from the Lord Strathcona's Horse armoured regiment. Based in Edmonton, these guys drove the Leopard 2 A6M tanks for a living. The news was on. There had been a kafuffle in Ottawa over something the prime minister had said. One of the guys was getting ready to blow a raspberry at the screen when he realized the piece was talking about Afghanistan.

"Shut the fuck up," he hollered and the tables around us settled down.

The day before, Stephen Harper had been interviewed by CNN's Fareed Zakaria for the program *GPS—Global Public Square*. The report covered the reaction to his comments and didn't replay the whole interview, but it was evident that the top end was about Afghanistan and the 2011 end date for combat operations. Harper put in his usual steady, understated performance when asked all of the boilerplate questions. Would Canada reconsider its policy now that Barack Obama was in office? Would you stay if asked? Show me an exit strategy, Harper said. What was support like for the mission? The issue wasn't whether Canada stayed or left; the question was whether it was a success, the prime minister countered. Was it a success?

That was when Harper dropped the bomb.

"We're not going to win this war just by staying. We're not going to—in fact, my own judgment, Fareed, is, quite frankly, we are not going to ever defeat the insurgency. Afghanistan has probably had—my reading of Afghanistan history, [is] it's probably had an insurgency forever, of some kind.

"What has to happen in Afghanistan is, we have to have an Afghan government that is capable of managing that insurgency and improving its own governance."

The mess hall had gone totally silent. Looking at the faces of the soldiers sitting around that table, you knew they weren't sure they'd heard him correctly. It took a brutally long moment for Harper's words to fully register. A lot went unsaid afterward, but just because it was unspoken didn't mean it wasn't there. The guys looked at each other in the pitiless way soldiers do and one by one slipped off of the benches and trudged into the Kandahar night.

* * *

A few days later, I was on a U.S. Black Hawk helicopter that swooped down to the base at Sperwan Ghar to pick up some Canadians going home at the end of their tour. A bunch of sweaty, exhausted-looking guys piled in and buckled up. They had their ballistic sunglasses on, which gave everyone a remote, anonymous quality. One guy pulled a silver digital camera from his pocket and started snapping pictures out the window. The helicopter lifted into the sky and swung low over the hardscrabble village, which is tucked up almost against the wire. Another soldier flashed the finger and kept it there until the place receded into the milky dust behind us. It was a spontaneous, gut-level gesture directed at the unseen tormentors who'd lobbed mortars and rockets and taken potshots at him for months. But it was also a unique summary of how we all felt about the place.

The political Opposition back in Ottawa made great hay with the Harper interview and paraded out all the tired clichés and exhausted references to Harper's 2006 "cut and run" speech. The NDP were the most vocal and took great delight in rubbing the prime minister's words in his face. What was evident from the clips I watched on-line—from the gestures, facial expressions, even from the way they held themselves—was that rhetoric and wishful thinking had finally given way to reality among the Conservatives. If someone wanted to chart the slide, I would suggest that it had started the previous fall, with Harper's startling if not wholly appreciated declaration at the beginning of the 2008 election campaign that all troops would leave Afghanistan in 2011. The distinction was lost on most people. The Parliamentary motion that the Conservatives had taken to hiding behind only required troops to leave Kandahar. The fact that Harper wanted everyone with a gun to go home was, in the estimation of most people who followed the war, the real clarion moment. It was a major policy decision that came thundering out of nowhere.

I remember sitting on Jack Layton's campaign bus in Montreal on that glorious September day, watching my BlackBerry fill up with notes from the families of dead soldiers: Is it true? Is it true what the prime minister said? Are they really leaving? There was nothing I could say that didn't sound hard or even stupid. You could sense the political calculation in every syllable of the prime minister's statement. Neutralizing politically explosive issues at the beginning was a textbook election strategy for the Conservatives in 2006. Taking Afghanistan off the table in 2008 was smart, short-term politics. But to those of us looking in from the outside, the move smacked of not having been thought all the way through. There was an utter indifference and clenched-teeth hypocrisy that was hard to fathom. What made it even more breathtaking was that few, if any, in the federal cabinet seemed to know it was coming. Later in the war, I asked Peter MacKay to explain the rationale.

"I don't know," he said. "I heard it at the same time you did."

MacKay said he witnessed a delayed reaction among politicians and the public in general because most didn't seem to grasp the nuance or the significance of what Harper had said. To them, the statement was in keeping with the motion passed fewer than six months earlier in the House of Commons with the help of the Liberals. But slowly the light went on. And from a domestic political standpoint, the message achieved the desired effect.

"It silenced people like Jack Layton because I think Jack was gearing up at that point to say let's make this a defining issue for [the NDP]," said MacKay.

The reverberations of the policy decision were felt almost immediately among NATO allies, who sat up and took notice and began asking in not-so-hushed terms whether Canada was serious about leaving entirely.

"When the prime minister said it in such emphatic terms I think it did have a ripple effect. It did. It was almost like a sonic boom. It echoed out," MacKay said.

As for the real motivation and the real strategy, they remained as much a mystery to MacKay as to the allies and the general public. The only insight he could offer was hindsight.

"I'm interpreting what was leading up to that moment and its impact."

Nowhere was the dismay among allies stronger than in Washington, which saw both the Canadian and Dutch exits from Afghanistan as a possible unravelling of the war. The departures meant that the bulk of the fighting against the Taliban and al-Qaeda would fall on U.S. and British soldiers who were just exiting an exhausting and poisonous war in Iraq. In public and even behind closed doors with Canadian ministers, the Obama administration was cool and deliberate throughout much of 2009, according to several defence and NATO insiders. Nobody came out and directly asked for an extension. Once or twice they may have hinted at it, but no one was going to lay the question on the table and put Ottawa in the uncomfortable position of having to say no.

Publicly and privately, Stephen Harper underlined he wanted to see a clear, unambiguous exit strategy, which, to that point in the war, nobody had delivered. NATO's Afghan commander, General Stanley McChrystal, was still months away from presenting his strategy to Obama. It was around mid 2009 when American officials showed up in Ottawa and quietly engaged a major research firm. They were looking for advice on how to convince war-weary Canadians to keep "boots on the ground" in Afghanistan after 2011. They were conscious of the deep political and public opposition to the war, but didn't really understand it. They wanted to identify the right arguments to make to the Harper government.

The questions they asked were meant to lay the groundwork for whatever request the Administration would make of Ottawa in either late 2009 or early 2010. The sophisticated, below-the-radar project reflected Washington's new approach to dealing with allies, and marked a sharp departure from the Bush Administration, which had treated Canada with a benign indifference. Hillary Clinton's appearance on CTV in March 2010 with a public plea for an extension and possibly a training mission was the culmination of that exercise. The secretary of state's carefully chosen venue was meant to take the case directly to the Canadian people, over the heads of the Harper government, which had proven intransigent.

There seemed to be a receptive audience among some members of the Harper cabinet who saw the inevitability of an extension—although none dared say so publicly. The crowd eventually grew to include the Liberals, most notably the party's foreign affairs critic, Bob Rae. He was won over during a whirlwind tour of Kandahar and Kabul, where the fruits of the American troop surge were offered up for display. How much he and the rest of the committee may have been suckered by the U.S. Army remains a matter of debate. An article in *Rolling Stone* pointed out that the head of NATO training mission, Lieutenant-General William Caldwell, had directed his staff to use PSYOPS—psychological information techniques—on visiting U.S. senators. Whether they did the same to Canadians is unclear, although Rae and company did meet with members of the training command. Americans using PSYOPS manipulation on Americans is a violation of U.S. law. Interestingly enough, however, it is not illegal in Canada. The Canadian military is restricted but not prohibited from using psychological and information warfare techniques on its own citizens. According to the *Canadian Forces Psychological Operations Manual*, the military cannot engage in PYSOPS in domestic operations "except at the direct request/approval of cabinet." Even then, the operations must be conducted within the boundaries of Canadian law. I was startled to read that.

The British were a little more circumspect in their attempts to convince Ottawa to remain engaged in Afghanistan. The silence from the Harper government throughout 2009 and 2010 confounded them, according to diplomats I spoke with in Ottawa, Brussels and Kabul. To a certain degree the British played with our heads, but they kept tightly focused on traditional Canadian insecurities toward Washington and the national desire to be seen as a player on the world stage. The Americans used rational, fact-based arguments and psychological mumbo-jumbo. The Brits just pushed our buttons. They probably thought they understood us better. To start with, there was nothing better than appealing to the sober Canadian sense of responsibility. I spoke with one senior diplomat in the fall of 2009, just after the Obama administration began debating McChrystal's request for 40,000 additional troops. As a member of the "inner circle'" of Western nations, there was a sense that Ottawa had an obligation to help Washington navigate the crisis.

"One would hope Canada would find a way of continuing beyond just development and political presence in the country," the seasoned diplomat said over tea.

The one point the allies were prepared to concede was that the Harper government's grasp on power remained tenuous. They didn't want to do or say anything to upset the balance, at least at that juncture.

"It's very tricky, you [may] have an election coming up."

Even still, the diplomats working the circuit were keen to underscore the urgency and sense of crisis. There was a growing perception among some

NATO countries at the time that Afghanistan had the potential to overwhelm the new U.S. Administration, which had spent the earlier part of the year facing down the worst economic crisis since the Great Depression. The McChrystal strategy was circulated in Ottawa in September 2009 and received what the diplomat described as a "sympathetic hearing," but officials and military commanders said they were "awaiting political direction." As everyone in Ottawa knows, that meant they were waiting for the prime minister.

Stephen Harper would not sit for a book interview. Attempts to understand his motivations on everything and anything have spawned an entire cottage industry of punditry. It is also the capital's favourite parlour game. There are those who fawn over Harper and declare his every move to be brilliant tactical politics, no matter how tone-deaf the argument. Others light him on fire at every opportunity and refuse to see any redeeming qualities, which is a shame no matter which side of the fence you're on.

How much of Stephen Harper there is in the Conservative political machine and how much he is a product of that machine has always perplexed me. There are many brilliant and insightful minds around Ottawa who can spin much more eloquently on that point than I. All I can tell you is what I've witnessed. In the very few brief private conversations I've had with the man, he was pleasant, thoughtful and painfully smart. He seemed to have an almost immediate grasp of details and subtlety, more so than I've ever seen in a politician, most of whom are content with small talk and the patently obvious. The impression I got was that he made time for you if you knew what you were talking about and could carry on an intelligent conversation with interesting arguments. Although I never saw it, I was told he could be brutal on staff who didn't have their facts straight and that he has a legendary temper.

In 2009, PMO insiders told me that Harper was a frustrated man when it came to Afghanistan. He was disillusioned with the allies, especially some of the larger European powers that wanted "a big say, but weren't willing to step up." He felt betrayed by their refusal to come south at a time when Canada had "trusted them to a certain extent" to be there. The painful divisions created by George W. Bush's Iraq adventure would last throughout his presidency and there was a sense in the Prime Minister's Office that Canada paid a price for it. Harper apparently told insiders that he and Bush never "argued about Afghanistan" but they came to have a fundamental difference as the war slid into stalemate in 2007. The American president was committed to building pluralistic, Western-style democracies in both Iraq and Afghanistan "no matter how long it took." That was, in Harper's estimation, a recipe for open-ended war. It was something Canada and ultimately the United States couldn't afford, the insiders explained.

At one point, Harper told insiders that "if Parliament and the Manley panel hadn't imposed an end date" on him, he would have done it himself because "all wars have to have an end." He didn't believe it was healthy for the country's tiny military to stay. Aside from the casualties, the enormous cost weighed on him. The numbers were nowhere close to what the Liberals had projected when they went into Kandahar. The military came to cabinet regularly with requests for necessary equipment, such as mine-clearing vehicles. The numbers over time became staggering. Words like "mission creep" began to get thrown around. Harper reportedly told one individual he would literally "gulp" when the equipment bills were laid on the table, and that came from a Conservative prime minister who was a fan of the military. Harper was also said to have lamented the notion that Canada went into Kandahar "totally unprepared," either militarily or from a development standpoint. General Rick Hillier had volunteered the Forces for the assignment to be on the front lines for the first time since Korea. Canada ended up mentoring the fledgling Afghan army, but the question that perplexed Harper was who was there to mentor the Canadians. The answer was no one. Insiders said he blamed the Liberals and in particular Paul Martin, whom he said went to Kandahar "for totally the wrong reason" of placating Washington over Iraq. In his estimation, the Conservatives had been mopping up ever since they'd come to office and Afghanistan was a major distraction from domestic concerns. His last frustration was the one most of us who'd intimately been entangled in this war could relate to: the inability of the Afghans to appeal to their better angels. Not long after Hamid Karzai's disastrously crooked re-election in September 2009, Harper's frustration would find a public voice in his repeated blistering attacks and lectures on corruption.

The insistence that the Canadian military would leave Afghanistan entirely in 2011 went off the absurdity scale when Chief of Defence Staff Walter Natynczyk issued overseas command an order to begin preparations for the withdrawal. He'd received no direction from the Harper government by the fall of 2009 and as a dutiful soldier, he needed to start planning. Word got out and, not to be outdone, the prime minister confirmed the instruction.

He told John Ivison of the *National Post* in January 2010: "We will not be undertaking any activities that require any kind of military presence, other than the odd guard guarding an embassy."

At roughly the same time as Harper gave the interview, he met newly minted NATO Secretary-General Anders Fogh Rasmussen in Ottawa. The secretary-general had come seeking Ottawa's continued involvement in Afghanistan. A summary of the discussion was sent to Washington by the U.S. embassy in Ottawa and released late in the war by on-line whistle-blower WikiLeaks.

"Harper promised that the government would look at the possibility" of becoming involved in the NATO training mission, U.S. diplomats reported.

It took a really long time for that to filter down, or so it seemed.

I walked into Lieutenant-General Marc Lessard's office for an interview at the Canadian Expeditionary Force Command later in the year. His staff closed the door and we sat opposite each other on a plush leather sofa set. Relaxed and confident, he looked at me with serious eyes.

"Not only are we not planning a follow-on military mission, we're not even planning to plan," he said. "Those are my orders from the CDS [Chief of Defence Staff]."

I couldn't help but wonder if this was any way to run a war.

The war came to an end, but nobody really seemed to notice. The thing that had consumed us, sapped so much energy, hammered us to our chairs with such horror and nearly driven everyone mad just ceased to be. It was almost like it never happened. The lights came up and the show was over and we were expected to stumble into the street and figure out what had become of the last five years. Bombs still went off over there; people still bled and died by the dozens, but it was about as remote as anything you'd see in a darkened room where they told you to shush and turn off your cellphone.

For most people, Afghanistan was over even before it was over. The public barely had the strength to lift a crooked finger of indignation at Stephen Harper for his sudden decision to keep troops in the country for training when he'd promised the opposite. The outrage of those who were always outraged lasted two days, and by the late fall of 2010, most people had just stopped talking about the place. The troops were going somewhere safe. That's all they knew. That's all they wanted to know. They believed the government's assurances that everything would be all right and carried on with life. That the war had truly come to end was captured neatly in a colleague's off-the-cuff remark as a group of us sat sipping wine during some down time during the 2011 federal election campaign.

"Afghanistan. I could never really get into that story," the colleague said, as though being at war was some kind of fashion statement. That's what it had become. And since it didn't look right, fit right or seem interesting and flattering enough, the war went back on the rack for somebody else to try on. The comment wasn't intended to sound as bad as all that—and I know she'd actually meant it as a backhanded compliment to the tenacity of those of us who'd stuck with the place—but it spoke so clearly that you couldn't help but grimace.

What my colleague didn't get was that you didn't have to invent drama in a war—not like on Parliament Hill. With war, the drama was real. It was there all the time, and it dug its nails into you so hard that when it was gone, you still felt the notches in your skin. You'd watch television, flip through Web pages or read the papers just hoping to catch a glimpse. You knew it was out there; you knew it was happening, but you couldn't see it. It was like the acoustic shadows they talked about in the Civil War—those haunting times when a battle would rage almost in front of you, but because of the folds of the land, you couldn't hear it.

For most people, a heavy curtain of indifference had been drawn around the war, and after a while you wondered whether it had really meant as much as you believed. You could see it in their eyes, the way they'd squint trying to remember the last thing they'd heard about the war and fail unapologetically. History has to be remembered in order to be forgotten and the brain dump that went on in the spring of 2011 was immeasurable. The Harper government had done everything it could to shove Afghanistan off the public agenda and it succeeded beyond anyone's wildest dreams. Just how devastatingly effective it had been was evident in a poll by Leger Marketing, conducted for National Defence. Nearly three-quarters of those asked—73 per cent—were aware of the war because they had heard or read something around the time of the survey.

"On the other hand, both focus groups and survey results demonstrated that the Afghanistan mission is not a top-of-mind priority for most Canadians," said the poll, conducted in September 2010. "Canadians appear more concerned with issues surrounding health care, the economy and education."

Most people, when it came right down to it, wanted an Afghanistan that could fit into their iPod, something that was easily explainable and would be wrapped up by the time their bus reached downtown. But the place stubbornly refused to conform.

"Discussions thus brought to light a complex mixture of emotions and opinions regarding Canada's mission in Afghanistan. These were dominated by confusion regarding the goals of the mission, and yet pride in Canadian troops and their work in Afghanistan also consistently came to the fore."

So that was the lesson, then. You could tell people what was going on, actually shove it in front of them, but there was no guarantee they'd hear, especially when they decided to tune out. The public had been shocked, jolted and overloaded with information for years to the point where it was no longer interesting and those who still craved the lurid spectacle of combat were more drawn to the details and comfortable familiarity of a UFC match. A sort of collective amnesia took hold, a grey, foggy recollection. People knew the war was coming to an end, they just didn't know how or when.

* * *

It's drilled into our heads by those who get off on ceremony that we shouldn't forget the dead, but in the spring of 2011 you got the sense only a handful of the cold and lonely would be left behind when everyone else had folded up their flags along the Highway of Heroes. It was a resentment you didn't talk about too much for fear of appearing morbid. Heaven forbid any of us made it personal and treated soldiers or even the Afghan people as more than cardboard cut-outs that were dragged out of the closet for photo-ops. Friends with cooler heads on Parliament Hill just shrugged and said to "chill out." But I saw what the gulf between the war and so-called real life did to my attitude and I couldn't imagine what it was like for the men and women who wrestled with real demons for a living.

I remember sitting across from Sergeant Jim Collins at a half-empty, cookie-cutter Western-style restaurant in Kanata, Ontario, late one October evening. He'd been promoted since the last time I saw him. It was one of those heavy fall nights when the darkness and the north wind came early. We drank pitcher after pitcher of beer, more than we should have, and tried to wash off everything that had gotten us in Kandahar. There are some stains that don't come out, no matter how hard you scrub. I'd hung off the back of Collins's LAV in 2008 before Sarpoza blew up and sent the war straight to hell and beyond. He'd gone back since then and, as fate had it, led the patrol the day journalist Michelle Lang was killed. He laid his forearm on the lacquered wooden table and pointed to a tattooed palm tree and maple leaf and what, through my bleary eyes, appeared to be a jumble of letters. They were initials. Each set represented the name of a person who'd died that day, under his command. "Kandahar. Always remembered. GC-GM-ZM-KT-ML."

I recall thinking what an awful burden that was for someone so young to carry. Collins had decided on the route they took that day and had jokingly traded insults with one of his soldiers over the radio in the moments before the explosion. Jim and Sergeant George Miok had just flashed each other the finger when the blast engulfed the 26-tonne armoured vehicle and cracked it open like a walnut. When he finished recounting the whole story, I felt faint. I could smell the diesel wash and sweat of the LAV, hear the hydraulic sucking sound of the ramp closing and the crackle of the radio. I knew the claustrophobic feeling of giving your life over time and again to a hazy fate and watching with amazement as it was handed back unbroken. We looked at each other across the table and marvelled, wondering what had separated us from them. My breath clotted at the thought of what the explosion must have been like that day. Jim had barely slept a full night since the attack, but talked about how he was eager to go back for the close-out mission. It was like he had some unfinished business there. We all had unfinished business with that place.

The next time I climbed into the back of a LAV, a few weeks after that October night, I was stopped short by the sight of a tan medical bag hanging on one of the metal cargo clamps just inside the ramp. The first-aid kits were always hung in that spot, but this one had a Velcro patch splashed with red crosses, a scarlet poppy and the words "Baby Girl Callou. 'The Love Boat.' RIP. June 26, 2010." It was a portable memorial to Master Corporal Kristal Giesebrecht, a medic who'd been killed the previous summer. You saw more and more of these reminders scattered about as the war drew to a close. I heard one guy refer to the impromptu cairns as "Afghanistan Post-it Notes" that implored us not to forget.

Giesebrecht had been a close friend of the medic who tended to the battle group headquarters where I found myself in the final months of fighting. Corporal Nicky Black was quiet, with a wry sense of humour and an intense brown-eyed stare. Her sun-bleached uniform was neat and tidy, but her flak jacket and the tactical vest that covered it were nicked and singed, as though somebody had been clipping at them with hot scissors.

She never talked about it, at least not to me, but her comrades couldn't get over how close she and the rest of the crew I rode with had come to death in an ambush the previous summer. They were the last of four vehicles in a convoy that had just crossed the narrow bridge over a wide, coursing irrigation canal that emptied into the Arghandab River in Panjwaii. There was the sound of gunfire. A pair of local kids swimming in the ditch on the sweltering afternoon dove for cover. A rocket-propelled grenade whizzed out of nowhere, struck the rear tire, bounced upward and slithered its way through the seams of the vehicle's extra armour plating. Fragments of the round burst into the cabin and set off the ammunition behind Corporal Black and one other soldier. Both went for the floor. The innards of the LAV were chewed as rounds cooked off indiscriminately. Power, hydraulics—it all failed. The LAV burst into flames and rolled to a stop. It couldn't even bring its turret and 25-mm chain gun around to defend itself.

Lieutenant-Colonel Conrad Mialkowski, the battle group commander, initially thought it had been a roadside bomb. The rest of the convoy halted and trained their guns north on a man who was running away—someone they assumed to be the bomb spotter. But as survivors poured out of the crippled LAV into a hail of AK-47 fire, it became clear it was an RPG strike and the other vehicles swung their turrets south to engage. That's when they realized they'd been caught at the perfect angle. A set of compounds blocked their field of fire and for a few brief seconds they were helpless. Mialkowski watched from an air sentry hatch as his team—including Chief Warrant Officer Stuart Hartnell, his regimental sergeant-major—dragged themselves out of the burning vehicle.

"The RSM took a 25 [mm] round to the back," Mialkowski said in amazement. "He picked it out. His gunner saw him picking this round out of his back."

The ramps went down on the other LAVs and the rest of the team charged into a curtain of dust, smoke and automatic weapons fire. They formed a skirmish line and advanced achingly toward the gunfire. It came to an end rather quickly. The troops overran the ambush point to find the Taliban had fled.

"These guys knew what they were doing," Mialkowski remarked afterward.

The insurgents were hard-core, the guys noted with some amazement. The engineers discovered a map model of the ambush in the dirt near the bridge; the pair had taken the time to sketch out how they were going to attack. It was the kind of thing that frosted nerves, especially then. The battle group had heard reports of "Waziris" in the area. They were an emerging breed of Taliban hailing from the battle-hardened camps of North and South Waziristan, a mountainous region of northwest Pakistan where al-Qaeda was entrenched and preached perpetual jihad. Waziris had nearly overrun a U.S. outpost in northern Afghanistan in a battle that made even the good ol' boys at NATO sit up and take notice.

The RPG team was eventually captured that day after fleeing to a mosque and trying to blend in with a seventy-person wedding party. Soldiers nabbed the pair as the procession meandered down an old dirt road toward a boarded-up market. They were the only ones looking "sweaty and suspicious," Mialkowski joked. They turned out to be locals, but it was never clear where they had received their training.

* * *

It was an anonymous kind of war that played out across Panjwaii as the hard heat of summer gave way to the dry, breathable fall. The colder the weather got, the fewer enemies you found lurking about. For a while, it seemed like only the hapless stuck around. A pair of bombers trying to dangle a booby trap in a tree accidentally blew themselves up. Soldiers watching from a nearby outpost guffawed into their binoculars. A squad of Taliban holed up in a compound within sight of a wretched mound of sand known as Three Tank Hill just up and left one day as the leaves withered and turned brown. The guys who manned the observation post saw them go; it was as though the insurgents were leaving for a winter vacation. The limiting of air and artillery strikes to prevent civilian deaths rubbed soldiers raw—a fact that was particularly true for those who'd been around in the free-ranging days of 2006 and 2007, when they could blast the land cold without blinking. Unlike those days, the sky overhead was now black with surveillance drones and static balloons—all equipped with HD cameras and infrared. For some of the guys, however, it seemed that the more they saw under the new rules, the less they did.

"You can see the enemy, you'd call in air attacks or artillery on to it and there'd be a fifteen-to-twenty-minute wait for some guy to get out of bed at KAF and then to try to talk him on to a view screen and by that time the enemy has already pulled off," said Sergeant Eric Coupel, who called in the fire for the guys of Bravo Company, 1 RCR, in the fall of 2010.

"There was one time we saw six fucking insurgents digging IEDs, [but] by the time a higher up got on to a Viewnet, he said 'Well, I didn't see them drop anything.' And then they'd send us out the next fucking day to go clear it."

I asked whether he thought the Taliban would be back for another fighting season.

"We've just let a lot of them walk away and go back to Pakistan," he said. "Those guys are going to come back. Good bet those fucking guys are coming back."

Coupel wasn't alone. Other guys repeated the refrain wherever you went in the area of operations in the fall of 2010. It was as though we were stuck in some kind of grim Groundhog Day scene, only with the amp turned up. The Americans were the difference. They made everything feel louder, bigger, more serious, more important and more deadly.

A Reuters photographer rolled into KAF one day in early December 2010. Irish and soft-spoken to the point where you had to lean in to hear him, he'd seen more war and misery than almost anyone I'd met and it was reflected in his dark, calm eyes. The photog spent weeks with the Marines in Marjah and told of how an Afghan police pickup truck had pulled up to their compound with Taliban dead stacked like cordwood in the back. Bloody arms and legs dangled out the sides and over the gate. The Marines, at first horrified but then pleased with the ghastly haul, dragged the bodies out on to the hard-packed ground and scanned the retina of each corpse. Biometrics would tell them whether the slaughter had been really worth anything.

My buddy Louie Palu spent time flying with and photographing the medevac aviation brigade, which, compared with earlier in the war, had gone all industrial. Everything about the nine-liner was bigger, more efficient and more precise than before. These days, the Role 3 Hospital was made of bricks, not plywood, and it was packed with enough diagnostic tools to make NASA blush. The helicopters were so efficient that a wounded guy could be in hospital twenty minutes after being hit on the battlefield, some of the medics bragged. But despite the wizardry, some guys still died. Louie watched them go into the back of the Black Hawk and wrote about how the blood used to seep under the cabin deck and pool in the aluminum wells below, just enough to stink up the place in the summer heat. After a while, no matter how hard they scrubbed, the air techs couldn't get rid of the stench. It was just another one of those things we were all glad to leave behind.

* * *

Somewhere in late 2010, the war took a darker turn, one that caused even the veterans of Kandahar to suck in their breath. Ahmed Wali Karzai and Tooryalai Wesa, supposedly fed up with the never-ending cycle of violence and assassination, went back to the future and unleashed Abdul Raziq, the self-appointed colonel of the Achakzai border police. His bloody rampage through Panjwaii in 2006 turned the insurgency toxic and layered a tribal war atop the insurgency the Canadians were already fighting. What apparently sent them over the edge was the murder of a friendly police commander in Daman district. AWK convinced his brother to invest Wesa with the powers of a provincial commander-in-chief, meaning he could call out the militia, so to speak.

Raziq had grown rich as the overlord of the pass between Afghanistan and Pakistan, one of the major opium routes out of the country. He gave himself a promotion to general sometime in 2008 and his appearance back on the battlefield rattled the Canadians who knew of his brutal reputation. As with any rock-star warrior, he had to be ruined before being redeemed. Raziq's ruin had been a bloody 2006 battle outside Bazaar-e-Panjwaii against rebellious Noorzai tribesmen. His reclamation was Mehlajat, a farming village on the outskirts of Kandahar. It was the home of some important provincial council members, including the soft-spoken but steel-willed Haji Mohammed Qasim. Mehlajat was lousy with Taliban and AWK wanted it cleared. Instead of turning to the army and the police—the very institutions NATO and the West had invested so much blood, sweat and tears into building—the president's brother looked to Raziq and his 1,700-man militia.

Raziq blew into Mehlajat in September 2010 and cleared the place out with an efficiency so brutal it made your skin crawl. The U.S. 5th Stryker Brigade, which took over for the Canadians in Spin Boldak, took an instant shine to him. Soon after the success of Mehlajat, they began pairing a section of American Special Forces with Raziq's militia. Soon he was all over the war-wasted province, acting as NATO's advance strike force, clawing away at Taliban commanders and their bomb makers. In background briefings, officers with the U.S. 10th Mountain Division gushed about Raziq and what he could do for them. They called him a "great partner." The Canadians who knew his history and the Afghans often at the opposite end of his rifle barrel had a different perception.

"He's been extremely effective," said Brigadier-General Dean Milner, the last Canadian combat general. "I think you always have a few concerns because he's had some challenges in the past."

AWK and the Americans had unleashed a shadowy proxy war within the war—and why not? That was how the U.S. had won Afghanistan in the first place, by letting the Northern Alliance do most of the fighting and dying. Yet Raziq made almost everybody fidget; you never quite knew if he was going to roar across that line between legitimate counterterrorism and ethnic cleansing. Raziq's father had been killed by the Noorzai, and his uncle was hanged from the barrel of a Taliban tank, according to one Kandahar provincial councillor. That made Raziq less than impartial when deciding the fate of the insurgents. Fear that his operations could rekindle a tribal war between the Achakzai and the Noorzai was so strong in Kandahar city near the end of the Canadian combat mission you could almost taste it. The people who ran reintegration programs for the handful of Taliban who gave themselves up watched everything unfold with a muted unease.

Soon after sipping Pepsi in Lalai's office, I was back at Regional Command South to ask what sort of rules of engagement were in place for the marauding militia. A soft-spoken colonel mumbled into his briefing book that Raziq was free to fight the "Afghan way." Even a generous interpretation of that meant there were no restrictions. As I wandered back to the Canadian headquarters that afternoon through the rutted dusty laneways, I couldn't stop laughing. How many times had we heard that the goal was to get the Afghans to take over their own security? Well, be careful what you wish for. They had—in their own special way. The best we could do now was close our eyes and pray.

* * *

MPs belonging to the House of Commons special committee on Afghanistan went to Kandahar halfway through 2010 like a group of wise men in cargo pants looking for a messiah. They wandered far and wide in search of something—anything—that would give this entire ruinous adventure some deep, satisfactory meaning. The transcripts made for insightful yet hilarious reading. The MPs were loaded up with metrics, briefings and binders full of qualitative analysis, perspective and qualification. There was no question the system was fabulous at writing reports and giving presentations, and a bunch of the MPs came away feeling like they'd *really* been to Afghanistan. I could just see some of the guys on the close-protection detail burying their faces in their hands at some of the things that got said. The soldiers hated those travelling circuses almost as much as they'd despised having to cart journalists around in the beginning.

The Afghans didn't quite know what to make of visiting Western politicians either. Most of them just plastered a strange hypnotic smile on their face. When the freezing wore off, they'd jabber among themselves like angry geese. Liberal foreign affairs critic Bob Rae drew the best reaction. After listening to one Afghan army kandak commander in Panjwaii, Rae apparently embraced the startled colonel and kissed him on both cheeks in traditional European fashion. It may have seemed like the culturally sensitive thing to do, but Afghan men are notoriously stoic and masculine. Colonel Muhameed Baris apparently thought he was being hit on, and his face took on a glassy, wide-eyed expression, according to some of the Canadian officers who couldn't stop laughing afterward. It was this trip that convinced Rae, a former NDP premier, to say that Canada needed to remain and help continue training the Afghan army.

One of the things that seemed to turn everybody off about staying was the sense that we were being fleeced by the Afghans. The stories about corruption—police chiefs and government officials on the take—had been repeated so often that they took on a life of their own. What was amusing to watch was the Afghan attitude, not only toward our barely disguised condescension but also toward the graft and clawing covetousness of their fellow citizens. Most would condemn payoffs and kickbacks. They'd harangue; they'd vilify—at least until they got one of their own. The most toxic kind of corruption was the stuff that fuelled the insurgency, the bribes that let government officials look the other way as drugs and weapons coursed through the streets and back alleys. Day-to-day irritants, such as checkpoint police shakedowns and paying under-the-table service fees to bureaucrats, were not as lethal, but they stoked a sense of grievance that has written itself into the Afghan DNA. Other forms of corruption were more easily recognizable to those of us from the outside, like ballot-box stuffing and shady land deals. Yet what grated most on Afghan sensibilities was the high moral tone struck by many Western leaders. They only needed a half-hour of satellite television to tell them we were no better, perhaps just a little more polished and sophisticated about it. The undeniable aftertaste of hypocrisy barely registered with many of the diplomats, war profiteers and scoundrels, but the sense of injustice was driven home one winter-scorched day in late December when I arrived at the governor's palace.

A half a dozen men had blocked the brushed concrete path with a partially dissected tree and a spray of sawdust. The neatly clipped, dead brown grass crunched under our feet as we skirted the sidewalk on the way to meet Kandahar's mayor. Ghulam Hayder Hamidi met us at the doorway. He embraced Khan, but when he saw me his face lit up as though we were old friends. He had a cold that day and clutched a tissue between his fingers while keeping a blanket firmly wrapped over his tweed sport coat. He gave me a hug and coughed on my shoulder.

"Come in. Come in, my friends," he said in clipped English. We stepped out of the marble foyer into his darkened office, where the shades were drawn tightly to guard against snipers.

Hamidi was slightly built, cheerful and grandfatherly, a man who'd spent three decades as an accountant in Arlington, Virginia. One of his daughters had moved back to Kandahar with him in 2007 to start a business; the other lived in Toronto and we had a fine conversation about the pleasant drives he'd taken from Virginia to Ontario. We'd met in passing over the years and his focused, precise manner had always made an impression. On that day, he was eager to talk about corruption.

The NATO summit in Lisbon had ended a week or so before and the mayor was still steamed. Stephen Harper had told the gathering the Afghan government didn't deserve a "dime" of direct foreign aid money until it cleaned up its act when it came to corruption. It was among the toughest statements I'd heard from the prime minister and was greeted with snorts of approval from other countries. Hamidi set down a medium-size file folder on the glass coffee table in front of us and opened it.

"Corruption?" the mayor said, his voice almost cracking.

"Your prime minister, President Obama and the prime minister of England are complaining that we didn't clean the corruption in Afghanistan [and] they will stop helping. Who is doing the corruption? You are doing the corruption."

He handed me a letter of complaint, written in Pashto and addressed to William Crosbie, the Canadian ambassador in Kabul. It suggested we were being taken to the cleaners by a few guileful Afghan companies that preyed upon the ignorance and fears of foreigners.

Near the end of Canada's involvement in Kandahar, the "good works" stampede was on, and it manifested itself in all sorts of weird ways. In spring 2010, Canadian civilians insisted Hamidi approve a contract with a Kabul-based consortium to install solar lights on the streets of Kandahar. It was the old bureaucratic reflex of spending the budget before the fiscal year ran out. The $1.9-million project looked promising on paper, but then again everything did. The mayor argued to have a Kandahar company do the work and was told the contractor was already arranged. By the time we spoke at the end of the year the work was nowhere near completed and 40 per cent of the lights that had been installed were on the fritz. Hamidi flipped through the inspections reports and pointed a frustrated finger at each page. The contractor was so inept that workers drilled holes for light standards and left them unattended overnight. He clasped his hands together.

"They start making holes in the sidewalk, and we said, 'Pleeeeease don't make the holes because of the security, because they put bomb[s] in them,'" he said.

Only in Kandahar could you have this kind of comic opera, where the most benign of municipal projects somehow morphed into a lethal menace. It spoke so loudly about how screwed up the place still was, even after all these years. Sure enough, the Taliban planted an explosive, which dutifully blew up outside the home of a municipal official.

"You see? You see what I deal with?"

It wasn't as though the Canadians were without good intentions. In fact, some days that was all we had. The Taliban had tried to take out Hamidi with a roadside bomb in March 2009 while Foreign Affairs Minister Lawrence Cannon was visiting. The minister ordered the department to buy the mayor an armoured SUV. Officials presented him with brochures and options and Hamidi settled on a U.S. $95,000 base model. The next thing he knew, it had been upgraded to the U.S. $139,000 luxury model.

"We told them, we didn't need a luxury model, but they insisted," said the mayor, his hands fluttering in exasperation. "And it came with no warranty."

It was flown to Kandahar Airfield, where he picked it up. On the way into the city it broke down and had to be restarted.

"After three weeks, the car completely stopped, not to be started," he said. "When they called to the company in Kabul, which they purchased [it from], they told us security is not that good, we cannot come to Kandahar."

The contractor eventually sent mechanics to Kandahar and Hamidi waited weeks for the repairs. In the interim, he borrowed a friend's car.

We talked more about some of the shady land deals that powerbrokers had cooked up and how the Afghan treasury, what little of it there was, was being raped. Although many liked to portray Hamidi as being in the pocket of the Karzais, he struck a fiercely independent tone that made me wonder how long he had left in this world.

"Are you ever afraid for your life?" I asked, sipping from a can of Red Bull while the mayor's assistant slipped him cold medication and bottled water.

He thought for a moment.

"If it happens, it happens," he said. "I could go back to America, but I choose to be here. I will fight, fight corruption. This is my city. Kandahar is my city and I will die here."

"I didn't do my job for Ahmed Wali Karzai. I did not do it for Mr. Hamid Karzai. I do my job because I owe this city. I [was] born here. I grew up here. I eat from this city. I was educated in this province and I had good times here. Now in the last times of my life, I want to spend it here, serving my city and city citizens."

It wasn't so much what he said as the tenor of his voice that made me look up from the notepad. His lined face had a serene expression, the kind you don't see very often in an exhausted country. He had come to accept his fate and how it was irrevocably entangled with this brutal place. You could tell he hated, just hated, what had become of Kandahar in his lifetime. Yet he didn't radiate despair or a thoughtless sense of optimism—just a healthy sense of outrage. Hamidi was a good, gentle, quick-witted man doing his best to make things right, someone who stood on the precipice and railed at the storm of consequence around him. There was something unsettling yet reassuring about the tone of his voice. That feeling followed me out as we warmly shook hands on the marble steps of the governor's palace, and it lingered as we stepped across the dry, wasted gardens and into the long shadows of the winter sunset.

The darkness did not come immediately. In fact it did not fully arrive until July 2011 when the mayor, like Wali Karzai weeks before him, was murdered. A man wearing an explosive-laced turban blew himself up in the same office where we had often sat.

By the time the end came, Khan was more than ready to check out of the life he'd made as a fixer. His career as a film star in Pakistan, while not blossoming, had afforded a much-needed distraction from the day-to-day misery of dodging bombs and stepping over broken glass and body parts. I think he never quite recovered from Jojo's murder. He dragged himself through his routines and mailed it in with me and my colleagues, all the while immersing himself in the make-believe world of films and screenplays. Who could blame him? He'd been wounded three times in our service. He'd been threatened and chased by the Taliban and roughed up by cops, and that life wasn't about to change.

* * *

Very late in the war, we paid a return visit to Tarnak Farms. I dragged along my friend Laurie Graham of CBC television and her cameraman, a tall, quiet Egyptian by the name of Ousama Farag. I had read that the Afghan agriculture ministry wanted to return the land around the old al-Qaeda compound back to the people and I asked Khan to round up both the provincial government director and the manager of the farms for an interview.

They picked us up at the gate to Kandahar Airfield and we drove the fifteen minutes along the winding desert trail and past the garbage dump to the isolated, silent monument of this war. The land to the south of the compound was alive and green, not the deathly grey it had been the last time I'd come. Every once in while you could see the heads of tenant farmers bobbing up and down among the waist-high wheat.

We stopped at a shack within the shadow of the still silent training camp, which hovered in the background like a powerful echo from another era. As we sat and drank tea and Pepsi, the compound was the focus of the director of agriculture's message. Abdul Hai Niamati argued that the old research station, with its ghostly skeletons of buildings, twisted columns, smashed masonry and unexploded bombs, needed to come down.

"The ruins mean the Taliban are still here," said Hai Niamati. "Destroying them would help convince people they are gone and not coming back."

The ministry had been trying to entice tenant farmers to come and work the land, but many were afraid. The ghost of Osama bin Laden, even though he hadn't yet been killed, loomed large in the minds of many Afghans. The raid by U.S. Navy SEALs that eventually killed the terrorist mastermind in Abbottabad, Pakistan, was still months away, and it was strange how the mere mention of bin Laden's name was enough to give the Afghans a jolt.

Laurie began scouting a place to do the stand-up portion of her report. She tiptoed up to a farmer kneeling in the fresh mud of a newly ploughed field and called to her cameraman.

"Ousama, could you come here?"

Both Khan and Mirwais, his cousin and driver, froze in their tracks. They'd been helping to set up, along with one of Hai Niamati's assistants.

"Sir, why does she keep calling him Osama?"

"Because that is his name."

In unison, each of the Afghans sucked in his breath and took a step back. They looked at the cameraman with a sort of supernatural horror that eventually gave way to maudlin curiosity. They played a guessing game over where he was from by judging the tint of his dark skin. It took them about five tries to get it right.

"Had I known his name, I would never have brought him," Khan mumbled.

"Just think, Khan. You are now infamous. You will forever be known as the fixer who brought Osama back to Tarnak Farms," I said quietly.

"That is not perfectly all right, sir."

We had to explain to Hai Niamati what was going on and, when he understood, his stone mask of reserve cracked with a great wail of laughter. Not far away was an irrigation ditch coursing with water and I took a few photos of him standing beside it. He looked rather thoughtful.

"Do you know where that water is coming from?" he asked in halting English. I let the camera dangle around my neck and shook my head.

"Dahla. It comes from Dahla dam," he said, referring to the dam in the north that Ottawa had paid to rebuild. "It started flowing ten days ago. Your people did that. You should be very proud."

I looked around at the greening fields under the white, hard heat of the Afghan sun. I couldn't say anything. There was nothing to say. This wasn't ending like any war story I'd ever known. But then again, Kandahar was unlike anything I'd ever known. So many had come here and never left, even if they had managed to walk out the door. The land under my feet tasted of both our blood and our tears and I couldn't figure out if it would ever get enough of either. Afghanistan had a shadowy embrace that was hard to escape.

On the way out, Laurie had Khan and Mirwais pull the car over near a group of farmhands weeding a field. Ousama jumped out to take some video and I followed. There was a strange peaceful vibe despite the workers' dead-eyed stares. But Mirwais gripped the steering wheel tight and looked at Laurie, who was huddled under a scarf on the back seat.

"Don't get out of the car," he told her. "Even though these are my people, I do not trust them."

Acknowledgements

No work is ever done in isolation and what you've just read is no exception. In some ways, there are just too many to thank; wonderful, generous individuals who've given their time, insight and support. I don't believe I could ever fully repay the gifts of advice and guidance bestowed upon me during this process.

My greatest debt is owed to the hundreds of soldiers, diplomats, aid workers, politicians, officials and ordinary Afghans who freely gave of their time.

I am grateful for the courage and conviction of my fixer, Abdul Raziq Khan, without whom most of this would not have been possible.

To my editors and colleagues at The Canadian Press: there are no words to describe how privileged I feel to work for a news organization that still values clear-eyed, uncompromising journalism. My fellow Afghanistan correspondents, folks on the foreign desk and everyone who calls the Ottawa bureau home have been constant sources of inspiration, kind words and encouragement, which have always arrived at just the right moments.

I owe a special debt of gratitude to my editors at John Wiley & Sons— Don Loney, Linda Pruessen and Pauline Ricablanca—whose good humour, patience and sharp eyes have lifted my words off the page and taken them to a higher a place.

To my good friend Gerald Weseen, without whose advice and thoughtful suggestions this work would not have been possible at all.

To my agent, Rick Broadhead, who continued to believe in me, and in this project, at times when I had doubts.

To my good friend Blair Patton, who poured equal measures of Scotch and encouragement.

To my long-time friend Nelofer Pazeria, for lighting the fire of imagination about Afghanistan and for having the courage to tell the stories of her people.

Index

Note: *Charles Company* in reference to the 1 RCR (Royal Canadian Regiment) is correct. Unlike other Canadian Army regiments, 1 RCR uses the more formal name to distinguish its "C" Company. *Charlie Company* in reference to PPCLI (Princess Patricia's Canadian Light Infantry) is correct.